A QUICK OVERVIEW OF THE SIGNIFICANT RULE AND GAME CHANGES IN THE 2013-2016 RACING RULES OF SAILING

The following is a list of the significant changes in the 2013-2016 edition of The Racing Rules of Sailing (RRS). These are changes from the 2009-2012 edition. NOTE: These brief summaries are not intended to be actual representations of the rules; nor is this a complete list of all the changes in the 2013-2016 RRS.

- **Basic Principles** A new Basic Principle has been added called "Environmental Responsibility" which reads, "Participants are encouraged to minimize any adverse environmental impact of the sport of sailing." This is supported by new rule 55 (Trash Disposal) which reads, "A competitor shall not intentionally put trash in the water." Rule 55 applies at all times when boats are on the water and subject to the RRS.

- **Finish** The definition has been revised to clarify that if a boat crosses the finishing line but then takes a penalty or corrects an error in crossing the finishing line, she has not "finished" yet and is therefore still "racing." She "finishes" when she crosses the finishing line after completing her penalty or correcting her error. And if a boat happens to cross the "finishing line" on her way to the next mark (say the start/finish line is in the middle of the beat), she doesn't "finish" until she crosses the finishing line and stops racing.

- **Keep Clear** The second part of the definition has been expanded to apply to port and starboard tack boats as well as windward and leeward boats. If a port-tack boat allows herself to get so close to a starboard-tack boat that the starboard-tack boat cannot change course in both directions without making immediate contact with the port-tack boat, the port-tack boat has failed to keep clear.

- **Mark** Now an object attached "temporarily" to a mark is considered part of the mark. For instance, if the race committee hangs a "keep-off buoy" off the back of the race committee boat, that buoy and the line attaching it to the boat are part of the race committee boat which is a "mark."

- **Mark-Room** This definition has been changed to remove the "to" / "at" convention from the previous definition. The new definition allows an inside boat "room" to leave the mark on the required side. In addition, when the inside boat's proper course would bring her close to the mark, as it would when a boat is rounding that mark, she is entitled to "room" to sail to the mark, i.e., the space she needs to get to the mark while s~ ~~ ~~ ~~ ~~ ~~ ~~ ~~ ~~ en "room" to round the mark as necessary ~~ ~~ ~~ he needs to round the mark and begin saili~ ~~ a- manlike way." Note, the reference to "pro ~~ er an inside boat is entitled to "room" to s~ ~~ ot include room for a boat to sail her "pro ~~ .in rules in rule 18 do permit an inside boat to sail her proper course near a mark).

- **Party** The definition has been expanded to include a boat for which redress has been requested, the race committee when it requests redress for a boat, and any body listed in rule 62.1(a) (Redress) when it is alleged to have made an improper action or omission.

- **Room** The definition now includes space for a boat to comply with her obligations under the rules in Part 2 (When Boats Meet) and rule 31 (Touching a Mark). For instance, rule 16.1 (Changing Course) now means that a right-of-way boat cannot change course if it causes the keep-clear boat to foul another boat or touch a mark.

- **Rule 14 (Avoiding Contact)** has been modified so that when a right-of-way boat or one entitled to room or mark-room breaks rule 14, but there is no damage or injury, she is to be "exonerated," which means freed from blame for breaking the rule. The previous rule said that the boat would not be "penalized."

- **Rule 18.2(c)(2) (Giving Mark-Room)** answers the question: when a boat is taking mark-room, how far can she turn to shut the door and still be exonerated under rule 21 (Exoneration) for breaking rule 16.1 (Changing Course) when a boat that owes her mark-room tries to sail in between her and the mark? Rule 18.2(c)(2) effectively says she can sail up to her "proper course," but if she sails higher than that, she will not be exonerated if she breaks rule 16.1.

- **Rule 18.2(e) (Giving Mark-Room)** adds that if a boat obtains an inside overlap by tacking to windward of another boat, and from the time the overlap began the outside boat has been unable to give mark-room, she is not required to give it.

- **Rule 20 (Room to Tack at an Obstruction)** has been reformatted but with very little change in meaning. The changes are:
  - if a boat is fetching an obstruction that is also a mark, but would not have to change course to avoid a boat that hailed for room and subsequently tacked, the hailing boat has not broken a rule;
  - from the time a boat hails until she has tacked and avoided the other boat, rule 18.2 (Giving Mark-Room) does not apply between them. In the previous rules, this was stated in the preamble to Section C;
  - and if a boat has been hailed to tack, but can't tack due to boats to windward of her, she can pass along the hail even when she herself does not need to take any action to avoid the obstruction.

- **Rule 21 (Exoneration)** This rule covers rules 18 (Mark-Room), 19 (Room to Pass an Obstruction) and 20 (Room to Tack at an Obstruction), and provides exoneration for a boat sailing within the room or mark-room to which she is entitled if she breaks a rule of Part 2, Section A (the basic right-of-way rules), or rules 15 (Acquiring Right of Way) or 16 (Changing Course), or if she is forced to break rule 31 (Touching a Mark). Previously, some of this exoneration needed to be handled by using rule 64.1 (Penalties and Exoneration).

- **Rule 22.3 (Starting Errors; Taking Penalties; Moving Astern)** now clarifies that it is only when you are moving backwards "through the water" by backing a sail that you can break this rule.

- **Rule 41(a) (Outside Help)** has been expanded to allow a boat to receive outside help when one of its crew is in danger, which obviously includes being in the water. The rule now also permits that boat to be protested, and the protest committee to penalize a boat, for gaining a significant advantage after receiving help under rule 41(a), but the penalty can be less than disqualification.

- **Rule 42.3 (Propulsion: Exceptions)** has been revised. Rule 42.3(c) clarifies that a boat may pump to surf down the "front" of a wave (the prior rule said the "leeward side" of a wave), which means a boat can, for instance, pump to surf a powerboat wake that is not moving directly downwind. And a boat can now pump her mainsail to "pop" an inverted compression batten, but not in a way that propels the boat.

- **Rule 44 (Penalties at the Time of an Incident)** has been clarified to say that a boat need only take one penalty per incident, regardless of the number of rules that may have been broken in that incident; and if the sailing instructions state a different alternative penalty is being used, such as the Scoring Penalty, then that penalty replaces the One-Turn and the Two-Turns Penalty.

- **Rule 48.2 (Fog Signals and Lights; Traffic Separation Schemes)** has been added. It reads, "A boat shall comply with rule 10, Traffic Separation Schemes, of the *IRPCAS.*" (*IRPCAS* are the *International Regulations for Preventing Collisions at Sea*).

- **Rule 49.2 (Crew Position; Lifelines)** has deleted the phrase "of wire," meaning the rule applies to lifelines whether they are wire or not. In addition, the rule has added this sentence: "If the class rules do not specify the material or minimum diameter of lifelines, they shall comply with the corresponding specifications in the *ISAF Offshore Special Regulations.*"

- **Rule 50.4 (Headsails)** now states, "For the purposes of rules 50 and 54 and Appendix G, the difference between a headsail and a spinnaker is that the width of a headsail, measured between the midpoints of its luff and leech, is less than 75% of the length of its foot." (Previously it was 50%.)

- **Rule 60.1 (Right to Protest; Right to Request Redress or Rule 69 Action)** now only permits a boat to protest under rule 31 (Touching a Mark) if it was involved in or saw the incident.

- **Rule 61.1(3) (Informing the Protestee)** now clarifies what to do when another boat allegedly isn't sailing the course correctly. It says, "if the incident was an error by the other boat in sailing the course, she need not hail or display a red flag but she shall inform the other boat before that boat finishes or at the first reasonable opportunity after she finishes."

- **Rule 62.1(a) (Redress)** has added "equipment inspection committee or measurement committee for the event" to the list of bodies whose improper actions or omissions can be the subject of a request for redress.

- **Rule 63.6 (Taking Evidence and Finding Facts)** now requires a member of the protest committee who saw the incident to state that fact while the parties are present.

- **previous Rule 67 (Rule 42 and Hearing Requirement)** has been deleted, which means that the protest committee may never penalize a boat under rule 42 (Propulsion) without a hearing (this does not preclude an event from using Appendix P, Special Procedures for Rule 42).

- **Rule 70.1 (Appeals and Requests to a National Authority)** now permits a boat to appeal when she is denied a hearing required by rule 63.1 (Requirement for a Hearing).

- **Rule 90.3(c) (Scoring)** Now, when the race committee determines from its own records or observations that it has scored a boat incorrectly, it can correct the error without going through the redress process.

- **Appendices** There are many appendices for specific disciplines within the sport of sailing. Many of these have been revised. Be sure to study the appendices that pertain to your racing.

- **Appendix T (Alternative Procedures for Dispute Resolution)** This appendix is a new US Sailing prescription, and includes systems for reducing the need for protest hearings, including post-race reduced penalties, expedited protest hearings, and arbitration (a short meeting held prior to a protest hearing to try to resolve the matter).

Dave Perry

Understanding the
Racing
Rules of
Sailing
through 2016

Illustrations by Brad Dellenbaugh

EIGHTH EDITION

AN OVERVIEW OF THE RULES...

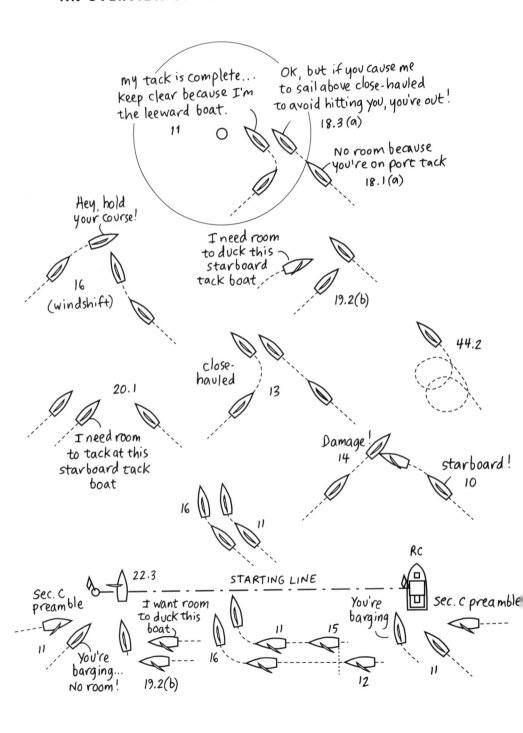

...FROM START TO FINISH

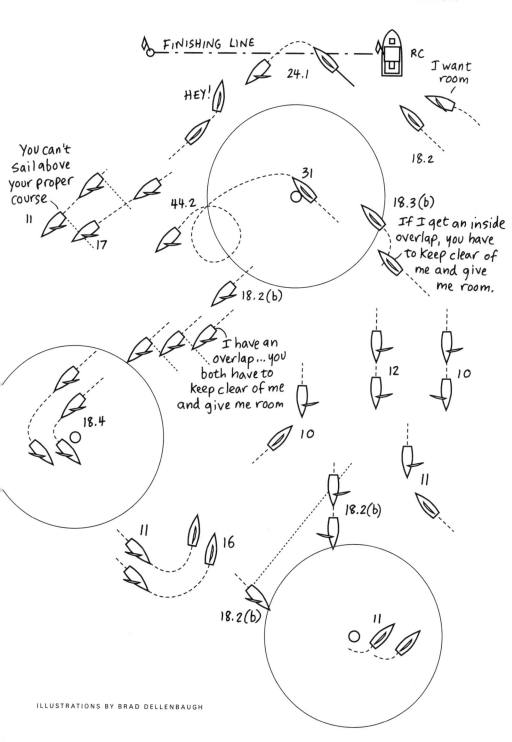

OTHER BOOKS BY DAVE PERRY

Dave Perry's 100 Best Racing Rules Quizzes

Winning in One-Designs

To order rulebooks, *US Sailing Appeals and ISAF Cases*, books by Dave Perry and other US Sailing publications, please call 800 US SAIL-1 or go to www.ussailing.org

TO CONTACT US SAILING

PO Box 1260, 15 Maritime Drive
Portsmouth, RI 02871 USA

Phone: 401 683-0800
Fax: 401 683-0840

info@ussailing.org
www.ussailing.org

ISBN 978-1-938915-04-8

Published by the United States Sailing Association

© 2012 by the United States Sailing Association and Dave Perry

Illustrations © 2012 by Brad Dellenbaugh

The Racing Rules of Sailing for 2013–2016 © 2012
by the International Sailing Federation (ISAF)

Previous editions published in 1985, 1989, 1993, 1997, 2001, 2004 and 2008

Cover photo: J/80 Worlds in Newport, RI © Paul Todd / outsideimages.com

Foreword

My hope is that each sailor who reads this book will be able to say honestly that they do finally know and understand the rules. I realize that a rules book doesn't often make for the best bedtime reading, but I've made a conscious effort to write in an easy-to-follow, conversational style. In addition, I've taken the time to go into each rule in enough depth so that you can feel confident that you actually do understand what the rule means and how it applies to your racing. And Brad Dellenbaugh has provided his usual clear and humorous diagrams that make understanding the rules even easier.

IN LEARNING THESE RULES and their tactical implications I strongly recommend an attitude that is positive about accepting that challenge, realistic about letting go of some of what was previously known about the rules, and willing to make the effort to fully study and understand them.

If you're new to sailboat racing, Chapter 2 covers the basic terms you'll hear throughout the book and around the race course; and it lists the basic rules which you will need to know so you can get out there and start having fun without feeling that you're lost and in everyone's way. But, after reading Chapter 2, I encourage you to take the extra time to read through the rest of the book. Obviously you won't be able to visualize all the situations discussed, but at least you will have been exposed to the big picture right off the bat; and I can promise that your understanding of the rules will happen much faster because you will know how to answer most of your own rule questions as they arise, which they will!

If you are already an experienced racer, I'm confident that you will find this book an informative and useful reference. Wherever possible, I have quoted from the US Sailing Appeals and International Sailing Federation (ISAF) Cases so that you will know their authoritative interpretation and explanation of the rules. I have also gone into depth in areas which commonly cause the most problems or raise the most questions. As a result, this reference will also be extremely useful to sailors serving as judges on a protest committee. The most useful appeals are quoted or referenced with the discussion of each rule; and each discussion goes into sufficient depth to provide the answers or at least the guidelines to resolve most protests or questions which come up. Both competitors and judges will find the extensive use and reference to the appeals very useful and timesaving when they are either lodging a protest or trying to resolve one in the hearing.

NOTE: *At the time this book was published, US Sailing and ISAF had not yet completed their revisions of their Appeals and Cases; therefore the quotes from the appeals may not be 100% accurate. I expect that the substance of the interpretations are accurate, but encourage you to double-check the actual Appeals and Cases. You can find both books at http://raceadmin.ussailing.org/ Appeals.*

I wish to point out that my opinions expressed in this book are my personal opinions, and not those of the US Sailing Appeals Committee of which I am a member.

It is nearly impossible to race sailboats without getting involved in some rules-related situations, whether it's in a crowded mark rounding, a protest hearing, a measurement problem, or an appeal. It is my hope that this book, which blends the rules and the appeals together, will answer most of your rules questions and expand your knowledge and awareness of what is in the US Sailing Appeals and ISAF Cases so that you can continue to satisfy your own rules curiosity into the future, and feel confident that you in fact do understand the rules yourself.

This book will be published every four years with the revisions of *The Racing Rules of Sailing*. As it is my goal to provide a useful and accurate reference for all sailors, I welcome your comments and suggestions concerning improvements and inaccuracies. Please send them to my attention by May 1, 2016, or sooner at: 239 Barberry Road, Southport, CT 06890.

And now, enjoy your understanding of the rules!

Good Sailing,
Dave Perry

Acknowledgements

I'D LIKE TO THANK the following people, and for the reasons given:

My father, Hop Perry, who began my rules interest and taught me the first rules I knew; my mother, Jan Perry, who, along with her father, Northrop Dawson, stimulated and encouraged my desire to write; and my wife Betsy, who has enhanced this book (and my life) with her contributions and her support.

Bill Bentsen and Dick Rose, members of both the US Sailing and ISAF Racing Rules Committees over the years, who have generously given me tremendous amounts of their time and insight as I have learned more about the rules; and who have inspired me to become a strict analyst of the exact word in each rule so as to learn and interpret only what the rule writers wrote.

Harry Anderson, who patiently tolerated my endless rule questions during his every visit to Yale from 1973-1977, and who answered each with the same high care and interest to explain exactly why he gave the answer he did. Gregg Bemis, whose countless hours of conversation on the rules I will always cherish. David and Brad Dellenbaugh, who have helped me gain tremendous insights into the rules by their high-minded approach to analyzing and interpreting the rules. Tom Ehman, who shares my insatiable curiosity to understand the rules. Andy Kostanecki with whom (along with Dick Rose) I shared my first experience at writing a rule and who was wonderful to work with. Goran Petersson, whose sincere dedication to listening to sailors and welcoming their input on the racing rules I admire and appreciate so much. And my fellow members on the US Sailing Appeals Committee past and present for their high level of rules interpretation and interest in the rules.

I would also like to thank the many friends with whom I've enjoyed much open-minded and friendly, thoughtful debate on the rules, completely devoid of any self-righteousness or the ill effects of taking debate personally; and all the sailors I've met while sitting on protest committees, who have given clear and honest testimonies so that the facts of what happened were clear, enabling everyone involved to learn from and enjoy the more intellectual challenge of applying the rules to the seemingly endless variety of situations we find ourselves in while racing.

I can't say enough about the talent and energy of my friend Brad Dellenbaugh, whose illustrations are an equal half of making this book fun and effective. I also thank Joy Shipman and the staff at US Sailing for all their efforts towards the publication of this book. Finally, I want to acknowledge all those sailors who took the time to write to me with their critical comments and suggestions for the improvement of this book.

As individual words form together to create a rule, so have all these people formed together to become my teacher in a subject that never ceases to give me pleasure each time I feel I know and understand a rule a little more clearly.

To all of you: Thank you!

Table of Contents

The Racing Rules of Sailing
Contents

This table indicates where discussion of each rule is located. Page numbers in **bold** indicate the page on which the text of the rule is quoted. The complete text of *The Racing Rules of Sailing* (RRS) is printed at the end of this book. "RRS" by a rule indicates that there is no specific discussion of that rule in this book; you will find the text of the rule in *The Racing Rules of Sailing*.

Section B – General Limitations

Section C – At Marks and Obstructions

PART 5 – PROTESTS, REDRESS, HEARINGS, MISCONDUCT AND APPEALS

Section A – Protests; Redress; Rule 69 Action

Section B – Hearings and Decisions

Section C – Gross Misconduct

Section D – Appeals

PART 6 – ENTRY AND QUALIFICATION

PART 7 – RACE ORGANIZATION

APPENDICES

Introduction

How to Learn the Most from This Book

Give me a fish and I'll eat for a day;
teach me to fish and I'll eat for the rest of my life.

It is one goal of this book to help you learn and understand the rules and the appeals better. It is an equal goal to help you see how you can continue to answer your own rules questions as they arise, whether in the position of a competitor, a race committee member or a judge. Here are some suggestions that will make it much easier for you to accomplish both.

DON'T TRY TO MEMORIZE THE RULES

It is the wrong approach to try to memorize the eight situations where a *port-tack* boat has right of way over a *starboard-tack* boat, just as it's confusing to try to simply memorize the entire text of rule 18.2 (Giving Mark-Room). Each rule has a clear purpose, which I have tried to explain thoroughly. You'll learn and remember the rules faster and more clearly if you take a step back and try to see exactly what actions each rule is trying to produce or elimi-nate. For example, when you are over the starting line at the gun you have taken an unfair head start on your competitors. You can remedy your mis-take simply by returning behind the line and starting properly; and it makes complete sense that while you are returning you have to stay out of the way of boats that have started correctly. This is the purpose of rule 28.1 (Sailing the Course) and rule 22 (Starting Errors; Penalty Turns; Moving Astern), which you can easily understand and apply in your racing without knowing the exact wording of each rule.

LET GO OF PREVIOUS INTERPRETATIONS OF THE RULES

My advice is: read this book with an open mind. Be careful not to hurry through sections that you feel you already know. Read each word and discussion carefully. It's very common and easy to superimpose what you "think" a rule says or should say; and in many cases this causes you to miss a subtle difference in what the rule is actually saying. Sailors seriously interested in understanding the rules will find real pleasure and benefit in learning a rule correctly.

WHEN ALL ELSE FAILS, READ THE DIRECTIONS

It is usually not difficult to answer your own rules questions if you follow this route. When you have a question, first look in the Index of Subjects in the ISAF *Racing Rules of Sailing* (RRS) to see which rule(s) may apply. Also look through the Contents of the RRS at the titles of the Parts, then the Sections and finally the rules themselves to find the one(s) that might pertain to your situation. For example, if it involves two or more boats, the appropriate rule(s) are probably in Part 2. To find the rule(s), first determine what the relationships of the boats are just before, during and just after the incident. For instance, have they been converging for some time or does one of the boats suddenly change course and cause the convergence; are they on the same or opposite *tacks*; are they *overlapped* or not, and so forth. Also determine where they are on the course; i.e., are they behind the starting line, near a *mark* or halfway down a reaching leg? Then look through the titles of the rules in Part 2 for the description most similar to the situation.

When you have found the rule you feel applies, read it out loud. As Bill Bentsen, member of the US Sailing and ISAF Racing Rules Committees for many years, says, "Before answering a rules question I always reread the rule first." Then read the discussion of the rule in this book, along with each appeal referenced in the discussion. It is also good advice to reread the definition of each italicized word in the rule. If you have access to the US Sailing Appeals and ISAF Cases (on-line at: http://raceadmin.ussailing.org/Appeals or available for purchase from US Sailing's on-line Store: store.ussailing.org/store), check the helpful index and read any appeals that may pertain to your situation. If you are still not confident in the answer, write down your question in the back of your rule book and discuss it with the local rules expert or one of the US Sailing Certified Judges in your area.

USEFUL FEATURES OF THIS BOOK

Brad and I have included the following features in the book with the hope that they will be useful to you:

1) **A "blimp's eye" chart** in the front of the book which shows an entire race course with the rule numbers for the situations that commonly arise in each location. This feature should be very useful when you're involved in a *protest* but you're not sure what rule number applies.

2) **A "question and answer" format,** indicated by the fish in the margin, in which I ask and answer the most commonly asked rules questions. Perhaps you'll recognize some as questions you may have.

3) When a term defined in the Definitions is used in its defined sense, I have printed it in *italic* type. To emphasize words or phrases throughout my explanations and discussions of the rules, I have used **bold** type.

4) **A Glossary of Terms** explaining the meaning of terms commonly used in discussing the rules but not defined in *The Racing Rules of Sailing*. (Located after this Introduction.)

5) **A table for calculating** boat speed, distance and time that will be useful when preparing for a *protest* or hearing one. (Located after this Introduction.)

6) **The complete text** of *The Racing Rules of Sailing*, including its appendices. (In the back of this book.)

7) **A detailed index** of rule subjects and the rule(s) in which they are located, prepared by ISAF and included in *The Racing Rules of Sailing*. (In the back of this book.)

8) **An index** listing each 2013-2016 rule number and where the primary discussion of that rule is located in this book. (Located after the Table of Contents in this book.)

9) **A summary** of the significant changes in the rules. (First few pages of this book.)

Glossary of Terms

To keep the rules short and simple, the rule writers use common terms when possible. When a term is not defined in *The Racing Rules of Sailing* (RRS), it is intended to be interpreted in its common, everyday dictionary meaning (see RRS Introduction, Terminology). The following is a glossary of some of the terms you will find in *The Racing Rules of Sailing* and their discussion in this book that are not defined in the RRS themselves:

Approaching a Mark getting closer to the time a boat will arrive at the *mark*

Bearing Away turning away from the direction of the wind

Beat to Windward a boat is on a "beat to windward" whenever she is racing upwind; i.e., when her fastest course to the next *mark* is close-hauled

Close-hauled Course the course a boat will sail when racing upwind; i.e., when sailing as close to the wind as she can and not lose too much speed

Heading Up another term for "luffing" (see below)

Inside Boat when two *overlapped* boats are near a *mark* or *obstruction*, the boat that is between the other boat and the *mark* or *obstruction*

Gybing the maneuver involving changing *tacks* with the boat's bow away from the wind; when sailing directly downwind, a boat changes *tacks* when her mainsail crosses her centerline

Leaving a Mark sailing past the *mark* in the final phase of the rounding or passing maneuver

Luffing turning toward the direction of the wind

May or Can means permissive; have option of doing it

Outside Boat when two *overlapped* boats are near a *mark* or *obstruction*, the boat that is not between the other boat and the *mark* or *obstruction*

Shall means mandatory; must do it

Tacking the maneuver involving changing *tacks* with the boat's bow toward the wind; when sailing upwind, a boat changes *tacks* the moment her bow passes head to wind

Code

Throughout this book, in order to consolidate space and to conform to the appeals, I have used the following code:

S	*starboard-tack* boat
P	*port-tack* boat
L	*leeward* boat
W	*windward* boat
A	boat *clear ahead*
B	boat *clear astern* (behind)
M	middle or intervening boat
I	inside boat (at a *mark* or *obstruction*)
O	outside boat (at a *mark* or *obstruction*)

When combined, the codes work like this:

S L	the boat is on *starboard-tack* and *overlapped* to *leeward* of the other boat.
P I	the boat is on *port-tack* and *overlapped* on the inside of the other boat.

Speed, Distance & Time Table

(based on the formula: distance = rate x time)

(1 knot = 6076 feet per hour)

Boat speed	Feet per second	Meters per second
1 knot	1.69	0.51
2 knots	3.38	1.01
3 knots	5.06	1.52
4 knots	6.75	2.03
5 knots	8.44	2.53
6 knots	10.13	3.04
7 knots	11.81	3.54
8 knots	13.50	4.05
9 knots	15.19	4.56
10 knots	16.88	5.06

In other words, if your boat is going 4 knots, you will travel 6.75 feet per second. One way to determine your boat's speed is to sail by a buoy or other fixed object and count how many seconds it takes for the buoy to go from your bow to your stern. If in a 24-foot boat it takes 3 seconds to go by the buoy, you are going 8 feet per second, or just under 5 knots.

It's very useful to know your boat's approximate speed on all points of sail in all wind and wave conditions, particularly in a protest hearing. For instance, in the above example you know that a *zone* that is three lengths wide is about 9 seconds' worth of sailing before the *mark*. You also know that if you tack in front of another boat and she claims to have hit you only 3 seconds after you became close-hauled, you can point out that, by her own testimony, she held her course for a full boat-length after you were close-hauled.

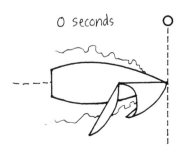

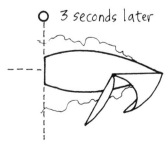

1

An Overview of the Rules System

Here is an overview of how the rules system works, and where the *rules* and their interpretations are located.

BRIEF HISTORY

Up through the early 1920s, different parts of the world had their own versions of racing rules. Then, as more sailors started traveling to other countries for international regattas, the European and United States yacht racing associations agreed on a common set of right-of-way rules in 1929. However, as racing grew in popularity and the boats were getting smaller, the existing rules were not clear and precise enough to make them easily enforceable.

In the mid-1930s Mike Vanderbilt, defender of the America's Cup in the J-boats *Enterprise* (1930), *Rainbow* (1934) and *Ranger* (1937) began work on a new draft of the rules based on the three basic relative positions boats can be in: on the same tack, on different tacks, and in the act of changing tacks. In 1948 the North American Yacht Racing Union (NAYRU), predecessor to the United States Sailing Association (US Sailing) and the Canadian Yachting Association (CYA), adopted Vanderbilt's draft as their official rules.

In 1949 the International Yacht Racing Union (IYRU), predecessor to the International Sailing Federation (ISAF), created a Racing Rules Committee to study the various racing rules that were being used throughout the world. From 1950 to 1959, Mike Vanderbilt and Gregg Bemis of the United States, Gerald Sambrooke-Sturges of Great Britain and others worked hard to draft one set of rules under which the entire world would race. In 1960 the IYRU adopted a draft, largely based on the "Vanderbilt draft," and these rules came into effect in 1961. Since then, racing throughout the world has been done under the same code of rules.

Beginning in 1961, the IYRU's policy became that these rules would be locked in place for four-year periods lasting through the Olympic Games. During these four-year periods, sailors would communicate their ideas for improvements to their Racing Rules Committees, which would also study the rules for areas of improvement. After each Olympics, the IYRU would adopt a revised set of rules for the next four-year period.

Over the years since 1961, in the process of being revised to clarify their meaning and to meet changes in the sport, the rules became longer and more filled with exceptions. As newcomers joined the sport, they (and those who taught them) found learning the rules to be a formidable task. In 1991, the International Sailing Federation (ISAF; formerly the IYRU) took formal action to simplify the rules. A draft of "experimental rules" was offered to sailors each year from 1993-1996 for their review, trial and input. This "world-wide" research project resulted in a highly refined and simpler set of rules that went into effect in 1997. The rules at *marks* and *obstructions* remained long and confusing to some, so a similar effort was made to simplify and clarify those rules in the 2009-2012 rules. It is ISAF's intention to minimize the changes to the racing rules as much as possible to enhance their understanding.

THE RULES AND HOW THEY ARE UPDATED

The rules are *The Racing Rules of Sailing*. They are published by ISAF. Each national authority (US Sailing in the United States) adopts these rules for racing in its own country. Some rules permit each national authority to make some additions or modifications, called "prescriptions." So when racing in a different country, a sailor need only learn what prescriptions, if any, that national authority has made. But notice that there are no modifications permitted to the Definitions and "right of way" rules in Part 2 (see rule 86, Changes to the Racing Rules), thus ensuring that these remain identical throughout the world.

Though rule 86 restricts which rules the sailing instructions can change, rule 86.3 says, *"If a national authority so prescribes, the restrictions in rule 86.1 do not apply if rules are changed to develop or test proposed rules."* US Sailing prescribes to rule 86.3: *"...proposed rules may be tested, but only in local races."* US Sailing Appeal 58 says, "Local races are those in which normally the same group of people from a limited geographic area regularly race together." The prescription goes on to say: *"However, proposed rules may also be tested at other events if, for each event, the organizing authority first obtains written permission from US Sailing and the proposed rules are included in the notice of race and sailing instructions."*

The ISAF and the national authorities are very interested in having sailors study the rules for improvements and give their input. In the U.S., suggestions or comments should be sent to the Racing Rules Committee, c/o US Sailing.

WHERE THE RULES ARE LOCATED

*The **rules** are located in the following places:*
*(See the definition **Rule**.)*

1. **The ISAF rule book (*The Racing Rules of Sailing*) and any prescriptions of the national authority.** US Sailing sells one "rule book" that includes the ISAF rules, appendices and US Sailing prescriptions. See its Contents for an overview of where each ISAF rule is located and what each Appendix covers. Notice that rule titles are not part of the *rules*.

2. **Class rules.** Each class publishes rules specific for that class, which are available from the class secretary, and generally on the class website.

3. **Club or "local" rules.**

4. **The Notice of Race. Appendix J** (Notice of Race and Sailing Instructions) lists the information contained in the Notice of Race.

5. **The Sailing Instructions.** The sailing instructions are required to tell you when class and "local" rules apply, as well as when parts or the whole of an Appendix apply. They may even change some of *The Racing Rules of Sailing* (see rule 86, Changes to the Racing Rules). Appendix J (Notice of Race and Sailing Instructions) lists all the information the sailing instructions must contain. Notice that rule 90.2 (Sailing Instructions) prohibits any oral instructions unless there is a procedure specifically set out in the sailing instructions; and even then, they can be given only on the water. This is obviously to avoid confusion and potential prejudice to sailors not hearing about a change.

   Every sailor should take a few minutes to read the sailing instructions for a race or event. Normally, a race committee will not answer oral questions concerning any rule or sailing instruction for the above stated reason. You should give them your question(s) in writing in ample time for them to consider their answer, seek the judges' opinions (when necessary) and post each question with its answer in writing on the official notice board.

6. **Any other conditions or documents that might apply to a particular race or series.** Note, ISAF Case 98 states: "Any other documents that will govern the event must be listed in the notice of race and the sailing instructions (see rules J1.1(3) and J2.1(2))."

PROTEST SYSTEM

A "*protest*" is merely the means of bringing an incident in which a boat may have broken a *rule* to a hearing after the race where the sailors involved and the members of the protest committee can review the incident and decide how the *rules* apply.

The rules for how to file a *protest* are clearly stated in Part 5, Section A (Protests; Redress; Rule 69 Action). Rules concerning how the protest hearing must be run, including a listing of all the sailor's rights, are in Part 5, Section B (Hearings and Decisions).

Appendix M (Recommendations for Protest Committees) contains detailed recommendations for how protest committees should conduct the hearing. The preamble to the Appendix clearly states the fundamental principle of "innocent until the jury is satisfied of guilt:" "*In a protest or redress hearing, the protest committee should weigh all testimony with equal care; should recognize that honest testimony can vary, and even be in conflict, as a result of different observations and recollections; should resolve such differences as best it can; should recognize that no boat or competitor is guilty until a breach of a rule has been established to the satisfaction of the protest committee; and should keep an open mind until all the evidence has been heard as to whether a boat or competitor has broken a rule.*"

APPEALS SYSTEM

If you are penalized in a protest hearing and you feel that the protest committee applied the *rules* incorrectly to the facts it found or failed to follow the correct procedures in hearing the *protest*, you can "appeal" its decision to a "higher court." All the rules and procedures for submitting an appeal are located in rule 70 (Appeals and Requests to a National Authority) and Appendix R (Procedures for Appeals and Requests).

Note that you cannot appeal the "facts" that were found by the protest committee. You can only appeal its interpretation and application of the *rules* to those facts, or its procedures (rule 63.6, Taking Evidence and Finding Facts;

rule 70.1, Appeals and Requests to a National Authority; rule 71.3, National Authority Decisions). If after a hearing you, as a *party* to the hearing, feel the protest committee found the wrong facts, you can ask it to reopen the hearing under rule 66 (Reopening a Hearing); and if you feel it used improper procedures (as opposed to disagreeing with its decision), you may request redress under rule 62.1(a) (Redress).

In the United States the "highest court" is the US Sailing Appeals Committee. When it decides a case that in its opinion sets a precedent or is a clear and useful interpretation of a rule, it publishes that decision. It can also submit the appeal and its decision to the ISAF Racing Rules Committee, which in turn can publish the appeal in its Case book. US Sailing's Appeals and ISAF's Cases are available on-line at: http://raceadmin.ussailing.org/Appeals or available for purchase from US Sailing's on-line store: store.ussailing.org.

"What is the status of US Sailing's Appeals and ISAF's Cases?"

The Appeals of the national authorities (US Sailing in the United States) and the ISAF Cases are not *rules*. The ISAF Cases are "authoritative interpretations and explanations of the rules" (see the Introduction to *The Racing Rules of Sailing*). The ISAF Cases carry supreme weight worldwide. When the facts from a protest are essentially similar to the facts of a Case, the interpretations in the Case should be accepted by the protest committee as the correct interpretation of the *rules* for that protest or request for redress. (See US Sailing Appeal 99.)

The decisions of national authority appeals committees are "final" (see rule 71.4). Therefore, when the facts from a protest are essentially similar to the facts of a US Sailing Appeal, and no ISAF Case conflicts with the interpretations in the appeal, a protest committee in the United States is well advised to follow the appeal in making its decision (US Sailing Appeal 99). Sailors and protest committees can and should refer to the appeals for guidance.

"What's the best way to use the appeals books?"

Both the US Sailing Appeals and ISAF Cases are designed for easy, quick reference. One index lists each appeal referring to a particular rule, and another gives a short description of each appeal. Instead of reading the appeals book from front to back, you should read each appeal pertaining to a particular rule. The appeals themselves are each very short. You are given the facts, a diagram when relevant, and then the decision. I like to read the facts, close the book, think out what my decision would be, then compare it with the actual decision.

 "Can the decision on an appeal change the results of a race or series?"

Absolutely yes. Rule 71.4 (National Authority Decisions) states, *"The decision of the national authority shall be final... all parties to the hearing and the protest committee... shall be bound by the decision."* In ISAF Case 61 it was asked, "May the organizing authority state in the notice of race or sailing instructions that, while appeal is not denied, final regatta standings and awards will not be affected by any appeal decision? ANSWER: No...An appeal involves not only the adjudication of a dispute on the meaning of a rule but also, in the event of a reversal of the decision of the protest committee, an adjustment of the results of the race and the final standings of the regatta on which the awards are based."

 "Can anyone appeal the decision of a protest committee?"

No. Only a *party* to the hearing can appeal the decision in that hearing (rule 70.1, Appeals and Requests to a National Authority). (For more explanation on who qualifies as a *party*, see the discussion of the definition *Party*.) In particular, if you weren't a *party* to a hearing, but the decision in that hearing affected you and you believe that the protest committee acted improperly, your recourse is to request redress under rule 62.1(a) (Redress). (See US Sailing Appeal 64 and ISAF Case 55.)

"If I'm a party to the hearing and I feel the protest committee is prejudicing, or has prejudiced, the outcome of the hearing by denying me any of my procedural rights under Part 5, Section B (Hearings and Decisions), do I have to 'object' at the time if I want to retain my right to appeal?"

You are not required to, but I strongly encourage you to do so. Remember that an appeals committee can only base its decision on the facts as presented to them by the protest committee. When a competitor appeals on the grounds that the protest committee made a prejudicial procedural error, generally there is little or no record of it in the protest committee's "facts found." As a result it becomes very difficult for the appeals committee to ever learn enough facts to uphold the appeal.

Therefore, if you are in a situation where the protest committee is denying you your procedural rights, you should state your "objection" right then, so that the hearing can continue properly. If, after the hearing, you feel the protest committee has prejudiced the outcome of the hearing by denying you any of your procedural rights, you should request redress under rule 62.1(a) (Redress). The reason for this is that a protest committee must give you a hearing and, more importantly, must find facts and give you a decision (rule 63.1, Hearings; rule 64.2, Decisions on Redress). Otherwise, you may never get any facts regarding the alleged improprieties on which to base an appeal. Note that the time limit for requesting redress for a protest committee action/omission is the protest time limit or two hours after the "incident," whichever is later (rule 62.2). The "incident" will be the improper action/omission of the protest committee (see US Sailing Appeal 90).

Note that, when seeking redress from the protest committee in a hearing in which you were a *party*, you are not allowed to base your claim on the committee's decision. Your claim must be based on an alleged procedural error (see rule 62.1(a)).

"Are there ever times when I am not allowed to appeal?"

Yes. Rule 70.5 (Appeals and Requests to a National Authority) is very clear on this:

There shall be no appeal from the decisions of an international jury constituted in compliance with Appendix N. Furthermore, if the notice of race and the sailing instructions so state, the right of appeal may be denied provided that

(a) it is essential to determine promptly the result of a race that will qualify a boat to compete in a later stage of an event or a subsequent event (a national authority may prescribe that its approval is required for such a procedure);

 US Sailing prescribes that its approval is required. Go to ussailing.org/racingrules/documents *and click on 'No Appeal' for more information or to obtain approval.*

(b) a national authority so approves for a particular event open only to entrants under its own jurisdiction; or

(c) a national authority after consultation with the ISAF so approves for a particular event, provided the protest committee is constituted as required by Appendix N, except that only two members of the protest committee need be International Judges.

2

A Simplified Version of *The Racing Rules of Sailing*

There's no disagreeing that there are a lot of rules to know when racing sailboats. But just as in every other sport, you don't need to know and completely understand them all before you go racing. I love to play soccer, and I've got the basic rules down: keep my hands off the ball, try to kick the ball into the goal to score, try not to kick the other guys in the shins, and stop when the referee blows the whistle. I'm still a bit hazy on what "offsides" means, what the difference between an "indirect" and a "direct" kick is, and just how many elbows in the ribs I'm supposed to peacefully accept as part of the game. But I still have a great time playing, and I learn a bit more about the rules each time I go out.

Here then are a few basic rules you should know so that you can get into racing without feeling like you're just in everyone's way. At first, take the racing easy just to get the feel of how it works; and never be worried about asking too many questions; that's exactly how we all learned what was up. Of course, the one danger in learning just the basic rules is that there will be places on the course where there are exceptions or where the actual rule has more detail. So you should really take the time to read through this book. It's written in language that is easy to understand. The more you race, the more situations you'll run into that are exactly as covered and described here, and the sooner you'll be comfortable enough to get in there and mix it up out on the course.

Now, if you are just getting into sailing and racing, you've probably noticed that there are a few different words and phrases used around the track. Clearly the rules wouldn't be using them if they didn't make things easier; so we've included some illustrations to help you understand what some of these terms mean.

BASIC RULES

These are simplified summaries of the basic rules that apply when you and another boat are about to hit. When one boat has the "right of way," that means that the other boat is required to "keep clear;" in other words to stay out of the way of the right-of-way boat.

1) If you are on **opposite** *tacks* (booms on different sides), the boat on *starboard tack* has the right of way over the boat on *port tack* (just as at a four-way stop, the car on the right gets to go first). (Rule 10.)

2) If you are on the **same** *tack* (booms on the same sides), the *leeward* boat has the right of way over the *windward* boat; and a boat coming up from behind can't hit the boat ahead (just as on the road). (Rules 11 and 12.)

3) If you are **tacking**, you have to stay out of the way of a boat sailing in a straight line (just as you cannot pull out onto a road immediately in front of a car driving down the road). (Rule 13.)

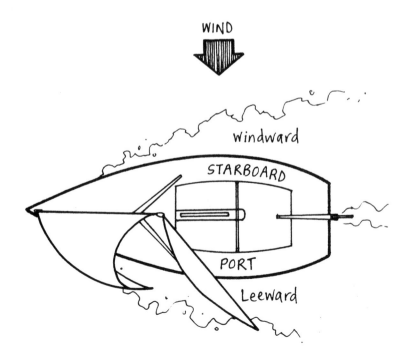

WIND

Windward

STARBOARD

PORT

Leeward

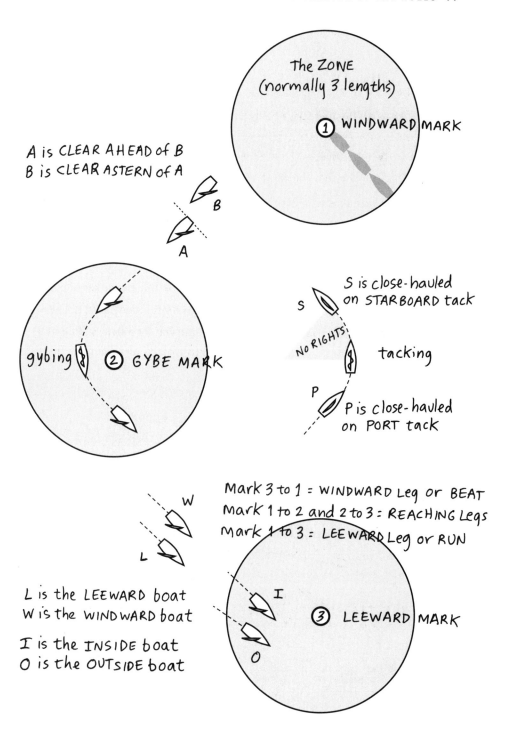

The ZONE (normally 3 lengths)

① WINDWARD MARK

A is CLEAR AHEAD of B
B is CLEAR ASTERN of A

B

A

S is close-hauled on STARBOARD tack

S

NO RIGHTS

tacking

P

P is close-hauled on PORT tack

gybing

② GYBE MARK

Mark 3 to 1 = WINDWARD Leg or BEAT
Mark 1 to 2 and 2 to 3 = REACHING Legs
Mark 1 to 3 = LEEWARD Leg or RUN

W

L

L is the LEEWARD boat
W is the WINDWARD boat

I is the INSIDE boat
O is the OUTSIDE boat

I

③ LEEWARD MARK

O

4) Before most races, the race committee will give each competitor a copy of the sailing instructions (SIs) that contain the specific information on how the races will be run. There will be an imaginary line between two marks called the "starting line," and a timing system to tell you when you can *start* the race (explained in rule 26 or the SIs). You must be completely behind this line when the starting signal is made. If you are not, simply turn back and get behind the line. However, while you are returning, you must stay clear of all boats that *started* correctly. (Rule 22.)

5) Anytime you have the right of way you may turn toward another boat, but you must be sure that the other boat has enough time and space to get out of your way. That's why *windward* boats must be very careful when they pass close by to *leeward* boats. (Rule 16.)

6) When you are three boat-lengths from a *mark*, or are passing an *obstruction* on the same side as another boat, you have to give any boat between you and the *mark* or *obstruction room* to round or pass it. (Rules 18 and 19.)

7) One large exception to number 6 (above) is at the starting *marks*, where you do **not** have to give *windward*/inside boats *room* to pass between you and the starting *mark* when you are about to *start*. If a *windward*/inside boat tries to squeeze in between you and the starting *mark* (like a race committee boat), they are "Barging," which is definitely illegal but unfortunately very common. (Rules 18 and 11.)

8) You must avoid all collisions if possible. (Rule 14.)

9) If you make a right-of-way boat have to **change their course** to avoid hitting you, you must take a penalty. Normally the penalty is to simply get away from the other boats immediately and sail two circles in the same direction. When you're done, get back in the race. (Rule 44.)

10) If you **touch any *mark*,** the penalty is just one circle. (Rule 44.)

If you have the right-of-way and another boat makes you change course to avoid hitting her, she has broken a rule. You can tell her this by "protesting" her. To do this, immediately hail the word "Protest." If you are racing on a boat 20 feet or longer you must also put up a red flag as quickly as possible (usually immediately) after the incident. Then at the finish tell the race committee which boat you are protesting, and onshore fill out the protest form the race committee will give you. Soon afterward, the protest committee (usually three knowledgeable sailors) will hold a hearing at which both boats have the opportunity to tell their story; the committee will then make its decision. (Rules 60 to 67.)

Hike hard, sail fast and enjoy!

3

Sportsmanship and the Rules

"You haven't won the race if in winning the race you have lost the respect of your competitors."

Four-time Olympic Gold Medalist, Paul Elvström

SPORTSMANSHIP AND THE RULES

Competitors in the sport of sailing are governed by a body of *rules* that they are expected to follow and enforce. A fundamental principle of sportsmanship is that when competitors break a *rule* they will promptly take a penalty, which may be to retire.

This statement of principle is located in the rule book just before Part 1 (Fundamental Rules). It is no coincidence that the subject of "sportsmanship" is given a status above all the rules in our sport. The history of sailboat racing is filled with the tradition of exciting competition played out with respect among the competitors and officials. In keeping with that tradition, when we race we agree to be fair and honest, to be good sports and to attempt to win using our own superior boat speed and racing skills.

At the heart of what makes our sport so fulfilling is the principle that we have a competitor-enforced, "no-referee" rules system; that is we have the responsibility to follow the *rules* on our own, to self-penalize ourselves when we break a *rule*, and to protest ("enforce" the *rules*) when we believe another boat has broken a *rule*. In this regard, our sport is unique compared with most other sports. I am constantly amused watching a pro tennis singles match (two players) when I count at least ten referees: one calling each of the four lines on each side, one calling the net, and an umpire to settle disputes. Even at the highest levels of racing we "call our own lines."

The *rules* are intended to provide for safe, fair and equitable racing world-wide; and to make competitor enforcement as easy as possible by clearly defining which boat has the right of way and which boat the requirement to *keep clear* when boats meet. When competitors know they have broken a *rule*, they are expected to promptly take a penalty (Two-Turns Penalty or 20% Scoring Penalty or retire). Competitors who "never drop out," even when they know they are in the wrong, because they think they have a chance to "win" the *protest* in the hearing just waste the time of all the people involved in the *protest* and diminish the quality of the racing for all. Furthermore, they break rule 2 (Fair Sailing) which says, "*A boat and her owner shall compete in compliance with recognized principles of sportsmanship and fair play.*" And if they are disqualified under rule 2, they cannot drop the DSQ from their series score (rules 2 and 90.3(b)).

Rule 44 (Penalties at the Time of an Incident) provides that the One (for touching a *mark*) or Two (for fouling a boat) Turns Penalty or other voluntary penalty will almost always be available to a boat. Given that often a boat does not realize she has broken a rule until returning ashore and consulting with a rules expert, etc., US Sailing has instituted an experimental system where a boat can take a Scoring Penalty on shore before a protest hearing begins, as well as providing for a lesser penalty on the water and an accelerated protest process. All of these options are in a US Sailing prescription to the racing rules, under Appendix T, Alternative Procedures for Dispute Resolution.

When a competitor believes that another boat may have broken a *rule*, she can protest. A *protest* is merely the means of bringing an incident in which a boat may have broken a *rule* to a hearing after the race where the sailors involved and the members of the protest committee can review the incident and decide how the *rules* apply. *Protests* that are the result of honest differences of opinions on the *rules* or observations of the incident should never have a negative taint to them. Quite the contrary, *protests* are an essential part of our competitor-enforced rule system and are expected, particularly in situations where a boat has gained an advantage in the race or series by breaking a *rule*.

When a boat is forced to break a *rule* through no fault of her own, she is known as the "innocent victim," and can be "exonerated" (meaning excused from blame) under rule 64.1(a) (Decisions: Penalties and Exoneration). If a boat feels her score has been made significantly worse through no fault of her own by the organizing authority, race committee, protest committee, equipment inspection committee, measurement committee or another competitor, she can request redress under rule 62 (Redress); in this case, rule 64.2 (Decisions on Redress) reminds the protest committee to make as fair an arrangement as possible for all boats affected.

The rule writers have taken some excellent measures to amplify the message that sailboat racing should be synonymous with good sportsmanship and integrity with regard to fair play. However, in the end of the day it is up to us, the sailors, to use the *rules* as they are written and intended. One problem is that some feel that the rewards from winning justify cheating, such as the "good feeling" of winning, the attention and hype, the benefit to business and sponsors and so on. Obviously, this is a personal decision that all sailors must make for themselves. The hope is that the temptations to cheat can't possibly overpower the realization that once people start bending or ignoring the *rules*, or develop their own "common law," the whole exercise of playing the game becomes meaningless for everyone involved.

Rule 2 (Fair Sailing) and rule 69 (Allegations of Gross Misconduct) provide the external "weight" to encourage strict and voluntary rule observance. However, people who race should want to know that everyone whom they've spent the time, money and energy to race against is sailing within the *rules*; and when they know or suspect that someone isn't, then rather than joining in, they should take action under the *rules* to encourage the others to stop.

4

Part 1
Fundamental Rules

The first rules in the rule book are appropriately called the "Fundamental Rules;" and they address five very important issues in our sport: safety and helping others when in a position to do so, fairness while racing, acceptance of the rules under which we race, responsibility for one's own safety, and drug use (primarily an issue of caution for Olympic-bound racers).

RULE 1 — SAFETY

RULE 1.1 — HELPING THOSE IN DANGER

A boat or competitor shall give all possible help to any person or vessel in danger.

This rule is the first fundamental rule, reaffirming that this principle must be the one to which all sailors hold above all others. Remember that the word "shall" is mandatory. If it were proved that a sailor was in a position to help another, but did not do so, he or she would be liable for disqualification. Note that the rule requires the giving of all "possible" help; this is to leave no question about the extent to which sailors should help each other when in danger.

The rule book is very supportive of this principle.

- Rule 22 (Capsized, Anchored or Aground; Rescuing) reads in part, "...*a boat shall avoid a boat that is...trying to help a person or vessel in danger.*"

- Rule 41 (Outside Help) reads, "*A boat shall not receive help from any outside source, except (a) help for a crew member who is ill, injured or in danger; (b) after a collision, help from the crew of the other vessel to get clear...*"

- Rule 42.3(g) (Propulsion, Exceptions) reads, *"Any means of propulsion may be used to help a person or another vessel in danger."*

- Rule 47 (Limitations on Equipment and Crew) reads in part, *"No person on board shall intentionally leave, except...to help a person or vessel in danger..."*

 "If I do stop and help a boat or person in danger, can I get some compensation for the places and/or time I may have lost?"

You bet! When you have lost places and/or time as a result of a rescue, you are permitted to request redress under rule 62.1(c) (Redress), and the protest committee, acting under rule 64.2 (Decisions on Redress), can give you appropriate compensation for the places and/or time lost. In the event you go to a rescue, try, if possible, to accurately note the time and your position when you began sailing to the rescue and when you got back in the race. On boats in offshore races it is common to keep a log, supported by GPS data, of times and positions to help the protest committee provide the fairest compensation.

A now famous instance of these rules at work is the rescue made by Canadian Finn sailor Larry Lemieux in the 1988 Summer Olympic Games held in the rough seas off Pusan, South Korea. While in second place midway through a race, Larry noticed a 470 sailor in the water separated from his boat and having great difficulty. Larry went to the sailor's rescue, succeeded in getting him safely back to his boat, and after the race requested redress. The Olympic Jury awarded Larry points equal to finishing second in that race!

ISAF Case 20 reads: "SUMMARY OF THE FACTS: Dinghy A capsized during a race and seeing this dinghy B sailed over to her and offered help. A accepted help and B came alongside, taking the crew of two aboard. Then all hands worked for several minutes to right A, whose mast was stuck in mud. Upon reaching shore, B requested redress under rule 62.1(c). The protest committee considered several factors in its decision. First, A's helmsman was a highly experienced sailor. Secondly, the wind was light, and the tide was rising and would shortly have lifted the mast free. Thirdly, she did not ask for help; it was offered. Therefore, since neither boat nor crew was in danger, redress was refused. B appealed, stating that rule 1.1 does not place any onus on a boat giving help to decide, or to defend, a decision that danger was involved.

"DECISION: B's appeal is upheld. A boat in a position to help another that may be in danger is bound to do so. It is not relevant that a protest committee later decides that there was, in fact, no danger or that help was not requested."

RULE 1.2 — LIFE-SAVING EQUIPMENT AND PERSONAL FLOTATION DEVICES

A boat shall carry adequate life-saving equipment for all persons on board, including one item ready for immediate use, unless her class rules make some other provision. Each competitor is individually responsible for wearing a personal flotation device adequate for the conditions.

Rule 1.2 gives the highest prominence to these safety issues. Note that it is each sailor's responsibility to decide when to wear his or her life-jacket (often referred to as a "personal flotation device" or "PFD"). Often class rules and/ or sailing instructions will require you to wear your life-jacket any time you go afloat. Be sure to check those rules.

Also, the race committee can require you to wear your life-jacket by displaying flag Y (rule 40, Personal Flotation Devices). Note, however, that though the race committee has the option to use this signal, it does not shift away from you any of your responsibility for your own safety (see rule 4, Decision to Race). Rule 40 also clarifies that wet suits and dry suits are not adequate personal flotation devices.

Finally, the US Sailing prescription to rule 40 reads, *"US Sailing prescribes that every boat shall carry life-saving equipment conforming to government regulations that apply in the racing area. Go to* **ussailing.org/racingrules/documents** *and click the 'PFD' link for more information."*

RULE 2 — FAIR SAILING

A boat and her owner shall compete in compliance with recognized principles of sportsmanship and fair play. A boat may be penalized under this rule only if it is clearly established that these principles have been violated. A disqualification under this rule shall not be excluded from the boat's series score.

As was discussed in Chapter 3, Sportsmanship and the Rules, when we race we should all agree to hold ourselves to the highest principles of fairness and good sportsmanship. Rule 2 is a clear statement of that premise. When a boat or competitor clearly violates these principles, he or she breaks this rule and is liable to penalty.

Note that a penalty for breaking this rule is more severe than for most other rules. Rule 2 clearly states that if you are in a series that allows you to discard your worst race, a disqualification for breaking rule 2 cannot be discarded. Notice also that a boat can be penalized under rule 2, even when another rule applies to the situation. Therefore, in any incident or situation where the principles in rule 2 have been clearly violated, regardless of what other *rules* may also have been broken, a boat is liable to disqualification under rule 2. This becomes very significant given that a boat has to count that disqualification in her final score (see rule 90.3, Scoring).

 "Could you give some examples of when you would consider the principles in rule 2 have been violated?"

Sure, recognizing that each protest committee is given the discretion to judge what they deem to be "recognized principles of sportsmanship and fair play." In deciding whether a competitor has competed in compliance with the principles in rule 2, I feel it is important to consider the motive for their actions; i.e., was it an intentional violation of one of the principles?

In ISAF Case 47, "An experienced helmsman of a port-tack boat hails 'Starboard!' to a beginner who, although on starboard tack, not being sure of himself and probably being scared of having his boat holed, tacks to port to avoid a collision. No protest is lodged. One school of thought argues that it is fair game, because if a helmsman does not know the rules, that is his own hard luck. The other school rejects this argument, on the grounds that it is quite contrary to the spirit of the rules to deceive a competitor in that way. It is known that such a trick is often played, particularly where novices are involved. In such as case, has the port-tack boat broken rule 2? ANSWER: A boat that deliberately hails 'Starboard' when she knows she is on port tack has not acted fairly and has broken rule 2. The protest committee might also consider taking action under rule 69."

Other examples:

- A *port-tack* boat is reaching by to *leeward* of a *starboard-tack* boat before the start. The *starboard-tack* boat does not change her course, but just as the boats are passing her boom suddenly flies out and hits the *port-tacker*'s shroud. Clearly there is no way for port to *keep clear* at that moment. If it is determined that S's skipper let the boom out **intentionally to hit the boat on port**, I would penalize S under rule 2. If it is determined that S was simply sailing her boat, perhaps responding to a gust of wind, etc., I would penalize P for not *keeping clear*.

- Two boats come off the starting line side by side in very light air. Suddenly, the *leeward* boat rocks hard to windward, the tip of her mast hitting the tip of the *windward* boat's mast. The *leeward* boat does not change course. Again, if it is determined that the action was done solely to try to touch the *windward* boat, I would penalize the *leeward* boat under rule 2. I would apply the same reasoning to a *leeward* boat whose crew goes out on the trapeze in light air or otherwise reaches out and touches the *windward* boat for the sole purpose of "fouling the other boat out."

- A boat is on a heavy-air overnight race. Each time the boat tacks, the crew down-below move the sails back and forth to the windward side to increase the boat's stability. Not only would I penalize this boat for breaking rule 51 (Movable Ballast), I would penalize her under rule 2 as well.

One common practice that is not a violation of rule 2 is the tactic whereby one boat tries to make it harder for another boat to do well in a race or series, including by trying to put boats between herself and the other boat at the finish, provided the boat tries to sail within the *rules* and provided her motive is to benefit her own series score. The following ISAF Q&A (2011-022), published November 28, 2011, addresses this question. Note that this Q&A replaces ISAF Case 78.

"Situation – In a fleet race, Boat A adopts tactics that clearly interfere with and hinder Boat B's progress in the race. While using those tactics, boat A does not break any rule, except possibly rule 2.

Question – In which of the following circumstances would Boat A's tactics be considered unsportsmanlike and a breach of rule 2?

(a) Boat A's tactics benefit her series result.

(b) Boat A's tactics increase her chances of gaining selection for another event.

(c) Boat A's tactics increase her chances of gaining selection to her national team.

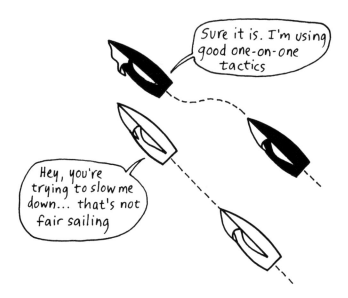

(d) Boat A and Boat C had agreed that they would both adopt tactics that benefited Boat C's series result.

(e) Boat A was attempting to worsen Boat B's race or series score for reasons unconnected with sport.

Answer – In circumstances (a), (b) and (c), Boat A would be in compliance with recognized principles of sportsmanship and fair play because there is a sporting reason for her actions. In circumstance (d), both Boat A and Boat C would clearly break rule 2. In addition, by receiving help prohibited by rule 41 (Outside Help) from Boat A, Boat C would also break rule 41. In circumstance (e) Boat A would break rule 2 because, with no good sporting reason, her actions would clearly break recognized principles of sportsmanship and fair play."

Though some may shiver at the notion that it is okay for one boat to actively try to hinder another boat's race, the racing rules themselves are in no way constructed to discourage, inhibit or prevent this. In fact, it is quite common for one boat to try to start close to leeward of another for the purpose of hindering the other's start, to intentionally tack on someone's wind on a beat, or to luff a boat downwind. In addition, it is quite common for sailors to be aware of "who their competition is" from the outset of a race or series and to actively seek opportunities to hinder them early on. As long as it's done within the racing rules, there is no problem.

"What happens if a boat hinders my race and causes me to finish worse than I would have otherwise finished, and is found to have broken the Fair Sailing rule (rule 2) in the process?"

Then you are entitled to redress under rule 62.1(d) (Redress)! You can request this yourself, or the race or protest committee can do it on your behalf (rule 60, Right to Protest; Right to Request Redress or Rule 69 Action).

When a protest committee feels that an individual competitor has acted in a way that is contrary to the sport, they can conduct a hearing under rule 69 (Allegations of Gross Misconduct).

RULE 69 — ALLEGATIONS OF GROSS MISCONDUCT

RULE 69.1 — OBLIGATION NOT TO COMMIT GROSS MISCONDUCT

a) A competitor shall not commit gross misconduct, including a gross breach of a *rule*, good manners or sportsmanship, or conduct bringing the sport into disrepute. Throughout rule 69, 'competitor' means a member of the crew, or the owner, of a boat.

(b) An allegation of a breach of rule 69.1(a) shall be resolved in accordance with the provisions of rule 69.

RULE 69.2 — ACTION BY A PROTEST COMMITTEE

(a) When a protest committee, from its own observation or a report received from any source, believes that a competitor may have broken rule 69.1(a), it may call a hearing. If the protest committee decides to call a hearing, it shall promptly inform the competitor in writing of the alleged breach and of the time and place of the hearing. If the competitor provides good reason for being unable to attend the hearing, the protest committee shall reschedule it.

(b) A protest committee of at least three members shall conduct the hearing, following the procedures in rules 63.2, 63.3(a), 63.4 and 63.6.

(c) If it is established to the comfortable satisfaction of the protest committee, bearing in mind the seriousness of the alleged misconduct, that the competitor has broken rule 69.1(a), it shall either

   (1) warn the competitor or

   (2) impose a penalty by excluding the competitor and, when appropriate,

disqualifying a boat, from a race or the remaining races or all races of the series, or by taking other action within its jurisdiction. A disqualification under this rule shall not be excluded from the boat's series score.

3) If the standard of proof in this rule conflicts with the laws of a country, the national authority may, with the approval of the ISAF, change it with a prescription to this rule.

(d) The protest committee shall promptly report a penalty, but not a warning, to the national authorities of the venue, of the competitor and of the boat owner. If the protest committee is an international jury appointed by the ISAF under rule 89.2(b), it shall send a copy of the report to the ISAF.

(e) If the competitor does not provide good reason for being unable to attend the hearing and does not come to it, the protest committee may conduct it without the competitor present. If the committee does so and penalizes the competitor, it shall include in the report it makes under rule 69.2(d) the facts found, the decision and the reasons for it.

(f) If the protest committee chooses not to conduct the hearing without the competitor present or if the hearing cannot be scheduled for a time and place when it would be reasonable for the competitor to attend, the protest committee shall collect all available information and, if the allegation seems justified, make a report to the relevant national authorities. If the protest committee is an international jury appointed by the ISAF under rule 89.2(b), it shall send a copy of the report to the ISAF.

(g) When the protest committee has left the event and a report alleging a breach of rule 69.1(a) is received, the race committee or organizing authority may appoint a new protest committee to proceed under this rule.

If the protest committee decides that the competitor has acted improperly, it can warn him, exclude him or disqualify his boat from one or more races in a series or the entire series, or take other action available to it. If it disqualifies his boat, the DSQ cannot be dropped from the series score. Notice that it must also report its action, other than a warning, to the national authorities involved.

Rule 69 is to be used when the competitor's conduct is "gross." "Gross" can be generally interpreted as follows: conspicuously obvious, flagrant, deliberate, referring to offenses or errors so bad they cannot escape notice or be condoned or actions exceeding reasonable or excusable limits.

In my opinion, any **deliberate infringement** of the *rules* is a gross infringement. For example: S deliberately rams P causing damage (perhaps because the skipper of S had been disqualified based on a protest by the skipper of P in a protest hearing the night before). Another example is when a competitor deliberately cuts a *mark* or *starts* ahead of the starting line for the purpose of hindering another competitor's race. See ISAF Case 34.

Further examples of a gross breach of good manners or sportsmanship include: **proven lying** in a protest hearing (as opposed to honest differences in recollection of the incident); **intentional cheating** (for instance, racing with an unmeasured sail or removing mandatory ballast, as opposed to class or racing rule violations caused by ignorance); **intentional damage to another boat** afloat or on shore, (for instance, cutting someone's shrouds in the night); **fighting,** particularly where there is injury or damage; **stealing** from another boat or from private property at a club or elsewhere; and **foul or threatening language,** particularly if it is continued after receiving a clear warning.

Obviously rule 69 is an important rule, but its effectiveness relies on the integrity of the protest committee that chooses to invoke it. Each case must be carefully examined to determine, as accurately as possible, exactly what happened, what events led up to the incident, and what the probable motives of the individuals involved were. The hearing and deliberations should be conducted as objectively as possible with an effort to keep emotions out. A competitor's previous actions should not be weighed in the case unless germane and accurately represented. Appeals that are cited as precedent must be closely examined to be sure that they are truly nearly identical in all ways. And before imposing a penalty under rule 69.2(c)(2), the protest committee must thoroughly consider if the weight of the punishment is justified by the competitor's action. See the ISAF and US Sailing Judges Manuals for guidance on holding rule 69 hearings.

Disqualification from a series for a gross infringement of the *rules* or a gross breach of good manners or sportsmanship is a strong penalty by itself, due to the effect it generally has on the individual(s) and from the adverse publicity it can create. But in addition, this penalty must also be reported to US Sailing or the appropriate national authorit(ies). In turn they can conduct an investigation and exclude the competitor(s) or boat(s) from the sport for a period of time. This is extremely strong as it will have an impact on the sailor's life beyond just their sailing, in ways that may extend beyond just the time period of their penalty.

Note that a sailor penalized under rule 69 is a *party* to a hearing (see the definition *Party*), and as such has the right to appeal the decision of the protest committee under rule 70.1(a) (Appeals and Requests to a National Authority). U.S. sailors may also file a grievance under Regulation 15 of the US Sailing Regulations when they feel actions have been taken against them that are not in accordance with the *rules*.

RULE 3 — ACCEPTANCE OF THE RULES

By participating in a race conducted under these racing rules, each competitor and boat owner agrees

(a) to be governed by the *rules*;

(b) to accept the penalties imposed and other action taken under the *rules*, subject to the appeal and review procedures provided in them, as the final determination of any matter arising under the *rules*; and

(c) with respect to any such determination, not to resort to any court of law or tribunal.

Rule 3 states that when you decide to race under the ISAF *Racing Rules of Sailing*, you agree to be governed by those *rules*, and to keep actions made in accordance with the rules within the rules system of the sport; i.e., not to take them to any outside court. Note that Appendix J (Notice of Race and Sailing Instructions) requires that the Notice of Race include, when appropriate, an entry form to be signed by the boat's owner or owner's representative, containing words such as: "'I agree to be bound by *The Racing Rules of Sailing* and by all other *rules* that govern this event'."

This agreement becomes especially important when an incident results in a high cost of repair or replacement. Rule 67 (Damages) states, "*The question of damages arising from a breach of any **rule** shall be governed by the prescriptions, if any, of the national authority.*"

In the United States, US Sailing prescribes "*...that responsibility for damages arising from any breach of the **rules** shall be based on fault as determined by application of the **rules**, and that she shall not be governed by the legal doctrine of 'assumption of risk' for monetary damages resulting from contact* *with other boats.*" Furthermore, the prescription states, "*A protest committee shall find facts and make decisions only in compliance with the **rules**. No protest committee or US Sailing appeal authority shall adjudicate any claim for damages. Such a claim is subject to the jurisdiction of the courts.*"

In other words, a protest committee can find only the facts; and a protest committee, or appeals committee acting on an appeal, can decide only which boat was at fault under the *rules*. They cannot decide issues of claims for damages.

When you disagree with a protest committee's application or interpretation of the *rules*, you may appeal under rule 70.1 (Appeals and Requests to a National Authority), unless the right of appeal has been denied under rule 70.5. If you feel that any of your rights as a competitor have been denied by the organizing authority, race committee, protest committee, equipment inspection committee or measurement committee, and it hurt, or may hurt, your score in a race or series through no fault of your own, you can request redress under rule 62 (Redress) and you can appeal that decision as well.

If ever you feel you've been aggrieved by an action not under the jurisdiction of the *rules*, you can take your grievance to the organizing authority for the race or series, or to US Sailing through Regulation 15 of the US Sailing Regulations.

RULE 4 — DECISION TO RACE

The responsibility for a boat's decision to participate in a race or to continue *racing* is hers alone.

There have been attempted lawsuits brought unsuccessfully against race committees by sailors who have had accidents during races in strong winds. Their contentions have been, in part, that the race committee has jeopardized their safety by holding races in severe conditions. The decision to start, postpone or abandon a race is within the jurisdiction of the race committee (see rule 90.1, Race Committee; Sailing Instructions; Scoring). Rule 62 (Redress) should not be interpreted to restrict or interfere with its authority and responsibilities in matters of race management. Under rule 4, each boat has the sole responsibility to decide whether or not to race. If a boat decides not to race, she cannot claim her score was made worse through no fault of her own. (See US Sailing Appeal 39.)

Notice that it is the **boat's** responsibility to decide. Every sailor on a boat has the responsibility to voice his or her opinion as to whether or not to *start* or to continue to *race*. Nothing in this rule protects an owner, skipper or helmsman from a liability suit by their crew.

RULE 5 — ANTI-DOPING

A competitor shall comply with the World Anti-Doping Code, the rules of the World Anti-Doping Agency and ISAF Regulation 21, Anti-Doping Code. An alleged or actual breach of this rule shall be dealt with under Regulation 21. It shall not be grounds for a *protest* and rule 63.1 does not apply.

Clearly, this is primarily of concern for Olympic-bound competitors. However, all competitors are wise to recognize that there is a strict rule forbidding the use of banned drugs in our sport. ISAF Regulation 21, Anti-Doping Code, is not included in the rule book because it can be changed at any time. ISAF regulations plus any updates or new versions can be obtained through the ISAF website (sailing.org/racingrules/documents) or the US Sailing website (ussailing. org/racingrules/documents).

5

The Definitions

The Definitions are the "dictionary" of the rule book. Words and terms like "racing," "obstruction" and "proper course" are specifically defined so that there is no question or debate as to their meaning. When a defined word or term is used in a *rule*, it is printed in *italic* type. Before studying the *rules*, be sure to study the Definitions and then actively check back to them as you go through each *rule*; you'll find that in a short time you will be confident of each *rule's* full meaning.

ABANDON

A race that a race committee or protest committee *abandons* is void but may be resailed.

N

A race committee can *abandon* a race before it starts (rule 27.3, Other Race Committee Actions Before the Starting Signal), while it is under way (rule 32, Shortening or Abandoning After the Start) or even after one or more boats have finished (rule 32.1). To signal an *abandonment*, the race committee will make three consecutive sound signals and display flag N (meaning return to the starting area for a new start), flag N over H (meaning return to the harbor and await further instructions) or flag N over A (meaning no more races that day). (See Race Signals.) A protest committee, acting on a request for redress, can *abandon* a race (rule 64.2, Decisions on Redress). A race that has been properly *abandoned* may be resailed.

N over H

N over A

Notice that once the race has started, the race committee is governed by rule 32 when deciding whether to *abandon* a race. Rule 32 lists the five scenarios in which the race committee may *abandon* a race:

1) because of an error in the starting procedure,

2) because of foul weather,

3) because of insufficient wind making it unlikely that any boat will *finish* within the time limit,

4) because a *mark* is missing or out of position, or

5) for any other reason directly affecting the safety or fairness of the competition.

 "Does rule 32.1(e) mean that the race committee can abandon a race in progress when a large wind shift occurs?"

Yes, when in its judgment the wind shift has made the race an unsatisfactory test of skill and therefore "unfair." However, in my opinion it is desirable to reduce the number of subjective decisions a race committee can make once the race has started and it can see who is or isn't doing well. Therefore, once a race has been started, race committees should make every attempt to anticipate and react to wind shifts and to reposition *marks* in order to keep the race "fair" before deciding to *abandon*, particularly after the first boat has rounded the first *mark*.

After at least one boat has sailed the course and *finished* within the time limit, if any, the race committee and protest committee are required, before *abandoning* the race, to consider the probable consequences for all boats affected and to take appropriate evidence when doubt exists (rules 32 and 64.2). (See US Sailing Appeal 100.)

CLEAR ASTERN AND CLEAR AHEAD; OVERLAP

One boat is *clear astern* of another when her hull and equipment in normal position are behind a line abeam from the aftermost point of the other boat's hull and equipment in normal position. The other boat is *clear ahead*. They *overlap* when neither is *clear astern*. However, they also *overlap* when a boat between them *overlaps* both. These terms always apply to boats on the same *tack*. They do not apply to boats on opposite *tacks* unless rule 18 applies or both boats are sailing more than ninety degrees from the true wind.

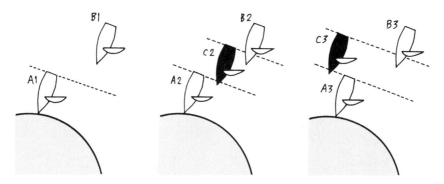

In position 1, A and B are not overlapped; A is clear ahead and B is clear astern.

In position 2, C is in between A and B and overlapped with both of them; therefore B is overlapped with A.

In position 3, C is not in between A and B; therefore B is overlapped with C, C is overlapped with A, and A and B are not overlapped.

Putting aside for a moment what *tack* the boats are on, let's look at two boats sailing near each other. To figure out if they are *overlapped,* take one of the boats and draw a line down her centerline. Then find the aftermost point of her hull or equipment in **normal position**. Draw another line perpendicular to the centerline and through the aftermost point. If the other boat's hull and equipment in **normal position** are completely behind that line, she is *clear astern* and the other boat is *clear ahead*. If she is across that line at all, then neither boat is *clear astern* of the other; therefore they are *overlapped.*

Now let's say one of the boats was *clear ahead* of the other boat by five feet. Put a third boat in between the two. If the boat that was *clear astern* now *overlaps* this middle boat and the middle boat *overlaps* the boat that was *clear ahead,* the definition says that now each boat is *overlapped* with each other.

One point worth discussing is determining the aftermost point of the hull and equipment in normal position. It literally means the point on the boat that is the farthest aft; i.e., the point that would hit a wall first if the boat were backed into one.

Notice also the term "normal position" (see the definition *Finish* for more discussion). If your auxiliary engine is tilted up, then in all likelihood the propeller is the aftermost point; and if you've been sailing the race with it up, you can't come into a *mark* and quickly swing the engine down just to break an *overlap* by making your boat shorter.

Finally, notice that the terms "clear astern," "clear ahead" and "overlap" do not apply to boats on opposite *tacks* unless either rule 18 (Mark-Room) applies (which is when one of the boats is in the *zone* at a *mark*), or unless both of the boats are sailing below a beam reach (90 degrees to the true wind), as they would be doing on a downwind leg. So two boats side by side on opposite *tacks* inside the *zone* at a leeward *mark* are considered to be *overlapped*.

FETCHING

A boat is *fetching* a *mark* when she is in a position to pass to windward of it and leave it on the required side without changing *tack*.

Assume you are on *starboard tack* approaching the windward *mark* to be left to port. You are sailing a close-hauled course and it is close whether you are going to make it around the *mark*. You luff up to head to wind, coast around the *mark*, and then bear away onto the next leg of the course. You "fetched" the *mark* because you never went past head to wind during your rounding maneuver. If you had gone past head to wind, you would have instantly changed *tack* from *starboard tack* to *port tack* and you would have failed to "fetch" the *mark*. Anytime you are in a position where you can "fetch" the *mark*, you are *fetching*.

Note: if a boat is approaching a port-hand windward *mark* on *port tack*, and has to tack to round the *mark* (i.e., change *tack*), she is not *fetching* the *mark*.

FINISH

A boat *finishes* when any part of her hull, or crew or equipment in normal position, crosses the finishing line from the course side. However, she has not *finished* if after crossing the finishing line she

(a) **takes a penalty under rule 44.2,**

(b) **corrects an error under rule 28.2 made at the line, or**

(c) **continues to sail the course.**

You *finish* when any part of your hull, or of your crew or equipment in normal position, crosses the finish line. Therefore, in a strong adverse current for example, all you need to do is get your bow across the finishing line to get your finishing position or time. Rule 28.1 (Sailing the Course) states, "*After finishing she need not cross the finishing line completely.*"

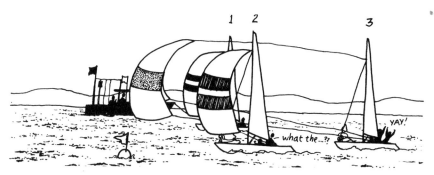

Boat 3's spinnaker is not in normal position.

Notice that your crew and equipment must be in "normal position." "Normal position" is generally defined as the position where your crew or equipment is normally located in the existing wind and sea conditions. Therefore boats can't come into a close downwind finish and suddenly let their spinnaker halyards and sheets out two feet, or come into a close upwind finish in light air and suddenly have their crews jump out on the trapeze to put their heads across the line.

If you foul a boat at the finishing line or touch a finishing *mark*, it's possible that you will cross the finishing line before doing your penalty turns (see rule 44.2, Penalties at the Time of an Incident). That is not a problem. Simply get clear of other boats, do your penalty turn(s) and then cross the finishing line again. You *finish* when you cross the finishing line after taking your penalty; i.e., the first time you crossed the line will be disregarded.

If you do not *finish* correctly, the race committee is allowed to score you DNF (Did Not Finish) without protesting you (rules A5, Scores Determined by the Race Committee). If you feel it has incorrectly scored you DNF, you can request redress under rule 62.1(a) (Redress). However, if you *finish*, but the race committee thinks it saw you touch a finishing *mark* and you do not take a penalty, or it thinks you skipped a *mark* or otherwise failed to sail the course correctly, it must score you as having *finished* and then protest you under rule 31 (Touching a Mark) or rule 28 (Sailing the Course) in accordance with rules 60.2 (Right to Protest; Right to Request Redress or Rule 69 Action) and 61 (Protest Requirements). (See ISAF Case 80.)

Sometimes, when coming up to a finishing line, it is not always clear which way to go across it. The definition says that a boat *finishes* when she crosses the finishing line in the direction of the course from the last *mark*. The last

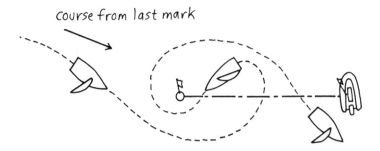

course from last mark

Boat X finishes when she crosses the finishing line the third time.

mark means the last *mark* of the course prior to the finishing line. Therefore, simply cross the line in the natural direction from the last *mark* you passed, regardless of any required sides either of the finishing *marks* may have had at other times during the race (see ISAF Case 45). And if you realize you have crossed the finishing line in the wrong direction, you can correct your error so that your course complies with rule 28 (Sailing the Course). Remember that this may require that you "unwind your string" first before crossing the line in the correct direction.

Finally, there are times when the course requires boats to sail through a gate after each lap. If the gate is the finishing line after the third lap, when the boats cross it after the second lap and continue sailing the course, they have not "finished."

INTERESTED PARTY

A person who may gain or lose as a result of a protest committee's decision, or who has a close personal interest in the decision.

Rule 63.4 (Interested Party) reads, "*A member of a protest committee who is an **interested party** shall not take any further part in the hearing but may appear as a witness.*" The purpose of this rule is clearly to provide competitors with the fairest possible hearing without any taint of prejudice or self-interest among the protest committee members.

Persons who, in my opinion, **could** be considered *interested parties* are parents (or offspring), instructors or coaches, employers or employees, and sponsors or financial contributors. Normally, members of the same yacht club or association or a fellow sailor with the same nationality are not considered "interested parties." However, in the right set of circumstances, any of these persons could be judged to be an *interested party*. (See US Sailing Appeal 107.)

There are times when protest committee members will have witnessed an incident or will have initiated a *protest* against a boat; for example, under rule 31 (Touching a Mark) if they see a boat touch a *mark*. In this context they are not *interested parties*. However the US Sailing prescription to rule 63.4 states: "*US Sailing prescribes that when practicable…no person who brings an incident to the attention of the protest committee or who will give evidence regarding an incident shall be a member of the protest committee for a hearing involving that incident.*" Therefore that person is not allowed to be **both** a member of the protest committee as well as the protestor or even a witness. However, if the sailing instructions specifically state that that prescription does not apply, the person **can** be a member of the protest committee and be the protestor or a witness, but they must give all their evidence and testimony in front of the *parties* to the hearing. Note, even if they are not the protestor, rule 63.6 requires them to state that they saw the incident (see rules 63.3(a), Right to Be Present and 63.6, Taking Evidence and Finding Facts, and US Sailing Appeal 39.)

"What can I do if I honestly feel a member of the protest committee might be an 'interested party'?"

If you feel any member of a protest committee is an *interested party*, you may object. Rule 63.4 reads, "*A **party** to the hearing who believes a member of the protest committee is an **interested party** shall object as soon as possible.*" The protest committee should then consider your objection before proceeding (Appendix M2, Recommendations for Protest Committees, Before the Hearing). In evaluating members of a protest committee as potentially *interested parties*, the important criterion is: will their hearing of the evidence, their finding of the facts and their application and interpretation of the *rules* be hindered by any prejudice or favoritism toward or against any of the *parties* to the hearing? If members of the protest committee honestly feel that any predisposition on their part will affect their decision in the hearing, they should respectfully decline to serve. Furthermore, rule 63.4 requires them to "*declare any possible self-interest as soon as they are aware of it.*" And when you honestly feel or suspect that a protest committee member's decision-making ability might be affected for some reason, you have a right to say so and to state your reasons (rule 63.4).

KEEP CLEAR

A boat *keeps clear* of a right-of-way boat

(a) if the right-of-way boat can sail her course with no need to take avoiding action and,

(b) when the boats are *overlapped*, if the right-of-way boat can also change course in both directions without immediately making contact.

The *rules* are structured so that when two boats converge on the race course, one has the right-of-way and the other must stay out of her way; i.e., *keep clear*. The preamble to Part 2, Section A reads, "*A boat has right of way over another boat when the other boat is required to* **keep clear** *of her.*" I call the boat that is required to *keep clear* the "keep-clear" boat.

The principle in the definition is clear: right-of-way boats should be able to sail their race without keep-clear boats getting in their way. That means that not only must a keep-clear boat not hit a right-of-way boat, she must also not get so close that the right-of-way boat can no longer sail her straight-ahead course because she has to take action to avoid contact with the keep-clear boat. Though this avoiding "action" will normally be a change of course, it could also be a change of speed or some other action.

On the issue of "need," I believe that when the right-of-way boat has a reasonable apprehension that contact will occur without action on her part, she is justified in saying she "needed" to take action, even if subsequent analysis of the situation shows that the keep-clear boat would have actually cleared her by inches (see ISAF Case 50).

The second part of the definition (part (b)) closes a possible loophole caused by rule 16 (Changing Course). Rule 16.1 requires that when right-of-way boats change course, they give other boats *room* to *keep clear*. The loophole is that a *windward* boat (W) or a *port-tack* boat (P) could position herself so close to a *leeward* boat (L) or a *starboard-tack* boat (S) such that the moment L or S changed course she would hit W or P. W or P could then claim that L or S had broken rule 16.1 by not giving her *room* to *keep clear*. The definition closes that loophole by addressing *overlapped* boats and telling W or P that she is not *keeping clear* if she allows herself to get so close to L or S that L or

S couldn't change course in **both** directions at that moment without "immediately" making contact with her. Keep in mind that boats on opposite tacks are considered "overlapped" when rule 18 applies, or when both of them are sailing more than 90 degrees from the true wind.

Note that the word "if" in part (b) of the definition suggests that L or S does not need to actually hit W or P to prove she couldn't change course without making immediate contact. If the protest committee decides that L or S couldn't have changed course without immediately hitting W or P, then W or P has broken rule 11 (On the Same Tack, Overlapped) or rule 10 (On Opposite Tacks) simply by their extreme close proximity to the right-of-way boats.

"Do I have to keep clear of the right-of-way boat's crew, sails, equipment,
spars, etc. even when they are clearly out of their 'normal position'?"

Yes. In the "Introduction" to the *Racing Rules of Sailing*, under "Terminology" it says "'*Boat' means a sailboat and the crew on board.*" And the definition makes no distinction regarding whether or not a boat is carrying her crew, sails, equipment, spars, etc. in "normal position" (see ISAF Case 91). The only exception is in the rare instance where a boat is *keeping clear* and suddenly something from the right-of-way boat flies out unexpectedly and immediately makes contact with the keep-clear boat. ISAF Case 77 describes such a case where just after rounding a leeward *mark*, the head of the spinnaker of the boat *clear ahead* (A) came loose and flew back and touched the headstay of the boat *clear astern* (B). The decision concludes, "[Rule 12] requires B to keep

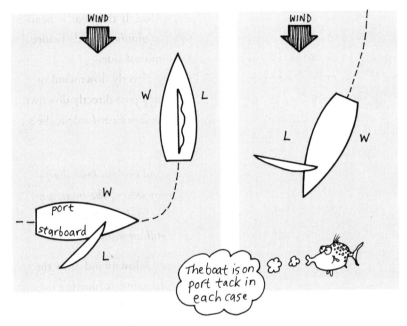

The boat on the left is reaching with her port side toward the wind; therefore her port side is her windward side and she is on port tack. When she luffs up to head to wind she remains on port tack. The boat on the right is sailing by the lee with her mainsail lying naturally on her starboard side. Therefore her port side is her windward side and she is also on port tack.

clear of A, which she is doing because nothing B did or failed to do required A 'to take avoiding action' (see the definition Keep Clear). This is shown by the fact that the contact between them results exclusively from A's equipment moving unexpectedly out of normal position."

LEEWARD AND WINDWARD

A boat's *leeward* side is the side that is or, when she is head to wind, was away from the wind. However, when sailing by the lee or directly downwind, her *leeward* side is the side on which her mainsail lies. The other side is her *windward* side. When two boats on the same *tack overlap*, the one on the *leeward* side of the other is the *leeward* boat. The other is the *windward* boat.

The definition *Tack, Starboard* or *Port* tells us that whether we are on *port* or *starboard tack* is determined by our *windward* side; i.e., if our *windward* side is our port side, we are on *port tack*.

This definition tells us that our *windward* side is the side closest to the wind, and that our *leeward* side is the opposite side. If the boat is heading directly into the wind, then whichever side **was** the *windward* side before the boat was head to wind is still considered the *windward* side.

The only exception is when the boat is heading directly downwind or "by the lee" (which means the boat has continued to turn past directly downwind without the boom changing sides). In that case, the *windward* side is the side opposite the side the boom is on.

"If I'm sailing close-hauled on port-tack in light air and heel the boat sharp- *ly to windward such that the boom falls to the port side of the boat, am I now on starboard tack; or if I'm sailing by the lee and forcibly holding the mainsail over the port side with my arm, am I still on starboard tack?"*

No. Remember that when you are not sailing directly downwind or by the lee, your *tack* is determined by the side of the boat the wind is blowing over. In your first case, when you are sailing close-hauled, the wind is blowing over your port side regardless of where your boom is located; therefore you are on *port tack*. The same would be true if you are sailing along on *port tack*, and then go head to wind and push your boom out on the port side to back down. You are still on *port tack* as long as your bow doesn't **pass** head to wind. The moment it **passes** head to wind, you are now on *starboard tack*.

When you are sailing directly downwind or by the lee, your *leeward* side is the side on which your mainsail "lies." "Lies" is used intentionally to indicate that it is the side where your mainsail would **naturally** lie; i.e., be pushed by the wind, as opposed to by the control of some other force such as your arm, the mainsheet or gravity. Therefore, in your second case, you are now on *port tack* because if you released the mainsail, it would lie on your starboard side. The same would be true if, while sailing directly downwind, you trimmed the mainsail in amidships. Your *tack* will be determined by where the mainsail would lie naturally; in this case, most likely it will want to go back out to the side it was on before you trimmed it in.

Finally, there is the definition of *windward* and *leeward* boat. If the boats are **on the same *tack*** and they are ***overlapped,*** the one on the *leeward* side of the other is the *leeward* boat. The other is the *windward* boat. Notice that if they are not *overlapped*, they are not "*windward*" and "*leeward*" boats; they are "*clear ahead*" and "*clear astern*."

MARK

An object the sailing instructions require a boat to leave on a specified side, and a race committee boat surrounded by navigable water from which the starting or finishing line extends. An anchor line or an object attached accidentally to a *mark* is not part of it.

A *mark* can be an inflatable ball, a bell buoy, a large power boat, an island or any object the sailing instructions so indicate. Notice that often the sailing instructions require that government *marks* be passed on their required side as you sail from one turning *mark* to the next. These government *marks* are *marks* of the course as well. Also note that the entire object is the *mark*, not just the above-water part.

On a starting line between a race committee boat and a buoy, the **entire** race committee boat is a *mark* even though the actual end of the line is marked by a flag or some other specific point on the boat. Note that anything that is **intentionally** attached to the object is also part of the *mark*; for instance, a flag, a long antenna or a swimming platform. This also includes something temporarily attached such as a Whaler tied up to the race committee boat, or a "keep-off buoy" hung off the transom of the race committee boat to keep boats farther away. However, the race committee's anchor line is not part of the *mark*.

MARK-ROOM

Room for a boat to leave a *mark* on the required side. Also,

(a) *room* to sail to the *mark* when her *proper course* is to sail close to it, and

(b) *room* to round the *mark* as necessary to sail the course.

However, *mark-room* for a boat does not include *room* to tack unless she is *overlapped* inside and to *windward* of the boat required to give *mark-room* and she would be *fetching* the *mark* after her tack.

This definition is central to applying rule 18 (Mark-Room). It describes the "space" (see the definition *Room*) a boat needs to give another boat when one of them is in the *zone*. The definition describes two different points in time: first, while the inside boat is sailing "to" the *mark*; and then while the inside boat is rounding the *mark*. Let's look at the first part of the definition first.

Rule 18 begins to apply when the first of the boats involved reaches the *zone* (rule 18.1), which is normally when she is three of her hull lengths from the *mark*. From that point, the outside boat or the boat *clear astern* must give the other boat *mark-room*. *Mark-Room* is the space the inside or *clear ahead* boat needs to leave the *mark* on the required side.

Furthermore, if the *proper course* of the inside or *clear ahead* boat is to sail close to the *mark* (let's say within a length or so), which will certainly be the case when the boat is rounding the *mark*, then *mark-room* includes the space needed to sail to the *mark* in a "seamanlike way," which means handling her boat in a normal way without risk of touching the boat giving her *mark-room* or the *mark*. Allowing her this space prevents an outside boat with luffing rights from luffing an inside boat inside the *zone* before she gets to the *mark*. Note, however, the use of the term "*proper course*" in the definition is purely a test for whether the boat is entitled to *room* to sail to the *mark*; it does not mean that the boat is entitled to space to actually sail her "*proper course*" to the *mark*.

Say, for instance, the inside boat was leaving the *mark* to port. Clearly, it would not be "seamanlike" to sail a course that will result in touching the *mark* or leaving the *mark* to starboard. Therefore, to sail "to" the *mark*, P will sail a course that will bring her slightly to the right of the mark in anticipation of her rounding or passing maneuver at the *mark*. See the discussion of the definition *Room* for a discussion on how far from the mark it is "seamanlike" to sail.

An example of a boat in the *zone* whose *proper course* is not to sail close to the *mark*, is a boat approaching the finishing line a couple lengths from one of the finishing *marks*. Clearly the boat is in the *zone* of the finishing *mark*, but her *proper course* will be to cross the finishing line as soon as possible, which may mean she will get no closer than two lengths to the actual *mark*. In that case, *mark-room* does not include space for her to sail "to" the *mark* (see the discussion of rules 18.2(b) and 18.2(c)(2) in Chapter 8 to understand why this is important).

"OK, I understand that when I'm a keep-clear boat and I'm approaching a rounding mark, I get room to sail "to" the mark in a seamanlike way. But how much room do I get when I am rounding the mark; and when have I taken all the room I am entitled to?"

You are entitled to *room* to round the *mark* as necessary to sail the course, which means just enough space to allow you to round the *mark* in a "seamanlike way" (see the definition *Room*). "Seamanlike way" means the space needed to not be at risk of touching the *mark* or the outside or *clear astern* boat during your rounding. Note, *mark-room* does not include the space you might want to sail your *proper course*; i.e., the course you might want to sail for tactical reasons. Once you have rounded the *mark* and can *keep clear* of a right-of-way boat without risk of touching the *mark* or fouling another boat, you have taken all the *room* available in *mark-room*. This might occur before you have left the *mark* astern.

Note that an inside boat is entitled to the space she needs to tack to round or pass a *mark*, but only when she is *overlapped* to *windward* of a boat that is required to give her *mark-room*, and she would be *fetching* the *mark* after her tack.

OBSTRUCTION

An object that a boat could not pass without changing course substantially, if she were sailing directly towards it and one of her hull lengths from it. An object that can be safely passed on only one side and an area so designated by the sailing instructions are also *obstructions*. However, a boat *racing* is not an *obstruction* to other boats unless they are required to *keep clear* of her, give her *room* or *mark-room* or, if rule 23 applies, avoid her. A vessel under way, including a boat *racing*, is never a continuing *obstruction*.

An *obstruction* can be **anything** on the race course including a moored boat, dock, breakwater, cruising boat, iceberg in the racing area or another boat in your race, large enough to qualify it as an *obstruction*. In determining whether the object can be considered an *obstruction*, the definition offers three criteria:

1) the object must be large enough to require you to change course substantially **if** you were aiming right at the largest part of it, regardless of whether you **actually** are or not. In other words, it is a hypothetical test. An object does not become an *obstruction* or cease to be an *obstruction* based on where you are actually aiming at the time in the race.

2) the amount of course change required is determined from a point one of your boat's overall lengths away from the object. This strongly suggests that you keep a lookout for anything ahead of you, as opposed to suddenly finding yourself about to hit something right in front of you and needing to slam your tiller over to miss it.

3) the size of the course change must be "substantial;" i.e., a large course change. In a 20-foot boat, a course change of 10 degrees moves the bow about three and a half feet. Done when one boat-length away, a 10-degree alteration will clear a seven-foot object on either side. **As my general rule** I would say that a course change less than 10 degrees is not "substantial;" i.e., a stationary object clearly less than one-third your boat's length would not be an *obstruction*, though a moving object will require a larger alteration to get around it. Obviously, a lobster pot or an average-size channel marker is not going to require you to change your course substantially, but a race committee boat, a breakwater or another sailboat in a race will.

A powerboat can be an *obstruction* if it's large enough. When a race committee decides to use a powerboat as one end of the starting line, the powerboat becomes a *mark* also. Notice that it doesn't cease to be an *obstruction*. It is always an *obstruction*, but now it also happens to be a *mark*.

"Can you clarify the times when a boat in a race can be considered an *'obstruction'?"*

Sure. A boat in a race, either your race or another race, is an "obstruction" when either:

1) it has the right of way over at least two boats in the situation; or

2) it is capsized or has not regained control after capsizing; or

3) it is anchored or aground; or

4) it is trying to help a person or vessel in danger.

Otherwise, boats in a race are not considered *obstructions*.

Furthermore, when *obstructions* are boats under way, including boats that are *racing*, they are never considered "continuing" *obstructions*. This pertains to the application of rule 19 (Room to Pass an Obstruction).

OVERLAP

See **Clear Astern** *and* **Clear Ahead; Overlap**

PARTY

A *party* to a hearing is

(a) for a protest hearing: a protestor, a protestee;

(b) for a request for redress: a boat requesting redress or for which redress is requested, a race committee acting under rule 60.2(b);

(c) for a request for redress under rule 62.1(a): the body alleged to have made an improper action or omission;

(d) a boat or a competitor that may be penalized under rule 69.2.

However, the protest committee is never a *party*.

It is important to understand exactly who is, and is not, a *party* to a hearing. The primary reason is that the rules in Part 5, Protests, Redress, Hearings, Misconduct and Appeals, provide many specific rights and obligations for *parties* to a hearing and many requirements of a protest committee regarding *parties* to a hearing. Furthermore, only a *party* to a hearing may appeal a decision of a protest committee under rule 70.1 (Appeals and Requests to a National Authority).

When boats lodge a *protest* they automatically become a *party* to the hearing (protestor), as do the boats they are protesting (protestee). The same is true when they request redress under rule 62 (Redress). When boats request redress under rule 62.1(a), claiming that an improper action or omission of the race committee, organizing authority, equipment inspection committee or measurement committee made their score significantly worse, those bodies also become a *party* to the hearing. Note that the protest committee is never a *party*, even when it is the subject of a request for redress under rule 62.1(a).

Often, in the course of a hearing, a third boat will become a "suspect." The protest committee has the right to protest that third boat. Rule 60.3(a)(2) (Right To Protest; Right to Request Redress or Rule 69 Action) says, "*[The protest committee] may protest a boat if during the hearing of a valid **protest** it learns that the boat, although not a **party** to the hearing, was involved in the incident and may have broken a **rule**.*" And rule 61.1(c) (Protest Requirements; Informing the Protestee) says, "*If the protest committee decides to protest a boat under rule 60.3(a)(2), it shall inform her as soon as reasonably possible, close the current hearing, proceed as required by rules 61.2 and 63, and hear the original and the new **protests** together.*" Once the protest committee protests the third boat, that boat (now a "protestee") becomes a *party* to the hearing.

"If, after acting on another boat's request for redress, the protest committee abandons the race in which I was first, can I consider myself a 'party to the hearing' because I was 'penalized,' and as such appeal the decision?"

Absolutely not. Rule 64 (Decisions) discusses "penalties," using disqualification as the usual penalty. You were not given a specific "penalty" when the race was *abandoned*. Obviously *abandoning* the race changes series results, moving some competitors up and some down. You may have been disappointed by the *abandonment*, but you were not "penalized" by it. A "penalty" results from a rule breach either accepted voluntarily or imposed by a protest committee decision. Because you were not liable to be penalized in the incident, you are not a *party* to the hearing and are not entitled to appeal.

On the other hand, you certainly can request redress under rule 62.1(a) (Redress), making you a *party* to your redress hearing. You must be prepared to demonstrate what "improper action or omission" the protest committee made in reaching its decision to *abandon* the race, and how the action/omission made your finishing place significantly worse through no fault of your own. Then, once the protest committee has made a decision on your redress request, you may appeal **that** decision. Note, however, that a boat is not entitled to redress if the claim is simply that the protest committee's decision made her score worse (see rule 62.1(a)).

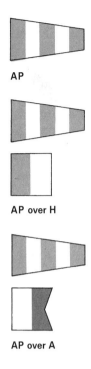

AP

AP over H

AP over A

Finally, boats or competitors who are liable to be penalized under rule 69.2 (Allegations of Gross Misconduct, Action by a Protest Committee) **are** a *party* to a hearing, thereby giving them standing to appeal the protest committee's decision should they want to do so.

POSTPONE

A postponed race is delayed before its scheduled start but may be started or *abandoned* later.

A race can be *postponed* only if it has not been started. Once a race has been started, it can only be stopped by *abandoning* it. To signal a *postponement*, the race committee will make two consecutive sound signals and display flag AP, flag AP over H (meaning return to the harbor and await further instructions) or flag AP over A (meaning no more races that day). (See Race Signals.)

PROPER COURSE

A course a boat would sail to *finish* as soon as possible in the absence of the other boats referred to in the rule using the term. A boat has no *proper course* before her starting signal.

This is the most subjective definition in the book. It is also very important, particularly in applying rule 17 (On the Same Tack; Proper Course). The concept is very straightforward: your *proper course* is the course you think will get you from the starting line to the finishing line as quickly as possible, taking into account all the factors that will affect your speed. Typically, different sailors will have different ideas on what their fastest course is; thus different boats will have justifiably different *proper courses*.

One way to visualize this concept is to imagine a Time Trial. You and nine other sailors show up to race around a fixed-length triangle course, one at a time; the one with the fastest time wins. Around the windward-reach-reach course there are wind shifts, grandstands and a small man-made island on the second reach for the press and photographers. You start. You've already calculated the fastest path up the first beat, accounting for wind shifts, waves,

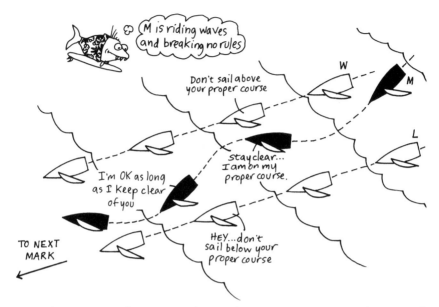

M is surfing waves in order to increase her speed in an attempt to arrive at the next mark and ultimately the finishing line as soon as possible. Therefore, her luffs are justifiable changes in her proper course; and when she bears away she is keeping clear of L. M has not broken any rule.

current, time lost while tacking and so on. Down the first reach, as you approach the grandstand area you notice it's creating a huge wind shadow so you bear away to avoid the light air and break through to leeward as quickly as possible. On the second reach, you've calculated that passing to leeward of the press island is the shortest, fastest route to the leeward mark. You finish.

The next boat starts. But this boat goes a different way up the beat. And it doesn't think the grandstand's wind shadow is that bad, so it doesn't bear off as much. And finally it passes the press island to windward and finishes. Both boats were trying to race and finish as quickly as possible and so they were both sailing *proper courses*. In fact, all the boats may have had different opinions as to the fastest course that day. The course each boat sailed was a *proper course*.

Clearly it is possible that there may be several *proper courses* at any given moment, depending upon the particular circumstances involved. However, because it is often difficult to prove when someone is actually on a *proper course* as opposed to sailing extra high or low for tactical purposes, ISAF

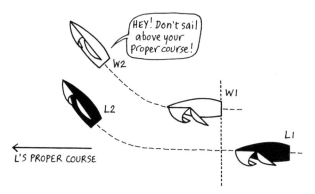

L became overlapped from clear astern and then luffed above her proper course solely to make it more difficult for W to stay ahead of her. In W's absence L would not have luffed at all. Therefore, L has broken rule 17 by sailing above her proper course.

Case 14 suggests, "Which of two different courses is the faster one to the next mark can not be determined in advance and is not necessarily proven by one boat or the other reaching the next mark ahead." For protest committees, two reasonable criteria for judging a *proper course* are whether the boat sailing it has a logical reason for its being a *proper course* and whether she applies it with some consistency.

The phrase "*in the absence of the other boats referred to in the rule using the term*" clarifies which boats to "remove" when determining whether a course is a *proper course* or not. Note that it certainly does not mean 'in the absence of all the boats in the race.' Let's say you and another boat are sailing down a reach. You catch up and become *overlapped* to *leeward* of the other boat (W). Rule 17 (On the Same Tack; Proper Course) tells you that you cannot sail above your *proper course* while *overlapped* with W. Because W is the "other boat" referred to in rule 17, your *proper course* is your fastest course in the absence of W.

As you and W continue down the reach, you begin catching up to a group of boats in front of you going slowly. Now you have to decide whether to head up and try to pass the group to windward, or bear away and try to pass them to leeward. You decide that you will arrive at the gybe *mark* faster by heading up and passing the group to windward, but by heading up, you will collide with the *windward* boat. In this case, heading up can be considered your *proper course* because you would do so even in the absence of W.

The point is: your *proper course* should be based on what will get **you** to

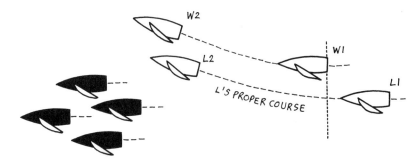

L is "limited" to sailing no higher than her proper course because she became over-lapped from clear astern. However, L decides that she will arrive at the gybe mark sooner by luffing and sailing to windward of the pack in front of her. Because she would do this even in the absence of W, it is a legitimate new proper course for L and W must keep clear under rule 11.

the next *mark* and ultimately to the finishing line as quickly as possible, not on a tactical consideration such as heading up to cut off a nearby *windward* boat. Note that the rules referring to *proper courses* are the definition *Mark-Room*, rules 17, 18.1(b), 18.2(c)(2), 18.4 and 24.2, Appendix C2.2 (match racing), and appendices B and F (windsurfing and kiteboarding) definition *Mark-Room* and *About to Round or Pass* and rule 18.4.

Notice also that there is no *proper course* **before** the starting signal. That is because a *proper course* is the course sailed to *finish* as soon as possible. Obviously, you can't start racing toward the finishing line until you are allowed to *start*; therefore, there is no *proper course* until after the starting signal is made.

PROTEST

An allegation made under rule 61.2 by a boat, a race committee or a protest committee that a boat has broken a *rule*.

For the most part, allegations and decisions on whether boats have broken any *rules* are handled after the race in a hearing called by a protest committee. The procedure to ask for such a hearing is called a *protest*. Rules 60 (Right to Protest; Right to Request Redress or Rule 69 Action) and 61 (Protest Requirements) clearly outline the rights and requirements for boats, race committees and protest committees who wish to protest.

Note that a "request for redress" under rule 62 is not a *protest*. For you to "request redress," you must make your request in writing, and state why you are claiming it, no later than the protest time limit or two hours after the incident, whichever is later. You don't need to fly a protest flag (rule 62, Redress).

RACING

A boat is *racing* from her preparatory signal until she *finishes* and clears the finishing line and *marks* or retires, or until the race committee signals a general recall, *postponement* or *abandonment*.

It is important to know when you are *racing* because you can be penalized for breaking a rule of Part 2 (When Boats Meet) only when you are *racing*, with the exception of rule 24.1, Interfering with Another Boat (see the preamble to Part 2).

You begin *racing* at your preparatory signal. In a "5-4-1-GO" sequence, the four-minute signal is the preparatory signal (Rule 26, Starting Races). In a "3-2-1-GO" sequence, it's usually the two-minute signal (Appendix S, Sound-Signal Starting System). Check the sailing instructions for the race to find out when your actual preparatory signal is.

You are no longer *racing* when you have *finished* and cleared the finishing line and *marks*. US Sailing Appeal 16 reads, "…when no part of a boat's hull, equipment or crew is still on the finishing line, she has cleared it."

 "When am I considered to be clear of the finishing marks?"

You have "cleared the finishing *marks*" when you are no longer at risk of hitting them during or just after an incident that occurred while you were *finishing*. US Sailing Appeal 26 says, "The official diagram shows that the boat in this case finished six hull lengths away from the mark that she subsequently touched. When she cleared the line, she was well clear of the mark. Thus, her contact with the mark occurred after she had finished and cleared the finishing line and finishing marks. Since she was no longer racing, rule 31 no longer applied."

ROOM

The space a boat needs in the existing conditions, including space to comply with her obligations under the rules of Part 2 and rule 31, while manoeuvring promptly in a seamanlike way.

This definition is central to applying rule 15 (Acquiring Right of Way); rule 16 (Changing Course); rule 18 (Mark-Room); rule 19 (Room to Pass an Obstruction); and rule 20 (Room to Tack at an Obstruction).

"Room" is "space." It is the space on the water a boat "needs" at the time. For instance, when the term is used in rule 15 and 16, it is the space the keep-clear boat needs to *keep clear* of the right-of-way boat. When the term is used in the definition *Mark-Room*, it is the space the inside boat needs to sail to and around the *mark*. When used in rule 19, it is the space the inside boat needs to pass between the outside boat and the *obstruction*.

Note the word "promptly" which means "performed readily, quickly, almost immediately." This builds in a time element to the definition. Therefore when a *leeward* boat (L) luffs or bears away near a *windward* boat (W), rule 16.1 requires L to give W *room* to *keep clear*, but W must respond "promptly" or risk losing the protection of *room*. The same is true when a *port-tack* boat (P) tacks close in front of, or to *leeward* of, a *starboard-tack* boat (S) and rule 15 applies.

To expand on "seamanlike," I would say "seamanlike" means "responsible, prudent, safety conscious." In other words, it is "seamanlike" never to put your or another boat's crew, boat or equipment at risk of damage or injury. Furthermore, "seamanlike" describes the way competent, but not expert, sailors handle their boat.

Note that "room" includes the space a boat needs to comply with the rules in Part 2, which include the right-of-way and *mark-room* rules, and rule 31 (Touching a Mark). For instance, if three boats are approaching a *mark*, and the inside boats are entitled to *mark*-room, the outside boat has to give the middle boat "room" to comply with her obligation to give the inside boat "room" to sail between her and the mark.

"Does the definition Room take into account the experience or the number of the crew on board the boat?"

No. ISAF Case 103 addresses this head on by saying, "Neither the experience of IW's crew nor their number is relevant in determining 'room'…the interpretation of 'seamanlike way' must be based on the boat-handling that can reasonably be expected from a competent, but not expert, crew of the appropriate number for the boat."

Furthermore, US Sailing Appeal 20 talks about tactical *mark* roundings and says in essence that *room* does not include all the space an inside boat might like to take to make a tactically desirable rounding.

RULE

(a) The rules in this book, including the Definitions, Race Signals, Introduction, preambles and the rules of relevant appendices, but not titles;

(b) ISAF Regulation 19, Eligibility Code; Regulation 20, Advertising Code; Regulation 21, Anti-Doping Code; and Regulation 22, Sailor Classification Code;

(c) the prescriptions of the national authority, unless they are changed by the sailing instructions in compliance with the national authority's prescription, if any, to rule 88;

(d) the class rules (for a boat racing under a handicap or rating system, the rules of that system are 'class rules');

(e) the notice of race;

(f) the sailing instructions; and

(g) any other documents that govern the event.

This is the complete list of the *rules* that govern a race. Note that the notice of race and the sailing instructions are *rules* so it is important to read them carefully before entering a race. Sailing instructions can change certain racing rules, **but they must refer specifically to the rule being changed** and state the change (see rule 86.1(b), Changes to the Racing Rules). Note that one of the rules sailing instructions cannot change is rule 42 (Propulsion). Note also that the term "racing rule" means a *rule* in *The Racing Rules of Sailing* (RRS) (see Introduction in the RRS; Terminology).

Also note that class rules are only permitted to change certain rules of *The Racing Rules of Sailing*, specifically: rule 42 (Propulsion); rule 49 (Crew Position); rule 50 (Setting and Sheeting Sails); rule 51, (Movable Ballast); rule 52 (Manual Power); rule 53 (Skin Friction) and rule 54 (Forestays and Headsail Tacks). They too **must refer specifically to the rule being changed** and state the change (see rule 86.1(c), Changes to the Racing Rules). Class rules that conflict with other racing rules do not apply.

START

A boat *starts* when, having been entirely on the pre-start side of the starting line at or after her starting signal, and having complied with rule 30.1 if it applies, any part of her hull, crew or equipment crosses the starting line in the direction of the first *mark*.

You cannot *start* until after the starting signal for your class. If any part of your hull, crew or equipment is on the course side of the starting line at the starting signal, you must return completely behind the line to *start* correctly (rule 28.1, Sailing the Course). If you don't, the race committee can score you OCS (On the Course Side) or DNS (Did Not Start) without needing to protest you (rule A5, Scores Determined by the Race Committee). If you feel the race committee has incorrectly scored you OCS or DNS, you can request redress under rule 62.1(a) (Redress).

Notice that you *start* when, having been entirely on the pre-start side of the starting line at or after the starting signal is made, **any** part of your hull, crew or equipment first crosses the starting line. There is no mention of **normal position** here. If your bow person is calling the line from the pulpit and inadvertently sticks his or her hand over the line just before the gun, or if your crew, by going out on the trapeze, mistakenly puts his or her head over the line one second before the gun, you are "on the course side." The same is true if anchored and your anchor and anchor line are over the starting line.

The definition refers to rule 30.1 (Starting Penalties; I Flag Rule), commonly referred to as the "round-an-end rule." Notice that the race committee can signal the "round-an-end rule" on any start it wants simply by displaying flag I as the preparatory signal. When it is lowered one minute before the starting signal, accompanied by one long sound signal, it means that the one-minute period of rule 30.1 has begun.

I

The purpose of the rule is to keep people from charging over the line early and making it difficult for the race committee to have a fair start. The way it works is, if you are on the course side of the starting line or its extensions during the minute before your starting signal, you must sail back to the pre-start side of the line outside one of the starting marks across the extension of the starting line before starting; i.e., you must **sail around one end of the starting line or the other at some point** before *starting* correctly. Notice you can get back around an end immediately; you don't have to wait for the starting signal to be made.

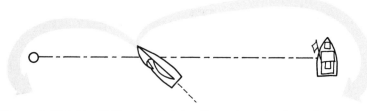

When rule 30.1 (the "I Flag Rule") is in effect, a boat that is on the course side of the starting line at any time during the final minute before the starting signal must sail back outside one of the starting marks across the extension of the starting line before starting. She may do this immediately if she chooses; i.e., she does not need to wait for the starting signal before going around an end.

Notice that anytime you are sailing back towards the pre-start side of the starting line or its extensions **after** your starting signal, you have to *keep clear* of any boats not doing so until you are completely on the pre-start side (rule 22.1, Starting Errors; Taking Penalties; Moving Astern).

Notice also the more stringent starting penalties available to race committees in rules 30.2 (Z Flag Rule) and 30.3 (Black Flag Rule).

TACK, STARBOARD OR PORT

A boat is on the *tack, starboard* or *port*, corresponding to her *windward* side.

When *racing*, you are **always** on either *starboard* or *port tack*, even when you are in the act of tacking or gybing. Your *tack* (*starboard* or *port*) is determined by your *windward* side; i.e., if your port side is your *windward* side, you are on *port tack*. For discussion on how to determine your *windward* side, see the definition *Leeward* and *Windward*.

Let's look at a boat (P) tacking from *port tack* to *starboard tack*. At some point during her tack, P will pass head to wind. At the moment she passes head to wind her starboard side becomes her *windward* side; therefore she is instantly on *starboard tack*. However, rule 13 (While Tacking) requires her to *keep clear* of other boats until she is on a close-hauled course; and rule 15 (Acquiring Right of Way) requires her to initially give other boats *room* to *keep clear* once she gets the right of way.

Note, in match racing (Appendix C), a boat sailing downwind that is gybing must *keep clear* of other boats from the time the foot of her mainsail crosses the centerline until the mainsail has filled, admittedly a very short period of time (rule C2.4).

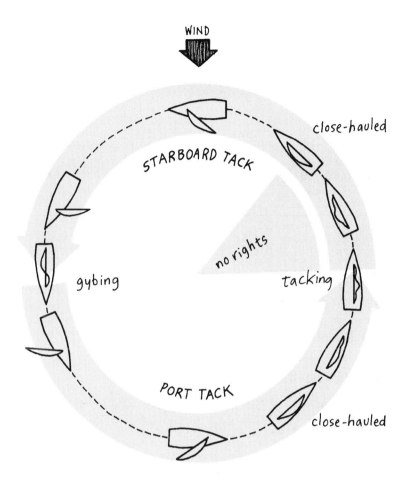

WINDWARD

See *Leeward* and *Windward*.

ZONE

The area around a *mark* within a distance of three hull lengths of the boat nearer to it. A boat is in the *zone* when any part of her hull is in the *zone*.

As boats near a *mark*, rule 18 (Mark-Room) provides specific instructions regarding which boats are entitled to *mark-room*, which must give *mark-room* to others, etc. These instructions begin to apply when the boats first enter the *zone*.

The *zone* is essentially a circle with the *mark* at its center whose radius is three hull lengths of the boat that is nearest to it. Therefore, if a 24-foot boat

The Zone is an imaginary area with the mark at its center, and extending out a distance equal to three hull lengths of the boat that is nearest the mark (unless team or match racing in which case the zone is two lengths, or radio sailing in which case it is four lengths).

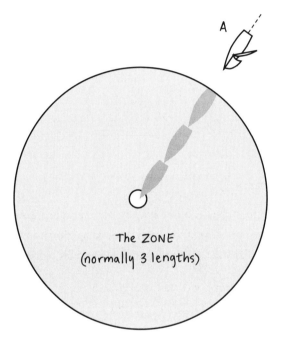

The ZONE
(normally 3 lengths)

and a 30-foot boat are approaching a *mark* and the 24-foot boat is nearer the *mark*, the *zone* is 72 feet (3 x 24 feet) from the *mark*. Obviously, if the *mark* were a boat, then the shape of the *zone* would be more oblong.

Note, a boat is in the *zone* based on her hull and not her spinnaker or bowsprit. Webster's dictionary defines the "hull" of a boat as its "frame or body, exclusive of masts, yards, sails and rigging." Furthermore, the use of the term "hull length" is intended to clarify that the *zone* is based solely on the length of the hull, and not the additional length of bowsprits, overhanging mizzen booms, etc.

Finally note that the *zone* in team and match racing is "two lengths" (rules C2.3, Match Racing Rules and D1.1(a), Team Racing Rules), and in radio-controlled boat racing it is "four lengths" (rule E1.3, Radio Sailing Racing Rules).

6

Part 2, Preamble and Section A
When Boats Meet – Right of Way

When boats that are **both** *racing* meet, the rules that apply are in Part 2 of the rule book.

PREAMBLE TO PART 2

The rules of Part 2 apply between boats that are sailing in or near the racing area and intend to *race,* are *racing,* or have been *racing.* However, a boat not *racing* shall not be penalized for breaking one of these rules, except rule 24.1.

When a boat sailing under these rules meets a vessel that is not, she shall comply with the International Regulations for Preventing Collisions at Sea (IRPCAS) or government right-of-way rules. If the sailing instructions so state, the rules of Part 2 are replaced by the right-of-way rules of the IRPCAS or by government right-of-way rules.

The preamble clarifies **which** *rules* apply **when** and to **whom.** Note that the "preambles" rank as *rules* (see the definition *Rule*). If the rules of Part 2 apply to you and you are approaching a vessel that is clearly not in any way a part of a race, e.g., a cruising boat or commercial tug, then you are required (note the word "shall") to comply with the Inland Navigational Rules (in U.S. waters) or the International Regulations for Preventing Collisions at Sea (outside of a country's waters) or other applicable government right-of-way rules. If you don't, you can be protested under rule 60 (Right to Protest; Right to Request Redress or Rule 69 Action) and penalized under rule 64.1 (Penalties and Exoneration).

When the Inland Navigational Rules (in U.S. waters) or the International Regulations for Preventing Collisions at Sea (outside of a country's waters) are to replace the *The Racing Rules of Sailing*, e.g., when the race will continue after sunset, the sailing instructions must specifically contain the numbers of the applicable INR or IRPCAS and state the time(s) or places(s) they will apply, as well as any night signals to be used by the race committee (Appendix J2.2(2), Notice of Race and Sailing Instructions).

Sailors wishing a complete copy of the INR or IRPCAS should contact the US Sailing office for information on how to get one.

 "Is it true that the rules of Part 2 apply between boats that are racing in different races?"

Yes. The rules of Part 2 apply between boats in different races as long as they both fit the description in the preamble of Part 2. Rule 63.8 (Protests between Boats in Different Races) reads, *"A **protest** between boats sailing in different races conducted by different organizing authorities shall be heard by a protest committee acceptable to those authorities."*

Also, notice that when you intend to *race*, the rules of Part 2 only apply from when you begin to sail in or near the racing area until you have left the racing area; and they only apply between boats intending to race. This distinction may be important in resolving a financial claim after a serious collision when the boats were not actually *racing*.

 "I realize I am technically 'racing' after my preparatory signal, but what happens if I accidentally foul a boat before or after I am racing?"

The preamble to Part 2 says, *"a boat not **racing** shall not be penalized for breaking one of these rules, except rule 24.1."* Rule 24.1 (Interfering with Another Boat) says that even if you aren't *racing*, you can't interfere with a boat that is; see discussion of rule 24.1. Rule 44.1 (Taking a Penalty) says, *"A boat may take a Two-Turns Penalty when she may have broken one or more rules of Part 2 in an incident **while racing** (emphasis added)."* Therefore, if you break a *rule* before your preparatory signal (i.e., before you are *racing*), other than rule 24.1, apologize and continue on. But if you break rule 24.1, you can't take a Two-Turns Penalty. You can be protested and penalized under rule 64.1 (Penalties and Exoneration). Note, rule 64.1 says *"If a boat has broken a rule when not **racing**, her penalty shall apply to the race sailed nearest in time to*

that of the incident."

Of course, if there is damage, you and/or the other boat may choose to protest so that the protest committee can find the facts and make a decision as to who was at fault. Though neither one of you can be "penalized" under rule 64.1 (Penalties and Exoneration), the facts and decision of the protest committee may be useful in determining who pays for the damage (rule 67, Damages).

Remember, under the definition of *racing*, you are *racing* from your preparatory signal until you have *finished* and cleared the finishing line and finishing *marks* or retired. So if your preparatory signal is four minutes before your starting signal and you foul someone with three and a half minutes to go, you can be disqualified if you don't take a penalty. Remember also that you are no longer *racing* the moment your transom clears the finishing line and finishing *marks* (US Sailing Appeals 16 and 26 and rule 28.1, Sailing the Course).

Note, however, that if you are not *racing* and break any other rules, other than those in Part 2 (When Boats Meet) and Part 4 (Other Requirements When Racing) and rule 31 (Touching a Mark), you will receive a penalty under rule 64.1 (Penalties and Exoneration). For instance, you will be penalized before or after you are *racing* for breaking the sailing instructions, or for violating the principles in rule 2 (Fair Sailing), or for committing a "gross breach of a *rule* or of good manners or sportsmanship" under rule 69 (Allegations of Gross Misconduct), or for not complying with the rules of Part 6 (Entry and Qualification) which include rules 75, 78 and 80 which concern eligibility, measurement compliance and advertising. And your penalty will be applied to the race sailed nearest in time to that of the incident (rule 64.1, Penalties and Exoneration).

"If five minutes before my preparatory signal I'm near the starting line on starboard tack and despite my best effort to avoid the collision my boat gets holed by a port tacker who is also intending to race, and as a result I can't sail in the race, do I have any recourse under the rules?"

You sure do. You should protest them under rule 10 (On Opposite Tacks) and request redress under rule 62.1(b) (Redress). Both of you were intending to *race* and were sailing in the racing area; therefore you were both governed by *The Racing Rules of Sailing* (preamble to Part 2, When Boats Meet). The *port-tack* boat (P) was required to *keep clear* of you while you were on *starboard tack* under rule 10. Though P cannot be penalized for breaking this rule as she was not *racing* at the time, the protest committee is required to hold a hearing, find facts and determine which boat, if either, was at fault (rules 63.1, Hearings; 64.1, Penalties and Exoneration; and 65.1, Informing the Parties and Others). Once P is found to have broken rule 10, the protest committee must turn to your request for redress (rule 63.1); and you should be granted redress as your race score was made significantly worse (you were unable to race!) through no fault of your own due to the physical damage caused by P, a boat that was breaking a rule of Part 2 at the time. Furthermore, the question of financial responsibility for damages may be helped by a finding of facts and fault by the protest committee (see rule 67, Damages).

 "If I'm racing and a boat definitely fouls me, and later in the race I am converging with them and I don't have the right of way, do I have to keep clear of them even though they were wrong in the first incident?"

You bet! When competitors know they have broken a *rule*, they are expected to promptly take a penalty (see Basic Principles, Sportsmanship and the Rules in the "Introduction of the RRS").

But while a boat continues to race, she maintains all her rights just as any other boat. US Sailing Appeal 1 reads, "*Pilgrim* (X) and Y were involved in an incident early in a race, and each protested the other. Later in the same race, *Maori* (Z), which had observed the incident and believed X to have been in the wrong, refused to yield right of way to her. X protested Z. The protest committee disqualified X for breaking a rule in the first incident. It then disqualified Z, despite her contention that X, having been disqualified for a breach of a rule in the first incident, was no longer entitled to rights under the rules. Z appealed. DECISION: The decision of the protest committee is upheld..."

ISAF Case 1 reads, "Boats A, B, and C are racing with others. After an incident between A and B, boat A hails 'Protest!' and displays her protest flag, but boat B does not take a penalty. Later, B protests a third boat, C, after a second incident. The protest committee hears A's protest against B and disqualifies B. Does this disqualification invalidate B's protest against C?

ANSWER: No. When a boat continues to race after an alleged breach of a rule, her rights and obligations under the rules do not change. Consequently, even though A's protest against B is upheld, the protest committee must hear B's protest against C and, if B's protest is valid and the protest committee is satisfied from the evidence that C broke a rule, she must be disqualified."

PREAMBLE TO SECTION A

A boat has right of way over another boat when the other boat is required to *keep clear* of her. However, some rules in Sections B, C and D limit the actions of a right-of-way boat.

The rules of Part 2 are written to clearly say which boat must *keep clear* of the other. (See the definition *Keep Clear* for a full discussion of the meaning of this phrase.) For example, rule 10 (On Opposite Tacks) says, *"When boats are on opposite **tacks**, a **port-tack** boat shall **keep clear** of a **starboard-tack** boat."* Therefore, in learning the rules, it is helpful to learn which boats do **not** have the right of way in meeting situations, as these are the boats with the requirement to stay out of the other's way. Note: "shall" when used in the *rules* means "must"; i.e., it is a mandatory requirement.

There are just four basic right-of-way rules (rules 10–13), and they are found in Section A. They cover the three basic relationships boats can be in (on the same tack, on the opposite tack or changing tacks), and they are:

- on *opposite tacks* .... *port tack keeps clear* of *starboard tack*
  – rule 10
- on same *tack*, overlapped .... *windward keeps clear* of *leeward*
  – rule 11
- on same *tack*, not overlapped .... *clear astern keeps clear* of *clear ahead*
  – rule 12
- changing *tacks* by tacking .... boat tacking *keeps clear* of other boats
  – rule 13

RULE 10 — ON OPPOSITE TACKS

When boats are on opposite *tacks*, a *port-tack* boat shall *keep clear* of a *starboard-tack* boat.

This basic rule applies to boats that are on **opposite** *tacks*. When boats are on the **same** *tack*, rules 11 *(windward/leeward)* and 12 *(clear astern/clear ahead)* apply. Thus, if on a downwind leg a *starboard-tack* boat comes up from behind and runs into a *port-tack* boat (assuming no damage or injury), who will be penalized under the rules? The *port-tack* boat under rule 10, because the two boats are on *opposite tacks*.

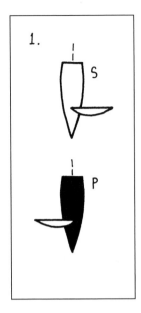

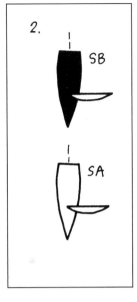

In position 1, the boats are on opposite tacks; therefore S has right of way over P under rule 10.

In position 2, both boats are on the same tack; therefore SB must keep clear of SA under rule 12.

  "If I'm on a beat converging with a port-tack boat and she hails "Hold your course," is that hail binding on me?"

US Sailing Appeal 27 reads, "In response to the questions regarding a boat that has been hailed to hold course, it is permissible to hail, but the rules do not recognize such a hail as binding on the other boat. S can tack or bear away at any time she is satisfied that a change of course will be necessary to avoid a collision."

My opinion is that in order for the *port-tack* boat to be liable for failure to *keep clear*, it is important that as they approach each other, the *starboard-tack* boat hold her course as long as she can do so with safety. I recommend that when *port-tack* boats are about to cross close in front of *starboard-tack* boats, P should hail "Hold your course" or otherwise alert S that P is there, she realizes it will be close, and she wants S to hold her course for as long as possible.

  "Okay, but do I have to hit the port-tacker to prove there was a foul; and if there is no contact, whom is the 'onus of proof' on?"

S does NOT have to hit P to prove that P failed to *keep clear*. S should avoid the collision and protest. Though the rule itself contains no specific "onus" (i.e., an assignment of responsibility to one boat or the other to prove the other boat's guilt), ISAF Case 50 discusses the whole issue, including the question

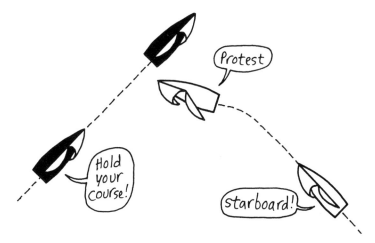

Though it is common for P to hail "Hold your course" to assure S that P is aware that she's there and to encourage S to give her every opportunity to try and cross, S is in no way bound by that hail to actually do so. S may bear away or tack at any time she has a reasonable concern that her change of course is necessary to avoid a collision.

of "onus of proof": "Rule 10 protests involving no contact are very common, and protest committees tend to handle them in very different ways. Some place an onus on the port-tack boat to prove conclusively that she would have cleared the starboard-tack boat, even when the latter's evidence is barely worthy of credence. No such onus appears in rule 10. Other protest committees are reluctant to allow any rule 10 protest in the absence of contact, unless the starboard-tack boat proves conclusively that contact would have occurred had she not changed course. Both approaches are incorrect.

"A starboard-tack boat in such circumstances need not hold her course so as to prove, by hitting the port-tack boat, that a collision was inevitable. Moreover, if she does so she will break rule 14 (Avoiding Contact). At a protest hearing, S must establish either that contact would have occurred if she had held her course, or that there was enough doubt that P could safely cross ahead to create a reasonable apprehension of contact on S's part and that it was unlikely that S would have 'no need to take avoiding action' (see the definition *Keep Clear*).

"In her own defence, P must present adequate evidence to establish either that S did not change course or that P would have safely crossed ahead of S and that S had no need to take avoiding action. When, after considering all the evidence, a protest committee finds that S did not change course or that there was not a genuine and reasonable apprehension of collision on her part, it should dismiss her protest. When, however, it is satisfied that S did change course, that there was reasonable doubt that P could have crossed ahead, and that S was justified in taking avoiding action by bearing away, then P should be disqualified."

In ISAF Case 88, P and S were converging on an upwind leg. When three and then two lengths away, S hailed "Starboard" but P held her collision course. When just under two lengths away, and fearing a collision, S luffed to try to minimize the contact at the same moment P bore away sharply. S then bore away sharply to pull her transom out of P's way. P passed astern of S within two feet; there was no contact. The protest committee dismissed S's rule 10 *protest* against P and S appealed.

In its decision, the appeals committee says, "Rule 10 required P to 'keep clear' of S. 'Keep clear' means something more than 'avoid contact;' otherwise the rule would contain those or similar words. Therefore, the fact that the boats did not collide does not necessarily establish that P kept clear. The definition Keep Clear in combination with the facts determines whether or not P complied with the rule. In this case, the key question raised by the definition is whether S was able to sail her course 'with no need to take avoiding action.'" After listing all the considerations it took into account, the appeals committee concluded that S did have a need to take avoiding action, and disqualified P for breaking rule 10.

RULES 11 AND 12 — ON THE SAME TACK

Rules 11 and 12 are the basic rules for boats on the **same** *tack*. When boats are on the same *tack* they can either be *overlapped* or not *overlapped*. If they are *overlapped*, they are either a *windward* boat or a *leeward* boat. If they are not *overlapped*, they are either *clear ahead* or *clear astern*.

RULE 11 — ON THE SAME TACK, OVERLAPPED

When boats are on the same *tack* and *overlapped*, a *windward* boat shall *keep clear* of a *leeward* boat.

When boats on the same *tack* are *overlapped*, rule 11 applies. When boats are on much different angles of sail, it is often difficult to know which is the *leeward* boat. The boat that will hit the other's *leeward* side or be hit on her own

 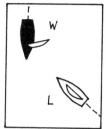 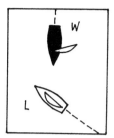 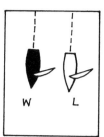

In each situation, both boats are on the same tack. The white boat is the leeward boat and the black boat must keep clear under rule 11.

windward side is the *leeward* boat. As a good rule of thumb, the boat that is on the point of sail closer to the wind is typically the *leeward* boat; i.e., between a boat sailing downwind and a boat sailing close-hauled, the close-hauled boat is usually the *leeward* boat.

"I realize that when I'm the windward boat I have to keep clear of the leeward boat, but how far away do I need to stay?"

Far enough away so that while the *leeward* boat (L) is sailing on a straight line, you do not hit L or force L to take any avoiding action to miss you; e.g., have to change her course, ease her spinnaker pole forward or require any of her crew to duck or move to avoid being hit.

Furthermore, you need to be far enough away so that the *leeward* boat can change course in **both** directions without **immediately** making contact with you. If you allow yourself to get so close to L that she is physically unable to change her course without immediately hitting you, you are not *keeping clear* under the definition *Keep Clear* and are breaking rule 11. Note that the word "if" in the second part of the definition suggests that L does not need to actually hit you to prove she couldn't change course without hitting you. If the protest committee decides that L couldn't change course without immediate contact, then you have broken rule 11 simply by your extreme close proximity to L.

More importantly, **anytime** L cannot sail her course without a need to take action to avoid you, you have not *kept clear* and have broken rule 11. Therefore, you will be smart not to allow yourself to get so close that you will possibly interfere with L in the least. Notice also that when L is head to wind, it is quite possible that you will be required to go **beyond** head to wind (i.e., change *tacks*) in order to *keep clear*. If this is the case, you must do so. Also, if you are converging with L and both of you are sailing on what you each believe to be your *proper course*, rule 11 requires you to *keep clear* of L.

RULE 12 – ON THE SAME TACK, NOT OVERLAPPED

When boats are on the same *tack* and not *overlapped*, a boat *clear astern* shall *keep clear* of a boat *clear ahead*.

In 1949 the rule read, "A yacht Overtaking another shall keep clear while she is Clear Astern." Now the rules only talk about boats that are *clear ahead* or *clear astern*; however, the concept is still the same. A boat, as in cars on the road, coming up from behind another boat on the same *tack*, must not hit her.

Rule 12 clearly identifies a boat or boats *clear ahead* as right-of-way boats, therefore making them *obstructions* to boats coming up from behind (definition *Obstruction*). ISAF Case 41 reads, "At positions 1 and 2, rule 12 requires both BL and BW to keep clear of A. Therefore, A is an obstruction to both BL and BW..." as the last sentence of the definition Obstruction makes clear. When they are at A, still overlapped, rule 19 will come into effect."

Note, rule 12 applies only to boats when they are on the **same** tack. If a *starboard-tack* boat (S) is astern but on a collision course with a *port-tack* boat (P), P must get out of S's way even though S is the "overtaking" boat. Because the boats are on **opposite tacks**, S is the right-of-way boat under rule 10 (On Opposite Tacks).

RULE 13 – WHILE TACKING

After a boat passes head to wind, she shall *keep clear* of other boats until she is on a close-hauled course. During that time rules 10, 11 and 12 do not apply. If two boats are subject to this rule at the same time, the one on the other's port side or the one astern shall *keep clear*.

Remember that under the definition *Tack, Starboard* or *Port*, you are always on one *tack* or the other. So if you are on *starboard tack* and turn your boat towards the wind, the moment your boat passes head to wind you are instantly on *port tack*.

Rule 13 provides a transitional rule that applies when a boat is changing *tacks* by tacking. "Tacking" is the maneuver by which a boat changes *tacks* with the bow passing head to wind. Generally that involves an approximately

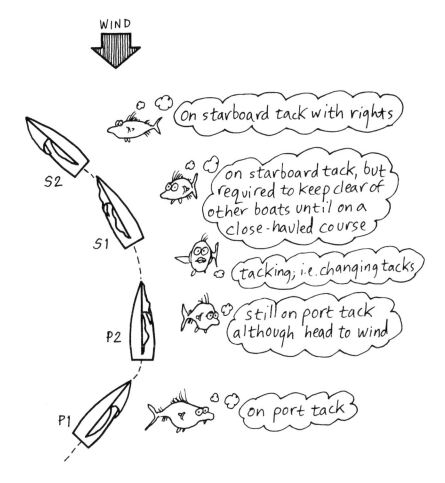

90-degree turn from a close-hauled course on one *tack* to a close-hauled course on the other *tack*.

Rule 13 simply says that while you are tacking, you must *keep clear* of other boats from the moment you pass head to wind until you are on a close-hauled course (on **either** *tack*). A "close-hauled course" is the course a boat will sail when racing upwind and sailing as close to the wind as she can. Notice that to be on a close-hauled course, the sails don't need to be full nor does the boat need any headway (see ISAF Case 17). Note that once you pass head to wind, rule 13 turns off rules 10, 11 and 12. Therefore, after you pass head to wind and before you're on a close-hauled course, if another boat hits you or has to change her course to avoid you, you have not *kept clear* and have broken rule 13.

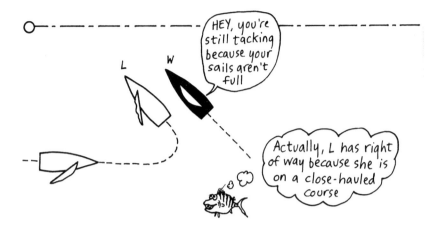

In the rare instance where two boats are tacking near each other and both are past head to wind but neither is close-hauled yet, the one on the other's port side must *keep clear*; or put another way, the boat on the right has the right of way. The same applies if the boats are not *overlapped*; the boat behind must *keep clear*.

"Gybing" is the maneuver by which a boat changes *tacks* with the bow turning away from the wind. For instance, when sailing downwind on *port tack*, the moment the foot of your mainsail crosses the centerline and can stay on the new side with no human force applied, you are on *starboard tack* (see the definition *Leeward* and *Windward* for a complete discussion on determining a boat's *tack* when sailing downwind or by the lee). Because the act of "gybing" is generally so momentary, there is no special transitional rule for "gybing" except in match racing under Appendix C. Rule C2.4 reads, "*After the foot of the mainsail of a boat sailing downwind crosses the centreline she shall **keep clear** of other boats until her mainsail has filled.*"

 "*When I tack or gybe into a right-of-way position, do I have to give other boats room to keep clear of me?*"

Absolutely yes. For a full explanation of the obligations of boats that acquire right of way, see the discussion of rule 15 (Acquiring Right of Way).

 "*Will you be discussing how the rules work in Slam Dunks?*"

You bet. That explanation occurs at the end of the discussion of rule 17 (On the Same Tack; Proper Course).

7

Part 2, Section B
When Boats Meet – General Limitations

In addition to the right-of-way rules, Part 2 also contains rules that **limit** the actions of right-of-way boats (rules 14-17). In other words, a right-of-way boat cannot just go anywhere she wants. These limitations are found in Section B. One example is that a right-of-way boat can be penalized when she's involved in contact that causes any damage or injury (rule 14). Another is that whenever a right-of-way boat changes her course, she is required to give the other boat *room* to *keep clear* (rule 16.1). Therefore, it is equally important to know what limitations the rules place on right-of-way boats in various situations.

RULE 14 – AVOIDING CONTACT

A boat shall avoid contact with another boat if reasonably possible. However, a right-of-way boat or one entitled to *room* or *mark-room*

(a) need not act to avoid contact until it is clear that the other boat is not *keeping clear* or giving *room* or *mark-room*, and

(b) shall be exonerated if she breaks this rule and the contact does not cause damage or injury.

This is a very strong rule regarding contact. It talks to all boats in a race, including right-of-way boats, and tells them to avoid any contact whatsoever if reasonably possible. The intent of the rule is to minimize the amount of collisions that occur during a race, and particularly the intentional ones. Collisions can be dangerous, expensive, frustrating to all sailors and particularly intimidating to newcomers and novice sailors. They are not part of the sport.

When two or more boats converge, the possibility of contact exists. The rules clearly assign the right of way and the requirement to *keep clear* or to give *room* or *mark-room* in each situation where boats could hit. Furthermore, when one boat is required to *keep clear*, the other shouldn't do anything to make the situation more dangerous. Rule 14(a) makes it clear that the right-of-way boat or one entitled to *room* or *mark-room* can hold her course until it becomes "clear" that the other boat is not going to *keep clear* or give *room* or *mark-room*. At that moment, the right-of-way boat or one entitled to *room* must take action herself to avoid contact if reasonably possible. For instance, when a *port-tack* boat is crossing a *starboard-tack* boat, if S holds her course and hits P, with no attempt to avoid the contact, P has broken rules 10 (On Opposite Tacks) and 14, and S has broken rule 14.

However, rule 14(b) states that a right-of-way boat or one entitled to *room* or *mark-room* shall be exonerated (freed from penalty) if the contact does not cause "damage or injury." "Damage" is what a boat suffers; "injury" is what a person suffers (see ISAF Case 110). Therefore, if the contact causes no physical damage or injury to any boat or person, the right-of-way boat or the one entitled to *room* or *mark-room* can be found to have broken rule 14 but cannot be penalized for doing so. On the other hand, if there is any damage or injury at all to **any** boat or person involved in the incident, no matter how slight and regardless of whether the damage or injury has any effect on the speed or handling of the boat or whether the damage or injury was to the right-of-way boat, the right-of-way boat or the boat entitled to *room* or *mark-room* will be penalized if it was found that it was reasonably possible for them to have avoided the contact.

Note that if the keep-clear boat fails to avoid contact, she technically can be disqualified under this rule; however, this is a moot point because she will be disqualified under the Section A rule she broke, and a boat can only be disqualified once in a race (rule 64.1(b), Penalties and Exoneration). Likewise, if she took a penalty for breaking one or more rules in the incident, she cannot be further penalized under rule 64.1; see rule 64.1(b) (Penalties and Exoneration).

 "If I'm involved in contact that causes damage or injury, can I do a Two-Turns Penalty or put up a yellow flag to avoid disqualification?"

If there is just "damage," then Yes! But if anyone got "injured" or if the damage was "serious," then No! Rule 44.1 (Penalties at the Time of an Incident) permits a boat that may have broken any rule in Part 2 while *racing* to take a penalty at the time of the incident. The penalty is the Two-Turns Penalty unless the sailing instructions specify the use of some other penalty (rule 44.1). So if you are a right-of-way boat or an inside boat entitled to *mark-room* and you cause damage in an incident, you can quickly do two turns in the same direction including two tacks and gybes and continue in the race. If you are the keep-clear boat, you can also do two turns which absolves you of all Part 2 and rule 31 (Touching a Mark) rule breaches you may have committed in the incident (even if you broke more than one rule in the incident; see rules 44.1 and 64.1(b).

There are two exceptions however. Rule 44.1(b) says, *"if the boat caused injury or serious damage or, despite taking a penalty, gained a significant advantage in the race or series by her breach her penalty shall be to retire."* In other words, you can't absolve yourself with a Two-Turns Penalty if anyone got injured in the incident or there was "serious" damage, or if you gained a significant advantage by breaking a *rule*.

See the explanation of rule 44 for a discussion on how to properly do a Two-Turns Penalty and what constitutes "serious damage."

"I understand that if I'm the right-of-way boat, I can be penalized for caus- *ing any damage or injury at all; what constitutes 'damage or injury'?"*

ISAF Case 110 says that "'Injury' in the racing rules refers only to bodily injury to a person, and 'damage' is limited to physical damage to a boat or her equipment." ISAF Case 19 offers an interpretation of the term "damage." "It is not possible to define 'damage' comprehensively, but one current English dictionary says 'harm or injury impairing the value or usefulness of something, or the health or normal function of a person.' This definition suggests questions to consider. Examples are:

1. Was the current market value of any part of the boat, or of the boat as a whole, diminished?
2. Was any item of the boat or its equipment made less functional?

In my opinion, a related question to number one above is, "Did the contact result in something needing to be repaired or replaced?"

Regarding "injury," I think an "injury" is something that physically hurts a person more than just briefly, and that ordinarily affects the person's ability to function normally and/or requires the person to be attended to at some point. A related question would be "Does the person need attending to; and/or is the effect on the person brief or longer lasting?"

Clearly, boats will have contact that will cause no damage or injury to either boat or crew. Examples will include two boats having light side-to-side contact while rounding a *mark*, or incidents where the crews fend off and the hulls never touch. On the other hand, there will be contact that clearly causes "damage or injury:" a hole or dent in the boat, a torn sail, a bent stanchion, a nick out of the rudder, a broken finger, etc. The hard calls will be the situations where the gel coat gets scratched, the sailors hear the fiberglass "crunch" though there is no visible sign of "damage or injury" or a crew member gets a temporary soreness from fending off, etc. Protest committees will need to exercise their best judgment in these situations. Notice that the judgment that "damage or injury" occurred is not a "fact found;" it is a conclusion based on the "facts found" and therefore subject to appeal.

 "As I understand the rule, even if I'm involved in contact that causes damage or injury, but it was not reasonably possible for me to avoid the contact, I won't be penalized under this rule; correct?"

Correct. The rule acknowledges that there may be times when it is simply not reasonably possible for a boat to avoid contact. However, this should not be viewed as a rationale for not making every effort to avoid collisions. Ultimately, whether or not it was reasonably possible to have avoided the contact will be decided by the protest committee.

The dictionary defines "reasonable" as "agreeable to reason; possessing sound judgment; not extreme or excessive." In judging whether it was "reasonably possible" for a boat to have avoided contact, it is implicit, to me, that as two boats near each other, the right-of-way boat settles on a straight-line or compass course or risk breaking rule 16.1 (Changing Course); and the keep-clear boat begins to take avoiding action. However, when, in her judgment, the right-of-way boat has a reasonable apprehension that contact will occur if she continues to hold her course, she may change her course to avoid the collision (ISAF Case 50). Rule 14(a) reinforces this by telling right-of-way boats and boats entitled to *room* or *mark-room* that they need not act to avoid contact until it is "clear" that the other boat is not *keeping clear*.

Therefore, as boats approach each other, they must continually assess the situation in terms of "what are the probable chances that I may hit this other boat or vice versa?" This judgment should factor in:

- what the response(s) have been from the other boat,

- whether the other boat is keeping a good lookout,

- what the sailing conditions are like and how well a boat of the class involved maneuvers in such conditions,

- who the sailors in the other boat are, and

- is there anything at all peculiar about the way the other boat is being handled?

In judging whether it was "reasonably possible" for a boat to have avoided contact, I'd consider whether the contact could have been avoided given the sailors' best attempts at avoiding or minimizing the impact of the collision, factoring in the amount of warning they had that a keep-clear boat might not *keep clear* or give *room* or *mark-room*, the time they had to consider what their best attempt might be, and the amount and difficulty of the boat and sail handling involved. Also factored in to a much lesser degree would be the competency of the sailors and the condition of their equipment and boat; i.e., their steering gear, cleats and so on. However, the rules do not make allowances for poor seamanship, and I would be hesitant to excuse a boat due to poor sailing skills or less than adequately functioning equipment. In other words, in my opinion, "reasonable" is defined in terms of what an average sailor possessing average sailing skills could be expected to do in a similar situation.

ISAF Case 87 addresses a situation where a *port-tack* boat (P) and a *starboard-tack* boat (S) are sailing upwind on a collision course. S expected that P would bear off and pass astern of her, but instead P "made no attempt to avoid S and struck her amidships at right angles, causing considerable damage. The protest committee disqualified both boats, P under rule 10 and S under rule 14. S appealed."

In its decision, the appeals committee says, "In P's case…P broke both rule 10 and rule 14. In S's case…[she] was required by rule 14 to avoid contact if it was 'reasonably possible' to do so. However, the second sentence of rule 14 allowed S to sail her course in the expectation that P would keep clear as required, until such time as it became evident that P would not do so...For that reason, the time between the moment it became evident that P would not keep clear and the time of the collision was a very brief interval, so brief that it was impossible for S to avoid contact. Therefore S did not break rule 14."

ISAF Case 26 concerns a collision where P, a 5-0-5, and S, a Soling, were rounding the same leeward *mark* in opposite directions. Needless to say, the 5-0-5 received most of the damage as the Soling's bow sliced through P's hull and side buoyancy-tank just aft of the mast, the force of the impact knocking P's crew overboard unhurt. The decision reads, "P, as the keep-clear boat, failed to keep a lookout and to observe her primary duties to keep clear and avoid contact. She broke both rule 10 and rule 14. An important purpose of the rules of Part 2 is to avoid contact between boats. All boats, whether or not holding right of way, should keep a lookout at all times.

"When it became clear that P was not keeping clear, S was required by rule 14 to act to avoid contact with P (see rule 14(a))...S could have luffed and avoided contact with P. Such a change of course by S would have given P more room to keep clear and would not have broken rule 16.1. The contact caused damage. Therefore, S broke rule 14 and must be penalized for having done so." (See US Sailing Appeal 52.)

ISAF Case 27 is an illustration of when it was not reasonably possible for a boat to avoid contact. It involves two boats sailing upwind on port tack approaching the starboard-tack layline. "AS, a hull length to leeward and a hull length ahead of BP, tacked as soon as she reached the starboard-tack lay line. Almost immediately she was hit and damaged by BP travelling at about ten knots." The Decision states, "When AS passed through head to wind, BP became the right-of-way boat under rule 13 and held right of way until AS assumed a close-hauled course on starboard tack. At that moment AS, having just acquired right of way under rule 10, was required by rule 15 to give BP room to keep clear. BP took no action to avoid a collision, but what could she have done? Given her speed and the distance involved, she had perhaps one to two seconds to decide what to do and then do it. It is a long-established principle of the right-of-way rules, as stated in rule 15, that a boat that becomes obligated to keep clear by an action of another boat is entitled to sufficient time for response. Also, while it was obvious that AS would have to tack to round the mark, BP was under no obligation to anticipate that AS would break rule 15…"

Another scenario in which it may not be reasonably possible for boats to avoid contact is in light air when boats have very little steerageway and large powerboat waves enter the racing area and toss the boats about.

In conclusion, to penalize a right-of-way boat or one entitled to *room* or *mark-room* under rule 14, two things must be decided. One, was the boat involved in contact that caused "damage or injury;" and two, was it "reasonably possible" for the boat to have avoided the contact? If either there was no "damage or injury," or if it is decided that the boat couldn't have reasonably avoided the contact, then the boat should not be penalized under rule 14. As a juror, I would have to be satisfied from the weight of the evidence submitted (in other words there is no onus) that a boat was negligent or had shown very poor judgment or seamanship before I penalized them. On the other hand, I expect jurors would not be very tolerant of situations where the right-of-way boat intentionally hits the keep-clear boat to prove the foul, causing any damage or injury as a result.

"If I'm on port tack, and a starboard-tacker hits me and causes damage or injury, and the damage or injury causes me to get a significantly worse score as a result, I realize that I have to do a Two-Turns Penalty because I was on port tack; but can I request redress because of the damage or injury?"

You can, but whether or not you receive it will depend on the facts found by the protest committee. Rule 62.1(b) (Redress) says that a boat is entitled to request redress when her *"score in a race or series has been or may be, through no fault of her own, made significantly worse by…injury or physical damage because of the action of a boat that was breaking a rule of Part 2…"* In the hearing, the protest committee must first decide if S broke rule 14; and if so, whether the injury or physical damage itself made your score significantly worse (see ISAF Case 110). Next it must decide if you contributed to the receiving of damage or injury. It may decide that you broke rule 14 as well because you misjudged the crossing and therefore failed to avoid the contact. Or it may decide that it was a close crossing, and though your misjudgment caused you to break rule 10 (On Opposite Tacks), S could have easily avoided hitting you, whereas there was very little you could have done to have prevented her actually hitting you.

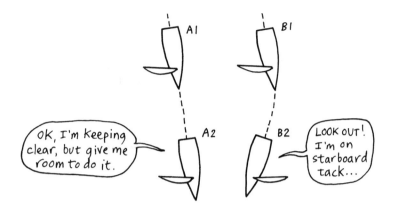

RULE 15 — ACQUIRING RIGHT OF WAY

When a boat acquires right of way, she shall initially give the other boat *room* to *keep clear*, unless she acquires right of way because of the other boat's actions.

This rule states one of the oldest and most fundamental principles in the rules, and it makes perfect sense. When a boat takes action that gives her the right of way over you, she must give you the chance to respond and *keep clear* of her. For example, you are sailing on a run on *port tack* with another *port-tack* boat just to windward. As the *leeward* boat, you have the right-of-way (rule 11, On the Same Tack, Overlapped) and everything is under control. You have the "sword," so to speak, and the *windward* boat must stay out of your way. Suddenly, the *windward* boat gybes. Now she is on *starboard tack* and you are on *port tack*. She now has the right-of-way; i.e., she now has the "sword" (rule 10, On Opposite Tacks), but she can't just gybe and hit you; her actions are limited by rule 15.

ISAF Case 24 describes a scenario where a boat (B) comes up from astern and becomes *overlapped* to *leeward* of the boat *clear ahead*. When B becomes *overlapped* she gains the right of way under rule 11, but also the limitation under rule 15 "which embodies the principle in the rules that when the right of way suddenly shifts from one boat to another, the boat with the newly acquired right of way must give the other boat space and time for response and thus a fair opportunity to keep clear." (See also ISAF Case 53.)

Note that a right-of-way boat does not have to anticipate that she will lose her right of way. ISAF Case 53 is clear on this point: "Allowing adequate time

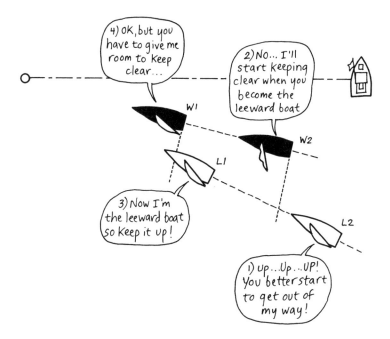

for response, when rights and obligations change between two boats, is implied in rule 15 by its requirement to allow the newly obligated boat 'room to keep clear.'" Therefore, in the example above, the *leeward* boat need not anticipate her requirement to *keep clear* as a *port-tack* boat before the *windward* boat gybes to *starboard*.

However, the use of the word "initially" clearly states that the protection of "*room* to *keep clear*" is not continuing. In the old video game *Deluxe Asteroids*, a tiny rocket ship tries to blast apart large rocks that will blow up the ship if they hit her. When there are just too many rocks about to hit, the player can press a button, putting a protective force shield around the ship. At first, the rocks bounce off the shield, but after a few seconds the shield begins to fade and disappear.

The room to respond to a newly acquired obligation to *keep clear* is a temporary "shield" for the new keep-clear boat. It is very strong initially, but fades in strength as the seconds go by. Also, for you to be entitled to the protection of the 'shield' you must, at the moment you become the keep-clear boat, make a prompt and careful attempt to begin to get clear of the right-of-way boat. If you delay at all, you lose the protection of "*room* to *keep clear*" and you run the risk of fouling the right-of-way boat.

LET'S LOOK at some common situations on the race course where this principle of transition comes into play:

Becoming *overlapped* to leeward of a boat from *clear astern* (common during pre-start maneuvering and when sailing downwind):

Two boats on the same *tack* are sailing near each other, one clear astern (BL) of the other (AW) and catching up. While BL is approaching AW, she must *keep clear*. When she becomes *overlapped* to leeward of AW, rule 12 *(clear astern/clear ahead)* ceases to apply and she **instantly** becomes the right-of-way boat under rule 11 *(windward/leeward)*. This is when rule 15 requires her to initially give AW *room* to *keep clear* of her. Remember that AW does not need to anticipate that BL will gain the right of way; therefore she does not need to take any evasive action **before** the *overlap* is created. And if AW luffs within the first few seconds of the *overlap* and her stern hits BL's bow, typically it will be decided by a protest committee that BL failed to give AW the space she needed to turn out of BL's way; i.e., that BL broke rule 15.

Rule 15 does not change the fact that W is required to *keep clear* of L. ISAF Case 53 makes the point that the keep-clear boat must respond immediately: "After L became overlapped to leeward of W, W immediately trimmed her sails, headed up, and thereafter kept clear. By taking these actions, W fulfilled her obligations under rule 11." ISAF Case 7 states, "... L was bound by rule 15 to allow W room to keep clear, but that obligation is not a continuing one, and in this case the overlap had been in existence for a considerable period during which W certainly had room to keep clear." (See ISAF Case 24 and US Sailing Appeal 43.)

Tacking into a right-of-way position to leeward of a right-of-way boat (commonly known as "lee-bowing"):

While a boat is tacking near another boat, rule 13 (While Tacking) requires her to *keep clear* of the other boat from the time she passes head to wind until she is on a close-hauled course. But, once she is on a close-hauled course, and if she has become the right-of-way boat, rule 15 applies. For a good analogy (though this may not be the actual highway law), picture yourself coming up the entrance ramp to a three-lane highway. Cars driving down the right-hand lane must stay clear of other cars in the right-hand lane in front of them.

While you're on the ramp you cannot interfere with cars driving in the right-hand lane. If, while you are moving across the white line into the right-hand lane, a car hits you or swerves to miss you, you are in the wrong. But once you get **all four wheels** across the line, you are now technically in the right-hand lane yourself and cars coming up from behind have to keep clear of you. However, these cars are not required to begin to avoid you or even to **anticipate** avoiding you until you are completely in the lane. Once you are in the lane they have to try reasonably hard to miss you. If they can't, then you've moved on too close in front of them.

The same is true in sailboats. Let's say I'm on *starboard tack*, you're approaching me on *port tack*, and you want to tack on my lee-bow or in front of me. If I could hit you before you passed head to wind (i.e., before you began to cross the white line), you'd be wrong under rule 10 *(port/starboard)*. If I could hit you after you'd passed head to wind but before you were aiming on your close-hauled course (i.e., while you were crossing the line), you'd be wrong under rule 13 (a boat past head to wind must *keep clear*). However, the moment you get to your close-hauled course (i.e., completely in my lane) and you are either *clear ahead* or to *leeward* of me, you have the right of way under either rule 12 *(clear astern/clear ahead)* or rule 11 *(windward/leeward)* and I have to promptly take action to *keep clear* of you. This is when rule 15 requires you to initially give me the *room* (space and time) I need to *keep clear* of you. Of course, in most situations it will take me only a second or two to react enough to luff or bear away slightly to avoid a collision.

In position 1, SL is past head to wind; therefore she is on starboard tack. However, rule 13 requires that she keep clear of SW until she is on a close-hauled course. If SW has to change course to avoid hitting SL before SL is on a close-hauled course, SL breaks rule 13.

In position 2, SL is on a close-hauled course; therefore, as the leeward boat, she is now the right-of-way boat. SW must now promptly try to avoid hitting SL, but SL must initially give her room to do so under rule 15.

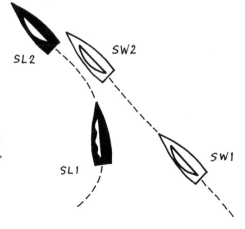

"In protests involving the situation where P tacks very close to leeward of S, it seems that P and S may often disagree on whether P was actually on a close-hauled course before S changed course to avoid her; or whether P, after acquiring right of way, actually gave S room to keep clear. Are there any onuses to help resolve these disagreements?"

No. In resolving these disagreements, most protest committees apply the principle in ISAF Case 50 (see rule 10 discussion), which is that they first put responsibility on S to satisfy the committee that the boats were close together. Then they put the responsibility on P to satisfy them that P was on a close-hauled course before S changed her course; and that once she was on a close-hauled course, she gave S *room* to *keep clear*. This responsibility on P is often difficult to win against. Hails to the effect of "complete-2-3-4, now you're changing course" and a witness are very helpful.

US Sailing Appeal 78 describes a situation where three *port-tack* boats (L, M and W) were sailing upwind and L (the leeward-most boat) tacked to *starboard* thereby acquiring the right of way. The middle boat (M) tacked to *starboard* and kept clear of L, but she tacked so close to the windward boat (W) that she and W could not avoid colliding, therefore breaking rule 15 (Acquiring Right of Way). The Appeals Committee said that L, by depriving M of the space necessary to maneuver without breaking a Part 2 rule, failed to give M *room* to *keep clear* (see the definition *Room*). L broke rule 15 against M and is disqualified. M was exonerated for breaking rule 15 against W under rule 64.1(a) (Penalties and Exoneration).

Gybing into a right-of-way position:

The same is true when gybing. If two boats are running side by side on *port tack* and the *windward* boat gybes, essentially the moment the foot of the mainsail crosses her centerline she is on *starboard tack* and the other boat (P) must promptly maneuver to get clear. However, S must plan to initially give P the *room* she needs to *keep clear*.

Completing penalty turns or starting after being over early:

Again, the principle applies when a boat is completing penalty turns for fouling another boat or touching a *mark* (rule 44, Penalties at the Time of an Incident). While making her penalty turn(s), she is required to *keep clear* of boats not doing so (rule 22, Starting Errors; Taking Penalties; Moving Astern). The moment she completes her last turn, she is no longer bound by rule 22. If she suddenly acquires the right of way over a nearby boat, she must give this boat *room* to respond. The same applies when she returns to the correct side of the starting line to *start* after being on the course side of the starting line at the gun (rule 22).

"What is the reason for the last phrase of the rule, 'unless she acquires right of way because of the other boat's actions'?"

This is to protect boats that suddenly become right-of-way boats solely because of an action by the other boat. For example, you are sailing upwind on *starboard tack* just to windward and slightly behind a boat to leeward. Suddenly, the *leeward* boat tacks and is now directly in front of you on *port tack*! Without the last phrase in rule 15, you would be required to give the boat that tacked *room* to *keep clear* of you, because you have just acquired the right of way! Clearly this would be unacceptable, hence the phrase. Therefore, in the example above, assuming you had to take action to avoid contact, the boat that tacked broke rule 10 *(port/starboard)*, and rule 15 did not apply to you.

Another situation where this applies is when two boats are on the same *tack* and the boat *clear ahead* (A) bears away and creates an *overlap* with the boat *clear astern* (B). The moment the boats are *overlapped*, B becomes the right-of-way boat under rule 11 *(windward/leeward)*. In this case, B was hold-

Because B acquires right of way as a result of A's tack, rule 15 does not require B to give A any room to keep clear.

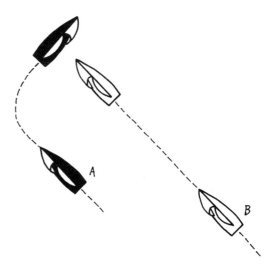

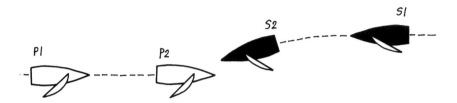

S has the right of way over P. But rule 16.1 requires that S not change her course so close to P that P does not have room to keep clear. So despite having the right of way, S needs to be careful when changing course near P.

ing her course and it was A's action that gave B the right of way. Therefore rule 15 does not apply to B, and if A were to suddenly luff and strike B's bow with her port stern quarter, A would be penalized for breaking rule 11 (On the Same Tack, Overlapped).

RULE 16 — CHANGING COURSE

RULE 16.1

When a right-of-way boat changes course, she shall give the other boat *room* to *keep clear.*

Rule 16.1 contains one of the most fundamental principles in the rules. Simply put, before a right-of-way boat changes her course near a keep-clear boat, she must be aware of the space and time the keep-clear boat will need to stay clear of her, assuming the keep-clear boat reacts and maneuvers promptly in a seamanlike way; and she must be sure to give her that **space** and **time**.

Let's get into this extremely important rule. Rule 16.1 is clearly talking to right-of-way boats (see ISAF Case 52). When two boats are about to collide, the keep-clear boat has the obligation to *keep clear*. The only way she can decide how to do this is if she can accurately figure out where the right-of-way boat is going. It would be chaos if just as a *port-tack* boat was reaching by a *starboard-tack* boat, S could suddenly and unexpectedly turn and hit P. The purpose of rule 16.1 is to protect keep-clear boats from unpredictable or last-second changes of course by right-of-way boats which, in essence, prevent the keep-clear boat from being able to *keep clear*.

 "So if I'm on starboard tack near a port-tack boat, rule 10 doesn't allow me to steer any course I want to?"

Absolutely not. That is exactly what rule 16.1 is designed to prevent. ISAF Case 60 says, "Tactical desires do not relieve a boat of her obligations under the rules. A (the right-of-way boat in the case) was free to adopt any course she chose to reach the leeward mark, but she did not have the right to luff into the path of B (the keep-clear boat) so close to B that B could not keep clear."

However, rule 16.1 does not shift the right-of-way between two boats; it is simply a common-sense "limit" on the right-of-way boat requiring her to limit her course changes when a keep-clear boat is close by and trying to *keep clear*.

Notice that rule 16.1 only applies to a "change of course." It in no way applies to a change in your boat's speed, sail trim or angle of heel. When P reaches by just to windward of S such that S momentarily loses her wind, thereby straightening up and hitting P's mast, P is wrong under rule 10 (On Opposite Tacks). Of course, rule 2 (Fair Sailing) is available to P if she suspects that S deliberately tried to hit her in an unfair manner (see the discussion of rule 2).

"If I'm making a smooth turn toward a keep-clear boat, am I considered to be 'changing course' if I continue the arc of my turn?"

US Sailing Appeal 33 says, "…a boat changes course when she sails the arc of a circle or any other course where she changes direction, whether or not she moves her helm…To change course means to change the direction in which the boat is heading…"

That tells us that "course" in rule 16.1 refers to the boat's straight-ahead or "compass" course. Therefore, whenever a boat is turning, it is changing "course." It also refers to its fore and aft or "directional" course; i.e., when a boat that was moving forward begins to move astern, it has also changed "course" (see US Sailing Appeal 33; see also rule 22, Starting Errors; Taking Penalties; Moving Astern).

"Okay, so if I'm a right-of-way boat and want to change course near another boat, what exactly does rule 16.1 require that I give her?"

You need to give her "*room* to *keep clear*" of you. She is *keeping clear* of you when you can sail your straight-ahead course with no need to take action to avoid hitting her; and if you are *overlapped*, if you can change course in both directions without immediately hitting her. The *room* you have to give her is the "space" and "time" she needs to get far enough away from you so that you can sail your course, assuming she acts promptly in a seamanlike way (see the definition *Room*).

Note that "promptly" means "performed readily, quickly, almost immediately" which builds in the time element. Therefore when a right-of-way boat changes course, rule 16.1 requires nearby boats to respond "promptly" or risk losing the protection of *room*.

However, "seamanlike" means "responsible, prudent, safety conscious." Therefore, you have to be sure that your course change doesn't force the keep-clear boat to put their or your boat's crew, boat or equipment at risk of damage or injury by the need to make a sudden, hurried or extreme maneuver. For instance, forcing a *windward* boat to sail head to wind with a spinnaker up in heavy air may be considered "unseamanlike" as it may put their spinnaker at great risk of tearing.

Also note that the definition *Room* makes it clear that your course change can't force a keep-clear boat to foul another boat or touch a *mark*. You need to be aware of the space the keep-clear boat has around her to get away from you.

 "Well, if I'm the right-of-way boat, how close to the keep-clear boat can I be and still change my course without breaking rule 16.1?"

Before I can answer that important question, we have to look at rule 16.2.

RULE 16.2

In addition, when after the starting signal a *port-tack* boat is *keeping clear* by sailing to pass astern of a *starboard-tack* boat, the *starboard-tack* boat shall not change course if as a result the *port-tack* boat would immediately need to change course to continue *keeping clear.*

The idea here is that if P has conceded that S is ahead in the race, and is steering a course that will take her astern of S, S can't change her course so close to P that P would "immediately" need to change her course to continue to avoid S.

So, there are basically two questions the right-of-way boat will need to consider before changing course near another boat (these will be the same two questions the protest committee will have to answer in a protest involving rule 16):

1) When I change my course, will the other boat have enough "space" and "time" to get away from me "promptly" without having to make an "unseamanlike maneuver" to do so?

2) If it is after the starting signal, and if I am on *starboard tack* converging with a *port-tack* boat that is about to safely pass behind me (upwind or downwind), will I be able to change my course without making the port-tacker have to make an "immediate" course change to continue safely passing behind me?

If the answer to either of these questions is "No," then the right-of-way boat will break rule 16.1 and/or rule 16.2 if she changes course near the other boat.

Clearly, the questions must be answered depending on the circumstances at the time, and for that reason it is impossible to project a hypothetical distance apart. The major considerations will be:

l) the distance between the boats;

2) the speeds and sizes of the boats;

3) the angles at which they are converging;

4) the visibility between the boats;

5) the amount of course change by the right-of-way boat;

6) the amount and difficulty of the boat handling required by the keep-clear boat to *keep clear*; and

7) the reasonableness of the keep-clear boat's attempt to *keep clear*.

Having said all this, I will say that as a conservative and safe rule of thumb in most boats, any course change by the right-of-way boat when closer than two lengths from the keep-clear boat is risky.

LET'S LOOK AT SOME COMMON SITUATIONS when rules 16.1 and 16.2 will come into play.

When a *port-tack* boat (P) and a *starboard-tack* boat (S) are converging on a beat:

Situation 1: P will cross S by half a boat-length or so. When about two lengths apart, S hails "Starboard" and makes a medium fast luff toward P. P, who has been watching S, continues for a couple of seconds, realizes she cannot cross

S safely, and makes a routine tack to *starboard tack* on S's lee-bow. S could continue straight-ahead, but decides to tack away to avoid P's bad air.

Resolution: When the boats are converging, P is required to *keep clear* under rule 10 (On Opposite Tacks). When S changes her course near P, she is required to give P *room* to *keep clear* (rule 16.1). P is able to tack in a seamanlike way to continue *keeping clear* of S. S is able to sail her course without concern of hitting P. Therefore S gives P the *room* she needs to *keep clear*, and P does *keep clear*. Neither boat breaks a *rule*.

Situation 2: Same scenario as above but the boats are a bit closer together when S luffs towards P. P tacks immediately in response to S's luff. P's tack is a routine tack to *starboard tack* on S's lee-bow. S tacks away to clear her air.

Resolution: Note that rule 16.2 does not apply (because P is not passing astern of S), so the fact that P had to "immediately" change course to avoid S is not, in and of itself, proof of a breach of rule 16.1 by S. If in fact P's tack was "seamanlike," then P properly *kept clear* under rule 10, and S properly gave P *room* to *keep clear* under rule 16.1. But part of sailing in a "seaman-like way" is looking before changing course. Keeping in mind that P does not need to anticipate the fact that S "might" change course near her, if S gets so close to P before luffing that P will need to tack immediately, typically P will not have time to look over her shoulder to see if she is clear to tack, let alone prepare her crew for the tack, and S will break rule 16.1 if P fails to *keep clear*. This is particularly true in a fleet race as opposed to a match race where there are no other boats besides P and S.

Situation 3: P will cross S by half a boat-length or so. When about one length apart, S hails "Starboard" and makes a medium fast luff toward P, putting the two boats on a collision course. P holds her course to get across S as quickly as she can (tacking would make matters worse because she would be turning directly in front of S). Just before contact, S bears away and protests.

Resolution: The first job of the protest committee will be to determine if P actually *keeps clear*. Clearly she doesn't because S needs to take action to avoid hitting her (see the definition *Keep Clear*). Therefore, P breaks rule 10 (On Opposite Tacks). Their next task is to decide if, when S changes course, she gives P *room* to *keep clear*. Clearly she doesn't because there is nothing P can

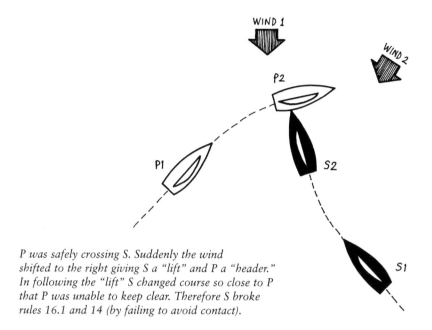

P was safely crossing S. Suddenly the wind shifted to the right giving S a "lift" and P a "header." In following the "lift" S changed course so close to P that P was unable to keep clear. Therefore S broke rules 16.1 and 14 (by failing to avoid contact).

do to get out of S's way. Therefore S breaks rule 16.1 and is disqualified; and because it was her "illegal" course change that compelled P to break rule 10, P is exonerated under rule 64.1(a) (Penalties and Exoneration).

NOTE: there does not have to be contact in order for a boat to break a rule. Anytime a right-of-way boat changes course near a keep-clear boat, rule 16.1 comes into effect. If it is determined that there would have been a collision if the right-of-way boat had not taken subsequent avoiding action, then that establishes that the keep-clear boat did not *keep clear*. At that point, either the keep-clear boat will be disqualified under the appropriate Section A – Right of Way rule, or the right-of-way boat will be disqualified under rule 16.1 (and the keep-clear boat exonerated under rule 64.1(a)). (See ISAF Case 60.)

Situation 4: P bears away to "duck" (pass astern of) S. When a length and a half away, S bears away towards P and P has to immediately bear away further to avoid S. S luffs back up to close-hauled and P safely passes close astern of her. P protests.

Resolution: By bearing away, P is *keeping clear* of S by sailing a course to pass astern of S. When S changes her course, P needs to immediately bear away further to *keep clear* of S. By causing P to have to immediately change her

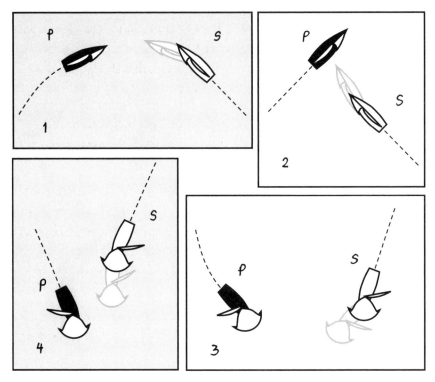

In diagrams 1 and 3, the starboard-tack (right-of-way) boat (S) is changing course while a port-tack boat (P) is keeping clear by passing astern of S. If P needs to "immediately" change course to continue keeping clear in reaction to S's course change, S breaks rule 16.2.

In diagrams 2 and 4, the starboard-tack (right-of-way) boat (S) is changing course while the port-tack boat (P) is keeping clear by passing in front of S. In this case rule 16.2 does not apply. If P can react to S's course change in a seamanlike way and keep clear of S, even if it requires an "immediate" course change, P must do so and S does not break rule 16.1.

course to continue *keeping clear*, S breaks rule 16.2. This is so even though S gives P space to *keep clear* in a seamanlike way; i.e., S does not break rule 16.1. (See ISAF Case 92.)

BOTTOM LINE: Rule 16 is very strict, and S must be very careful with her course changes when near P. Again, course changes when closer than two lengths from the keep-clear boat are risky.

 "I assume from all this that if I get a wind shift on a beat, I can't follow the shift and hit a port-tack boat that is just crossing my bow?"

That's absolutely right. Rule 16.1 applies to any course change, regardless of the reason (with one exception when rounding a mark; see discussion of rule 21, Exoneration). If you find yourself in the situation where P is crossing you and you get a favorable wind shift and want to head up and pass close astern of P, but you know that P doesn't have *room* to tack away after you head up, simply let P know, with a hail or a wave, that she can continue on across you as you head up to pass close astern of her.

"Do I have to hail before changing my course? And if I do warn the *other boat with a hail that I am about to change course toward them, does that count as 'giving room' ?"*

No and No. First, the rule does not require a hail. Second, the rule is about "changing course," which means that the test of whether you gave *room* will begin at the moment you actually change your course. However, a clear hail alerting the keep-clear boat that you are about to change course is strong evidence that you intend to give her *room* to *keep clear* when you do change course, and is therefore strongly recommended.

When a port-tack boat (P) and a starboard-tack boat (S) are on a downwind leg:

Situation 1: P will cross S by half a boat-length or so. When one length away, S bears away such that the boats are now on a collision course. P immediately makes a routine gybe to *keep clear* of S, and protests.

Resolution: Again note that rule 16.2 does not apply (because P is not passing astern of S). When S changes her course, the question is whether P is able to get out of her way in a seamanlike way. P makes a routine gybe and therefore is able to properly *keep clear* of S in a seamanlike way. Neither boat breaks a *rule*.

Situation 2: P and S are converging and P is sailing a course that will take her astern of S. When one and a half lengths apart, S luffs slightly which causes P to have to immediately luff slightly to continue safely passing astern of S, which she does.

Resolution: Because P was sailing to pass astern of S, rule 16.2 applied; and because S's course change required P to immediately change her course, S breaks rule 16.2, even though P is able to safely *keep clear* of her.

When a *leeward* boat (L) and a *windward* boat (W) are sailing on the same *tack*:

Situation 1: L is sailing along on a reach. W catches up and *overlaps* her to windward, but far enough away so that L can change her course toward her (luff) without immediately hitting her. L begins to luff medium fast and W promptly responds and *keeps clear*. At some point during the luff, L gets closer to W (either because W slows down her response rate, or L increases her luffing rate or because of the boats simply getting closer as they rotate up). L realizes that if she continues her luff she will get so close to W that she could then immediately hit W if she luffed even more. She stops her luff and protests.

Resolution: When L luffs (changes course toward W), W must respond "promptly" (i.e., very quickly) and make her best effort to get out of L's way. Furthermore, L can luff as quickly as she chooses **provided** she allows W the space and time needed to get out of her way, assuming W is responding promptly. However, L can never luff so suddenly or fast that, despite W's best efforts, W physically cannot *keep clear* of her.

The first job of the protest committee will be to determine if W actually *keeps clear* of L. Clearly she does because L can always sail her course; i.e., her straight-ahead course, with no apprehension of collision. Furthermore, throughout the incident L can always change course in either direction without making immediate contact with W. Once it is decided that W has *kept clear* throughout the incident, it then means that L has complied with rule 16.1. Neither boat breaks a *rule*. (See US Sailing Appeal 108.)

NOTE: If L had allowed herself to get so close to W that L could not change course any more without immediately making contact with W, it would have been a much different situation. This is often called the "lock-up" position. First, by definition W was not *keeping clear* (see part (b) in the definition *Keep Clear*), and she breaks rule 11 (On the Same Tack, Overlapped). Therefore, either W will get disqualified for breaking rule 11, or L will get disqualified for breaking rule 16.1 (and W will get exonerated under rule 64.1(a), Penalties and Exoneration). This *protest* will be resolved by the protest committee's determination of whether W was maneuvering promptly in a seamanlike way or not (an admittedly difficult protest at best). If yes, then L failed to give her enough *room* to continue *keeping clear* and is disqualified under rule 16.1;

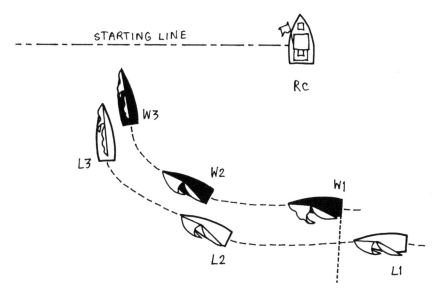

When L becomes overlapped to leeward of W and then luffs, L must initially give W room to keep clear when she first becomes overlapped; and then L must give W any additional room she needs to keep clear when she luffs.

if no, then W failed to *keep clear* by her own actions and is disqualified under rule 11.

"If L luffs, then stops luffing to give W more room to respond, is L still bound by rule 16.1 to give W room to keep clear when L begins luffing again?"

Yes. Rule 16.1 applies to L whenever she changes her course. The use of the word "initially" in rule 15 (Acquiring Right of Way) makes the requirement in rule 15 a temporary one at the outset of the overlap. However, rule 16.1 does not contain the word "initially." Therefore, each time L stops and then changes her course again, she must give W *room* to *keep clear* once again. W, on the other hand, will put herself at great risk by remaining too close to L over an extended period of time, and should make every effort to get well clear when L first luffs.

"What if, despite the fact that L has given W plenty of room, W allows herself to get so close to L that L can't change course at all without hitting W?"

Part (b) in the definition *Keep Clear* tells W that she is not *keeping clear* if she allows herself to get so close to L that L can't change course in **both directions** at that moment without **immediately** making contact with her. Note the use

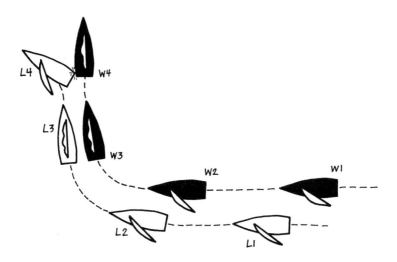

When L bears away, she cannot do so as suddenly and fast as she pleases. She is required by rule 16.1 to give W room to keep clear (unless she is changing course to round a mark; see rule 21(a)). She is also required by rule 14 to avoid contact. If, however, W has allowed herself to get so close that L can't luff and bear away at that moment without immediately hitting W, W has failed to keep clear and has broken rule 11 by her extreme close proximity to L.

of the word "if" in the definition suggests that L does not need to actually hit W to prove she couldn't change course without contact. If the protest committee decides that L couldn't have changed course without immediately hitting W, then W has broken rule 11 (On the Same Tack, Overlapped) simply by her extreme close proximity to L.

Furthermore, any time L has a reasonable apprehension that contact with W may occur if she holds her course, W fails to *keep clear* and breaks rule 11; and when W allows herself to get that close to L, L will generally be justified in being concerned about the masts touching, the boats being tossed together by waves, etc., etc.

However, when L is luffing and her bow is getting closer to W's stern quarter, there will come a point that, due to the way boats rotate, it will become impossible for W to *keep clear* if L continues to luff (the "lock-up" position). At that point, L must cease her luff and allow W the *room* she needs to move away from L before she continues her luff again (see US Sailing Appeal 108).

"Is it true that the rules regarding the rate of L's luff are the same before and after starting?"

Yes. Rule 16.1 is the rule that deals primarily with the rate of L's luff, and there is absolutely no difference in the application of rule 16.1 before or after *starting*.

"What if a boat to windward of W, or some other object, restricts her *ability to respond to a luff by L?"*

This is commonly the situation as boats begin to tightly line-up in the final minutes before a start or as they approach a crowded downwind *mark*. The room that rule 16.1 requires L to give W often must include time for W to wait for boats to windward of her to respond; or for W to sail past an object (e.g., something in the water) that prevents her from *keeping clear* of L. A hail by W to the effect, "I am trying to *keep clear* but I have these other boats, or this object, to windward of me!" will be useful and is strongly encouraged.

Situation 2: W is slowly sailing along the starting line about a minute before starting. L catches up from *clear astern* and becomes *overlapped* to leeward of W. After about five seconds, L begins to slowly luff toward W.

Resolution: Prior to the overlap, W, as the boat *clear ahead*, is the right-of-way boat under rule 12 (On the Same Tack, Not Overlapped); therefore she doesn't need to take any action in anticipation of L's leeward *overlap*. When L becomes *overlapped*, L is required by rule 15 (Acquiring Right of Way) to initially give W *room* to *keep clear*. This includes the "space" and "time" necessary for W to trim her sails and otherwise get steerageway to get away from L. After W has had *room* to *keep clear*, L may luff, provided she gives W any **additional room** W needs to *keep clear* under rule 16.1. The bottom line is that when *leeward* boats "come in the back door" (i.e., establish leeward *overlaps* from *clear astern* on *windward* boats) and then want to luff, they must plan to be very patient. (See ISAF Case 7.)

 "Can L ever bear away with no limitation and hit W with her transom?"

No, with one exception discussed below. When L bears away near W, L must comply with rule 16.1 as well; i.e., she must bear away in a way that gives W *room* to *keep clear*. Normally, if L bears away slowly and with some caution not to swing her stern into W's *leeward* side, L will not break rule 16.1. And if W has left herself so close to windward of L that L can't luff and bear away without immediately hitting her, W has failed to *keep clear* and has broken rule 11 (On the Same Tack, Overlapped).

 "Sounds like there could be some difficult protests involving rule 16.1; are there any onuses to help resolve these disputes?"

No. In a dispute over whether W *kept clear* or whether L provided enough *room* to *keep clear*, neither the *rules* nor the appeals place any "onus" on either boat. The protest committee will have to determine the facts and use its best judgment. Remember that a *windward* boat's right to *"room* to *keep clear"* under rule 16.1 is a 'shield' and not a 'sword' for W. Also, to be entitled to the protection of *room*, W must respond as soon as she can to L's change of course and make a reasonable attempt to get clear. From there it will be up to the protest committee to decide from the weight of the evidence on (a) the wind and sea conditions, (b) the nature of the incident and (c) the exact actions of both boats as to whether or not W had '*room* to *keep clear.*' Hails by both boats at the time will be very helpful in resolving such conflicts and are strongly encouraged. And to be safe, I always assume that the benefit of any doubt will go to the right-of-way boat (L).

 "Are there any exceptions to rule 16?"

Well, in fact, there is one exception to rule 16, and that is found in rule 21 (Exoneration). This will be discussed in detail in the discussion of rule 18 (Mark-Room) in Chapter 8. But in a nutshell, rule 21 says that a boat will be exonerated (freed from blame) if she breaks rule 16 when she is changing course to round a *mark*. So as L is bearing away around a windward *mark*, she does not need to give W *room* to *keep clear* of her transom as she bears away. She does however have to avoid contact with W under rule 14 (Avoiding Contact).

RULE 17 — ON THE SAME TACK; PROPER COURSE

If a boat *clear astern* becomes *overlapped* within two of her hull lengths to *leeward* of a boat on the same *tack*, she shall not sail above her *proper course* while they remain on the same *tack* and *overlapped* within that distance, unless in doing so she promptly sails astern of the other boat. This rule does not apply if the *overlap* begins while the *windward* boat is required by rule 13 to *keep clear*.

Rule 16.1 (Changing Course) is about limiting **how fast** a right-of-way boat can turn near a keep-clear boat; rule 17 is about limiting **where** a *leeward* boat can sail when near a keep-clear boat. Note that rule 17 simply puts a "limit" on where a *leeward* boat can sail when near a *windward* boat in certain situations. It does not shift any right-of-way to the *windward* boat. When near each other, W must remember that rule 11 (On the Same Tack, Overlapped) requires her to *keep clear* of L.

The concept in rule 17 is simple: either L is "limited" to sailing no higher than her *proper course* or she is "free" to sail up to head to wind if she pleases; it is always one or the other for L whenever L and W are *overlapped* on the same *tack* and within two of L's lengths of each other.

Whether L is "limited" or "free" depends on the following five factors:

1) whether the boats are *overlapped* on the same *tack* (note: two boats sailing downwind on opposite *tacks* can be *overlapped* (see the definition *Clear Astern and Clear Ahead; Overlap*); but rule 17 does not apply to them;

2) whether the boats are within two of L's hull lengths of each other;

3) whether L became *overlapped* from *clear astern* within two of her hull lengths of W and was on the same *tack* as W at the time;

4) whether W was subject to rule 13 (While Tacking); i.e., past head to wind but not yet close-hauled, when L became *overlapped*; and

5) whether the starting signal has been made.

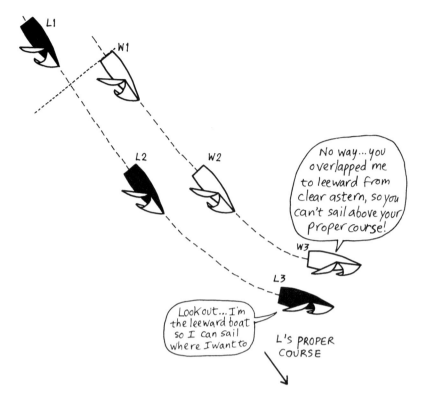

Whenever L becomes overlapped to leeward of W from clear astern within two of her lengths of W, she cannot sail above her proper course while less than that distance apart, unless she promptly sails astern of W.

A few clarifying points on the five factors listed above:

- When L is not "limited" under rule 17, she is "free" to sail up to head to wind if she pleases (commonly described as having "luffing rights"), provided if she changes course she gives W *room* to *keep clear* in a seamanlike way (rule 16.1, Changing Course). To clarify, even if L is only *overlapped* with W by two feet, L can sail up to head to wind. US Sailing Appeal 17 says, "A boat is head to wind when her bow is facing the wind, and the centerline of her hull is parallel to it, irrespective of the position of her sails." This clarification is helpful because often when a boat is head to wind her sails will blow momentarily to the other side giving the **illusion** that she is past head to wind and therefore subject to rule 13 (While Tacking).

  Remember that when L is head to wind, it is quite possible that W will be required to go **beyond** head to wind in order to *keep clear* under rule 11

(On the Same Tack, Overlapped). If this is the case, W must do so. If it's not possible for W to *keep clear* without fouling other boats to windward of her, W should clearly alert L that she needs more *room* to *keep clear* (as required by rule 16.1).

- The only time L is "limited" is when she is **on the same *tack*** as W and becomes *overlapped* **to leeward of W from *clear astern* within two of her lengths** of W. That's it! The "limit" does not apply when L *overlaps* W when more than two lengths apart, or when W becomes *overlapped* to windward of L, or when L becomes *overlapped* to leeward of W on the opposite *tack* and then gybes.

- Note that rule 17 uses the phrase "becomes *overlapped*." This means that any time a boat that was *clear astern* crosses a line perpendicular to the *clear ahead* boat's centerline drawn through the boat's aftermost point in normal position, it is considered that the boat has "become *overlapped*" to leeward of the boat that was *clear ahead*, regardless of how that line came to be in front of the boat *clear astern* (see the definition *Overlap*). So even in the situation where a boat *clear astern* is holding her course and a boat *clear ahead* and to windward turns down and creates an *overlap*, it is considered that the *leeward* boat has become *overlapped* with the *windward* boat.

- The "limit" in rule 17 only applies to boats that are *"overlapped"* **on the same *tack***. The terms *clear ahead, clear astern* and *overlap* apply to boats on opposite *tacks* when sailing below beam reaches or when rule 18 applies; but rule 17 does not apply to those boats. So when a *starboard-tack* boat and a *port-tack* boat are half way down a downwind leg and they are sailing side by side, neither has a *proper course* limitation. This also means that if two boats are *overlapped* on the same *tack* and rule 17 applies, and the *leeward* boat (L) gybes, now the two boats are on opposite *tacks* (i.e., they did not "remain" on the same *tack*) and rule 17 ceases to apply; and if L gybes back while remaining *overlapped* with W, rule 17 does not apply and L has "luffing rights."

- The "limit" only applies when L and W are **within two lengths of each other**. The "two lengths" distance is determined by two of L's **hull** lengths; i.e., the length of L's hull, and not the additional length of any bowsprits, overhanging mizzen booms, etc. This is particularly important when boats of different sizes are near each other. That means that if rule 17 applies and the two boats remain *overlapped* but sail more than two of L's lengths apart, rule 17 ceases to apply; and if the two boats remain *overlapped* and converge again, rule 17 does not apply and L has "luffing rights."

- The "limit" in rule 17 is that L **cannot sail above her** *proper course*. Because a boat does not have a *proper course* until the starting signal is made, there is never any "limit" on L before her starting signal (see the discussion of definition *Proper Course*). Therefore, before the starting signal, L can sail up to head to wind at all times, regardless of how she became overlapped.

  But at the starting signal, L will be "limited" or "free" depending on how the *overlap* began (whenever it began). Note that this applies regardless of whether the boats have actually *started*; i.e., have crossed the starting line or not. If with 20 seconds to go before the starting signal L becomes *overlapped* from *clear astern* within two lengths of W, then at the starting signal L is "limited" and must sail no higher than her *proper course*. If with 20 seconds to go W *overlaps* L to windward, then at the starting signal L continues to be "free" to sail up to head to wind if she pleases.

"So it sounds like the starting signal is the key moment in time for determining whether L is 'limited' or 'free;' and that it is pretty important for overlapped boats to remember how they first became overlapped as the starting signal approaches!"

Exactly right. Before the starting signal, L is not "limited" in any way; i.e., she can sail up to head to wind if she pleases. But after the starting signal, L is "limited" to sailing no higher than her *proper course* if she originally became *overlapped* from *clear astern*. The advantage of having L's limitation begin at the starting signal is that it is a precise and predictable moment in time.

And the moment the starting signal is made, L instantly gets a *proper course* (see the definition *Proper Course*). At that moment it is critical for L and W to remember how they became *overlapped*! Hails when the *overlap* first begins and throughout the *overlap* are going to be critical for producing orderly starts and reducing disputes!

"Do I have to bear away to my proper course before the starting signal is made; i.e., do I have to anticipate my obligation not to sail above my proper course after the starting signal?"

No. You do not have a *proper course* before the starting signal, and therefore you are not "limited" as to where you can sail. When the starting signal is made, and if you are now "limited" because you originally became *overlapped* from *clear astern*, you are required to sail no higher than your *proper course*. The course you will sail to *finish* as soon as possible will include the course you are on at the moment the starting signal is made. If you must then bear away to a lower course to get to the next *mark* and ultimately the finishing line as soon as possible, you must do so immediately. For instance, if you are head to wind before an upwind start, your *proper course* will be to bear away to a close-hauled course or even slightly lower to build speed and sail upwind.

"What is the purpose of the last sentence in rule 17, the one about rule 13?"

This sentence specifically addresses the tactic known as the "Slam Dunk." (A detailed analysis of the Slam Dunk can be found at the end of this chapter.) Consider two close-hauled boats on opposite *tacks* (S and P) converging. P bears away to pass astern of S. When P gets near S's stern, S tacks. At some point during S's tack, P becomes *overlapped* to leeward of S. Is P "limited" or "free" under rule 17?

Well, once S passes head to wind and until she is on a close-hauled course, S is required by rule 13 (While Tacking) to *keep clear* of P. And the last sentence in rule 17 says that if P becomes *overlapped* to leeward of S while S is required by rule 13 to *keep clear* of her, then rule 17 doesn't apply. So in this case, P would be "free" for as long as the boats remained *overlapped*; i.e., she could sail up to head to wind, subject of course to rule 16.1 (Changing Course). If S was already down to a close-hauled course **before** P became *overlapped*, then P would be "limited" under rule 17 throughout the *overlap*. The net effect of this rule is that it discourages Slam Dunks, which are very aggressive and often contentious.

"What happens in the situation where L and W are both sailing their proper courses and the two boats are converging; who has to keep clear?"

W must *keep clear* of L under rule 11 (On the Same Tack, Overlapped). Rule 17 only requires that L not sail **above** her *proper course*. As long as L is **on** her *proper course*, she is complying with rule 17. Note that the phrase in rule 17 "her *proper course*" clarifies that it is L who gets to sail her *proper course*.

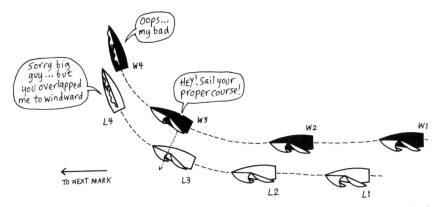

Whenever W becomes overlapped to windward of L, L can turn all the way up to head to wind for the duration of the overlap, provided she gives W room to keep clear in the process.

Therefore, when L is sailing on "her" *proper course*, W must *keep clear* under rule 11, even when W's proper course may be a **lower** course than L's. (See ISAF Cases 7 and 14.)

Remember that a *proper course* is essentially any course a boat chooses to sail in order to get to the next *mark* and ultimately to *finish* as quickly as possible. Therefore it is possible that there may be several *proper courses* at any given moment depending upon the circumstances involved. It is also obvious that two *overlapping* boats sailing for the same *mark* will converge. Note also that a boat's *proper course* is not necessarily a straight-line course. It can change with changes in the breeze, current or waves, or with a change in the boat's

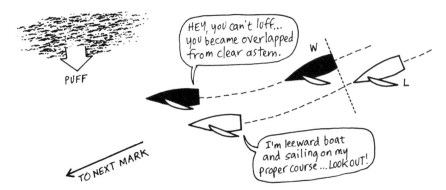

L is slowly luffing up to a new proper course in order to get to a puff of wind sooner. Because she is not sailing above her proper course, she is not breaking rule 17; and because she is giving W room to keep clear, she is not breaking rule 16.1. W must keep clear under rule 11.

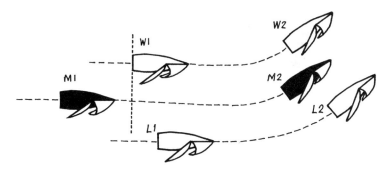

Because M becomes overlapped to leeward of W from clear astern, she is "limited" to sailing no higher than her proper course. When L luffs, M is required to keep clear of her under rule 11. Even in the absence of W, M would luff to keep clear of L. Therefore, M is not sailing above her proper course and W must keep clear of M under rule 11 and give her room under rule 19.2(b).

strategy (see the discussion of definition *Proper Course*). However, whenever L wants to change her course to a new *proper course*, she must give W *room* to *keep clear* under rule 16.1 (Changing Course). A hail that she intends to change course is strongly recommended.

If L is "limited" and W thinks that L is sailing above L's *proper course*, W must still *keep clear* (rule 11) and she can protest under rule 17. If the two boats hit, and it were decided by the protest committee that L was sailing above her *proper course*, both boats will likely be disqualified: W for failing to *keep clear* of L (rule 11), and L for illegally sailing above her *proper course* (rule 17).

"What happens when L wants to luff two or more boats and one of the middle boats is 'limited' to where she can sail?"

Good question! Let's take the situation where L and W are sailing down a reach about two lengths or so apart. A boat from astern (M) catches up and becomes *overlapped* between them. When M becomes *overlapped* on W, W is clearly able to give M *room* to pass L such that she is entitled to *room* from W to pass L (rule 19.2(b), Giving Room at an Obstruction). Now L begins to luff toward M and W. M responds by luffing. W must *keep clear* of M under rule 11 (On the Same Tack, Overlapped) and give her *room* under rule 19.2(b). And M is not breaking rule 17 because in fact M is not sailing above her *proper course*. Here's the reason. Take the two boats involved, M and W. M became *overlapped* on W to leeward from *clear astern*. Rule 17 requires M, therefore, not to sail above her *proper course*. In determining her *proper course,* the definition *Proper Course* instructs us to remove the boats referred to in the rule using the term *"proper course."* In this case, rule 17 uses the term and refers to the *windward* boat W, so we remove W. As M was sailing a course to *keep clear* of L, she would have been sailing the same course in the absence of W; therefore, M was sailing her *proper course* and not above it.

"What's the purpose of the phrase in rule 17, '...unless in doing so she promptly sails astern of the other boat'?"

This is to close a very subtle, undesirable loophole in the rule. Here's a potential scenario: on a beat to windward, a boat crosses you and tacks just ahead and about half-a-length to *windward* of you. Due to your greater speed you become *overlapped* to *leeward* from *clear astern,* but you realize that you won't be able to sail past them enough to get your air clear. You want to tack out of there. Assuming that when sailing upwind your *proper course* is a close-hauled course, without an exception to the rule the question would be: "could you sail above close-hauled and tack while you're *overlapped* to *leeward* of W; or would you have to wait until you were no longer *overlapped* so you didn't break rule 17?" Rule 17 clarifies that you can certainly luff and tack (i.e., sail above your *proper course*) provided you break the *overlap* with W at some point during your turn. If you luff and then realize that your bow won't clear W's transom and have to pull your bow back down, you have broken rule 17.

"I thought there was a rule that said you couldn't sail below your proper course if you were to windward of another boat or clear ahead of a boat that was trying to pass you to leeward?"

You are right; there **was.** It was rule 17.2. But it was removed from the rule book entirely in the 2009–2012 rules. The reason it was removed is that it wasn't widely known, it was very difficult to prove a boat was breaking it, and with far fewer races run on triangular courses (where the rule balanced the game coming into the gybe mark), the need for the rule is far less.

What that means is that if two boats (W and L) are sailing downwind *overlapped,* W can sail as low as she pleases in order to more effectively slow L down by blanketing her wind, as long as she *keeps clear* of L under rule 11 (On the Same Tack, Overlapped), even if she is sailing below her *proper course.* And if one boat (A) is *clear ahead* of another (B), not only does B need to *keep*

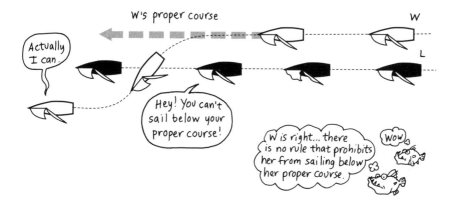

clear under rule 12 (On the Same Tack, Not Overlapped), but A can sail as low as she pleases to make it more difficult for B to become *overlapped* to *leeward* and perhaps gain an inside overlap at a *mark*, even if she is sailing below her *proper course*.

Section A and B Rules In Action

Now that we've had a thorough explanation, let's look at how the rules in Section A and B work in various common situations on the race course.

STARTING MARK SITUATIONS

For the purposes of these following explanations, it will be assumed that the starting *mark* is surrounded by navigable water, and that the boats are approaching the starting *mark* to *start*. For a full explanation of the rules at starting *marks*, see the discussion of the preamble to Section C (At Marks and Obstructions).

UPWIND STARTS, INCLUDING A DISCUSSION ON "BARGING"

When boats are on their final approach to *start*, Section C rules (At Marks and Obstructions) do not apply, meaning that a *leeward*/outside boat (LO) does not have to give a *windward*/inside boat (WI) *room* to pass to leeward of the starting *mark* (say a race committee boat). If W tries to squeeze between L and the *mark* and hits L or forces L to bear away to avoid a collision, W has broken rule 11 (On the Same Tack, Overlapped). This is what is called "Barging."

If Barger tries to squeeze in between the race committee boat and L, and hits L or causes L to bear off to avoid a collision, Barger breaks rule 11.

 "I understand that when I'm the windward boat, a leeward boat does not have to give me room to pass to leeward of the race committee boat; but does that mean she can do anything she pleases to 'shut the door' on me?"

Absolutely not. As we've discussed above, the rules in Sections A and B apply. There are no other special rules that apply at this starting *mark*. Therefore, L must behave in exactly the same way that she must behave anywhere else on

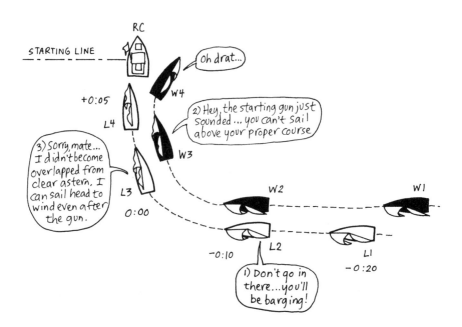

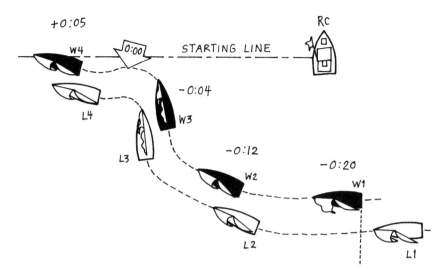

Before the starting signal, even though L becomes overlapped to leeward from clear astern she is permitted to sail up to head to wind provided she gives W room to keep clear. However, after the starting signal, L may not sail above her proper course which, when sailing to windward, is normally a close-hauled course.

the race course. Rule 11 (On the Same Tack, Overlapped) gives L the right of way; and L can sail up to head to wind if she pleases, even when only *overlapped* with W by two feet.

However, rule 16.1 (Changing Course) tells L when and how fast she can luff near other boats; i.e., she must give them *room* to *keep clear* whenever she changes course near them. Consider L and W approaching the race committee boat. If L holds her course W will be able to pass between L and the committee boat without touching either. Just as W sticks her bow in behind the race committee boat, L luffs slowly, but W is unable to *keep clear* due to her proximity to the race committee boat and hits both it and L. L has broken rule 16.1 by changing course (luffing) without giving W *room to keep clear*, and rule 14 (Avoiding Contact) by not avoiding a collision with W. If L wants to prevent W from passing between her and the committee boat, she must put herself on a course to "shut the door" **before** W gets her bow stuck in to leeward of the committee boat.

"Now, what about after the starting signal?"

If L is not "limited" under rule 17, then she can continue to sail where she pleases. She is under **no obligation** to turn down to her *proper course* at the

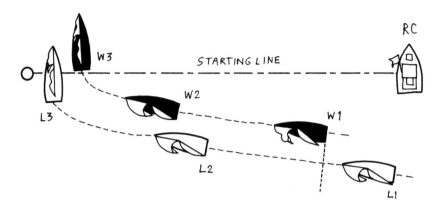

L becomes overlapped to leeward from clear astern on W. Before the starting signal she may sail up to head to wind whenever she pleases. After the starting signal she cannot sail above her proper course, which, when sailing to windward, is normally close-hauled. However, in order to pass the starting mark L's proper course may be to momentarily luff up to head to wind. In this case W must keep clear but L must give her room to do so.

starting signal. Therefore, L can sail head to wind after the gun, even if it forces W onto the wrong side of the race committee boat, before turning down to *start* herself!

Now, if L is "limited" under rule 17, then she must not sail above her *proper course* after the starting signal. Therefore, if she is "limited," and sailing above close-hauled before the starting signal, she must immediately turn down to her *proper course* when the starting signal is made. She does not have to anticipate this obligation; she need only react when the signal is made. However, if L is sailing her *proper course* after the starting signal, and there is no *room* for W to squeeze in between her and the committee boat, tough luck on W; W is not allowed to go in there.

"Anything special I should know when I'm starting near the leeward end of the starting line?"

Well, one thing that often happens at the leeward end of the starting line for an upwind start is that L gets into a position where she cannot make it around the starting *mark* after the starting signal goes off without sailing above close-hauled.

Remember that in this situation, sailing above close-hauled to get around the *mark* can certainly be considered L's *proper course*, and W must *keep clear* regardless of how the *overlap* began. However, L has to remember that her

Whether L is "limited" to sailing no higher than her proper course or not depends on how the overlap began. If L became overlapped to leeward from clear astern, then she cannot sail above her proper course after the starting signal. If the overlap began in any other way, L is free to sail up to head to wind, and can even cause W to pass on the wrong side of the committee boat before bearing away to start.

luff is limited by rule 16.1 (Changing Course) in that she must give W *room* to *keep clear* when she changes her course. This may be difficult when W is close by or when there is a pack of boats to windward of her.

DOWNWIND STARTS

On downwind starts, it is especially critical that boats remember how they became *overlapped*! If L is not "limited" under rule 17, she may sail where she pleases; i.e., she is under no obligation to head for the first *mark* or sail her *proper course* at the gun. W must beware, especially before setting her spinnaker if L has not set her spinnaker yet!

As *overlapped* boats approach one of the starting *marks* (which can include the race committee boat) and the starting gun goes off, remember that L is under **no obligation** to give W *room* at the starting *mark*! If L is not "limited" under rule 17, then L can force W onto the wrong side of the *mark* before turning down to start herself. And if L is "limited," then she need only turn down to her *proper course* (not to the compass course to the first *mark*). As *proper course* is so subjective, especially around a starting line, *windward* boats will be well advised to try and avoid becoming *overlapped* to *windward* of *leeward* boats near the starting *marks*. If ever W feels L is sailing above her *proper course*, she must *keep clear* and protest.

ON UPWIND LEGS ("BEATS")

Again, coming off the starting line it will be essential that L and W remember how they became *overlapped*. If L originally became *overlapped* from *clear astern*, then she is "limited" under rule 17 and cannot sail above her *proper course* (most likely close-hauled). If she is not "limited," she can turn all the way to head to wind and W must *keep clear*.

A common situation on beats is when a *port-tack* boat (PL) tacks on the lee-bow of a *starboard-tack* boat (SW). Because PL did not become *overlapped* from *clear astern*, she is not "limited" under rule 17 and therefore can luff up to head to wind at any time during the *overlap*, even when only *overlapped* with SW by a couple of feet. *Windward* boats will have to be a bit more cautious when rolling over *leeward* boats in this situation.

If P tacks in front of S, and S chooses to *overlap* her to leeward, then S must comply with rule 15 (Acquiring Right of Way) and furthermore must not sail above her *proper course* during the *overlap* unless she chooses to luff and pass astern of P (rule 17, On the Same Tack; Proper Course).

 "Can you walk me through how the rules apply to a Slam Dunk?"

Sure. The Slam Dunk is an aggressive and often contentious tactic used upwind by S to gain control over P. It is more commonly used in match and team racing than in fleet racing. The relationship between S and P is rapidly changing in this maneuver such that the rules analysis gets quite complicated. However, the last sentence in rule 17 (On the Same Tack; Proper Course) is designed to greatly discourage S from using this tactic (see discussion of rule 17). See the illustration opposite for a detailed analysis of the "Slam Dunk."

ON DOWNWIND LEGS (REACHES & RUNS)

L and W are sailing down a reach. L did not become *overlapped* from *clear astern* and therefore L is "free" to sail where she pleases, subject to rule 16.1 (Changing Course); i.e., she has "luffing rights." W begins to pass L and L luffs to prevent her from doing so. W is about three-quarters of the way past L and

THE SLAM DUNK

POSITION 1: *Position 1: P has borne away to pass astern of S. The moment P is steering a course to clear S's transom, S luffs preparatory to tacking. As long as when she luffs, S does not cause P to have to immediately change her course to continue to keep clear, S does not break rule 16.2.*

POSITION 2: *S is not past head to wind and is therefore still on starboard tack; P must still keep clear of her under rule 10.*

POSITION 3: *S has just passed head to wind. She is now on port tack, i.e., the same tack as P, and P is clear astern. S must keep clear of P under rule 13 until she is close-hauled, and then under rule 11 as the windward boat. P, now the right-of-way boat, does not need to give S room to keep clear under rule 15 if she maintains her straight-line course because she acquired the right of way by S's actions. However, if P changes course toward S, she is required by rule 16.1 to give S room to keep clear (i.e., not to prevent S from being able to keep clear or cause her to make an unseamanlike maneuver to do so).*

Furthermore, if P becomes overlapped to leeward of S before S is down to a close-hauled course, P is not "limited" under rule 17, because S is required by rule 13 to keep clear of her. Therefore P can sail up to head to wind, provided she complies with rule 16.1. If S is on a close-hauled course when P becomes overlapped, then P is "limited" to sailing no higher than her proper course (most likely a close-hauled course) for the duration of the overlap because she became overlapped from clear astern.

POSITION 4: *P has become overlapped with S before S is on a close-hauled course; and P has luffed above her proper course towards S. Rule 17 does not apply. Whether or not she broke rule 16.1 will be decided by the protest committee based on their determination of whether P gave S enough space and time to cease her turn towards P and begin her turn away from P in a seamanlike way. If the collision was avoidable, P and/or S may be found to have broken rule 14; and if there was any damage or injury, both could get penalized under rule 14.*

NOTE: *If, in position 3, P and S were overlapped the moment S passed head to wind, then P would not be "limited" under rule 17 (because P did not become overlapped from clear astern while on the same tack as S), and would be permitted to sail up to head to wind provided she gave S room to keep clear under rule 16.1. Again rule 15 wouldn't apply to P; but P could still be penalized under rule 14 if the contact caused damage or injury.*

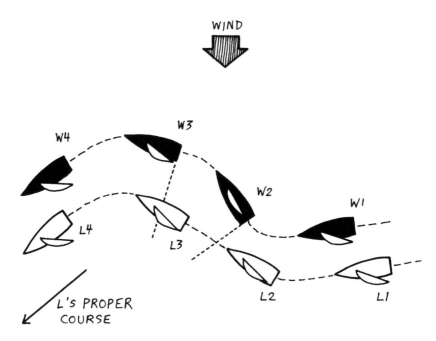

In this situation it is W's luffing that breaks the overlap and her bearing away that causes the overlap to begin again. When L acquires the right of way at position 3, she does not need to give W room to keep clear under rule 15 because she acquires right of way as a result of W's actions. However, rule 17 is not concerned with how the overlap was established. Therefore, because L became overlapped from clear astern, she must immediately bear away and continue to sail no higher than her proper course during the overlap.

W luffs quickly and "breaks" the *overlap*. W then turns back down, thereby creating an *overlap* once again (being sure to *keep clear* under rule 11, On the Same Tack, Overlapped, and remembering that her actions have given L the right of way such that rule 15, Acquiring Right of Way, does not require L to "give" W *room* to *keep clear*!). Now, L has become *overlapped* to *leeward* from *clear astern* and therefore is required to immediately comply with rule 17 (On the Same Tack; Proper Course) and turn back down to her *proper course*, which includes gybing when that is necessary for L to sail her *proper course* to the next *mark*.

Anytime a boat becomes *overlapped* to *leeward* from *clear astern* within two of her lengths of a *windward* boat, she is not permitted to sail above her *proper course*. However, prior to becoming *overlapped*, L is free to sail where she pleases. Therefore, the moment the *overlap* begins, the course she will sail to *finish* as soon as possible will include the course she is on at that moment.

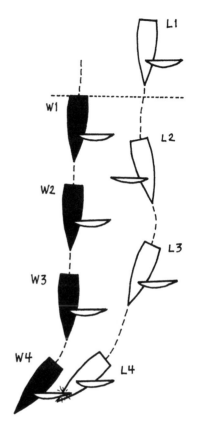

In position 1, L is clear astern of W. When L becomes overlapped on W she is "limited" under rule 17 to sailing no higher than her proper course.

In position 2, L gybes so that the two boats are on opposite tacks and rule 17 no longer applies.

In position 3, L gybes back. Though she has remained overlapped with W, she has not been clear astern since rule 17 turned off in position 2. Therefore, L is not "limited" and can sail up to head to wind if she pleases.

In position 4, L luffs, giving W room to keep clear under rule 16.1. W fails to keep clear thereby breaking rules 11 and 14. L also breaks rule 14 (for failing to avoid contact) but will be exonerated if there is no damage or injury.

If she must then bear away to a lower course to get to the next *mark* and ultimately the finishing line as soon as possible, she must do so immediately. Rule 15 (Acquiring Right of Way) builds in a cushion to protect W while L is bearing away.

Here are three common situations where a boat can catch up from astern and sail in to leeward of a boat ahead and be "free" to sail up to head to wind if she chooses (i.e., have "luffing rights"), subject to rules 15 (Acquiring Right of Way) and 16.1 (Changing Course):

1) The boat behind (BL) *overlaps* the boat ahead (AW) more than two of her lengths to *leeward* of AW. Rule 17 (On the Same Tack; Proper Course) does not apply because the *overlap* did not begin when BL was within two of her lengths of AW. Now BL turns toward AW and maintains her *overlap* as she gets within two lengths. BL is not "limited" and

can sail up to head to wind, even when she may be *overlapped* with AW by just two feet. As a defense, AW can "break" the *overlap* by heading up just before BL comes within two lengths of her; and then "create it" again by bearing off thereby causing BL to "become *overlapped* within two of her hull lengths" of AW.

2) BL overlaps AW to *leeward* within two of her lengths. At that point BL is "limited" to sailing no higher than her *proper course*. BL then gybes and gybes right back, maintaining her "overlap" throughout the maneuver. Now, BL is not "limited" and can sail up to head to wind, even when she may be *overlapped* with AW by just two feet. The reason is that when BL gybed the first time, she did not remain on the same *tack* as AW and therefore rule 17 ceased to apply (see rule 17). When she gybed back onto the same *tack* as AW, she was still *overlapped*; i.e., she did not become *overlapped* again from *clear astern*. Therefore she was not "limited" by rule 17 (On the Same Tack; Proper Course). However, BL did acquire the right of way by her own actions, so she must initially give AW *room to keep clear* under rule 15 (Acquiring Right of Way); and if she changes her course toward AW, she must give AW additional *room* to *keep clear* under rule 16.1 (Changing Course).

3) Halfway down a run, a *port-tack* boat (PL) is converging with a *starboard-tack* boat (SW). PL, after passing very close astern of SW, turns down thereby creating an "overlap" on SW's *leeward* side. The boats, though on opposite tacks, are now *overlapped* because they are both sailing more than 90 degrees from the true wind (see the definition *Clear Astern* and *Clear Ahead; Overlap*). Maintaining her "overlap," PL gybes. When her boom crosses her centerline and she is on the same *tack* as SW, the two boats are already *overlapped*; i.e., PL did not become *overlapped* with SW from *clear astern* while on the same *tack* as SW. Therefore PL is not "limited" and can sail up to head to wind, even when she may be *overlapped* with SW by just two feet. However, the same "limitations" under rules 15 (Acquiring Right of Way) and 16.1 (Changing Course) apply to PL as in the example above. And SW can employ the same tactic as in example one above of breaking the *overlap* with PL just as PL is about to gybe and then re-creating it the moment PL gybes.

8

Part 2, Section C
When Boats Meet at Marks and Obstructions – Mark Room

Section C contains the rules that apply when boats converge at *marks* and *obstructions,* and are intended to provide for safe and orderly transitions from one leg to the next in these tight-quartered situations. In order for that to happen, there are times when a right-of-way boat may find herself with a **limit** on her right of way or a temporary obligation to give *room* or *mark-room* to a keep-clear boat. An example is when a *leeward* boat is on the outside of a *windward* boat while rounding a *mark* or passing an *obstruction*. The *leeward*/outside boat may have to give that *windward*/inside boat *mark-room* to round the *mark* (rule 18, Mark-Room) or *room* to pass the *obstruction* (rule 19, Room to Pass an Obstruction). Another example is when a *starboard-tack* or *leeward* boat is on the inside at a *mark*, and she has just tacked in the *zone* and she has certain obligations (rule 18.3, Tacking in the Zone), or she must gybe to sail her *proper course* and she cannot sail any farther from the *mark* than needed to sail her *proper course* (rule 18.4, Gybing). Finally, there are times when a boat may need to tack to avoid hitting an *obstruction*, but other boats are too close for her to tack without fouling them. Rule 20 (Room to Tack at an Obstruction) gives special permission in certain circumstances that permits the boat to tack.

Section C contains four distinct rules:

Rule 18........ this rule applies at **marks**, including *marks* that are also *obstructions*, other than continuing *obstructions* such as an island that boats are required to round or pass on the same side.

Rule 19........ this rule applies at **obstructions**, unless the *obstruction* is a *mark* that is not a continuing *obstruction*.

Rule 20........ this rule applies when a boat sailing **close-hauled or above** wants to tack to avoid an *obstruction*.

Rule 21........ this rule provides exoneration (freeing from blame) to a boat that breaks a rule of Section A, or rules 15 (Acquiring Right of Way) or 16 (Changing Course), or rule 31 (Touching a Mark) when she is taking *mark-room* to which she is entitled.

Rule 18 is broken into the following distinct sections:

18.1............ states **when** rule 18 does and does not apply

18.2............ states which boats need to **give *mark-room*** to which boats

18.3............ a rule about **tacking** inside the *zone*

18.4............ a rule about **gybing** inside the *zone*

I'll cover rules 18.1 (When Rule 18 Applies), 18.2 (Giving Mark-Room) and 21 (Exoneration) in this chapter. I'll cover rules 18.3 (Tacking in the Zone) and 18.4 (Gybing), as well as the exceptions to rule 18 in chapter 9. And I'll cover rules 19 (Room to Pass an Obstruction) and 20 (Room to Tack at an Obstruction) in chapter 10.

RULE 18 — MARK-ROOM

RULE 18.1 — WHEN RULE 18 APPLIES

Rule 18 applies between boats when they are required to leave a *mark* on the same side and at least one of them is in the *zone*.

This is the rule that governs boats when they are near *marks*. Though rule 18 is the longest rule in Part 2, it is very clearly written and fits very sensibly with the basic right-of-way rules in Section A. Again, the key to understanding it is not to try to memorize its every detail, but to stand back and see how the rule is trying to create orderly sailing when boats converge at *marks*.

"How do I know on which side the mark or obstruction is to be left?"

Good question. First of all, "side" in rule 18.1 refers to the boat's side, not the *mark*'s side. Therefore, when two boats are rounding or passing a *mark* going in the opposite direction (as they might when they are in different races using the same *mark* but leaving it on opposite sides, as in ISAF Case 26), rule 18 does **not** apply, and the rules of Section A and B apply.

As for which way to "leave" a *mark*, the sailing instructions must indicate that (definition *Mark*; rule 28.1, Sailing the Course; and rule J2.1(5), Sailing Instruction Contents).

"Am I always required to leave all marks on a certain side?"

No. Rule 28.1 (Sailing the Course) only requires you to leave all the *marks* of the course on the required side in order to *start* and after *starting*. As for the starting *marks*, rule 28.2 says, *"A string representing a boat's track from the time she begins to approach the starting line from its pre-start side to* **start** *until she* **finishes** *shall, when drawn taut...pass each* **mark** *on the required side and in the correct order..."* Therefore, when there are still two minutes to the starting signal, you can pass a starting *mark* on either side you wish; and because you and other boats are not "required" to leave the *mark* on the same side, rule 18 does not apply. (Note, if the starting *mark* is also an *obstruction* such as the race committee boat, rule 19, Room to Pass an Obstruction, applies when the boats are not "required" to leave it on the same side but are choosing to pass it on the same side.)

The same is true for other racing *marks* that are on your leg but that you are not required to round or pass. Rule 28.1 says, *"...[a boat] may leave on either side a* **mark** *that does not begin, bound or end the leg she is sailing."* So if you are on the final leg to a finishing line that is set to leeward of the leeward *mark*, the leeward *mark* does not define your leg such that you can pass it on either side. Again, rule 18 does not apply at that *mark*.

"To whom is rule 18 talking?"

Rule 18 is "talking" to all the boats involved in the rounding or passing maneuver, but fundamentally it is talking to the outside or *clear astern* boats. When rule 18 applies, outside and *clear astern* boats, whether on *port tack* or *starboard tack* and whether *leeward* or *windward* boats, must give *mark*-room to inside or *clear ahead* boats. Rule 18 also tells inside or *clear ahead* boats how much *room* they are entitled to.

Remember, rule 18 is a rule of exception. In some situations at *marks*, an outside boat otherwise holding right of way must nonetheless yield to an inside keep-clear boat and even change course to move far enough away from the *mark* to give the inside keep-clear boat the *mark-room* she needs to round or pass it. At a downwind *mark*, a *starboard-tack* boat with a *port-tack* boat inside and a *leeward* boat with a *windward* boat inside are examples of this sort of situation that put a "limit" on the right-of-way boat. So, even though you are the right-of-way boat approaching a *mark* or *obstruction*, when rule 18 begins to apply, your right of way may be temporarily "limited."

 "As I approach a mark, when does rule 18 begin to apply to me?"

Rule 18 begins to apply between boats when at least one of them is in the "*zone*." The "*zone*" is the area around the *mark* within a distance of three (3) hull lengths of the boat nearer to it; and a boat is "in the *zone*" when any part of her hull (not her sails or equipment) first is in the *zone* (see the discussion of the definition *Zone* in chapter 5).

 "Will the zone always be three hull lengths in every race?"

Normally the *zone* will be three lengths. But the *zone* in team and match racing is "two lengths" (rules C2.3, Match Racing Rules and D1.1(a), Team Racing Rules), and in radio sailing racing rules it is "four lengths" (rule E1.1, Radio Sailing Racing Rules).

 "So does that mean that rule 18 does not apply between boats if none of them have reached the zone yet?"

Yes, that's right! A *leeward* boat that may be an outside boat at the *mark* that has luffing rights may luff a *windward* boat, subject to rule 16.1 (Changing Course) right up until the point either of them first reaches the *zone*. Note, this could be during or after the boats have taken their spinnakers down, etc. in preparation for the *mark* rounding.

But note that when either of the boats enters the *zone*, rule 18.2(b) (Giving Mark-Room) requires the outside boat to give the inside boat *mark-room* from that moment on, which in most situations is the space the inside boat needs to sail to the *mark* in a "seamanlike way" (see the definition *Mark-Room*).

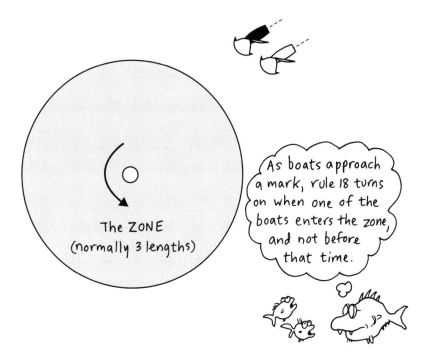

The ZONE
(normally 3 lengths)

As boats approach a mark, rule 18 turns on when one of the boats enters the zone, and not before that time.

Therefore, in order to comply with rule 18.2(b), boats will have to anticipate this by sailing a course **prior** to entering the *zone* so that they will be in compliance with the rule at the moment the first one reaches the *zone*.

"I understand now about the significance of the 'zone;' but how do I know where the 'zone' actually is on the water?"

Well, at first it's difficult, and then after you've raced more and more it becomes easier to judge. Let's say you race a 30-foot boat. Three lengths is 90 feet. That's the distance from home plate to first base on a baseball diamond, or approximately a third of a football field. Doing 6 knots (about 10 feet per second) you'll cover three lengths in just under 10 seconds. Measure it out and mark it with two orange poles or something at your club so everyone will learn to "guesstimate" it better. And remember that when the first part of your hull is three lengths from the *mark*, the helmsman will be almost four lengths away.

"Okay, but what if two boats simply can't agree on whether an over-lap was obtained or broken before reaching the zone?"

Competitors and protest committees should try their hardest to remember and determine the facts. However, realizing that there will be disputes, the rule

writers built in some "guidance" to help resolve such disputes. Rule 18.2(d) reads, *"If there is reasonable doubt that a boat obtained or broke an* **overlap** *in time, it shall be presumed that she did not."*

In other words, if you come up from behind and claim that you got the inside *overlap* before the outside boat reached the *zone*, but the outside boat disagrees saying that you were still *clear astern* when she arrived at the *zone* and that you subsequently obtained the *overlap*, rule 18.2(d) states that if there is "reasonable doubt," it shall be presumed by the sailors that the *overlap* was **not** obtained in time. Similarly, if it goes to a protest hearing and the protest committee has "reasonable doubt," it shall presume that the *overlap* was **not** obtained in time. In other words, in a *protest* you will have to satisfy the protest committee that there is no doubt that you obtained the *overlap* in time. See US Sailing Appeal 92.

By the same token, if you have an *overlap* on an outside boat at say five and then four lengths away, she will be required to give you *mark-room* under rule 18.2(b) unless she pulls *clear ahead* before reaching the *zone*. If she claims to have "broken" the *overlap* just before she reached the *zone*, but you disagree saying that you were still *overlapped* when she reached the *zone*, then it is she who must satisfy the protest committee that there is no doubt that the *overlap* was broken in time.

Satisfying the protest committee is generally very tough to do as it is usually one person's word against the other's. Hails to each other regarding the *overlap* situation as the boats near the *zone* are very helpful to the point that they are almost expected by good protest committees. Also, witnesses can be very useful, particularly independent witnesses who were positioned exactly at the *zone* and in a position to determine *overlaps*. But the bottom line is that boats that will have the "burden of proof" should yield on the water to be safe.

WHEN THE BOATS ARE OVERLAPPED

"When rule 18 applies between two or more overlapped boats, what rights and requirements do the inside and outside boats have?"

That's the key question, and it's covered in rules 18.2(a) and 18.2(b). Let's get into it.

When boats get to the *zone*, they will either be *overlapped* or not *overlapped*. Let's look at those two situations.

RULE 18.2 — GIVING MARK-ROOM

(a) When boats are *overlapped* the outside boat shall give the inside boat *mark-room*, unless rule 18.2(b) applies.

(b) If boats are *overlapped* when the first of them reaches the *zone*, the outside boat at that moment shall thereafter give the inside boat *mark-room*. If a boat is *clear ahead* when she reaches the *zone*, the boat *clear astern* at that moment shall thereafter give her *mark-room*.

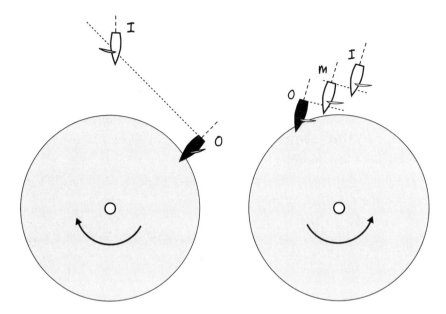

Even though I is well behind O, I has an inside overlap when O reaches the zone; therefore O must give I mark-room.

M is in between O and I and overlaps both of them; therefore, I is overlapped with O when O reaches the zone. O and M must keep clear of I and give I mark-room.

Note, rule 18.2(a) and the first sentence in 18.2(b) are "talking" only to *overlapped* boats. The second sentence in rule 18.2(b) deals with boats that are not *overlapped*.

Remember, a boat is *overlapped* with another if her bow or equipment in normal position (such as the spinnaker or extended bowsprit) is on or across a line drawn abeam through the aftermost point of the other boat's hull and equipment in normal position. Also, two boats that otherwise are not *overlapped* suddenly become *overlapped* when a boat **in between them** *overlaps* both of them. So if you are approaching a *mark* to be left to port and are just *overlapped* on the port transom of the boat ahead of you, and she is just *overlapped* on the port transom of the boat ahead of her, you are technically *overlapped* with the boat ahead of her (see the definition *Clear Astern and Clear Ahead; Overlapped*). Therefore you are entitled to *mark-room* from both boats if you are *overlapped* when the **farthest boat ahead** arrives at the *zone*.

Also remember that, by definition, two boats *overlap* when the bow or equipment in normal position of one is over the line drawn through the after-most part of the other, even when the boats are a quarter of a mile apart; and that when rule 18 applies or both boats are sailing more than ninety degrees from the true wind, the boats are considered *overlapped* even when they are on opposite *tacks*. This becomes important as boats approach the leeward *mark* on opposite *tacks* on widely differing angles. (See the definition *Clear Astern* and *Clear Ahead; Overlap*.) For instance, say that two boats are reaching on opposite *tacks* to a leeward *mark* to be left to starboard. When the *starboard tack* boat (S) reaches the *zone*, the *port tack* boat (P) is five lengths from the *mark*, but based on the angle of S's course, P is *overlapped* on the inside of S. Therefore, P is entitled to *mark-room* from S under rule 18.2(b) if she needs it!

"Are there any limitations on obtaining an overlap and becoming *entitled to the rights in rule 18.2(a) or 18.2(b)?"*

Yes, there are two:

1) the boat astern cannot obtain an inside *overlap* and become entitled to *mark-room* once the boat ahead reaches the *zone clear ahead* of the boat astern (18.2(b)); and

2) the outside boat is not required to give *mark-room* if she has been physically unable to give the inside boat *mark-room* from the time the *overlap* began (18.2(e)).

Up to 1965, a boat *clear astern* could get a legal inside *overlap* as long as it was (a) in time to enable the outside boat(s) to give *room*; (b) before the boat ahead changed her course in the act of rounding; and (c) before any part of the boat ahead came abreast of the *mark*. Things were often a tad out of control as boats came barreling up from astern yelling for "buoy room" at the last second.

In 1965 the rule writers took a creative step. Realizing that there ought to be some cutoff "point" after which a boat *clear astern* could not obtain an inside *overlap*, they devised a safety zone now simply called "the *zone*," which has proved to work very effectively. And because the "point" can be in any direction from the *mark*, the *zone* is an imaginary area with the *mark* in the center and having a radius of three of the nearer boat's hull lengths; for instance, 72 feet in a Melges 24 (see the definition *Zone*). Note the fact that it is the nearer boat's hull lengths; this becomes important when the boats are different sizes.

The second sentence in rule 18.2(b) says, *"If a boat is **clear ahead** when she reaches the **zone**, the boat **clear astern** at that moment shall thereafter give her **mark-room**."* So the game ends at the *zone*. If you are catching up from astern but don't get the inside *overlap* before the boat ahead of you gets to the *zone*, then you are not entitled to the rights in rule 18.2(b) and must give the boat ahead *mark-room* under rule 18.2(b). If you do get the *overlap* before she gets to the *zone*, then you are entitled to the rights in rule 18.2(b). So often the race is to the *zone*!

 "What if I physically can't give room to the boat that just obtained the inside overlap on me?"

That's the second exception to rule 18.2(a) and 18.2(b). When a boat obtains an inside *overlap* from *clear astern*, the boat ahead has a "protective shield" if she needs it. When a boat gets an *overlap* at the zero-moment before you enter the *zone*, she becomes entitled to *mark-room* under rule 18.2(b) as an inside boat. However, you are not required to anticipate her arrival. There are times, though rare, when you may be physically unable to give her the *room* she needs to round or pass the *mark* from the time the *overlap* began, based on your situation at that moment. Rule 18.2(e) says, *"If a boat obtained an inside overlap from clear astern or by tacking to windward of the other boat and, from the time the overlap began, the outside boat has been unable to give mark-room, she is not required to give it."* In this situation, she is not entitled to *mark-room* and the applicable rules of Section A and B apply. If she is a right-of-way boat, she must comply with rule 15 (Acquiring Right of Way) which means she won't get inside at the *mark* because if the outside boat could have created enough *room* to do so, she would have done so in the first place. And if she is a keep-clear boat, she must *keep clear*.

One example of where this situation might occur is a tightly packed *mark* rounding in light air where a boat astern gets an inside *overlap* on a boat that is three-and-a-half boat-lengths from the *mark*, but there's just no way the outside boat can get everyone else outside of her to move away from the *mark* in time to create *room* for the new inside boat. Another example is when two boats are going so fast that by the time the outside boat can react to her new obligation and make the *room*, the inside boat is already past the *mark* on the wrong side. Twelve knots of boat-speed equals about 20 feet per second, so on a windy reach a Hobie 18 will chew up three boat-lengths in less than three seconds!

A similar situation is when you are approaching a starboard-hand windward *mark* on *starboard-tack*, and a *port-tack* boat crosses you in the *zone* and tacks to *windward* of you, or ducks you and then tacks into a *windward overlap*. Rule 18.2(a) requires you to give them *mark-room* unless you are physically unable to do so from the moment the *overlap* began.

"What if at a windward mark I am fetching the mark and the boat ahead of me, or overlapped outside of me, didn't reach the zone clear ahead of me, but instead they approached me on the opposite tack and then tacked inside the zone?"

If you are *fetching* the *mark* (i.e., you can pass to windward of the *mark* leaving it on the required side without sailing past head to wind to do so; see the definition *Fetching*) and a boat tacks inside the *zone* and is *clear ahead* of you when she completes her tack, you can obtain an inside *overlap* and become entitled to *mark-room* under rule 18.3(b) (Tacking When Approaching a Mark). Note, in this one instance if the boat that tacked is unable to give you *mark-room*, she breaks rule 18.3(b). And if a boat tacks within the *zone* into an outside *overlap* on you, it must give you *mark-room* at the *mark* as well under rule 18.3(b).

Another possible scenario is two boats (P and S) approaching a windward *mark* to be left to port on opposite *tacks*. S is about two lengths below the *starboard-tack* layline (i.e., she is not *fetching* the *mark*); P is close to the *port-tack* layline. When S nears the *port-tack* layline she tacks. When she passes head to wind she is within the *zone*. She completes her tack *clear ahead* of P. P, moving faster, *overlaps* S to windward about one length from the *mark*. Or in a similar approach, when S completes her tack she is *overlapped* to leeward of P. In both scenarios, S is required to give P *room* at the *mark* under rule 18.2(a).

The reason is that rule 18.2(a) makes no reference to **where** the boats were when they reached the *zone*. It just talks about *overlapped* boats. (Rule 18.2(b) contains references to the *zone* but it does not apply in the scenarios described above.) S and P are *overlapped* with S on the outside, so rule 18.2(a) requires the outside boat to give the inside boat *mark-room*. Note that in these scenarios, P is not *fetching* the *mark*, so rule 18.3 does not apply.

"OK, I get all that. So if I'm the outside boat, can you remind me when I have to start giving the inside boat mark-room?"

You have to start giving *mark-room* the moment rule 18 begins to apply, which is when the hull of the first of the boats involved is in the *zone*, which is normally three lengths from the *mark*. It is at this point that outside/right-of-way boats need to have yielded and provided the inside/keep-clear boats the space they need to sail to and around the *mark*.

"So if I'm the outside boat and required to give mark-room, how much room do I have to give the inside boat?"

Well first you have to understand what *"room"* means; then what *"mark-room"* means. *"Room"* is *"the space a boat needs in the existing conditions, including space to comply with her obligations under the rules of Part 2 and rule 31, while maneuvering promptly in a seamanlike way"* (see the definition *Room*). *"Mark-room"* is *"**Room** for a boat to leave a **mark** on the required side. Also (a) **room** to sail to the **mark** when her **proper course** is to sail close to it, and (b) **room** to round the **mark** as necessary to sail the course* (see the definition *Mark-Room*)."

So first, assuming the inside boat's *proper course* is to sail close to the *mark*, say within a length or so as it will be when she is rounding the *mark*, you have to give her the space she needs to sail to the *mark* in a "seamanlike way" (meaning safe; not putting her boat or crew at risk of damage or injury, or at risk of touching the *mark*; sailed the way competent sailors would sail to the *mark*) in the prevailing conditions. A boat will need more space if it is windy and wavy, and less space if it is light air and smooth; just as a boat will need more space if it has a lot of sail handling to do, and less space if it has only one sail to deal with. *Room*, however, does **not** include space for the inside boat to sail her *proper course* to the *mark*; i.e., the space the inside boat might like to set up for a tactically desirable "swing wide-cut close" type rounding, though in actual practice most outside boats are a little more forgiving.

Then you have to give her the space she needs to round the *mark* as necessary to sail the course, which means just enough space to allow her to round the *mark* in a "seamanlike way" (see the definition *Room*). Again, "seamanlike way" means the space needed to not be at risk of touching the *mark* or the outside or *clear astern* boat during her rounding, and not the space she might want to sail her *proper course*; i.e., the course she might want to sail for tactical reasons.

Once she has rounded the *mark* and can *keep clear* of a right-of-way boat

O is right... I is only entitled to room to round the mark as necessary to sail the course, not room to sail her proper course

Careful... they've changed the definition mark-room; don't gybe too close!

Yeah! what he said...

Don't I still get to sail my proper course while rounding the mark?

without risk of touching the *mark* or fouling another boat, she has taken all the *room* available in *mark-room*. Note, this might occur before she has left the *mark* astern when there are no mitigating circumstances; or it might occur after she has left the *mark* astern, for instance in strong adverse current.

Note that a boat is not entitled to more space than usual just because her crew is short-handed or inexperienced. ISAF Case 103 addresses this head on by saying, "Neither the experience of IW's crew nor their number is relevant in determining '*room*'... the interpretation of 'seamanlike way' must be based on the boat-handling that can reasonably be expected from a competent, but not expert, crew of the appropriate number for the boat."

"What if I need to gybe; do I get room for that too?"

If you need to gybe to round the mark in order to sail the course, then yes, *mark-room* includes enough space for your boom to come across and your stern to swing when you gybe to round the *mark*. But let's say you are rounding the windward *mark* onto a run (where you will spend time on both tacks). You do not need to gybe to round the *mark* onto the run, even though gybing may be your *proper course*. Therefore, *mark-room* does **not** include *room* to gybe in that situation.

"How about when I'm a windward/inside boat coming into the wind- *ward mark or rounding the leeward mark; am I entitled to room to tack around the mark?"*

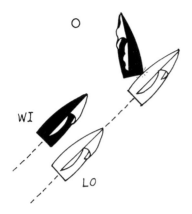

LO must give WI mark-room under rule 18.2, which includes room to tack. However, the moment WI passes head to wind, she and LO are on opposite tacks and rule 18 shuts off. At that point rule 13 requires WI to keep clear of LO while tacking; and rule 14 always requires both boats to avoid contact. If WI makes a normal tack and her transom touches LO, it is likely a protest committee will decide that LO failed to give WI room to tack. But to be safe, WI should try not to let her transom touch LO after she passes head to wind.

At the windward *mark*, Yes; at the leeward *mark*, No. If you are the inside boat and are **overlapped** to *windward* of the boat required to give you *mark-room*, and you need to tack to round the mark as necessary to sail the course, then *mark-room* includes *room* to tack as long as you are *fetching* the *mark* after your tack (see the definition *Mark-Room*). Note, if you have pulled *clear ahead*, you are still entitled to *mark-room* (see rule 18.2(c)(1)), but not to *room* to tack. However, at a leeward *mark* going onto a beat to windward, you do not need to tack around the *mark* in order to sail the course; therefore, *mark-room* does **not** include *room* to tack.

At the windward *mark*, note that once the inside *overlapped* tacking boat passes head-to-wind, rule 18 no longer applies because the boats are now on opposite tacks on a beat to windward (rule 18.1(a)). If contact occurs during the tack, the inside boat will have a good argument that the outside boat was failing to give her *mark-room* before she passed head-to-wind; i.e., while rule 18.2(a) or 18.2(b) still applied, and that she should be exonerated under rule 21 (Exoneration) for her breach of rule 13 (While Tacking). However, it is possible that a protest committee might decide that the inside boat could have tacked without causing contact (i.e., that she had *room* to tack), and therefore disqualify the inside boat for breaking rule 13 because rule 18 no longer applied once she passed head to wind. The bottom line in this situation is that the outside boat should be sure to give the inside boat enough space to make a normal tack without hitting her; and the inside boat should be careful not to hit the outside boat while she is tacking to be safe.

Next, the question of how much *room* an outside boat must give to an inside boat depends on whether the outside boat is a "right-of-way" boat or a "keep-clear" boat.

WHEN THE OUTSIDE BOAT IS THE RIGHT-OF-WAY BOAT:

When the outside boat has the right-of-way, she only needs to give the inside boat *mark-room*; and no more space than that (see the discussion above). Note that rules 18.2(a) and 18.2(b) do not shift the right of way from the outside/right-of-way boat to the inside/keep-clear boat. But clearly the obligation to give *mark-room* conflicts with rule 10 (On Opposite Tacks) and rule 11 (On the Same Tack, Overlapped) in Section A. In other words, when a *starboard-tack* (S) and a *port-tack* boat (P), or a *leeward* (L) and a *windward* boat (W), are rounding a *mark* with P or W on the inside, S or L has a "temporary obligation" to give P or W *mark-room*. After fulfilling that obligation, S and L will get their full rights back under rules 10 or 11.

Furthermore, if a keep-clear boat sails farther from the *mark* than allowed under *mark-room*, and she breaks a rule in Section A or rule 15 (Acquiring Right of Way) or 16 (Changing Course), she is not entitled to exoneration under rule 21 (Exoneration). For instance, when a *windward*/inside boat (WI) is slow in coming up to close-hauled around a *mark* and contact occurs between her and a *leeward*/outside boat, WI breaks rule 11 (On the Same Tack, Overlapped); and if it is found that she took more *room* than was needed to round the *mark*, she will not be exonerated under rule 21. (See ISAF Case 25 and US Sailing Appeals 3 and 20.)

WI is the windward/inside boat. Because she does not have right of way over LO, she is entitled only to enough space to sail to the mark in a seamanlike way, as opposed to the space she might like to take in order to make a tactical "swing wide-cut close" type of rounding. WI is taking too much room while sailing to the mark, and by hitting the leeward boat she breaks rules 11 and 14 and is not exonerated under rule 21.

Remember, the primary purpose of rule 18 is to allow boats to round or pass a *mark* without the inside boats getting wedged in between the outside boats and the *mark*, or getting forced onto the wrong side of the *mark*; and to create an orderly transition from one leg of the race to the next. As discussed above, sometimes these outside boats are going to otherwise have the right of way. Rule 18 requires them to give only enough *room* for the inside boat to round or pass the *mark*. The moment the inside boat has completed her rounding or passing maneuver, the purpose of rule 18 has been served. At that moment the outside/right-of-way boat gets her full rights back, and the inside/keep-clear boat must *keep clear*.

For example, let's say that two *overlapped* boats on *port tack* are rounding the leeward *mark* onto a beat. The *leeward*/outside boat (LO) is allowing enough space for the *windward*/inside boat (WI) to round the *mark* as quickly as possible, but LO is trying to keep her bow just ahead of WI. As WI comes up to close-hauled, LO luffs at a medium rate. WI responds by luffing and tacking onto *starboard-tack*. She *keeps clear* of LO and does not hit the *mark* or tack too close to any boat about to pass the *mark*. No foul. LO gave WI *room* to round the *mark*, and when LO asserted her rights as a *leeward* boat, WI was able to *keep clear* without hitting the *mark*.

Note that the circumstances will weigh heavily in determining exactly when the outside boat can assert her rights. If there are a lot of boats near the *mark* such that WI could not tack without fouling them under rule 15 (Acquiring Right of Way), LO will have to be careful to allow WI the *room* needed to sail between LO and the *mark* without tacking. If there is current or strong wind or waves, LO will again have to wait until WI can clear the *mark* without risk of losing speed and being pushed back into the *mark*. But if there are no mitigating circumstances, WI may be able to respond safely to LO's luff even before she has left the *mark* astern.

 "Well, if I'm the inside boat and required to keep clear and the outside boat is not giving me mark-room, what should I do?"

You should sail to the *mark* in a seamanlike way expecting the outside boat to give you *mark-room* as required under rule 18.2. If you are not allowed to sail to the *mark*, or there is contact between you and the outside boat, you should protest. The outside boat should be penalized for breaking rule 18.2(a)

or 18.2(b); and if there is contact, you should be "exonerated" which means freed from blame for breaking a rule. Rule 21 (Exoneration) says, *"When a boat is sailing within the* **room** *or* **mark-room** *to which she is entitled under a rule of Section C, she shall be exonerated if, in an incident with a boat required to give her that* **room** *or* **mark-room***, (a) she breaks a rule of Section A, rule 15 or rule 16, or (b) she is compelled to break rule 31."*

Note, however, that you only get exonerated for breaking a rule in Section A (Right of Way), or rule 15 (Acquiring Right of Way) or 16 (Changing Course), or rule 31 (Touching a Mark). If at the moment it became clear to you that the outside boat was not going to give you *mark-room* it was possible to have avoided the contact, and if the contact resulted in damage or injury to either boat, you will also be penalized for breaking rule 14 (Avoiding Contact). In other words, both boats will be penalized in this circumstance.

Note also that by avoiding the contact this may result in you not being able to round or pass the *mark* on that approach. Though the outside boat's rule breach caused you to sail on the wrong side of the *mark* on that approach, it hasn't prevented you from ultimately rounding the *mark* correctly as required by rule 28.1 (Sailing the Course); i.e., she didn't compel you to break rule 28.1. Therefore, unfortunately, you are not entitled to exoneration under rule 64.1(a) (Penalties and Exoneration) or redress under rule 62 (Redress); you must circle around and try again. You should certainly win your *protest* against the outside boat, but there is nothing the protest committee can do to compensate you for the distance/places/time lost while making a second try to round or pass the *mark*.

And remember, if you hit the *mark* you have broken rule 31 (Touching a Mark). But you can be exonerated under rule 21 (Exoneration) if the protest committee finds that the outside boat compelled you to touch the *mark* by failing to give you *mark-room*.

"What happens when I have an inside overlap when the boats reach the zone, but once inside the zone the outside boat breaks the overlap?"

You are still entitled to *mark-room* under rule 18.2(b). Rule 18.2(c)(1) says, *"When a boat is required to give* **mark-room** *by rule 18.2(b), she shall continue to do so even if later an* **overlap** *is broken or a new* **overlap** *begins."* So as long as you are *overlapped* when one of the boats reaches the *zone*, your

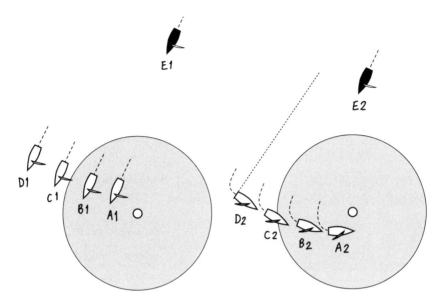

A, B, C and D are in a bunch at a mark. D is keeping clear of the three boats inside her, and as a result is outside the zone. E is well astern. In position 2, the four boats gybe and line up to pass the mark one behind the other. The position of A, B and C make it obvious that D is still outside the zone. Because E is overlapped on D's inside and is the right of way boat, D must give her mark-room and keep clear of her. E must gybe when it is her proper course to do so.

right to *mark-room* under rule 18.2(b) is "locked in" until the rule no longer applies, or until you pass head to wind or sail out of the *zone* (rule 18.2(c)).

"What happens when boats on the outside that are giving room to boats on the inside never get to the zone until after they've turned and begun heading for the mark; now can a boat that was well clear astern suddenly claim room?"

Yes! ISAF Case 59 clarifies this very common situation at crowded *marks*:

"QUESTION: Five boats were approaching a leeward mark dead before the wind. Four of them were overlapped in line with A nearest the mark. The fifth boat, E, was clear astern of A, B and C when those three boats reached the zone. When D came abreast of the mark and turned to round it, E became overlapped inside D. This occurred after E had already reached the zone and before D reached it. E rounded the mark behind A, B and C but inside D, which was able to give mark-room to E. Is E entitled to mark-room under rule 18.2(b) from D?

"ANSWER: Because E was clear astern of A, B and C when they reached the zone, she was required by rule 18.2(b) to give each of them mark-room. Between E and D, however, a different relationship developed. In order to leave room for the three inside boats with their booms fully extended, D had to approach the mark on a course that brought her abreast of it outside the zone. When E reached the zone, she was clear astern of D and D was still outside the zone. Therefore, rule 18.2(b) did not apply between D and E. When D changed course towards the mark, E obtained an inside overlap and rule 18.2(a) began to apply between D and E. E was entitled to mark-room under that rule, which D was able to give."

"Does the inside boat have to call for mark-room in order to get it?"

No. When you are on the inside at a *mark*, you are not required to call for *room*, although that is a prudent thing to do to avoid misunderstandings. Boats are expected to know their obligations under the *rules*, which includes outside boats at *marks*.

"Now is any of this different when the inside boat also has the right of way?"

Well, everything we've talked about regarding *mark-room* is the same; but the fundamental difference is that when the inside boat has the right of way, she can sail her *"**proper course**"* from the moment she enters the *zone* (and she can sail even farther from a gate *mark* than her *proper course* would take her if she is not subject to rule 17, On the Same Tack; Proper Course; see rule 18.4, Gybing). Whereas if the inside boat does **not** have the right-of-way, she can only sail a **"seamanlike"** course from the time she enters the *zone*. That permits the inside right-of-way boat to set up for a more tactical "swing wide/ cut close" type of rounding before she is at the *mark*, whereas the inside keep-clear boat will have to begin her rounding closer to the *mark*.

WHEN THE INSIDE BOAT IS THE RIGHT-OF-WAY BOAT:

When the inside boat has the right-of-way under Section A (Right of Way) of the rules, the outside boat must *keep clear*. This does not change just because the boats are rounding or passing a *mark*. Therefore, not only is the inside/ right-of-way boat entitled to *mark-room*; she is free to sail where she pleases, with just a couple of possible limits. Therefore, the right-of-way boat has more freedom in the *zone*.

There are two situations where the inside right-of-way boat will have a "limit" as she sails to and around a *mark*:

- One such "limit" is in rule 17 (On the Same Tack; Proper Course) which limits L to sailing no higher than her *proper course* when she becomes *overlapped* from *clear astern*. Therefore, at a windward *mark*, if LI (*leeward/inside*) becomes *overlapped* on the inside of a boat that has just tacked in front of her inside the *zone* such that rule 18.3(b) (Tacking in the Zone) applies, LI must sail her *proper course* around the *mark*. Note that, in this situation, her *proper course* may be to sail head to wind momentarily to get up and around the *mark*.

- The other "limit" is in rule 18.4 (Gybing) which says that if an inside *overlapped* right-of-way boat must gybe to sail her *proper course* around the *mark*, she is required to sail no farther from the *mark* than needed to sail her *proper course* until she gybes; i.e., she can't continue on straight past the *mark* or luff away from the *mark* if that takes her farther from the *mark* than necessary to sail her *proper course*. (For a full discussion, including an exception at a gate *mark*, see the explanation of rule 18.4.) This "limit" commonly arises at offwind *marks* whenever L or S is on the inside and her *proper course* is to gybe around the *mark*.

But the bottom line is that an inside right-of-way boat is allowed to swing a bit wider and then cut closer around the *mark* (often called a "tactical rounding"). The reason is because inside right-of-way boats always have the right to sail their *proper course* while they remain the right-of-way boat, and outside boats must both *keep clear* of them and give them *mark-room*. Setting up to round this way allows boats to make a smooth turn and will get them into the most strategically desirable position (clear air, ability to tack, etc.) as they begin the beat, which will help them to *finish* as soon as possible (see the definition *Proper Course*).

Note, however, that the moment an inside/right-of-way boat gybes to round the *mark* and becomes an inside/keep-clear boat, she is only entitled to *mark-room*, which does **not** include *room* to sail her *proper course*; and if she takes more space than she is entitled to, she will not be exonerated under rule 21 (Exoneration) if she breaks rule 11 (On the Same Tack, Overlapped).

WHEN THE BOATS ARE NOT OVERLAPPED

"Okay, I've got it so far; now how about when the boats are not over-lapped when they get to the zone?"

The second sentence in rule 18.2(b) covers the situation where the boats are not *overlapped* when the boat *clear ahead* reaches the *zone*. It says, *"If a boat is **clear ahead** when she reaches the **zone**, the boat **clear astern** at that moment shall thereafter give her **mark-room**."*

So, between two boats (A and B), if they are not *overlapped* when the first of them reaches the *zone*, and assuming the *proper* course for the one ahead (A) is to sail close to the *mark* (within a length or so), the one behind (B) must give A the space she needs to sail to the *mark* in a seamanlike way; and if it is a rounding mark, the space A needs to round or pass the *mark* in a seaman-like way as well. And, if A has the right of way, then B must also *keep clear* of her, and A is not "limited" to sailing her *proper course*; i.e., she can swing as wide as she pleases as long as she stays in the *zone*.

Before reaching the zone, S has right of way over P under rule 10. However, the moment P reaches the zone clear ahead of S, rule 18.2(b) requires S to give P mark-room.

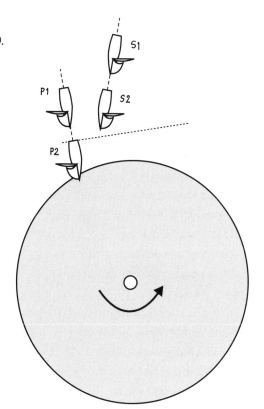

Note that rule 18.2(b) does not shift the right of way from the boat *clear astern* to the boat *clear ahead*. If the boat *clear ahead* is the keep-clear boat, she is simply entitled to *mark-room* from the *clear astern* right-of-way boat.

"What happens when the boat ahead is on port tack approaching a downwind finishing line with a boat on starboard tack right behind her, and the port-tack boat will pass through the zone about two lengths from the finishing mark?"

Good question. First of all, the *port-tack* boat (PA) is the keep-clear boat under rule 10 (On Opposite Tacks). This does not change just because she is in the *zone* of the *mark*. Because she reached the *zone clear ahead* of the *starboard-tacker* (SB), she is entitled to *mark-room*. However, because her *proper course* is to sail straight across the finishing line, and because she is two lengths away from the *mark*, her *proper course* is not to sail close to the *mark*. Therefore, she is not entitled to *room* to sail to the *mark*; only to the space needed to leave the finishing *mark* on the required side (which she has plenty of). PA will need to *keep clear* of SB as she *finishes* and clears the finishing line and *marks*, which she can easily do by either heading up or bearing away or gybing. And if she fails to *keep clear*, she breaks rule 10 and will not be exonerated under rule 21 (Exoneration).

"What happens if the boat that was clear astern becomes overlapped on the inside of the other boat inside the zone?"

Note that rule 18.2(b) has a "lock-in" provision (*"...shall thereafter give her mark-room"*), and the first sentence of rule 18.2(c) makes it clear that the lock-in provision continues to apply even if the boat *clear astern* later becomes *overlapped*, either on the inside or outside, with the boat that was *clear ahead* at the *zone*. Rule 18.2(c) says, *"When a boat is required to give **mark-room** by rule 18.2(b), she shall continue to do so even if later an **overlap** is broken or a new **overlap** begins..."* Therefore, if a boat is *clear ahead* when she reached the *zone*, the boat that is *clear astern* at that moment must continue to give her *mark-room*, even if she *overlaps* her later during your rounding or passing maneuver.

"So if I'm entitled to mark-room at a leeward mark, can I go head to wind to 'shut the door' on a boat trying to sneak inside of me?"

Yes, but you have to be careful! Assuming the boat trying to sneak inside of you owes you *mark-room*, she still must give you that *room*, which is just

enough space for you to round the *mark* as needed to sail the course. Furthermore, she must also give you *room* to sail your *proper course* while you two are *overlapped* (see rule 18.2(c)(2)). If you break rule 16.1 (Changing Course) while taking the *room* you are entitled to, you will be exonerated under rule 21 (Exoneration). So as long as you don't sail above your *proper course*, you can "shut the door" even if you break rule 16.1 in the process.

However, when rounding a leeward *mark* to start a beat, once you have sailed up to a close-hauled course (usually your *proper course*), you've been given the *room* you need to round the *mark* and sail your *proper course*. If you choose to sail above close-hauled, you are no longer sailing within the *room* you are entitled to, and you will **not** be exonerated if you break rule 16.1. So if when you luff above close-hauled, the windward boat cannot *keep clear* of you because she is stuck between you and the windward *mark*, you will break rule 16.1. And you get no *room* to tack, so if you sail past head to wind, you risk breaking rule 13 (While Tacking).

"Rule 18.2(c)(2) is a new rule. Can you explain in more detail what it means?"

Sure. Imagine two boats (PA and SB) approaching a downwind finishing line with PA *clear ahead* on *port tack* when she reaches the *zone* of the committee boat to be left to port. Let's say her *proper course* is to cross the finishing line a boat length from the committee boat. Now SB, *clear astern* on *starboard tack*, sails in between PA and the committee boat. Even though she is now the inside boat, the "lock-in" provisions in rules 18.2(b) and 18.2(c) require SB to continue to give PA *mark-room*. Furthermore, rule 18.2(c)(2) says, "*if [a boat that is required to give **mark-room** under rule 18.2(b)] becomes **overlapped** inside the boat entitled to **mark-room**, she shall also give that boat **room** to sail her **proper course** while they remain **overlapped***. That means that PA can sail her *proper course* to *finish* and SB must give her *room* to do that; and if PA breaks rule 10 (On Opposite Tacks), she will be exonerated under rule 21 (Exoneration). But it also means that if PA sails **above** her *proper course* to try to "shut the door" on SB, and forces SB to avoid her, she will break rule 10 and will not be exonerated under rule 21.

Note that if SB were to gybe to port tack before PA sailed above her *proper course*, then PA would become the right-of-way boat under rule 11 (On the Same Tack, Overlapped), and could luff and "shut the door" on SB as long as she gave SB *room* to *keep clear* under rule 16.1 (Changing Course).

 "Is it true that a boat entitled to mark-room can change course to round a mark as quickly as she wants, with no regard to boats overlapped with her (other than avoiding contact that causes damage or injury)?"

Essentially yes!

RULE 21 – EXONERATION

When a boat is sailing within the *room* or *mark-room* to which she is entitled under a rule of Section C, she shall be exonerated if, in an incident with a boat required to give her that *room* or *mark-room*,

(a) she breaks a rule of Section A, rule 15 or rule 16, or

(b) she is compelled to break rule 31.

"Exonerated" means freed from blame for breaking the rule. So if the boat ahead or the inside boat (AI) is a keep-clear boat and while rounding the *mark* in a seamanlike way she fouls the other boat (BO), BO breaks rule 18.2(b) (Giving Mark-Room) and AI is exonerated for the Section A rule she broke.

If AI is a right-of-way boat and while rounding the *mark* in a seamanlike way (i.e., within the *mark*-room she is entitled to) she fails to give BO *room* to *keep clear*, BO breaks rule 18.2(b) and AI is exonerated for breaking rule 16.1 (Changing Course).

This is a common sense rule. If you are entitled to *room* at the *mark*, you should be able to sail your course around that *mark* without concern for the boats required to give you *mark-room*. And those boats should be able to easily anticipate the course you are going to sail around the *mark*.

Remember also that rule 14 (Avoiding Contact) always applies, so even right-of-way boats rounding *marks* must be careful to avoid any contact, and particularly any contact that causes damage or injury.

Note that exoneration for breaking rule 16 only applies when rule 18 applies. For instance, when boats are approaching a starting *mark* surrounded by water (like a race committee boat) to *start*, rule 18 does not apply (preamble to Section C). So both before and after the starting signal, rule 16.1 applies and right-of-way boats must give *keep clear* boats *room* to *keep clear* **anytime** they change course. The same applies at a windward *mark* when a *starboard-tack* boat (S) is bearing away around the *mark* and a *port-tack* boat (P) is approaching the *mark*. Because P is "approaching" the *mark* and S is "leaving" it, rule 18 does not apply (rule 18.1(c)), and therefore rule 16.1 does apply to S; i.e., S must be careful as she changes course near P (see discussion of rule 16).

Let's look at some examples of this rule 16 (Changing Course) exception in action:

- A and B, two *port-tack* boats not *overlapped*, are approaching a leeward *mark* to be left to port. A reaches the *zone clear ahead* of B. As A swings wide to make a "tactical" (swing wide-cut close) rounding, B puts her bow in between A and the *mark*. As A changes course to round the *mark*, B yells that A must give her *room* to *keep clear* under rule 16.1 (Changing Course) and that B can't *keep clear* of A due to the proximity of the *mark* on her port side. B is wrong. Rule 18 applies and B is required to give A *mark-room* under rule 18.2(b). Therefore, A is free to round the *mark* and if in doing so she fails to give B *room* to *keep clear* of her, she will be exonerated under rule 21 (Exoneration).

- L and W, two *overlapped starboard-tack* boats, are approaching a gybe *mark* to be left to port. They enter the *zone overlapped*. L then bears away to gybe around the *mark* and her transom hits W's *leeward* side with no damage or injury. Again, rule 18 applies and L is entitled to *mark-room*. W is wrong for breaking rules 11 and 18.2(b), and L will be exonerated for her breach of rule 16.1. Note that L has broken rule 14 (Avoiding Contact), but she cannot be penalized under rule 14 unless the contact causes damage or injury (see discussion of rule 14).

- PL and SW, two opposite *tack* close-hauled boats, are approaching a windward *mark* to be left to port. PL safely lee-bows SW (i.e., tacks to *leeward* of SW) outside the *zone*. As the boats enter the *zone* PL realizes she will not make the *mark* without luffing up to head to wind. When near the *mark*, PL luffs and collides with SW with no damage or injury. As PL was changing course to round the *mark*, SW breaks rules 11 and 18.2(b) as above, and PL is exonerated for her breach of rule 16.1.

In the same scenario, SW does *keep clear* of PL's luff, but as PL begins to pass the *mark* she bears away to round the *mark* and her transom swings up and hits the *leeward* side of SW, again with no damage or injury. Same answer as above. SW must *keep clear* (as well as give *mark-room*), PL is rounding the *mark*, and therefore PL is freed from blame for her breach of rule 16.1.

 "What if the boat ahead wants to tack around the mark?"

She must be very careful! A boat that is *clear ahead* when she reaches the *zone* that tacks around a *mark* gets no protection from rule 18.2(b) what-so-ever. In fact, rule 18.2(c) says, *"However, if the boat entitled to **mark-room** passes head to wind...rule 18.2(b) ceases to apply."* In other words, the moment the boat ahead passes head to wind, rule 18.2(b) instantly shuts off, and the boat is subject to the rules in Sections A and B thereafter, beginning with rule 13 (While Tacking). This can happen at a windward *mark* when the boats need to tack to round the *mark*; or at or just after a leeward *mark* when the boats are beginning the beat.

Notice also that at the windward *mark* the boat *clear astern* can sail above close-hauled to make it more difficult for the boat *clear ahead* to tack. Let's say you (A) and another boat (B) are sailing close-hauled on *port tack* into the windward *mark* to be left to port, not *overlapped*. You thought you were

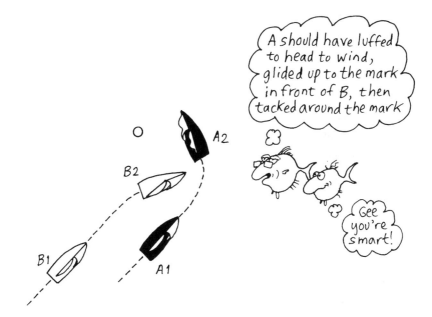

allowed to just tack around the *mark*. After you had passed head to wind but before you were close-hauled, B had to bear away to miss your transom. You have fouled B by breaking rule 13 (While Tacking). Notice, though, that you can luff up to head to wind just prior to tacking around the *mark*, which will make it difficult for a boat close astern to prevent you from tacking. Tactically speaking for a moment, in this situation your best move is to luff to head to wind, glide up to the *mark*, then tack around making it difficult for a boat close astern to prevent you from tacking.

ISAF Case 81 discusses the situation where two boats, A and B, close reaching on *starboard tack* into a windward *mark* to be left to starboard. A enters the *zone clear ahead* and to leeward of B, then proceeds to tack to *port tack* in order to round the *mark*. B (still on *starboard tack*), collides with A (now on *port tack*), causing no damage or injury. The Appeals Committee said, "… from the time A reached the zone until she passed head to wind, rule 18.2(b)'s second sentence applied, requiring B to give A mark-room. B fulfilled [this obligation]. Shortly before position 5, when A passed head to wind, rule 18.2(b) ceased to apply (see rule 18.2(c)). At that time B acquired right of way and A became obligated to keep clear of B, first by rule 13 and later, after A was on a close-hauled course, by rule 10. Rule 15 did not apply because B acquired right of way as a result of A's tack."

"What if a boat that is entitled to mark-room in the zone sails out of the zone before rounding the mark; when she re-enters, does she retain her original rights or is it a whole new ball game?"

It's a whole new ball game. Rule 18.2(c) says, *"if the boat entitled to **mark-room**... leaves the zone, rule 18.2(b) ceases to apply."* Note, it doesn't matter **why** she left the *zone*. She could have been giving *mark-room* to several boats inside her, or she could have been carried out by the current, or she may have lost control of her boat. In every case where she leaves the *zone*, she does not carry back in any rights or obligations she had before she left; it is a whole new situation.

"Now I understand when I can and cannot be entitled to 'room,' but what if an outside boat leaves enough space between her and the mark; is it a foul to sneak in there?"

Absolutely not, as long as you don't hit the *mark* or the outside boat or force the outside boat to change course to avoid hitting you. US Sailing Appeal 5 is clear: "…when a boat voluntarily or unintentionally makes room available to another boat that, under the rules, has no right to that room and makes no claim to it, that other boat may take advantage, at her own risk, of the room so given. In that case, she breaks no rule."

9

Part 2, Section C
When Boats Meet at Marks and Obstructions — Tacking and Gybing, and Other Exceptions to Rule 18

Rule 18 (Mark-Room) also has rules for when boats tack inside the *zone* of a windward *mark* (rule 18.3, Tacking in the Zone) or have to gybe inside the *zone* of a leeward *mark* in order to sail their *proper course* (rule 18.4, Gybing). It also contains some exceptions, such as when boats are approaching a starting *mark* to *start* (preamble to Section C) or when a boat leaving a *mark* encounters a boat approaching a *mark* (rule 18.1(c)). I will cover all these special rules in this chapter.

WHEN ONE OF TWO OPPOSITE TACK BOATS TACKS WITHIN THE ZONE AT THE WINDWARD MARK

RULE 18.3 — TACKING IN THE ZONE

If a boat in the *zone* passes head to wind and is then on the same *tack* as a boat that is *fetching* the *mark*, rule 18.2 does not thereafter apply between them. The boat that changed *tack*

(a) shall not cause the other boat to sail above close-hauled to avoid contact or prevent the other boat from passing the *mark* on the required side, and

(b) shall give *mark-room* if the other boat becomes *overlapped* inside her.

The concept in this rule is to improve the racing by trying to minimize the frustrating and sometimes dangerous congestion that can occur at crowded windward *mark* roundings, especially when the *mark* is to be left to port. Problems are often caused by *port-tack* boats approaching on or near the port layline and trying to squeeze their boats in between the *starboard-tack* boats on the starboard layline and the *mark*. Too often, these *port-tackers* shoot right back up after tacking to try to make it around the *mark*, or they get hung up on the *mark* itself, or worse: they fall back onto *port tack* directly in front of the approaching *starboard-tackers*! Too many otherwise excellent close races have been ruined by these actions; and with the popular trend toward shorter courses and more races, the rule writers put this rule in the book to improve the game.

IN A NUTSHELL, RULE 18.3 works like this (we'll get into the technicalities below):

A boat that passes head to wind while tacking in the *zone* near other boats that are "*fetching* the *mark*" must do it in a place that allows the other boats to pass the *mark* on the required side with no physical interference and without ever having to sail above close-hauled to avoid contact with another boat.

If the boat that tacked causes other boats to sail above close-hauled to keep from making contact or prevents other boats from being able to pass the *mark* on the required side, the boat that tacked has broken rule 18.3(a).

Furthermore, if any of the other boats gets an inside *overlap* on the boat that tacked at **any time** during her rounding, the boat that tacked must give her *mark-room* (*room* to round the *mark*) (rule 18.3(b)). And if the boat that tacked is unable to give the inside boat *mark-room*, tough luck on the boat that tacked. Rule 18.2(e) (about not having to give *mark-room* if unable to do so) does not apply because none of rule 18.2 applies. Furthermore if the *leeward*/inside boat breaks rules 15 (Acquiring Right of Way) or 16 (Changing Course) while taking *mark-room*, she is exonerated under rule 21 (Exoneration). In other words, the boat that tacked becomes more or less a "sitting duck" for the *leeward*/inside boat!

The bottom line is: if you are going to come into a crowded windward *mark* on *port tack*, it is better to cross nearby *starboard tackers* if you can, and tack safely to *windward* of them. And if you can't cross them, then it is better to duck

them then to try to tack close to leeward of them. And to be safe, approach the *mark* four or more boat lengths below the *port-tack* layline.

"Okay, I'm ready to have you lead me through this rule!"

OK, let's consider just two boats to begin with. First, the two boats must have been on opposite *tacks*, and then one of them passed head to wind in the *zone* and became on the same *tack* as the other boat, as will happen at a windward *mark* when two boats on opposite tacks approach the *mark*. Remember that rule 18 doesn't apply at all while the boats are on opposite *tacks* on a beat to windward (rule 18.1(a), When Rule 18 Applies).

Note, if the tacking boat passes head to wind **outside** the *zone* and then completes her tack inside the *zone*, rule 18.3 does **not** apply. However, rule 13 (While Tacking) applies, and if a boat needs to avoid the tacking boat before she completes her tack (gets to a close-hauled course), the tacking boat has broken rule 13. Rule 18.3 applies only when the boat passes head to wind inside the *zone*. It can be argued that it is difficult to know exactly where the *zone* is, but that is the case when applying the *zone* in any *mark* rounding or passing situation. Sailors approaching port-hand windward *marks* on *port tack* will be well advised to be conservative when the *mark* area is congested and to complete their tacks clearly outside the *zone*.

Next, the boat that didn't tack must be "*fetching*" the *mark*. "*Fetching*" means the boat can pass to windward of the *mark* leaving it on the required side without sailing past head to wind to do so (see the definition *Fetching*).

In interpreting and applying rule 18.3(a), it can be viewed as one obligation on the boat that tacks not to do either of two things; i.e., she breaks rule 18.3(a) if either:

1) she causes the other boat to sail above close-hauled to avoid hitting another boat, meaning the other boat actually sails above close-hauled to avoid contact, or

2) she prevents the other boat from passing the *mark* on the required side.

In my opinion, "causes" means "is the primary and reasonable reason for;" and "prevents" means "physically prevent," as opposed to prevent as a result of disturbing the air and water, etc.

 "I thought that if a boat tacked in front of me inside the zone and caused me to change course at all, she broke rule 18.3(a)."

No! She breaks rule 18.3(a) only if she causes you to sail above a **close-hauled** course. If you are overstood, for instance, and avoid contact by luffing up to a close-hauled course, she has not broken rule 18.3(a).

LET'S LOOK AT SOME SCENARIOS that will involve rule 18.3.

P approaches S at a port-hand windward *mark*, and passes head to wind in the *zone* just to *leeward* of S who is *fetching* the *mark*:

Let's say that when P gets to close-hauled, the boats are now one length from the *mark*. As P (now the *leeward*/inside boat) approaches the *mark*, she realizes she won't make the *mark* unless she luffs above close-hauled. She does so, thereby clearing the *mark*, but as a result of her luff, S sails above close-hauled to avoid hitting her. P has broken rule 18.3(a). Note that even though she's an inside/right-of-way boat, P is not entitled to *mark-room* under rule 18.2(a) (Giving Mark-Room) because rule 18.3 specifically states that rule 18.2 does not apply. The same would be true if S sailed above close-hauled to avoid P's transom as P bore off around the *mark*.

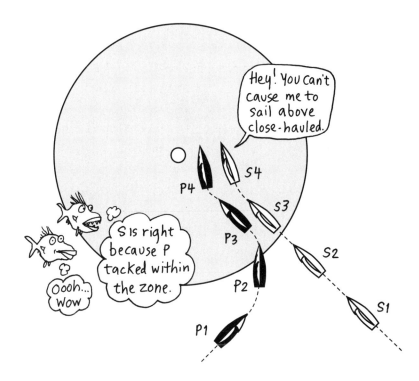

Had S been able to pass the *mark* without having to sail above close-hauled to avoid P, then P would not have broken rule 18.3(a), and S would simply be required to *keep clear* under rule 11 (On the Same Tack, Overlapped). Note that if P changed course to round the *mark*, she would not be exonerated if she broke rule 16.1 because she is not taking *mark-room* (see rule 21, Exoneration).

P passes head to wind in the *zone* of a port-hand windward *mark* directly ahead of S who is *fetching* the *mark*; once P is close-hauled, S must change course either up or down to avoid colliding with her:

First of all, once P gets to a close-hauled course *clear ahead* of S, S is required to *keep clear* of her under rule 12 (On the Same Tack, Not Overlapped). If, despite her best efforts to avoid P beginning the moment P is close-hauled, S is unable to do so and she hits P on the transom, P has "tacked too close" and broken rule 15 (Acquiring Right of Way), and S is exonerated under rule 64.1(a) (Penalties and Exoneration). If S does have *room* to *keep clear* of P but hits P on the transom anyway, then S is not exonerated for breaking rule 12, and also breaks rule 14 (Avoiding Contact).

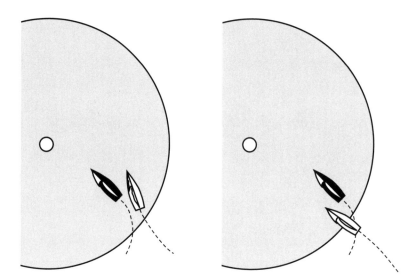

When a boat passes head to wind within the zone and a boat that is fetching the mark approaches her, the boat that tacked breaks rule 18.3(a) if the other boat has to sail above close-hauled to avoid hitting her or is prevented from passing the mark.

It could happen that when P gets to a close-hauled course, S can avoid hitting P but is faced with the choice of *overlapping* P to leeward and probably not being able to pass the *mark* or sailing above close-hauled to avoid hitting P. If S chooses to sail above close-hauled, then P has broken rule 18.3(a) by causing S to sail above close-hauled to avoid hitting her, because it isn't reasonable to expect S to bear away and not make the *mark*. And if S chooses to *overlap* P to *leeward*, but once there finds that she can't pass the *mark* due to P's physical presence, even when she luffs up to head to wind, P has "prevented" S from passing the *mark* thereby breaking rule 18.3(b). (Note that S is not allowed to sail past head to wind as she would be tacking onto *port tack* and required to *keep clear* first under rule 13, While Tacking, and then under rule 10, On Opposite Tacks.)

Now if P tacks far enough to windward of the layline such that S can clearly *overlap* P to leeward and pass the *mark*, then P has not caused S to sail above close-hauled to avoid contact with her because it would be reasonable to expect S to bear away and pass the *mark*. However, if S chooses to sail above close-hauled and protest, it will be the **protest committee** who decides whether S would have been "prevented" from passing the *mark* had she chosen to *overlap* P to *leeward* (and my guess is they will give S the benefit of the doubt). So *port-tack* boats will want to be very conservative with where they

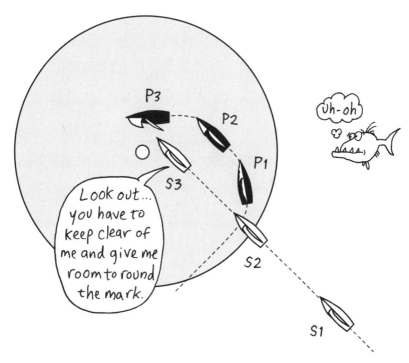

Because P passed head to wind within the zone, and S is fetching the mark, P must keep clear of S and give S mark-room if S gets an inside overlap. Furthermore, S can change course in either direction necessary to round the mark, and if she breaks rules 15 or 16, she will be exonerated (see rule 21(a)).

choose to tack in the *zone* near opposite-*tack* boats!

Finally, if S is *fetching* the *mark* and P tacks sufficiently far ahead of her such that S is not required to take any action to avoid hitting P after the tack, but then S fails to make the *mark* due to the disturbed air and water caused by P, P has not "prevented" S from passing the *mark* due to her physical presence, and therefore has not broken rule 18.3(a).

P passes head to wind in the *zone* of a port-hand windward *mark* and one length later, as P is bearing off around the *mark*, S sails in to *leeward* telling P to *keep clear* of her and to give her *mark-room*:

Once P is past head to wind within the *zone*, then for the duration of her rounding or passing maneuver a boat *clear astern* (S) is allowed to obtain a *leeward/* inside *overlap* on P, and P must *keep clear* of her and give her *mark-room* (i.e., *room* to round or pass the *mark*)!

Note that when S becomes *overlapped* with P she instantly gets the right of way, so rule 15 (Acquiring Right of Way) requires her to initially give P *room to keep clear*. But as she is entitled to *mark-room* to round the *mark*, S is exonerated (freed from blame) if she happens to break rule 15 (see rule 21, Exoneration). Note also that if S needs to luff slightly to get up and around the *mark*, that too is part of her rounding maneuver, and if she happens to break rule 16.1 (Changing Course), she will also be exonerated under rule 21.

The only "limit" on S is that, because she became *overlapped* from *clear astern*, she cannot sail above her *proper course* under rule 17 (On the Same Tack; Proper Course), which means she must bear away to follow her *proper course* around the windward *mark*. And if the boats collide, remember that both boats are subject to rule 14 (Avoiding Contact).

In summary, once S *overlaps* P to *leeward*, if S makes contact with P, or if S is unable to round or pass the *mark* because she would hit P, then P has not given *mark-room* nor *kept clear* and has broken rules 11 and 18.3(b). If P can stay out of S's way such that S has no need to take action to avoid P and is not prevented from rounding or passing the *mark*, then P has not broken rule 18.3(b).

Two *overlapped port-tack* boats (PL to *leeward* and PW to *windward*) are approaching a port-hand *windward mark* with S approaching as well, and both PL and PW pass head to wind in the *zone*:

Let's say PW tacks to *starboard tack* first, immediately followed by PL. When they complete their tacks, S is *overlapped* to *windward* of PL. PW, now on the inside of the three boats, luffs above close-hauled to make the *mark*. PL responds and is able to *keep clear*, but her luff causes S to also luff above close-hauled to avoid contact with PL. Both PW and PL have broken rule 18.3(a) because both of them passed head to wind in the *zone* and both caused S to sail above close-hauled to avoid contact. PL directly caused S to sail above close-hauled; and it was PW's luff that caused PL to luff that caused S to sail above close-hauled to avoid contact with PL. In this case, because it was PW's breach of rule 18.3(a) that compelled PL to break rule 18.3(a), PL is exonerated under rule 64.1(a) (Penalties and Exoneration). Note that between PW and PL, PW was entitled to *mark-room* from PL under rule 18.2(a) (Giving Mark-Room); and though she arguably broke rule 16.1 (Changing Course) by changing course and forcing PL to break rule 18.3(a), PW would be exonerated

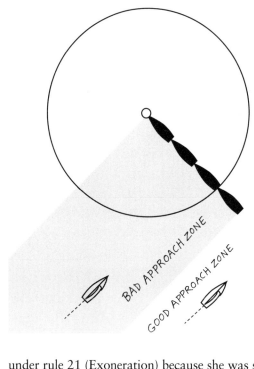

Rule 18.3 encourages port-tackers approaching a congested port-hand windward mark to approach about four hull lengths below the port-tack layline so that they can pass head to wind during their tack when clearly outside the zone.

BAD APPROACH ZONE

GOOD APPROACH ZONE

under rule 21 (Exoneration) because she was sailing within the *mark-room* to which she was entitled.

"It sounds like this rule eliminates the port-tack layline and a port-tacker's tactic of lee-bowing a starboard tacker right at the mark!"

I don't think the rule dramatically changes the way the top of the beat is sailed. If you are doing well in the race, the windward *mark* rounding won't be that congested, and you will probably approach it as close to the layline as you want. If you are farther down in the pack (out of the top 10, let's say), coming in right on the *port-tack* layline isn't a great look anyway. For at least some of the time, you are sailing more slowly in the disturbed air and water of the boats going down the reach or offset leg, or trying to pick your way through the *starboard-tack* boats as they turn and go down the run. So for tactical reasons, as well as because of rule 18.3, you will want to approach a port-hand windward *mark* at least four lengths below the *port-tack* layline.

To me, the most significant effect of this rule is on the decision the *port-tacker* makes on whether to duck the nearby *starboard-tackers* and tack safely up to *windward* of them or to lee-bow them (i.e., tack just to *leeward* of them)

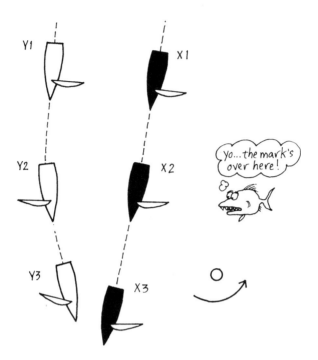

When boats are sailing below 90 degrees to the true wind or when rule 18 applies, the term "overlap" applies to boats on opposite tacks. Therefore, X and Y are "overlapped" at the mark. When the inside boat has the right of way and when she must gybe to sail her proper course, rule 18.4 requires her not to sail any farther from the mark than needed to sail her proper course until she gybes. By not gybing, i.e., not sailing her proper course, X breaks rule 18.4.

and hope to make the *mark* from there. My personal experience (and I've been there myself!) is that too often sailors choose the (dare I say) "greedier" choice (lee-bowing), and end up not only not making the *mark*, but causing a real mess for others at the *mark*. I think the net effect of rule 18.3 is that fewer *port-tackers* tack right at the *mark* in crowds, which is a welcome situation for all.

WHEN AN INSIDE RIGHT-OF-WAY BOAT NEEDS TO GYBE TO SAIL HER PROPER COURSE AROUND A MARK

RULE 18.4 — GYBING

When an inside *overlapped* right-of-way boat must gybe at a *mark* to sail her *proper course*, until she gybes she shall sail no farther from the *mark* than needed to sail that course. Rule 18.4 does not apply at a gate *mark*.

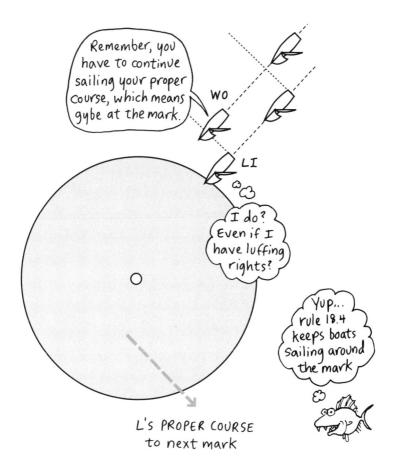

L's PROPER COURSE
to next mark

First of all, rule 18.4 puts a "limit" on inside right-of-way boats; i.e., *leeward* boats and *starboard-tack* boats. Essentially, that "limit" is that whenever their *proper course* is to gybe at a *mark*, they must do so. Actually, the instruction in the rule is that up until she actually gybes, the right-of-way boat "shall sail no farther from the mark than needed to sail [her *proper course*]." This means that not only does she have to gybe when it is her *proper course* to do so, but she can't luff (turn) away from the *mark* prior to gybing if that takes her farther from it than necessary to sail her *proper course*. This applies even when the outside/*windward* boat initially obtained the *overlap* to *windward* such that L would otherwise have the right to sail above her *proper course*. (See ISAF Case 75.)

Note that rule 18.4 has a clear "shut off" time built in. The rule no longer applies once the inside boat gybes (i.e., the boom crosses the centerline). After that, the inside boat is not limited by rule 18.4, though she will continue to be entitled to *mark-room* under rule 18.2(b) (Giving Mark-Room).

The situation will commonly arise at gybe *marks* and leeward *marks* to be left to port when the *leeward*/inside boat or the *starboard-tack*/inside boat will be required to gybe in order to round the *mark*. Notice that a boat's *proper course* is the course she thinks will get her to the finishing line as quickly as possible. Therefore, especially if there are boats just ahead of her, she can certainly swing wide to set up for a "tactical" cut-close rounding.

Note that rule 18.4 applies any time boats are *overlapped*. Therefore, if the boats are not *overlapped* when the boat ahead enters the *zone*, but the boat astern obtains an outside *overlap* later, rule 18.4 applies. Similarly, if the boats are *overlapped* as the boats enter the *zone* and then the *overlap* is broken at any time during the rounding, rule 18.4 does not apply.

Note also that rule 18.4 applies only when the inside right-of-way boat **must** gybe to sail her *proper course*. Therefore, at a windward *mark* going onto a run, when either tack could be a *proper course*, the inside right-of-way boat needs to gybe only if she decides it is her *proper course* to do so. The same applies at a gybe *mark* going onto a very broad reach where it may be faster for a boat to delay her gybe.

Finally note that the Team Racing Rules (Appendix D) delete rule 18.4 entirely (rule D1.1(c), Team Racing Rules, Changes to the Racing Rules). This enables team racers to continue setting "mark traps" by entering the *zone clear ahead* and then stopping their boats. "Enemy boats" astern must *keep clear* of them. They can't *overlap* them on the inside because of rule 18.2(b); and if they *overlap* the boat ahead on the outside, the boat ahead can luff or otherwise sail them past the *mark*, meanwhile letting teammates round the *mark* on the inside.

 "Does this apply at a gate mark as well?"

Good question! Rule 18.4 does **not** apply at a gate *mark*. A "gate" is two *marks* set close to each other, typically at the end of the downwind leg. The boats are required to sail between the *marks*, and then can choose to exit the gate around one *mark* or the other. When inside right-of-way boats are sailing to round a gate *mark*, rule 18.4 does not apply, meaning an inside right-of-way boat is not "limited" to sailing no farther from the *mark* than her *proper course*. She can sail as far as she pleases from the *mark*, force a *windward*/outside boat outside

the *zone* if she pleases, then gybe and round the *mark*. Outside keep-clear boats are well advised to not remain *overlapped* with inside right-of-way boats when approaching gate *marks*.

However, if the inside right-of-way boat became *overlapped* from *clear astern*, then she is subject to rule 17 (On the Same Tack; Proper Course), and she is not allowed to sail above her *proper course* for as long as the boats remain *overlapped*. Therefore, at a gate *mark*, even though rule 18.4 does not apply, the inside boat is required by rule 17 to gybe at the *mark* if that is her *proper course* at the time. If she goes further from the *mark*, she is sailing **above** her *proper course* and is breaking rule 17. Note that the outside keep-clear boat must still *keep clear* and protest.

EXCEPTIONS TO RULE 18

"I notice there seem to be some exceptions to rule 18 listed in the pre- *amble to Section C and in rule 18.1; could you go over those please?"*

You bet. There are very narrow situations when boats are rounding or passing *marks* when rule 18 does not apply at all. When rule 18 does not apply at a

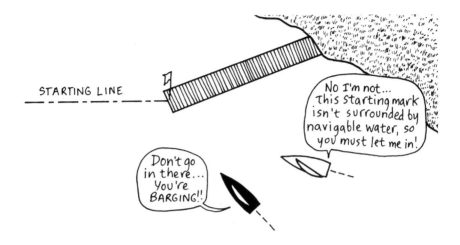

mark, the rules in Section A (Right of Way) and Section B (General Limitations) apply.

PREAMBLE TO SECTION C

Section C rules do not apply at a starting *mark* surrounded by navigable water or at its anchor line from the time boats are approaching them to *start* until they have passed them.

The preamble makes it clear that none of the rules in Section C (18, 19 and 20) apply when boats are approaching a starting *mark* that is surrounded by navigable water or its anchor line to *start* until they have passed them.

"So does this having something to do with Barging?"

Yes. I will explain what "Barging" is. The preamble to Section C "shuts off" the "mark-room" rules at the starting *marks*. The reason is that it would lead to chaotic starts if *windward* / inside boats were entitled to *room* to pass between the committee boat and *leeward* / outside boats at the start (it's often chaotic enough without them having that right!). When two boats are about to *start* and a *windward* boat tries to sail in between a *leeward* boat and a starting *mark* (often a race committee boat), and hits the *leeward* boat or causes her to bear away to avoid being hit, we say the *windward* boat is "Barging." In fact, she is breaking rule 11 (On the Same Tack, Overlapped). (For more discussion on "Barging" see the discussion in Chapter 7 entitled "Section A and B Rules in Action.")

To accurately apply this rule, be sure you understand that an object large enough to satisfy the definition *Obstruction* is **always** an *obstruction*, even when it is used as a *mark*; i.e., it does not cease being one when it becomes the other. Therefore a race committee boat used as one end of the starting line is **both** a starting *mark* and an *obstruction* at the same time.

Now, having said that the preamble "shuts off" rule 18 (Mark-Room) and rule 19 (Room to Pass an Obstruction), there are in fact two narrow situations when, for reasons of safety, the rules do entitle a *windward*/inside boat to *room* at a starting *mark* from a *leeward*/outside boat.

Let's look at those first.

1) At a starting *mark* not surrounded by navigable water:

Though this situation is not common, it will arise when one end of the starting line is the end of a long dock or breakwater, or is a bell buoy that marks some shallow rocks or sandbars. "Not surrounded by navigable water" means there isn't enough water for the inside boat to sail around the *mark* without running aground or hitting a dock or other object. At such a *mark*, an inside *overlapped* boat **is** entitled to *mark-room* under rule 18.2 (Giving Mark-Room) from an outside boat. And if the starting *mark* is a "continuing" *obstruction* (such as the end of a long dock), then the inside boat is entitled to *room* under rule 19.2(b) if there was space to pass between the outside boat and the *obstruction* in safety at the moment the *overlap* began (see rules 18.1(d) and 19.2(c)).

2) At a starting *mark* that is also an *obstruction* when the boats are not approaching it to *start*:

Again, when the starting *mark* is large enough to be an *obstruction* (such as most committee boats), rule 19 (Room to Pass an Obstruction) applies **before** boats are "approaching it to *start*." Therefore, an inside *overlapped* boat is entitled to *room* at such a *mark* under rule 19.2(b) (Giving Room at an Obstruction) from an outside boat, provided the outside boat has been able to give the *room* since the *overlap* began. If the starting *mark* is a "continuing" *obstruction*, then the inside boat is entitled to *room* if there was space to pass between the outside boat and the *obstruction* in safety at the moment the *overlap* began (rule 19.2(c)). This is for safety purposes while boats are sailing past the *marks* well before *starting*.

So, if say at three minutes before the starting signal you were sailing along to leeward of W and were about to sail to leeward of the race committee boat, and for whatever reason W wanted to pass to leeward of it also, you would have to give her *room* to do so under rule 19.2(b), unless you were unable to do so from the moment the *overlap* began. Now to play this out, because boats aren't required to pass the starting *mark* on its "required" side yet (rule 28.2, Sailing the Course), you can choose to pass it on either side (see rule 19.2(a)). You, as the *leeward* boat, have the right to sail where you please provided you make no sudden, fast course changes (rule 11, On the Same Tack, Overlapped and rule 16.1, Changing Course); therefore, you can choose to luff and pass to windward of the committee boat. If, however, you choose to pass to leeward of the committee boat and fail to provide enough *room* for W to do likewise if she wishes to, you have broken rule 19.2(b).

Note that when you break a *rule* before the starting signal, you can take your Two-Turns Penalty immediately; i.e., you do not have to wait until the starting signal to do so (rule 44, Penalties at the Time of an Incident). If W happens to hit the *mark* (i.e., break rule 31, Touching a Mark) because you didn't give her enough *room*, she can ask the protest committee, normally by protesting you, to exonerate her under rule 64.1(a) (Penalties and Exoneration).

 "When is a boat considered to be 'approaching a starting mark to start?'"

Though this question has never been discussed in an appeal, I would develop my opinion as follows. What is the purpose of the rule? Clearly it is preventing the situation where *windward*/inside (WI) boats can reach in and demand *room* at starting *marks* from *leeward*/outside boats (LO) that are trying to *start* there. And "when approaching the starting *mark* to *start*" is establishing the period of time during which these *windward*/inside boats know that they are not entitled to any *room*. Before LO is "approaching the starting *mark* to *start*," WI is entitled to *room* at the *mark* (provided it is also an *obstruction*); and the rules are consistently clear in providing predictable and specific times when a boat's rights change. To me, this is no exception. When LO is clearly on her final approach toward the line with the intention of *starting*; i.e., crossing the line after the gun, it will be obvious to WI and she will know to *keep*

clear. Furthermore, a boat that is "approaching the starting *mark* to *start*" and is close enough to the starting *mark* to shut out a *windward* boat, will clearly be *starting* in close proximity distance-wise to the starting *mark.*

Therefore, in my opinion, a boat that in 15 knots of breeze goes reaching full-speed by the committee boat with one-and-a-half minutes to go before the starting signal, and ends up *starting* halfway down the starting line, was in no way "approaching the starting *mark* to *start*" at the moment she went by the starting *mark.* But a boat that is passing the starting *mark* with ten seconds to go certainly is on her final approach to *start* very near to the starting *mark.* In addition, I feel that a boat that in light air sits nearly wayless behind the race committee boat may be approaching the line to *start* at one minute to go, and it will be more obvious and predictable that she plans to *start* near the *mark,* and the *windward*/inside boats can see this and *keep clear* accordingly.

This is a distinction that in general has caused very few problems, and in general has been very liberally interpreted in the *leeward*/outside boat's favor. But until it is officially interpreted, the safe move on LO's part would be to allow WI *room* up to one minute before the starting signal; and the safe move for WI would be not to try to force *room* with much less than two minutes to go. Both boats have the option to protest, and the protest committee can then decide whether LO was "approaching the starting *mark* to *start*" in the particular circumstances.

"OK, any other exceptions?"

Yes, a couple more. They are listed in rule 18.1 (When Rule 18 Applies).

RULE 18.1 — WHEN RULE 18 APPLIES

Rule 18 applies between boats when they are required to leave a *mark* on the same side and at least one of them is in the *zone*. However, it does not apply

(a) between boats on opposite tacks on a beat to windward,

(b) between boats on opposite tacks when the proper course at the mark for one but not both of them is to tack,

(c) between a boat approaching a mark and one leaving it, or

(d) if the *mark* is a continuing *obstruction*, in which case rule 19 applies.

 "Does rule 18.1(a) mean that 'mark-room' doesn't apply at the windward mark?"

No; rule 18.1(a) means that if two boats are coming into a windward *mark* on opposite *tacks* (including a finishing *mark* when the finish is at the end of a beat), rule 18 (Mark-Room) doesn't apply. But if the boats are coming into a windward *mark* on the same *tack*, then rule 18 applies just like at any other *mark*.

Though the phrase "on a beat to windward" has never been interpreted by an appeal, my opinion is that a boat is on a "beat to windward" if her *proper course* to the *mark* is to sail close-hauled or above.

Picture a windward *mark* to be left to port or the left end of an upwind finishing line, looking upwind. It would be chaos if suddenly a *port-tack* boat could come in and call for *mark-room* from a *starboard-tack* boat while still on *port tack*. While the boats are on opposite *tacks*, rule 10 (*port/starboard*) applies; and if the *port-tack* boat (PI) *tacks* to *leeward* of the *starboard-tack* boat (SO) within the *zone*, she is subject to rule 18.3 (Tacking in the Zone).

Notice that the exception in rule 18.1(a) applies only when opposite-*tack* boats are approaching a *mark* on a beat to windward. The reasoning is that at all the other *marks* (offwind *marks*), even though the boats may be on opposite *tacks*, they are going in more or less the same direction, or at least generally converging at much smaller angles. Therefore, at leeward *marks*, inside/*port-tack* boats **are** entitled to *room* under rule 18.2 (Giving Mark-Room) from outside/*starboard-tack* boats.

"What does rule 18.1(b) refer to?"

This is a bit of a "loophole closer." It covers situations that rarely arise, but can. For instance, on a windward leg the wind shifts 60 degrees to the right. Boats that were near the starboard-tack layline are now reaching on the leg. They are no longer "beating" to windward or "on a beat to windward." However, the boats in the left are now beating up to the *mark*, so they are still "on a beat to windward." When a *port-tack* boat (P) from the left meets a *starboard-tack* boat (S) from the right at the *mark*, the exception in 18.1(a) doesn't apply because **both** boats are not "on a beat to windward." But because P's *proper course* is to tack at the *mark*, and because S does not have to tack, the exception in rule 18.1(b) applies, meaning that rule 18 does not apply, P is not entitled to *mark-room*, and she needs to *keep clear* of S under rule 10 (Opposite Tacks).

The same is true when two boats are sailing to a gybe *mark* and a boat finds herself below the *mark* (due to current or a windshift or strong wind carrying her lower than she wanted to be), and she has to tack to get up to the gybe *mark*. Now she will be on the opposite *tack* from boats approaching the *mark*, and because she will have to tack to sail her *proper course* around the *mark*, she is not entitled to *mark-room*.

"Can you explain what the terms "approaching" and "leaving" mean in rule 18.1(c)?"

Sure. The rule writers wanted to make it clear that rule 18 does not apply to boats that aren't rounding the *mark* at essentially the same time. The rule clarifies that if one boat is just completing her rounding maneuver and is "leaving" the *mark* and she meets a boat that is just "approaching" the *mark* to begin her rounding maneuver, neither boat needs to give each other *mark-room*. The rules in Section A and B apply, including rule 16 (Changing Course) which requires a right-of-way boat to give the keep-clear boat *room* to *keep clear* when she changes course. This commonly comes up at port-hand windward *mark* roundings when the boat rounding the *mark* will be on *starboard-tack*. She must watch for nearby *port-tackers* when she bears away around the *mark*. Note that the exoneration from breaking rule 16 offered in rule 21 (Exoneration) does not apply, because rule 18 does not apply due to the exception in rule 18.1(b). (See ISAF Case 60.)

Finally, the exception in rule 18.1(d) clarifies that if the *mark* is a "continuing *obstruction*," such as an island that must be passed on a required side, rule 18 does not apply and rule 19 (Room to Pass an Obstruction) applies. This is primarily because it is tough to apply a *zone* at an island. Also, it is an undesirable situation to require a boat that was astern or *overlapped* on the outside when first arriving at the island or long *obstruction* to continue to give the other boat(s) *mark-room* even if she gets ahead of them while passing the *obstruction*.

We've discussed thoroughly how rule 18 applies slightly differently in certain situations, primarily at windward *marks* (including windward **finishing** *marks*), leeward *marks* where inside boats need to gybe to sail their *proper* course, starting *marks* and continuing *obstructions*. These are its only exceptions. Otherwise, the rules for "mark-room" are exactly the same at every other *mark* on the course, including the finishing *marks*.

10

Part 2, Section C
When Boats Meet – Room to Pass and Tack at an Obstruction

Rules 19 and 20 are the rules that apply when you are sailing near *obstructions*. Remember, an *obstruction* is an object large enough to require you to make a substantial course change to miss it **if** you were one of your lengths away and aiming directly at the largest part of it, whether or not you are **actually** aiming right at it on the water. In other words, it is a hypothetical test to determine if the **physical size** of the object qualifies it as an *obstruction*. For instance, imagine a 50-foot barge. If you were in a 20-foot boat aiming at the middle of its side, you would obviously have to make a large course change to avoid hitting the forward or aft 25 feet of it. So it ranks as an *obstruction* even if during the race you were only aiming at the last foot of its transom. (See discussion of the definition *Obstruction*.)

Also remember that a boat *racing* is an *obstruction* to you only when she has the right-of-way over **both** you and the boat(s) near you that are about to pass her (see the definition *Obstruction*), or if you and the other boat(s) have to avoid her under rule 23 (Capsized, Anchored or Aground; Rescuing). But note that no vessel under way, including a boat that is *racing*, is ever considered a "continuing" *obstruction*.

Finally note that an object that can be safely passed on only one side, such as a buoy that marks rocks, is an *obstruction*. So is an area so designated as an *obstruction* in the sailing instructions (see the definition *Obstruction*). But note that the "area" must be specifically designated as an "*obstruction*" in the sailing instructions. If the sailing instructions merely say "boats shall not pass between buoy X and the shore," or "shall not cross the starting/finishing line on the downwind leg," these areas are **not** "*obstructions.*"

Rules 19 and 20 are rules of safety. If two boats are passing an *obstruction* (such as a seawall, moored boat or *starboard-tacker* that is *racing*), it is reasonable to require the outside boat to give the inside boat *room* to pass in safety between her and the *obstruction*. Just as it is sensible to allow a boat sailing upwind that is about to hit an *obstruction* to call for *room* to tack to avoid the *obstruction*.

RULE 19 — ROOM TO PASS AN OBSTRUCTION

RULE 19.1 — WHEN RULE 19 APPLIES

Rule 19 applies between boats at an *obstruction* except when it is also a *mark* the boats are required to leave on the same side. However, at a continuing *obstruction*, rule 19 always applies and rule 18 does not.

19.2 — GIVING ROOM AT AN OBSTRUCTION

(a) A right-of-way boat may choose to pass an *obstruction* on either side.

Rule 19.1 is a clear statement of when rule 19 applies. Note it does not apply at *marks* that boats are required to leave on the same side unless the *mark* is a "continuing" *obstruction*. At all other marks rule 18 (Mark-Room) applies (see Chapter 8). Also note, as boats approach an *obstruction*, the right-of-way boat gets to choose on which side she will pass the *obstruction*.

 "So when does rule 19 begin to apply; is there a 'zone' around obstructions as there is around marks?"

No, there is no "*zone*" around *obstructions*! Rule 19 applies when boats are "at" the *obstruction* which is when one of them reaches the point where she must commit to passing on one side or the other of the *obstruction* and will need space from the other boat(s) to do so.

 "Which boat gets to choose which side of the obstruction the boats will pass on?"

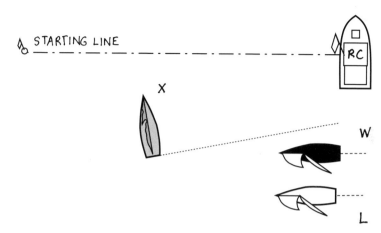

X is clear ahead of both L and W; therefore, as the right-of-way boat over both L and W, she is an obstruction to both. As L and W approach X, L, as the right-of-way boat over W, gets to choose on which side of X she will pass. If she chooses to pass to leeward of X, rule 19.2(b) requires her to give W room to do likewise if W also wants to pass to leeward of X.

Before one of the boats needs to commit to passing on one side or the other, the rules of Section A and B apply and the right-of-way boat can sail where she pleases, subject to rules 16 (Changing Course) and 17 (On the Same Tack; Proper Course). Rule 19.2(a) reminds of this by saying "*A right-of-way boat may choose to pass an* **obstruction** *on either side.*" So, approaching an *obstruction*, the right-of-way boat (*leeward* boat or *starboard-tack* boat) gets to choose on which side she wants to pass the *obstruction*, and the other boat(s) must *keep clear*.

"OK, so when does the outside boat have to begin giving room to the inside boat?"

RULE 19.2(b) — GIVING ROOM AT AN OBSTRUCTION

When boats are *overlapped*, the outside boat shall give the inside boat *room* between her and the *obstruction*, unless she has been unable to do so from the time the *overlap* began.

The outside boat, whether the right-of-way boat or not, must give the inside boat *room* to pass between her and the *obstruction* when she needs it, which will be when she needs to commit to sailing on one side or the other of the *obstruction* and needs *room* to do so.

A common example is two *overlapped* boats sailing upwind on *port-tack* (PL and PW) approaching a *starboard-tack* boat (S). As the boats near each other, PL bears away to pass astern of S. When PW gets to the point where she must commit to either bearing away also or tacking, rule 19.2(b) requires PL to give PW *room* to pass astern of S if PW chooses to do so (ISAF Case 11).

Another common example is on the starting line. Two *overlapped starboard-tack* boats (SL and SW) are reaching down the line and approaching another *starboard-tack* boat *clear ahead* (A). If SL wants to pass or stop on the *windward* side of A, she may do so by luffing, subject to rule 16.1 (Changing Course), and SW must *keep clear*. If SL chooses to pass astern of A, then she must give SW *room* to do so if SW chooses to pass astern as well. This is true even if SW's bow is ahead of SL's such that she will reach A before SL.

"What happens if it is not clear on which side the right of way boat will pass the obstruction?"

Good question! Rule 19.2(b) is premised on there being an "inside" and an "outside" boat. If neither boat is clearly the "outside" boat, then it is not possible to apply rule 19.2(b). It will be up to the protest committee to decide, based on the facts, whether there was an "outside" boat. If, in the starting line example above, SL is aiming at the aft portion of A when SW needs to commit to passing A on one side or the other, I would say it is reasonable for her to assume that SL will pass astern of A; i.e., on the "outside."

However, consider the situation where two *overlapped port-tack* boats (PL and PW) are sailing downwind and approaching a boat ahead on the same *tack* (PA), with PW half a length ahead of PL. As both PL and PW are required to *keep* clear of PA under rule 12 (On the Same Tack, Not Overlapped), PA is an *obstruction*. If PL is clearly sailing a course to pass to *leeward* of PA, then PW is entitled to *room* to do likewise when she arrives at PA. If PL is clearly sailing a course to pass to *windward* of PA, then PW must *keep clear* under rule 11 (On the Same Tack, Overlapped); and when PL must commit to passing PA to *windward*, she is also entitled to *room* from PW to do so. However, if PL is aiming directly at PA's transom such that it is not possible to determine by the positions of the boats on which side of the *obstruction* PL will pass, there is no clear "outside" boat. As PW will arrive at PA before PL does, she should *keep clear* under rule 11 and should not anticipate receiving *room* under rule 19.2(b). She may end up *overlapping* PA to *windward* as a result of *keeping clear* of PL. If when PL arrives at PA she chooses to pass PA to *leeward*, she must give *room* to PW (assuming the boats are still *overlapped*), but that may be a moot point as PW may not be able to take advantage of that space if she is *overlapped* close to *windward* of PA. Hails between PW and PL regarding PL's intentions as the boats approach PA may be helpful, but are not mandatory under the *rules*.

"If I am the outside boat, remind me how much space I need to give the inside boat?"

You have to give her *"room,"* which is enough space for her to sail between you and the *obstruction* in the prevailing conditions in a "seamanlike way;" i.e., sailing her boat in its normal way without risk of touching either you or the *obstruction*.

"Does the inside boat have to call for room in order to get it; what if I don't know the inside boat is there?"

There is no requirement in the *rules* that an inside boat has to call for *room* in order to get it, though I recommend hailing in advance to avoid problems later. Boats are expected to know their obligations under the rules, which includes outside boats at *obstructions*. ISAF Case 41 reads, "QUESTION 2: Does BW have to hail for room to pass to leeward of A? If not, would BL risk disqualification by not giving room? ANSWER 2: BW is not required to hail for room, although that is a prudent thing to do to avoid misunderstandings. Rule 19.2(b) requires BL to give room to BW when they both pass to leeward of the obstruction, whether or not BW hails for room."

In US Sailing Appeal 7, L and M were passing astern of another *starboard-tacker* that had been *clear ahead*. In this case M didn't know L was there or that she was even entitled to *room* at the *obstruction*. She bore off inadvertently and came within inches of hitting L. The Appeals Committee stated, "The fact that M was unaware of L's presence in no way changed L's obligation under the rules or justified her not giving M room to pass the obstruction." Clearly, outside boats must be aware at all times to be sure they give each inside boat *room* when required to.

"How does it work when I want to establish an overlap between two boats on the starting line?"

Let's say you were on *starboard tack* approaching two other *starboard-tack* boats (L and W) sitting side-by-side near the starting line. You need to *keep clear* of L under rule 12 (On the Same Tack, Not Overlapped), and W needs to *keep clear* of L under rule 11 (On the Same Tack, Overlapped). Because you **both** need to *keep clear* of L, she is an *obstruction*; but as a vessel under way, she is not a "continuing" *obstruction* (see the definition *Obstruction*). There- fore, rule 19.2(b) applies, meaning that you can establish an *overlap* between L and W even if there is not *room* at that moment to sail all the way between them in safety.

If you become *overlapped* to *leeward* of W, she needs to *keep clear* of you under rule 11; and you need to initially give her *room* to *keep clear* of you under rule 15 (Acquiring Right of Way). W also needs to give you *room* to pass the *ob- struction* (L) if she is able to do so from the moment you became *overlapped* with her. If she is able to *keep clear* of you and give you *room* to pass L, then she must. However, if despite her best effort she is unable to do so, then you break rule 15 if you hit W, or rule 11 if you hit L or force L to avoid you.

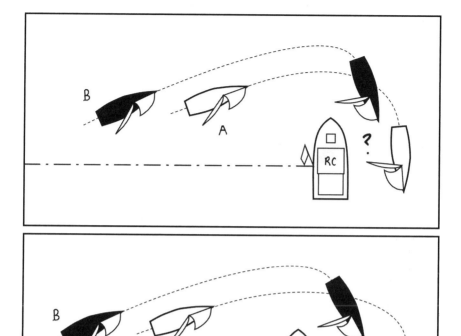

Because A and B are only passing the obstruction (race committee boat) for a very short time, it is not a "continuing obstruction." B is permitted to establish an inside overlap and become entitled to room only if A can initially keep clear under rule 11 when B becomes overlapped to leeward of her, and is able to give B room from the time the overlap is established (see rule 19.2(b)).

"So if the inside boat gets her overlap so close to the obstruction that *I physically can't give her room, I don't have to?"*

That's right. Rule 19.2(b) says that if an outside boat is "unable" to give *room* from the time the *overlap* begins, she doesn't have to do so. This is a safety feature intended to discourage boats from creating last-minute inside *overlaps* near *obstructions*. Note also that if the boat astern is acquiring the right-of-way when it establishes an inside *overlap*, it also has to comply with rule 15 (Acquiring Right of Way). So again, if the outside keep-clear boat is unable to respond promptly and *keep clear* (which would likely result in them also giving *room)*, the inside boat breaks rule 15 and the outside boat does not break rule 19.2(b).

"OK, but what do I do if I'm entitled to room but the outside boat doesn't give me room; can I get exonerated if I am forced to break a rule?"

Let's say you (PW) and a *leeward* boat (PL) are on *port tack* approaching a *starboard-tack* boat (S). It looks clear to you that PL is going to duck S; i.e., pass astern of her. At the point in time that it becomes clear to you that PL is not going to give you *room*, it is not possible for you to tack without hitting S. You continue ducking S and your boom touches PL. You both protest. First, at the point in time that it becomes clear to you that PL is not going to give you *room*, it is not possible for you to avoid contact with either S or PL; therefore you did not break rule 14 (Avoiding Contact) (see rule 14(a)). Second, PL failed to give you *room* to pass the *obstruction* (S) and therefore broke rule 19.2(b). Third, though you failed to *keep clear* of the *leeward* boat (PL) and broke rule 11 (On the Same Tack, Overlapped), you were compelled to do so because PL broke rule 19.2(b); therefore you will be exonerated (freed from blame) under rule 21 (Exoneration).

Note, if it becomes clear to the inside keep-clear boat that the outside boat is not going to give *room*, either by the position of the boat or a hail, and if the inside boat **can** avoid fouling the outside boat, she must do so and protest. If she does foul, when she could have avoided doing so, she can't blame the outside boat for that, and she won't be exonerated.

"When does rule 19 cease to apply such that I no longer have to give the inside boat room?"

Once the inside boat no longer needs *room* to sail between the outside boat and the *obstruction*, the boats are no longer "at" the *obstruction* and rule 19 ceases to apply. For instance, take the upwind situation where PL and PW are passing astern of S. Once PW has passed S such that she no longer needs space from PL to avoid S, PL may assert her rights under rule 11 (On the Same Tack, Overlapped) and can luff subject to rule 16.1 (Changing Course) and rule 17 (On the Same Tack; Proper Course).

"If I'm on port tack sailing as close to a shoreline or dock as I can, can I call for 'sea-room' from a starboard-tacker?"

Absolutely not! First, there's no such thing as "sea-room" in the rules. "Sea-room" is just a term for "*room*." Rule 19.2(b) applies only to boats that are "*overlapped*." Boats sailing upwind on opposite *tacks* are not *overlapped* (see the definition *Clear Astern* and *Clear Ahead; Overlap*). Therefore, if you are sailing close-hauled on *port tack* as close to the shore or a dock as you can get, you cannot call for *room* from a converging close-hauled *starboard-tack* boat. Rule 10 (On Opposite Tacks) applies and you must slow down or bear off and take their stern. (See ISAF Cases 9 and 43.)

WHEN PASSING A CONTINUING OBSTRUCTION

RULE 19.2(c)

While boats are passing a continuing *obstruction*, if a boat that was *clear astern* and required to *keep clear* becomes *overlapped* between the other boat and the *obstruction* and, at the moment the *overlap* begins, there is not *room* for her to pass between them, she is not entitled to *room* under rule 19.2(b). While the boats remain *overlapped*, she shall *keep clear* and rules 10 and 11 do not apply.

First of all, we need to discuss what a "continuing *obstruction*" is. It is an *obstruction* that a boat "continues" to sail next to for a longer period of time, as opposed to one that is passed in a matter of seconds. For instance, a break-water that a boat is sailing along is a "continuing *obstruction*," whereas a small spectator boat that gets sailed by in a few seconds is not a "continuing *obstruction.*" Note that a vessel under way, **including a boat *racing***, is never a "continuing *obstruction*" (see the definition *Obstruction*).

ISAF Case 33 interprets the situation where boats are sailing by the very end of a long breakwater protruding from shore as follows, "Although the breakwater is a continuous structure from the shore to its outer end, it does not qualify as a continuing obstruction because the boats pass close to it only briefly, near its outer end. Therefore, rule 19.2(c) does not apply."

 "So when can a boat come up from clear astern and obtain an inside overlap between a boat ahead and a continuing obstruction and be entitled to room?"

The answer depends on whether the boat astern has the right of way or not. When boats are passing an *obstruction* and are not *overlapped*, rule 19 places no obligations on the boats, meaning that the rules in Sections A and B apply. For instance, if two boats are running downwind along the shore or a breakwater or dock and the boat astern is on *starboard tack* (SB) and the boat ahead is on *port tack* (PA), PA must *keep clear* of SB under rule 10 (On Opposite Tacks). Of course, PA can defend her position close to the *obstruction* by gybing so that she too is on *starboard tack*. Then SB would need to *keep clear* of her under rule 12 (On the Same Tack, Not Overlapped).

However, if the boat astern is a keep-clear boat, then rule 19.2(c) applies. In that case, the boat *clear astern* (B) can obtain an inside *overlap* between the boat *clear ahead* (A) and a continuing *obstruction* only when, at the moment the *overlap* is obtained, there is enough *room* for B to pass **completely** between A and the *obstruction* without touching either. In other words, imagine that the moment the *overlap* between A and the *obstruction* is made, you could "freeze" the motion of A and the *obstruction*. If there is enough physical space for B to sail through between them in a seamanlike way (meaning sailing the boat in its normal way without risk of touching either the *obstruction* or the outside boat) without touching either, then the *overlap* is legal and A must give B *room* under rule 19.2(b) for as long as they are *overlapped* and B needs the *room* to keep from touching the *obstruction*; i.e., hitting the wall, running aground, etc. If B loses the *overlap* on A, then A ceases to be required to give *room* until B obtains another legal *overlap* and again needs *room*.

One sensitive situation occurs when A is sailing as close as she dares to shore but it's not obvious how close a boat of her class can really go without

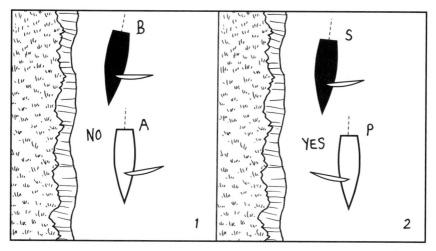

In situation 1, B is the keep-clear boat. There is not room for B to sail between A and the shoreline (a continuing obstruction) without hitting one or the other. Therefore, if she did establish an overlap between them, she would not be entitled to room under rule 19.2(b) and she would be required to keep clear of A under rule 11 (see rule 19.2(c)).

In situation 2, S is the right-of-way boat. P must keep clear of her under rule 10.

running aground. Boat B comes up and wants to obtain an inside *overlap*. The question becomes, "How do you determine if there is *room* for her to pass inside of A?" The essence of *room* is whether, under the conditions existing, the inside boat can safely sail between the outside boat and the *obstruction*. If B decides to risk it and obtains the *overlap*, and then immediately runs aground, she has demonstrated that there was not *room* for her at the time she obtained the *overlap*. But after she has sailed inside for a couple of lengths, she has clearly demonstrated that there was *room* for her to pass safely between the outside boat and the continuing *obstruction*, and therefore, having met the criterion in rule 19.2(c), is entitled to *room* for as long as the *overlap* continues to exist.

"If I'm a keep-clear boat and I obtain an overlap when there isn't *room to sail between the outside boat and the continuing obstruction, have I broken rule 19.2(c)?"*

No. You don't break rule 19.2(c) merely because you obtained an *overlap*. However, if you are not entitled to *room*, then you are required to *keep clear* of the outside boat under rule 19.2(c). If the outside boat has to take action to avoid you, now you have broken rule 19.2(c).

RULE 20 — ROOM TO TACK AT AN OBSTRUCTION

RULE 20.1 — HAILING

When approaching an *obstruction*, a boat may hail for *room* to tack and avoid a boat on the same *tack*. However, she shall not hail if

(a) she can avoid the *obstruction* safely without making a substantial course change,

(b) she is sailing below close-hauled, or

(c) the *obstruction* is a *mark* and a boat that is *fetching* it would be required to respond and change course.

RULE 20.2 — RESPONDING

(a) After a boat hails, she shall give the hailed boat time to respond.

(b) The hailed boat shall respond even if the hail breaks rule 20.1.

(c) The hailed boat shall respond either by tacking as soon as possible, or by immediately replying 'You tack' and then giving the hailing boat *room* to tack and avoid her.

(d) When the hailed boat responds, the hailing boat shall tack as soon as possible.

(e) From the time a boat hails until she has tacked and avoided the hailed boat, rule 18.2 does not apply between them.

RULE 20.3 — PASSING ON A HAIL TO AN ADDITIONAL BOAT

When a boat has been hailed for *room* to tack and she intends to respond by tacking, she may hail another boat on the same *tack* for *room* to tack and avoid her. She may hail even if her hail does not meet the conditions of rule 20.1. Rule 20.2 applies between her and the boat she hails.

This is the rule that is used when calling for "sea-room" or *room* at a shore, breakwater or dock. However, it is also commonly used when two *port-tack* boats are sailing side-by-side up a beat and are converging with a *starboard-tacker*. It is a "safety" rule. The purpose of the rule is to permit a close-hauled boat caught between another boat on the same *tack* and an *obstruction* to avoid the *obstruction* without loss of distance when a substantial change of course is required to clear it.

Notice that rule 20.1 does not apply to boats on opposite *tacks*. ISAF Case 43 describes a situation where a *port-tack* boat (P) is sailing close-hauled as close to shore as possible. A *port-tack* boat to leeward (S) tacks to *starboard tack* onto a collision course with P. S hails "Starboard" and P hails for "searoom." In ISAF Case 43, the Appeals Committee said, "P is subject to rule 10 and must keep clear… S establishes right of way over P when she tacks onto starboard, but must observe rules 13 and 15. S meets rule 13's requirement by not tacking so close that P has to take avoiding action before S reaches her close-hauled course. After S acquires right of way over P under rule 10, S complies with rule 15 by initially giving P room to keep clear." Therefore, P is not entitled to hail for *room* to tack since rule 20.1 applies to two boats on the "same" *tack* approaching an *obstruction*. So, in this situation P must slow down or bear away and pass astern of S.

When all the conditions in rule 20.1 are met, a *leeward* boat or one *clear ahead* will be able to call for "*room* to tack" from a nearby boat that is otherwise preventing her from tacking.

Here is how rule 20 works:

1) Two boats must be on the **same** *tack* and approaching an *obstruction*, and the *leeward* boat (L) or the boat *clear ahead* (A) must be sailing close-hauled or above (rule 20.1(b)).

2) Rule 20.1 is intended for the use of L or A when she is about to hit, or be hit by, an *obstruction*, e.g., a sandbar, a dock, a fishing boat, or a *starboard-tack* boat that is *racing*. When there is any doubt as to whether L or A actually is in imminent danger of colliding with an *obstruction*, I would always expect the protest committee to give L or A the benefit of the doubt, and I would encourage sailors on the water to do the same.

3) Rule 20.1 only provides a boat enough *room* to tack without fouling a nearby boat. Let's say the boats are on *starboard tack*. L or A hails for *room* to tack and W or B responds, "You tack." If the course of L or A is sufficiently to leeward of W's or B's course such that after tacking onto *port tack* she has *room* to immediately bear away and pass astern of W or B, she is required to do so, since she has the *room* she needs to tack and avoid the other boat. (See ISAF Case 35.)

4) Rule 20.1(a) prohibits L or A from hailing the other boat for *room* to tack unless safety requires L or A to make a "substantial change of course" to avoid the *obstruction*. Here, the course change is simply that needed not to hit the *obstruction*. In this case, as my general guideline, a course change of less than 10 degrees is not very "substantial." That's only three feet, six inches, in a 20-foot boat. Therefore, in a 20-foot boat, if L or A can bear away and miss an *obstruction* that she would otherwise hit only three feet from its edge, it is questionable whether she is entitled to hail under rule 20.1. But if she needs to tack to avoid the last three feet, then that's more "substantial." (See US Sailing Appeal 15 and ISAF Case 11.)

 "What happens if a boat hails for room to tack, and the boat being hailed doesn't think the boat that hailed needed to make a course change at all to avoid the obstruction?"

First of all, the boat that was hailed **must respond** to the hail by tacking or replying "You tack" (see the following discussion on 20.2(b)). This is for safety. But, the hailed boat (or any boat) can protest the hailing boat for breaking rule 20.1(a). If the protest committee finds that the hailing boat did not need to make a substantial course change to ensure her safety, or if "safety" was not an issue, the hailing boat will be disqualified. Note the word "shall" in the rule's second sentence.

"Is there anything I should know about the hail itself?"

Well, first of all the hail must be **adequate**, which implies that it must be loud enough for the other boat to hear it above the wind and noise of the boats, and it must be absolutely clear as to what the hail means. I personally try to turn my head toward the other boat, use their helmsman's name if I know it, and say to the effect, "I have a dock or a *starboard-tacker* coming up; I need *room* to tack." ISAF Case 54 reads, "Concerning the hail, when the hailed boat fails to respond in any way… the hailing boat should hail again, more loudly."

Secondly, the hailing boat must give the hailed boat **time to respond**; i.e., she cannot hail and tack simultaneously. US Sailing Appeal 45 reads, "PL was at fault [by]…hailing and tacking simultaneously, contrary to rule 20.2(a)." The purpose of this is to provide time for the specific response called for under rule 20.2(c) (to tack or reply 'You tack'). This requires boats to keep a good lookout so they are not "surprised" by an *obstruction*. Furthermore, it requires boats to be aware of the hailed boat's ability to respond as well. Obviously it will require more time if the hailed boat will have to subsequently hail a boat or boats to windward of them, as permitted in rule 20.3.

Though the failure of a hailed boat to hear an adequate hail does not relieve her of her obligations under rule 20, before she is hailed a boat is under no obligation to anticipate that another boat is going to hail for room to tack. US Sailing Appeal 45 reads, "[The finding] that PW should have been prepared to respond is unwarranted." Therefore a boat does not have to anticipate that another boat might be approaching an *obstruction*; and if the other boat does not adequately hail in time and subsequently runs aground or fouls a *starboard-tack* boat, she cannot blame the hailed boat (see ISAF Case 54). Therefore, a boat must not sail into a position, before hailing, where she cannot allow sufficient time for a response.

"I thought that when two port-tack boats were approaching a starboard-tacker, it was whoever hailed first that got to tell the other what to do."

No! Rule 19.2(a) gives the right-of-way boat the right to choose on which side she will pass the *obstruction*. And if she wants to tack, rule 20.1 gives L or A the right to call for *room* to tack whenever she will have to make a substantial course change to avoid the *obstruction*; and requires W or B to respond to L or A's hail. When two port-tack boats (PW and PL) are approaching a *star-*

board-tack boat (S), US Sailing Appeal 24 says, "PW established an inside overlap on PL when the two boats were several lengths from the obstruction. However, this fact alone did not give PW right to room under rule 19.2(b). Therefore, PL was under no obligation to give PW room to pass astern of the obstruction if in fact PL desired to tack."

If PL chooses to pass astern of S and PW wants to pass astern of S also, then ISAF Case 11 reminds PL that, as an outside boat passing an *obstruction*, "Under rule 19.2(b) PW was entitled to room to pass between PL and the stern of S." But if PL chooses to hail for *room* to tack under rule 20.1, PW must comply by tacking or replying "You tack" and giving PL *room* to tack even when PW would rather duck.

When L or A adequately hails, rule 20.2 tells W or B how to respond.

So when L or A adequately hails, W or B has only two choices for a response: either tack as soon as possible or **immediately** reply "You tack" (rule 20.2(b)). W or B does not have the option of disputing L or A's judgment about her need to hail. When W or B feels L or A's hail is not proper (e.g., she is not really near an *obstruction* or she will not have to make a substantial course change to go around an *obstruction*) she nevertheless must respond. She can then protest under rule 20.1 claiming L or A hailed when she was not permitted to do so.

Notice that if you choose to reply "You tack," you must make that hail **immediately**; i.e., without delay. Note also that you must use those **exact two words** in your hail.

However, if you choose to respond by tacking, you need only do that "as soon as possible." The reason is that sometimes it will **not** be possible for W or B to respond by tacking "immediately" after hearing a hail. Examples would include: (a) when there are several boats to windward of W or B that need to be hailed; (b) when coming in on *port tack* to a windward *mark* where the boats already going down the first reach are so close that tacking is impossible; (c) when PW is still ducking one *starboard-tacker* when PL hails for *room* to tack at a second *starboard-tacker*; or (d) when some object in the water such as a log or the windward *mark* momentarily restricts her ability to respond. When it is not possible for W or B to respond by tacking immediately, it is good seamanship for them to inform L or A.

Notice also that it makes no difference whether the hailed boat (W or B) can "fetch" the *obstruction* herself (unless it is also a *mark*; see rule 20.1(c)). If the hailing boat (L or A) cannot clear the *obstruction* without tacking or bearing away sharply, she is entitled to hail and to get a response, regardless of whether the hailed boat can clear the *obstruction*.

Now let's say that you are L and have hailed W for *room* to tack because of a converging *starboard-tacker*. Upon hearing your hail, W tacks. You must begin your tack as soon as you can without hitting W. In other words, you must put your helm down within a couple of seconds after W puts hers down. You break rule 20.2(d) if you continue another couple of boat-lengths before tacking, or if you don't tack at all.

If W responds to your hail with the reply "You tack," again you must put your helm down and tack as soon as it is possible, which normally will be immediately. If you don't, you break rule 20.2(d). Once W hails "You tack" she assumes all the obligation to give you *room* to tack and clear her; so if you hear her reply and immediately put your helm down and hit her, she is wrong under rule 20.2(c) and you will be exonerated (freed from blame) for any Section A rule, or rule 15 or 16, you may have broken (rule 21, Exoneration). And if you decide to stop your tack or otherwise change course before completing your tack in order to avoid her, she is wrong as well under 20.2(c).

"Could you discuss the situation where two port-tackers (PW and PL) are sailing close-hauled side by side on a converging course with a starboard-tacker (S). PL hails PW for 'room to tack,' gets no response, and ultimately S must change course to avoid hitting PL. Who should be penalized?"

The answer will depend on the protest committee's judgment as to whether PL hailed adequately and gave the hailed boat enough time to respond.

ISAF Case 3 states, "Having decided to tack and having hailed for room to do so three times, PL was entitled by rule 20.2(c) to expect that PW would respond and give her room to tack. She was not obliged to anticipate PW's failure to comply with rule 20.2(c). PL broke rule 10, but she is exonerated as the innocent victim of another boat's breach of a rule, under the provisions of rule 64.1(a)."

US Sailing Appeal 19 is another good example of how PL fulfilled her obligation to adequately hail, but then was forced to foul S by PW's failure to respond. "FACTS: [PW and PL] were close-hauled on port tack. S, which was to leeward and ahead of both PW and PL, tacked to starboard. S completed her tack in compliance with rule 15 (Acquiring Right of Way). Twice, PL hailed PW to tack, so that she also could tack and avoid S. By the time it was clear that PW would not respond, it was too late for PL to make any alternative maneuver without interfering with the oncoming S. PL called to S that she could not respond, whereupon S tacked back to port to avoid a collision.

"DECISION: Inasmuch as PL would have had to make a substantial course change to pass astern of S, even if she had borne away instantly when S tacked to starboard, she had the right to hail PW as she did. However, by the time it was clear that PW would not respond, it was too late for PL to avoid S by bearing away. PW was properly disqualified for breaking rule 20.2(c)... Since PL was compelled to break a rule as a consequence of PW's breaking 20.2(c), PL is exonerated under rule 64.1(a)."

However, PL must remember that her primary obligation is to *keep clear* of S under rule 10 (On Opposite Tacks). In US Sailing Appeal 2 the protest committee found that after realizing PW was not responding to her hail, PL could have borne away and passed astern of S. Instead S was required to luff to avoid contact with PL. The Decision reads, "When PW failed to respond to PL's hail for room to tack, PL was faced with the necessity of taking alternative action to avoid S. This raises the question of whether she should be exonerated under rule 64.1(a) as the innocent victim of another boat's breach. We think not, since the protest committee found that she could have gone astern of S. A boat breaking a rule is not entitled to exoneration unless she was compelled by another boat to break a rule."

The key to all this is that L or A must keep a good lookout and begin hailing in time for W or B to hear and understand the hail and then respond. If L or A waits until the last second to hail, and then immediately fouls S, she cannot blame W or B. But if after two clear hails W or B does not respond, L or A must make a reasonable effort to *keep clear* of S. If she cannot *keep clear* she should be exonerated under rule 64.1(a), and W or B should be penalized for breaking rule 20.2(c). If, however, L or A did have enough time and space to *keep clear* of S after getting no response from W or B but failed to make an effort to use it, she should also be penalized under rule 10 (On Opposite Tacks).

This situation commonly occurs at the windward *mark*. Note that when PW and PL are in the *zone*, PW is entitled to *mark-room* from PL under rule 18.2 (Giving Mark-Room). However, remember that from the moment a boat

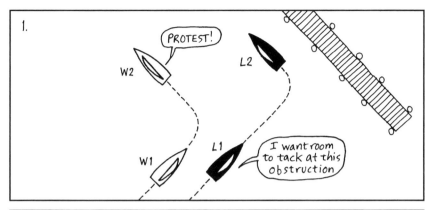

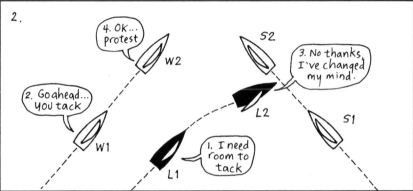

In situation 1, L breaks rule 20.2(d) by delaying her tack to starboard. After W tacks in response to L's hail, L must tack as soon as possible.

In situation 2, L breaks rule 20.2(d) by not tacking as soon as possible after W replies "You tack."

hails for room to tack until she has tacked and avoided the hailed boat, rule 18.2 does not apply between them (see rule 20.2(e). So if PL wants to tack to avoid a converging S, she can hail PW for *"room* to tack," and as long as it is possible for PW to respond, PW must do so, even if it means sailing to the wrong side of the *mark.* (See US Sailing Appeal 2.)

"What about when the obstruction is also a mark; can I still call for *room to tack?"*

Good question. The answer is in the preamble to Section C and in rule 20.1(c). Notice that the preamble to Section C says that none of the rules in Section C (which includes rule 20) apply at a "starting" *mark* surrounded by naviga-

ble water or at its anchor line once a boat is approaching them to *start* until the boats have passed them. When rule 20 does not apply, none of the hails in rule 20 have any meaning under the rules. Therefore a call for "*room* to tack" at a "starting" *mark* when you are about to *start* or have just *started* places no obligation on other boats. This situation usually develops when there is a race committee boat anchored as the port or "leeward" end of the starting line. A *leeward* boat is truly in "coffin corner" if she sails into a position where she can neither tack without fouling the *windward* boat nor bear away and pass astern of the race committee boat.

But if any other *mark* is a boat or other object large enough to qualify as an *obstruction*, then rule 20 applies. However, rule 20.1(c) says that a boat shall not hail if "*the **obstruction** is a **mark** and a boat that is **fetching** it would be required to respond and change course.*" Let's say you are approaching a *mark/obstruction* and cannot pass it on its required side without tacking, and that you want to tack but can't without colliding with the boat just to windward of you (W). First you must check to see if W is *fetching* the *mark/ob-*

struction (able to pass it without passing head to wind). If she is, then you are not allowed to hail for *room* to tack (rule 20.1(c)). In this case you are going to have to gybe or bear away and tack around to try it again. If W cannot *fetch* it herself, then you **can** hail W for "*room* to tack" under rule 20.1.

However, let's say you think you could tack and duck W; i.e., you could tack without making her change course to avoid you. If you choose to call for *room* to tack, and W responds by saying "You tack," and you don't require her to change course to avoid you, then you have not broken rule 20.1. But if W does need to change course to avoid you, you have broken rule 20.1(c).

Finally, it is important for W or B to remember that even if they are "*fetching* the *mark*" and would be required to change course to avoid L or A if they tacked, if L or A hails for *room* to tack, W or B must respond to the hail by tacking or hailing "You tack" (rule 20.2(b)), and then they can protest L or A for breaking rule 20.1(c).

"Now do I know everything there is to know about room at marks and obstructions?"

Yes!

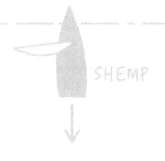

SHEMP

MOE   LARRY   CU

11

Part 2, Section D
When Boats Meet —
Other Rules

Section D contains rules that apply in special situations that arise on the race course (rules 22-24). Again, these rules contain times when a right-of-way boat may find herself with a **temporary obligation** to *keep clear* of, or otherwise avoid, a keep-clear boat. An example is if you are on *port tack* shortly after the start and a *starboard-tack* boat is sailing back to the line because she was over early, rule 22 (Starting Line Errors; Taking Penalties; Moving Astern) requires her to *keep clear* of you because you have *started* correctly, even though she is on *starboard tack* and you are on *port tack*. In this case you become the right-of-way boat and she the keep-clear boat for as long as the rule requires her to *keep clear*. Another example is that all boats are required to avoid a boat that is capsized, whether holding right of way over her or not (rule 23, Capsized, Anchored or Aground; Rescuing).

PREAMBLE TO SECTION D

When rule 22 or 23 applies between two boats, Section A rules do not.

This preamble clarifies that whenever rule 22 (Starting Errors; Taking Penalties; Moving Astern) or rule 23 (Capsized, Anchored or Aground; Rescuing) applies, it takes precedence over the basic right-of-way rules in Section A. Note, however, that the rules of Section B still apply, which most significantly means that rule 16 (Changing Course) applies to a boat given the right of way in rule 22.

RULE 22 – STARTING ERRORS; TAKING PENALTIES; MOVING ASTERN

RULE 22.1 – A boat sailing towards the pre-start side of the starting line or one of its extensions after her starting signal to *start* or to comply with rule 30.1 shall *keep clear* of a boat not doing so until she is completely on the pre-start side.

RULE 22.2 – A boat taking a penalty shall *keep clear* of one that is not.

RULE 22.3 – A boat moving astern through the water by backing a sail shall *keep clear* of one that is not.

Rule 22 is actually three rules in one. Let's look at rule 22.1 first. Rule 28.1 (Sailing the Course) reads in part, *"A boat shall start...."* So, if you aren't completely on the pre-start side of the starting line or its extensions at the starting signal, you have to get there before you can *start* the race. However, even when you and everyone else knows you are on the course side of the starting line at the starting signal (OCS), you keep all your right of way until you are sailing **back towards** the pre-start side of the starting line or one of its extensions; i.e., you are converging with it. This means that you continue to have rights even while slowing down or luffing in order to get clear enough to turn back. When it is obvious that you are sailing back towards the starting line, you must then *keep clear* of all boats that have *started* properly or are on the pre-start side of the starting line.

Once you are completely on the pre-start side of the starting line or its extensions, you are instantly subject to the Section A rules again; however, remember that if you acquire the right of way over another boat, you have to initially give her *room* to *keep clear* of you under rule 15 (Acquiring Right of Way).

Notice that when rule 30.1 (I Flag Rule), commonly referred to as the "one minute rule" or "round-an-end rule" is in effect, the requirement to *keep clear* in rule 22 applies only when you are sailing towards either end of the starting line to comply with rule 30.1 **after** your starting signal. Before your starting signal you have your normal right of way, even when you are over the line and obviously sailing toward an end to comply with rule 30.1.

Between two or more OCS boats sailing towards the pre-start side of the line after the starting signal, the Section A rules apply in the usual way.

"I realize that if another boat fouls me and forces me over the starting
line just before the gun I'm OCS, but do I have to go back and restart?"

I'm afraid you do. If you don't, then you haven't *started* the race and have broken rule 28.1 (Sailing the Course). And you can only be exonerated for breaking a *rule* when another boat "compels" you to break a *rule* (rule 64.1(a), Penalties and Exoneration). In your case, the other boat may have forced you over the line, and you certainly should win your *protest* against her, but she hasn't caused you to not return to the pre-start side and *start*. Therefore no exoneration is available. This is similar to the situation when an outside boat wrongfully fails to give you enough *room* at a *mark* and forces you on the wrong side of it. Though you were clearly fouled, you still must round the *mark* on the correct side.

These are two examples of situations where you can be right under the *rules* but have your finishing place seriously hurt by a keep-clear boat with no way for a protest committee to compensate you. At these times I'm reminded of the old saying, "He was in the right as he sped along; but he's just as dead as though he were wrong!"

Rule 22.2 talks to boats that are doing either a One-Turn Penalty for breaking rule 31 (Touching a Mark) or a Two-Turns Penalty for possibly breaking a rule of Part 2, under rule 44.2 (One-Turn and Two-Turns Penalties). It clearly tells them that, while they are taking their penalties, they have to *keep clear* of other boats, which makes sense.

Notice that when you hit a *mark* or possibly break a rule of Part 2, you still have all your rights as long as you continue sailing the course and while you are sailing well clear of the other boats in preparation to doing your penalty turn(s). But the moment it is obvious to other boats that you are clearly beginning to make a penalty turn, you must then *keep clear* of other boats in the race. You get your rights back when you have completed your last turn; but remember that if you acquire the right of way over another boat, you must initially give her *room* to *keep clear* of you under rule 15 (Acquiring Right of Way).

Note that if you touch a starting *mark* or possibly break a rule of Part 2 before the starting signal, you can make your penalty turn(s) immediately, as opposed to waiting for the starting signal before doing them. And when two boats are making a penalty turn, the Section A rules apply in the usual way, as does rule 24.2 (Interfering with Another Boat).

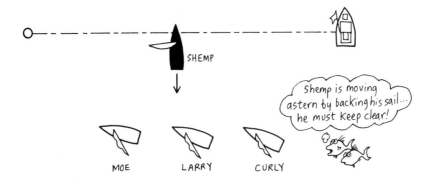

Rule 22.3 covers the situation where a boat actually backs its sail (i.e., holds the sail against the wind) and thereby causes the boat to move backwards through the water. When a boat does this, she must *keep clear* of any other boat that is not doing likewise. Furthermore, she must remember that when she begins sailing backwards, her action gives the right of way to boats astern; therefore they do not have to give her any *room* to *keep clear* of them under rule 15 (Acquiring Right of Way) because they acquired the right of way by the action of the boat moving astern.

Note that if a boat begins to move backwards due to the backing of her sail, she continues to be subject to this rule for as long as she is moving astern, even if she lets her boom come amidships. However, if a boat simply begins to move backwards because she has lost her headway, rule 22.3 does not apply to her (unless she is doing umpired match racing using the rules in Appendix C, Match Racing Rules; see rule C2.9).

RULE 23 – CAPSIZED, ANCHORED OR AGROUND; RESCUING

If possible, a boat shall avoid a boat that is capsized or has not regained control after capsizing, is anchored or aground, or is trying to help a person or vessel in danger. A boat is capsized when her masthead is in the water.

Rule 23 is a common sense rule of safety, and as such it complements rule 1 (Safety). These two rules place the safety of sailors and their boats well above the importance of any race they may be in. The rationale for rule 23 is clear: if a boat is anchored, aground or capsized it cannot very well "move" to get out of another boat's way, and it may be in peril; and if one boat is in the act of rescuing another boat or person, no other boat should hinder the rescue in any way.

Note that rule 23 requires you to "avoid" the boats described in the rule. In my opinion, this means not only avoid contact but keep away from them as well. However, the rule's opening phrase ("If possible…") clarifies that if for whatever reasonable reason it is not possible for you to avoid them, you should not be penalized. This further emphasizes the safety principle in that if you are attempting to assist a boat that otherwise has right-of-way over you, you should not be penalized.

Also note that the definition *Obstruction* states that boats which others must "avoid" under rule 23 are considered *"obstructions."* This is a further safety aspect requiring outside boats to give inside boats *room* to avoid these boats in distress under rule 19 (Room to Pass an Obstruction).

Finally, note that a sailboat is considered "capsized" based on the location of its masthead. Given that it is possible to "capsize" a boat without the very top of the mast ever touching the water, I interpret "masthead" to include the top few feet of the mast. Note also that rule 23 offers protection to a sailboat while she is regaining control after capsizing.

RULE 24 — INTERFERING WITH ANOTHER BOAT

Rule 24 states two situations in which a boat cannot interfere with other boats.

RULE 24.1

If reasonably possible, a boat not *racing* shall not interfere with a boat that is *racing*.

Rule 24.1 makes it clear that before you begin *racing* and once you are no longer *racing*, you cannot interfere with boats that are *racing*. "Interfere" means that you have adversely affected a boat's forward progress or maneuverability. The principle of the rule is that a boat that is not *racing* should not adversely affect a boat that is *racing*.

Note that any "interference" will potentially break this rule. Particularly after *finishing*, boats need to be very careful where they sail so that their wind-shadow and physical presence do not hurt boats still *racing*. However, the rule's opening phrase ("If reasonably possible…") means that boats do not need to go to unreasonable measures to avoid interfering. If they are careful, they should have no problems.

Remember, the preamble to Part 2 says, *"a boat not **racing** shall not be penalized for breaking one of these rules, except rule 24.1."* Rule 44.1 (Taking a Penalty) says, *"A boat may take a Two-Turns Penalty when she may have broken one or more rules of Part 2 in an incident **while racing** (emphasis added)."* Therefore, if you break rule 24.1 you can't take a Two-Turns Penalty. You can be protested and penalized under rule 64.1 (Penalties and Exoneration). Note, rule 64.1 says *"If a boat has broken a rule when not **racing**, her penalty shall apply to the race sailed nearest in time to that of the incident."*

RULE 24.2

Except when sailing her *proper course*, a boat shall not interfere with a boat taking a penalty or sailing on another leg.

Rule 24.2 is intended to provide some protection to boats while they take penalties, and to try to stop boats from interfering with a competitor who is a leg or more ahead of them. If you are sailing your *proper course* (i.e., the course that will get you to the finishing line the fastest) and you interfere with a boat taking a penalty or sailing on another leg, you do not break this rule. But, if you are not sailing your *proper course* and interfere with them, you break this rule.

Note that before the starting signal a boat does not have a *proper course* (see the definition *Proper Course*). Therefore you can never interfere with a boat taking a penalty before the starting signal.

12

Part 3 and Part 4
Conduct of a Race and Other Requirements When Racing

Part 3 contains the rules that govern the conduct of a race (rules 25-36). Part 4 contains other rules that govern us while we are *racing* (rules 40-55). Most of the rules are straightforward and simple to understand. I'll focus on the five for which an explanation might be helpful: rule 31 (Touching a Mark), rule 42 (Propulsion), rule 44 (Penalties at the Time of an Incident), rule 50 (Setting and Sheeting Sails), and the new rule 55 (Trash Disposal).

RULE 31 — TOUCHING A MARK

While *racing*, a boat shall not touch a starting *mark* before *starting*, a *mark* that begins, bounds or ends the leg of the course on which she is sailing, or a finishing *mark* after *finishing*.

Prior to the 1969-73 rules, if you touched a *mark* and it was your fault, you had to drop out of the race. In the 1968 Olympics in Mexico, the late Carl Van Duyne, sailing the Finn for the United States, saw the leech of his main touch the windward *mark* as he rounded it in first place. Despite the claims of the race officer at the *mark* who insisted that Carl did not touch the *mark*, Carl withdrew from the race. From this example and others, the rule writers saw the obvious over-severity of this penalty for the infraction, and changed the rule to permit sailors to take a penalty when they accidentally touch a *mark*.

Notice that the rule applies only while you are *racing*, which is the time from your preparatory signal until you have *finished* and cleared the finishing line and finishing *marks*. Also, if the starting line is set to leeward of the leeward *mark* on the first leg or the finishing line is set to windward of the windward *mark* on the last leg, that leeward or windward *mark* does not begin, bound or end that first or last leg so there is no penalty for touching it. Otherwise, when you touch a starting or finishing *mark*, or any *mark* that begins, bounds or ends a leg on which you are sailing, you have broken rule 31.

When you've broken rule 31 and want to take a penalty, rule 44 (Penalties at the Time of an Incident) tells you how to do that. You must first get well clear of other boats as soon as possible after touching the *mark* (not half-way down the leg!). Then, once clear you must **promptly** (i.e., without delay) make a turn including one tack and one gybe. Notice that your turn does not need to be a complete 360 degree turn. Nor does it matter whether you do the tack or gybe first. As long as you have completed one tack and one gybe, you are all set. (See rule 44.2 for full discussion). While you are making your turn, you have to *keep clear* of other boats under rule 22 (Starting Errors; Taking Penalties; Moving Astern). Once you have completed your turn, you have completed your penalty and the rules of Section A apply to you again. Remember, if you acquire right of way over another boat after your turn, you have to initially give them *room* to *keep clear* under rule 15 (Acquiring Right of Way).

"If I hit one of the starting marks after the preparatory signal but well before the starting signal, when can I make my penalty turn?"

As soon as possible! In fact you are required to do so under rule 44.2 (One-Turn and Two-Turns Penalties). The rationale is that the penalty should fit the crime. Touching the *mark* three minutes before your start probably has little effect on anyone's race; likewise your penalty turn will be of little adverse consequence to you. However, touching it ten seconds before the start means that you are probably somewhere you shouldn't be and are likely adversely affecting the start for others; by the same token, making a penalty turn while others are *starting* will be of more negative consequence to you.

"What do I do if I accidentally hit the finishing mark after I've finished but before I've cleared the mark?"

If you touch a finishing *mark* **before** you have cleared the finishing line and

The penalty for touching a mark is a One-Turn Penalty that includes a tack and a gybe. The turn does not need to be a full 360 degree turn; i.e., after the boat has done a tack and a gybe (in either order) it may continue in the race.

marks (i.e., while you are still *racing*), you should take a One-Turn Penalty. You can make your penalty turn anywhere, but you then have to cross the finishing line again from the course side of the line. The second time you cross will be your finishing place or time. (See rule 44.2, the definition *Finish*, and the discussion of the definition *Racing* for a discussion on when you have cleared the finishing *marks*.)

Notice rule 44.1(b), "*However, if the boat…despite taking a penalty, gained a significant advantage in the race or series by her breach her penalty shall be to retire.*" This is clearly intended to deter boats from sailing into situations where they calculate that they can hit the *mark*, do a quick penalty turn and still come out well ahead of where they would be had they not done so. One example is at a crowded windward *mark* with a long line of *starboard-tackers*, where there is not enough space for a *port-tacker* (P) to tack in to leeward of the *starboard-tackers* and make it around the *mark* without either fouling the *starboard-tackers* or hitting the *mark*. P could probably come out ahead by hitting the *mark* and doing a quick penalty turn as opposed to ducking the line of *starboard-tackers*, but this wouldn't be fair; hence the rule against it in 44.1(b).

"What happens when I'm forced to touch a mark by another boat that was required to keep clear of me or give me mark-room?"

Whenever you touch a *mark*, you have three options:

1) If you think it was your own fault that you touched the *mark*, you can get clear of other boats and take your penalty as described in rule 44.2; or

2) If you believe another boat wrongfully compelled you to hit the *mark*, you can choose to not take a penalty. But you must protest the other boat (by hailing the word "Protest" and, if required, flying your flag at the first reasonable opportunity). If the other boat acknowledges breaking a rule of Part 2 and takes a voluntary penalty (Two-Turns or Scoring Penalty, etc. under rule 44) or retires from the race, the protest committee should exonerate you for breaking rule 31 under rule 64.1(a) (Penalties and Exoneration), provided it decides that it was that breach that caused you to touch the *mark*. If the other boat does not take a penalty, you must hope the protest committee decides that in fact it was the other boat's Part 2 rule breach that compelled you to touch the *mark*, in which case it will disqualify the other boat and exonerate you under rule 64.1(a). If it doesn't, you will be disqualified for breaking rule 31.

3) If you believe another boat wrongfully compelled you to hit the *mark*, you can do a penalty turn; i.e., take the penalty in rule 44.2 as "insurance," and protest the other boat. If the protest committee decides the other boat broke a *rule*, she will be disqualified. If the protest committee decides she didn't break a *rule*, you will not be disqualified for breaking rule 31 because you already took a penalty for that (see rule 64.1(b), Penalties and Exoneration).

"Does it count if just my head brushes against the mark?"

Absolutely yes. In the Introduction of *The Racing Rules of Sailing* under 'Terminology' it says, "*'Boat' means a sailboat and the crew on board.*" In fact, if you have a late spinnaker take-down and your spinnaker sheet trails behind the boat and rubs against the *mark* after you're already around and a boat-length away from it, you still have to take your penalty. ISAF Case 77 sums it up, "A boat touches a mark within the meaning of rule 31 when any part of her hull, crew or equipment comes in contact with the mark. The fact that her equip-

ment touches the mark because she has maneuvering or sail-handling diffi-
culties does not excuse her breach of the rule."

"If I get the mark's anchor line caught on my centerboard but quickly
raise my board and clear the line before I touch the mark, have I hit
the mark? What happens when I'm not so quick and the mark is
dragged in and touches my boat?"

Remember that the anchor line of a *mark* is not part of the *mark* (see the definition *Mark*). So, on a race committee boat with a high bow, where 15 feet of
anchor line may be above the water, the *mark* begins at the bow of the boat. The
same is true when a *mark*'s anchor line is partially or wholly submerged. In
both cases, there is no penalty for touching the line. However, if touching its
anchor line causes the *mark* to be drawn against your boat, you have touched
the *mark* and must do a penalty turn or protest. US Sailing Appeal 10 reads,
"If, however, fouling its anchor line causes the mark to be drawn against the
boat, the boat has broken rule 31."

"What if I foul another boat and hit a mark in the same incident?"

Good question. Rule 44.1(a) (Taking a Penalty) says, *"However, when a boat*
may have broken a rule of Part 2 and rule 31 in the same incident she need not
take the penalty for breaking rule 31." Therefore, when a Two-Turns Penalty
or a Scoring Penalty under rule 44 is available, and you choose to accept that
penalty, you do not have to also do an additional penalty turn for hitting the
mark.

RULE 42 — PROPULSION

RULE 42.1 — BASIC RULE

Except when permitted in rule 42.3 or rule 45, a boat shall compete by using
only the wind and water to increase, maintain or decrease her speed. Her crew
may adjust the trim of sails and hull, and perform other acts of seamanship,
but shall not otherwise move their bodies to propel the boat.

Rule 42 is the "pumping, rocking, ooching, sculling" rule. The rule specifically
tells sailors how they can, and cannot, propel their boats in a sailboat race. The
principle behind rule 42 is simple: the rule writers (and most sailors themselves)

want people to race their sailboats by sailing them (i.e., using the natural wind) as opposed to by propelling or slowing them in other ways. If you are a bit too early for a start, it is more of a sport if you have to slow down using your sails and rudder than if you could just stick your arms in the water and backpaddle; just as it's more challenging and fun to try to ride the waves on a windy reach as opposed to handing all the sheets to Igor and telling him to "pump" nonstop to the leeward *mark*.

 "It seems that there could be a variety of interpretations and applications of rule 42 by competitors and judges; are there any official interpretations of rule 42 that helps get all the competitors and officials reading and applying the rule the same way?"

In fact there is. ISAF has published a comprehensive document entitled *Interpretations of Rule 42, Propulsion* and it is available at the ISAF website (sailing.org/racingrules/documents) or by mail upon request. The intention of the document is to provide a clear and consistent interpretation of rule 42 as it applies to specific commonly-used actions while sailing a boat. This permits sailors and judges alike to prepare for events with confidence that they will be sailing and officiating properly under rule 42. I strongly encourage all who race or officiate boats that can be propelled by kinetic actions to read and study this document carefully.

Compliance with rule 42 continues to be a major issue facing the sport. In my opinion, the rule and the *Interpretations* clearly state what is permitted and what is prohibited. After an explanation of the rule, I will discuss the more central issue of competitor self-control and self-policing vs. the growing reliance on putting judges on the race course to police the kinetics.

Rule 42.1 clearly states the basic premise: *"A boat shall compete by using only the wind and water to increase, maintain or decrease her speed. Her crew may adjust the trim of sails and hull, and perform other acts of seamanship, but shall not otherwise move their bodies to propel the boat."* This is the way sailboats are to be raced; i.e., they can be powered only by the natural action of the wind and water. The last phrase in the rule serves to prohibit any crew action that **in and of itself** propels the boat. Paddling is an obvious example. But even one good hard roll of the boat that propels the boat as one stroke of a paddle would be illegal as well. Note that the term "crew" refers to **all** sailors on board, including the helmsman.

Notice that it is just as illegal to slow yourself down ("decrease speed") unnaturally as it is to propel yourself. So if you're early for a start or trapped on the outside of a crowd at a *mark*, you can't stick your leg in the water to slow down. Likewise, if you luff a boat before the start and hit them, you can't hang on to them to slow yourself down so you're not early. However, there are legal ways to slow yourself down using the natural action of the wind and water. One is to physically hold the boom out so the wind pushes against the sail; another is to turn the rudder hard over against the flow of the water provided it is not done repeatedly back and forth (see discussion of "sculling" in rule 42.2(d)). (See US Sailing Appeal 25.)

Note also that a boat can be penalized for breaking rule 42 only while she is *racing* (see preamble to Part 4). ISAF Case 69 says, "During the period in which the boat was racing she was using wind as a source of power as required by rule 42.1. Her motion also resulted from momentum created by engine power that propelled her before she began racing. Nothing in the rule requires that a boat be in any particular state of motion or non-motion when she begins racing."

Likewise, in light air and adverse current, a boat can just get its bow across the finish line (thereby *finishing*), drift backwards, and, when clear of the finishing line and finishing *marks* (i.e., no longer *racing*), turn on her engine and power out of the course area. The only exception to this is that in match racing under Appendix C, Match Racing Rules, rule 42 also applies between the warning and the preparatory signals, which means it applies during the minute **before** the boats are *racing* as well (rule C2.10).

There are some common sense exceptions built into rule 42 for safety reasons.

RULE 42.3(g) — Any means of propulsion may be used to help a person or another vessel in danger.

RULE 42.3(h) — To get clear after grounding or colliding with another boat or object, a boat may use force applied by the crew of either boat and any equipment other than a propulsion engine.

These reinforce the overriding safety principle that you should get to a boat or person's rescue as fast as you can using any means available, including paddling, rocking, or an engine when you have one. Obviously, this is not intended to be misused as a deceitful way to advance along the race course. ISAF Case 20 and the discussion of rule 1.1 (Safety, Helping Those in Danger) are clear as to the responsibility all racing sailors have, and when and how a boat that renders assistance should be compensated.

Also, when you go aground or hit another boat, you may use whatever means of force is necessary to clear yourself, except that you can't use your engine to propel yourself. Note that you can use the power from your engine to run a winch or windlass, etc. if necessary.

 "Can I anchor?"

Yes. Rule 45 (Hauling Out; Making Fast; Anchoring) states, *"[A boat] may anchor or the crew may stand on the bottom."* Rule 42.1 specifically permits the actions described in rule 45. Generally boats anchor either as a safety measure or to decrease the speed at which they are moving away from their destination (as in adverse current). Note that a means of anchoring is the crew standing on the bottom. Of course if that crew starts walking the boat around, rule 42.1 is broken.

Note, recovering an anchor, whether it was lowered or thrown forward, so as to gather way over the ground, breaks rule 42.1. Anchoring should be a means of keeping you where you are, and not a means of advancing yourself along the race course. Clearly, if you throw your anchor forward and then recover the anchor, you will be "pulling yourself" forward past where you were when you threw out the anchor. Therefore, when *racing*, the anchor should be **dropped straight down**. Likewise, when you pull the anchor back up, you can't generate momentum that will cause the boat to move **past** the point where the anchor was on the ground; i.e., where it was dropped.

 "Now what about the actions listed in rule 42.2; are they always prohibited, or only when they are actually capable of propelling the boat?"

Rule 42.2 lists five specific types of actions which are **always** prohibited, regardless of whether they are capable of propelling the boat or not. This makes it easier for sailors to know what they can't do, and for judges to administer the rule on the water and in protest hearings. The five are the major "offenses."

RULE 42.2 — PROHIBITED ACTIONS

Without limiting the application of rule 42.1, these actions are prohibited:

(a) pumping: repeated fanning of any sail either by pulling in and releasing the sail or by vertical or athwartships body movement;

(b) rocking: repeated rolling of the boat, induced by

(1) body movement,

(2) repeated adjustment of the sails or centreboard, or

(3) steering;

(c) ooching: sudden forward body movement, stopped abruptly;

(d) sculling: repeated movement of the helm that is either forceful or that propels the boat forward or prevents her from moving astern;

(e) repeated tacks or gybes unrelated to changes in the wind or to tactical considerations.

Let me re-emphasize: if you do any of these above-listed actions, you have broken rule 42.2. It does not matter whether the action actually propelled the boat, or even if it was capable of propelling the boat! Therefore, it applies to boats of all sizes. Note that class rules (but not sailing instructions!) can change rule 42, including some of the prohibitions in rule 42.2 (see rule 86.1(c), Changes to the Racing Rules).

To understand these descriptions, notice the use of the word "repeated" throughout. The ISAF *Interpretations of Rule 42* define "repeated" as "more than once in the same area on a leg." "Ooching" is the only action prohibited by rule 42.2 that involves a singular movement.

(a) **Pumping:** the ISAF *Interpretations of Rule 42* define "fanning" as "moving a sail in and out not in response to wind shifts, gusts or waves." So for a sail to be "pumped," it must be repeatedly pulled in and then released with no apparent connection with wind shifts or gusts, and this is illegal. This can be done using the sheets, or by using body motions. Bouncing up and down on the rail is an example of "vertical" movement; and crossing the boat quickly from side to side is "athwartships" movement. In a small boat with a flexible mast, bouncing can "pump" the top of the sail. Likewise, movement side to side will commonly cause the angle of heel to change, which in turn can act to "pump" the sail. These means of "pumping" are also illegal. Rule 42.3(c) allows you to pump in certain conditions.

Note, this rule is not designed to inhibit good sailing techniques. On a puffy or shifty day, the mainsail can be trimmed in and out constantly to keep the boat flat or the sails well trimmed, provided it doesn't become a "fanning" action. Similarly, downwind, the spinnaker sheet can be constantly played in response to changes in apparent wind.

(b) **Rocking:** Your boat is "rocking" when it is repeatedly rolling back and forth. You may be intentionally doing it with your body, or you may have simply encouraged it by pulling your centerboard up, letting your boom way out, and then starting the action like a pendulum with one lean back of your shoulders. It doesn't matter whether your body continues to move; if you started your boat rhythmically rolling back and forth, it's "rocking," and that is illegal at all times. Obviously, waves themselves will cause the boat to toss about. You do not have to run all over the boat counteracting every wave action. If you watch a fleet of boats on a broad reach or run, you will see that they all are being tossed in a similar way. If one boat is being intentionally "rocked," she will stand out instantly as being different from the others.

(c) **Ooching:** "Ooching" is a "sudden forward body movement, stopped abruptly." The key to "ooching" is that it is forward motion, it is sudden, and it is stopped abruptly. Even just one "ooch" is illegal. Pushing or pulling on the mast or shrouds (forward hand movements), slamming forward on the front of the cockpit, mast shrouds or forestay, and subtle abrupt forward motions with the rear or feet are all examples of "ooching" and are illegal at all times.

(d) **Sculling:** First of all, any "repeated forceful movement" of the helm is "sculling" and is illegal, with two exceptions (see below). Second of all, repeated movement of the helm that is turning the boat is not movement that is propelling the boat forward; therefore, it is legal to repeatedly move your tiller back and forth to turn your boat as long as you don't do it "forcefully." In that situation, typically your tiller won't cross centerline and your bow will be clearly moving to one side or the other. Finally, note that if you are stopped, you can't wiggle your tiller to keep from moving backward.

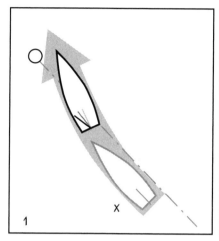 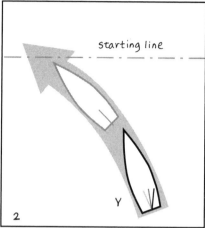

In diagram 1, Boat X is repeatedly forcefully moving her tiller to turn the boat toward the wind to get past the mark. Even though this action is solely to change the boat's direction, it is being done "repeatedly" and "forcefully" and is therefore "sculling" which is prohibited under rule 42.2(d).

In diagram 2, Boat Y is moving slowly and is repeatedly forcefully moving her tiller to turn the boat down from almost head to wind to a close-hauled course. Though this action is "sculling" it is permitted, under rule 42.3(d), as an exception to rule 42.2(d).

One exception is that you are allowed to "scull" if you are trying to turn back down to close-hauled after getting very slow or stopped above close-hauled (rule 42.3(d)). This will often happen on the starting line or when shooting head to wind to try to get around a windward *mark*. Also, it is legal to slow yourself down by repeatedly moving your helm (rule 42.3(e)).

Note that in match racing under Appendix C, Match Racing Rules, there is a slightly different, more liberal, rule for "sculling" (rule C2.11) which reads, "*Sculling: repeated movement of the helm to propel the boat forward.*" This means that forceful movement of the helm is legal as long as it is not propelling the boat forward.

(e) **Repeated tacks or gybes unrelated to changes in the wind or to tactical considerations:** You cannot repeatedly tack or gybe back and forth in quick succession unless you can justify your maneuvers based on changes in the wind (windshifts, etc.) or tactical considerations (covering another boat, etc.). Notice, you can tack or gybe for any reason you want; you just can't do it "repeatedly" without the specific reasons listed in this rule.

"Are there any exceptions to the prohibitions in rule 42.2?"

Yes. They are in rule 42.3, Exceptions.

RULE 42.3 — EXCEPTIONS

(a) A boat may be rolled to facilitate steering.

(b) A boat's crew may move their bodies to exaggerate the rolling that facilitates steering the boat through a tack or a gybe, provided that, just after the tack or gybe is completed, the boat's speed is not greater than it would have been in the absence of the tack or gybe.

(c) Except on a beat to windward, when surfing (rapidly accelerating down the front of a wave) or planing is possible, the boat's crew may pull in any sail in order to initiate surfing or planing, but each sail may be pulled in only once for each wave or gust of wind.

(d) When a boat is above a close-hauled course and either stationary or moving slowly, she may scull to turn to a close-hauled course.

(e) If a batten is inverted, the boat's crew may pump the sail until the batten is no longer inverted. This action is not permitted if it clearly propels the boat.

(f) A boat may reduce speed by repeatedly moving her helm.

(g) Any means of propulsion may be used to help a person or another vessel in danger.

(h) To get clear after grounding or colliding with a vessel or object, a boat may use force applied by her crew or the crew of the other vessel and any equipment other than a propulsion engine. However, the use of an engine may be permitted by rule 42.3(i).

(i) Sailing instructions may, in stated circumstances, permit propulsion using an engine or any other method, provided the boat does not gain a significant advantage in the race.

 "Can I change the angle of my boat's heel to steer the boat more efficiently than using the rudder?"

Yes. Rule 42.3(a) permits "rolling" the boat to facilitate steering. For instance, sailing downwind in waves it is legal to heel the boat to leeward to head up over a wave, then heel it to windward to steer down the backside, etc. Notice also that on a run most boats sail faster when heeled to windward, and the crew can position their weight to do this, provided the boat doesn't start "rocking" back and forth as a result.

"So it is legal to roll-tack and roll-gybe?"

Absolutely yes. Rule 42.3(b) specifically permits you to exaggerate the rolling provided it helps you steer the boat onto the new *tack*, and provided you don't come out of your tack or gybe going faster than just before you began it. Therefore, you can begin your tack with a slight heel to leeward to begin the boat heading up. Then, as the boat is at or near head to wind, you can roll the boat hard to the new leeward side to help "pivot" the boat onto its new close-hauled course. Finally, you can bring the boat upright or even past upright as it gets to its close-hauled course.

The most important thing is that once the boat is brought up from its roll, the mast cannot make a major dip to leeward and back up again. This second "pump," which serves to accelerate the boat rather than steer it, is illegal.

"Does rule 42.3(c) permit one pump of each sail per wave?"

Yes. Rule 42.3(c) permits "pumping," but only to initiate surfing or planing. The rule permits one "pump" for each sail (main, spinnaker and jib if desired, though pumping the jib is generally slow unless you are winging it). However, if the "pump" on the main gets the boat surfing, a subsequent "pump" on the spinnaker sheet would not be legal. If the main and spinnaker were "pumped" simultaneously, there would be no problem.

Notice that you must be just ready to launch down the front of the wave (the "downhill side"). You can't "pump" up the backside of the wave claiming it will get you over the top and down the front side faster. A "planing" boat will be lifted partly out of the water by its own bow wave, and its stern wave will disappear. Visually it will look like the boat is skimming across the surface of the water. The phrase "except on a beat to windward" prohibits you from "pumping" upwind at all for any reason.

Also you can "pump" using anything controlling the sail, including the vang or a special "pumping" line, unless prohibited by class rules.

"What if after a tack or gybe my compression batten is inverted; can I repeatedly pull in on the main to 'pop' it?"

Yes. But you break rule 42.2(a), pumping, if you clearly propel the boat as a result (rule 42.3(e)).

 "Is it true I can never ooch?"

That's right. Rule 42.3 makes no exception for ooching.

 "Why is rule 42.2 so restrictive, and can the rule ever be made more permissive other than the exceptions in rule 42.3?"

The rule writers have taken this step to reduce the strength factor required to race sailboats successfully, and to ensure that the sport remains a sailing contest. Notice that sailing instructions cannot change rule 42 (rule 86.1, Changes to the Racing Rules). Only **class rules** can make rule 42 more permissive by modifying it with a specific reference to it (rule 86.1(c), Changes to the Racing Rules). Therefore a class can permit more than one pump per wave or ooching or more liberal rules about roll tacking and gybing, etc. Additionally a class can permit pumping, rocking and ooching when the wind speed exceeds a specified limit (see Appendix P5, Flags O and R). This is an issue the members of each class should thoroughly discuss.

 "I heard that a protest committee can throw me out under rule 42 without a hearing, and that a DSQ under rule 42 can't be used as a 'throwout' race; is this true?"

Absolutely not! Under previous editions of *The Racing Rules of Sailing* this was permitted, but not under the 2013-2016 edition of the rules. If a judge sees an apparent infringement of rule 42 on the water and Appendix P (Special Procedures for Rule 42) is in effect, he or she can act as permitted (see next paragraph). Otherwise, the judge must protest the boat; and if the protest committee decides the boat broke rule 42, it will disqualify her under rule 64.1 (Penalties and Exoneration), just as with any other rules breach.

 "So how does the Appendix P (Special Procedures for Rule 42) work?"

The system, found in Appendix P (Special Procedures for Rule 42), gives judges on the water the authority to penalize boats for alleged breaches of rule 42. Note that Appendix P is in effect **only** if the sailing instructions state that it is. It has been used successfully at the international level, including the Olympics and ISAF class World Championships for several years now. Many sailors and judges feel that competitors break rule 42 far less when they know the judges are watching for potential breaches of the rule and have the authority to penalize them on the spot, and as a result the racing is cleaner and fairer. Of course this requires knowledgeable judges to ensure correct interpretations and applications of rule 42.

APPENDIX P — SPECIAL PROCEDURES FOR RULE 42

All or part of this appendix applies only if the sailing instructions so state.

P1 — SIGNALLING A PENALTY

A member of the protest committee or its designated observer who sees a boat breaking rule 42 may penalize her by, as soon as reasonably possible, making a sound signal, pointing a yellow flag at her and hailing her sail number, even if she is no longer *racing*. A boat so penalized shall not be penalized a second time under rule 42 for the same incident.

P2 — PENALTIES

P2.1 — FIRST PENALTY

When a boat is first penalized under rule P1 her penalty shall be a Two-Turns Penalty under rule 44.2. If she fails to take it she shall be disqualified without a hearing.

P2.2 — SECOND PENALTY

When a boat is penalized a second time during the regatta, her penalty shall be to promptly retire from the race. If she fails to take it she shall be disqualified without a hearing and her score shall not be excluded.

P2.3 — THIRD AND SUBSEQUENT PENALTIES

When a boat is penalized a third or subsequent time during the regatta, she shall promptly retire from the race. If she does so her penalty shall be disqualification without a hearing and her score shall not be excluded. If she fails to do so her penalty shall be disqualification without a hearing from all races in the regatta, with no score excluded, and the protest committee shall consider calling a hearing under rule 69.2(a).

P3 — POSTPONEMENT, GENERAL RECALL OR ABANDONMENT

If a boat has been penalized under rule P1 and the race committee signals a *postponement,* general recall or *abandonment,* the penalty is cancelled, but it is still counted to determine the number of times she has been penalized during the regatta.

P4 – REDRESS LIMITATION

A boat shall not be given redress for an action by a member of the protest committee or its designated observer under rule P1 unless the action was improper due to a failure to take into account a race committee signal or class rule.

P5 – FLAGS O AND R

(a) If the class rules permit pumping, rocking and ooching when the wind speed exceeds a specified limit, the race committee may signal that those actions are permitted, as specified in the class rules, by displaying flag O before or with the warning signal. The flag shall be removed at the starting signal.

(b) If the wind speed exceeds the specified limit after the starting signal, the race committee may display flag O with repetitive sounds at a *mark* to signal to a boat that the actions are permitted, as specified in the class rules, after she has passed the *mark.*

(c) If the wind speed becomes less than the specified limit after flag O was displayed, the race committee may display flag R with repetitive sounds at a *mark* to signal to a boat that rule 42, as changed by the class rules, applies after she has passed the *mark.*

 "Now I understand what rule 42 allows and doesn't allow; but what do I do when another competitor starts to rock or pump by me?"

Most active racers believe that the rule itself is clear enough and is not the cause of the problem. The real problem is the enforcement of the rule. There are several extreme positions, and there have been many creative attempts made at resolving this issue. Some say the enforcement should be left completely up to judges around the course; i.e., flood the course with referees. Others argue that it is impractical to put that many judges on the course; and that because competitors will never police themselves, the rule itself should be abolished altogether and the race committees given the authority to proclaim before or during a race that either "anything" or "nothing" goes.

Fortunately, the majority of us believe that the racing is best when the sailors themselves have the responsibility to sail within the *rules*. We have seen too many regattas with either too few judges or poorly qualified ones. More to the point, we like the concept of competitor-enforced *rules* which makes the sport unique from almost all others.

But it takes only a few people in each fleet to ruin it for the rest. If some decide that doing well in the race by cheating is okay, and they start pumping and sculling off the starting line and rocking downwind, it puts the other sailors in a very awkward position. Either they can join in, or warn and then protest the other boat, or do nothing. To join in, they have to admit that the problem is not worth their effort to fight it. To do nothing is frustrating because those sailors will feel that not only are they being left behind, but that nothing is being done to enforce the rule.

I strongly recommend sailors take these three steps: 1) first warn the other boat; 2) then get the attention of some other boats nearby with the hopes that they'll say something too; and 3) then protest if the illegal actions continue. You are not being the "bad guy" for simply doing what you'd do if a *port-tacker* hit you when you were on *starboard-tack*. It is destructive to the racing when people feel they can get away with cheating; and they will continue to only get worse if no one calls them on it.

In the hearing the protest committee should (a) find out exactly what the wind and wave conditions were; (b) discuss what the sailing characteristics of the boat are from their shared experiences, competitors' testimony and expert witnesses when useful; and (c) determine what the exact actions of the protestee were. Witnesses are useful to everyone and are desired. Keep in mind that when judges see an apparent infringement, the US Sailing prescription to rule 63.4 precludes them from being on the protest committee if they will also be the protestor or will give evidence in the hearing. Note also that rule 63.6 (Taking Evidence and Finding Facts) says, "*A member of the protest committee who saw the incident shall, while the parties are present, state that fact and may give evidence.*" Even if the protest committee member does not offer evidence, a *party* or the protest committee can call them as a witness, in which case they can no longer be on the protest committee for that hearing. Furthermore, when the sailing instructions state that the US Sailing prescription to rule 63.4 is not in effect, it is permissible for members of the protest committee to also be the protestor, but they must be sure to give their entire testimony while all the *parties* to the hearing are present and able to ask questions and otherwise respond. (See rule 60, Right to Protest; Right to Request Redress or Rule 69 Action; rule 63.3, Right to be Present; and rule 63.6, Taking Evidence and Finding Facts.)

The bottom line to the rule 42 issue is that everyone who races should make the effort to understand exactly what the rule does and does not allow, and then sail within the rule's limits. The rule is not that complex to understand, and my guess is that most sailors who have studied it have a good sense of what is right and wrong. Where it breaks down is when sailors intentionally ignore the rule for their own personal gain. All fleets of sailors should talk about this issue.

RULE 44 — PENALTIES AT THE TIME OF AN INCIDENT

RULE 44.1 — TAKING A PENALTY

A boat may take a Two-Turns Penalty when she may have broken one or more rules of Part 2 in an incident while *racing*. She may take a One-Turn Penalty when she may have broken rule 31. Alternatively, sailing instructions may specify the use of the Scoring Penalty or some other penalty, in which case the specified penalty shall replace the One-Turn and the Two-Turns Penalty. However,

(a) when a boat may have broken a rule of Part 2 and rule 31 in the same incident she need not take the penalty for breaking rule 31;

(b) if the boat caused injury or serious damage or, despite taking a penalty, gained a significant advantage in the race or series by her breach her penalty shall be to retire.

Rule 44.1 states that if you think you may have broken one or more rules of Part 2 in an incident while *racing*, you can **always** take a voluntary penalty at the time of the incident. This is sensible. Mistakes happen, and there should be a consequence for breaking a rule; but forcing sailors to retire and sail in for a minor infraction is not in balance with the great effort, time and expense that goes into participating in a race.

Rule 44.1 states that the voluntary penalty is the One or Two-Turns Penalty (see the discussion of rule 44.2) unless the sailing instructions specify the use of some other penalty. Another common penalty is the Scoring Penalty, often known as the "percentage penalty." When the Scoring Penalty is in effect, it replaces the One or Two-Turns Penalty as the voluntary penalty. This is clearly described in rule 44.3 (Scoring Penalty) and won't be discussed in this book.

Note that even a right-of-way boat can need to take a penalty. If a right-of-way boat fails to avoid contact with another boat when it was reasonably possible for her to do so, she breaks rule 14 (Avoiding Contact). If damage results from the contact, she is liable to being penalized and can do a Two-Turns Penalty to absolve herself.

"Can I ever take a voluntary penalty on shore?"

Check the sailing instructions for your race or event to see if the new US Sailing Appendix T, Alternative Procedures for Dispute Resolution, is in effect. The rules in this appendix are intended to improve compliance with the Basic Principles, Sportsmanship and the Rules, and to encourage boats to enforce the rules by protesting. The appendix provides alternative penalties that encourage competitors to take a penalty on shore when they realize they may have broken a rule of Part 2 or rule 31; and provides a modified hearing procedure that is less formal and less time-consuming than the usual hearing procedure.

"Is there a situation where a boat can't take a voluntary penalty?"

Yes. If a boat has broken a rule of Part 2 (including rule 14) and has caused "injury" or "serious damage" or has gained a "significant advantage" in the race or series by her breach despite taking a penalty, **she must retire**; i.e., she cannot exonerate herself by taking a voluntary penalty. This is a clear reminder to all competitors, whether holding the right of way or not, to be careful and sportsmanlike.

"Before going on, could you discuss the terms 'injury' and 'serious damage'?"

Sure. Understand, however, that these terms are difficult to define precisely. I will discuss what, in my opinion, are the important considerations based on the rule, the appeals, the dictionary and my interpretation. In a *protest*, protest committees will need to exercise their best judgment in these situations. Notice that the judgment that "injury" or "serious damage" occurred is not a "fact found;" it is a conclusion based on the "facts found" and therefore subject to appeal.

An "injury" is something that physically hurts a **person**, and more than just briefly, and in a way that ordinarily affects the person's ability to function normally and/or requires the person to be attended to at some point. The reason the rule does not refer to "serious" injury is that "injury" implies that the hurt is "serious." "Damage" refers to physical damage to a **boat or its equipment**. (See ISAF Case 110.)

Regarding "serious damage," the dictionary offers the following definitions:

"serious": having significant or dangerous possible consequences, not trifling or inconsequential.

"damage": harm impairing the value or usefulness of something.

The three primary considerations are:

1) what was the extent of the damage; i.e., how much damage was done, did the damage require immediate repair to prevent further damage, what was the cost of the repair, and what affect did the damage have on the boat in future races.

2) was it feasible or prudent for the boat to continue in the race; and

3) did the damage markedly affect the boat's speed, performance or maneuverability; i.e., did the damage significantly worsen her finishing place in the race?

Certainly, if the damage causes the boat to discontinue the race, it is "serious." If the boat can safely continue in the race and loses no finishing places as a direct result of the damage, and the nature and cost of any necessary repair isn't too high, the damage is not "serious." (Note that it is impossible to put a price tag on "serious;" that will have to be decided by the protest committee after considering all the relevant factors.)

If the damage is a deep scratch that penetrates the fiberglass, thereby requiring immediate repair after the race so that further damage doesn't result or so that the future speed, performance or maneuverability of the boat isn't affected, that damage would begin to fall into the "serious" category. If the extent of the repair were such that it could be handled that evening by the sailors involved with a minimum of hassle and expense, I would be inclined to rule it not "serious." But if the repair required more professional work and became a more costly and time-consuming affair, I would be more inclined to rule it

The Two-Turns Penalty is two turns in the same direction (in either direction) that include two tacks and two gybes. The second turn does not need to be a full 360 degree turn; i.e., after the last tack and gybe, the boat may continue in the race.

"serious." If, however, the damage is a 12-inch surface scratch in the gelcoat, which does not affect the overall speed, performance or maneuverability of the boat, I would not be as inclined to rule it "serious."

If the damage is a broken boom near the finish and the boat loses no places but cannot repair or replace the boom before the second race of that day, I'd consider the damage to be "serious;" but if the damage was to something that could normally be repaired or replaced on the water, such as a bent guyhook, the damage would not be "serious." (See Case 19.)

"Thanks! Now how do I take a One or Two-Turns Penalty?"

RULE 44.2 — ONE-TURN OR TWO-TURNS PENALTIES

After getting well clear of other boats as soon after the incident as possible, a boat takes a One-Turn or Two-Turns Penalty by promptly making the required number of turns in the same direction, each turn including one tack and one gybe. When a boat takes the penalty at or near the finishing line, she shall sail completely to the course side of the line before *finishing*.

When you want to do a One or Two-Turns Penalty you must first get well clear of other boats as soon **as possible** after the incident (not half-way down the leg!). Remember that while you are getting clear you still have all your Section A rights; i.e., your penalty does not begin until you clearly begin making your turns (see rule 22, Starting Errors; Taking Penalties; Moving Astern).

Once you are clear, you must **promptly** (i.e., without delay) make one or two turns in the same direction, each turn including a tack and a gybe. Notice that the turn does not need to be a complete 360-degree turn. Once you complete your final tack or gybe, your penalty is complete and you may continue in the race. This is why it is not called a "360" or "720." Note that you have to do one turn immediately after the other, though it is generally acceptable to build enough speed after the first turn to be able to sail efficiently through the second one. While you are making your turns, you have to *keep clear* of other boats (see rule 22).

 "What if I am not sure I have broken a rule; do I get some time to think about it before deciding to take a penalty?"

Unfortunately No! US Sailing Appeal 60 says "Rule 44.1 permits a boat to take a penalty at the time of the incident. Rule 44.2 requires the boat to sail well clear of other boats as soon as possible after the incident and promptly make two turns as described in the rule. Together, these rules require a boat that decides to take a penalty to do so as soon as possible after the incident. The rule does not provide for time for a boat to deliberate whether she has broken a rule. If she delays in doing her penalty turns, she is still liable to be disqualified."

Once you have completed your turns; i.e., your final tack or gybe, you have completed your penalty and the rules of Section A apply to you again. Remember, if you acquire right of way over another boat after your second turn, you have to initially give them *room* to *keep clear* under rule 15 (Acquiring Right of Way).

Note that if you break a rule before the starting signal, you can do your Two-Turns Penalty immediately; i.e., you don't have to wait until after the starting signal. As in touching a *mark*, the rationale is that the penalty should fit the crime. Breaking a rule three minutes before your start probably has little effect on anyone's race; likewise your turns penalty will be of little adverse consequence to you. However, breaking a rule ten seconds before the start means that you are probably somewhere you shouldn't be and are likely adversely affecting the start for others; by the same token, doing a Two-Turns Penalty while others are *starting* will be of more negative consequence to you.

If you break a *rule* near the finishing line, including while or just after you have *finished* but are still *racing*, you can do your Two-Turns Penalty anywhere, but you then have to cross the finishing line again from the course side of the line. The second time you cross the finishing line will be your actual *finish* (see the definition *Finish)*.

"How many penalty turns do I have to take if I break more than one rule in the incident; and if I take a penalty on the water, can I still be disqualified for that incident?"

You only need to take one penalty per "incident," regardless of how many rules you may have broken in that incident (first sentence of rule 44.1). Therefore, when a give-way boat breaks rule 10 (On Opposite Tacks) and fails to avoid a collision, thereby breaking rule 14 (Avoiding Contact), she need only do one Two-Turns Penalty. The same is true if you break a rule of Part 2 and rule 31 (Touching a Mark) in the same incident. Rule 44.1(a) is in effect saying, "You know you got yourself in trouble; do your two turns for fouling the other boat but there's no need to do a third turn for touching the *mark*!"

US Sailing Appeal 65 discusses the question of when two occurrences are considered one or two incidents, saying in essence that the test is whether the second occurrence was the "inevitable result" of the first.

If you have taken an applicable penalty on the water, you cannot be further penalized on shore unless the protest committee decides a voluntary penalty was not available to you or that you took it incorrectly, in which case it can disqualify you for the Part 2 rule(s) you broke.

"If I'm not sure who's right, can I do a One or Two-Turns Penalty and still protest the other boat, or am I admitting guilt by taking a penalty?"

Excellent question. You can definitely protest the other boat and your penalty turns are not an admission of guilt. Rule 44.1 carefully says, *"A boat may take a…[p]enalty when she **may** (emphasis added) have broken one or more rules…"* Furthermore, the US Sailing prescription to rule 67 (Damages) says, *"A boat that retires from a race or accepts a penalty does not, by that action alone, admit liability for damages."* Let's say you do a Two-Turns Penalty and protest, and that the other boat did neither. If the protest committee finds that the other boat was wrong in your incident, she will be disqualified; but you cannot be compensated for anything you lost by taking your penalty. However, if the protest committee decides that you actually were wrong, you can't be further penalized because you already took a voluntary penalty (rule 64.1(b)). Therefore, you can view your Two-Turns Penalty as "insurance" against further penalty in an incident where you're not 100% certain how the protest committee will decide it.

RULE 50 — SETTING AND SHEETING SAILS

RULE 50.1 — CHANGING SAILS

When headsails or spinnakers are being changed, a replacing sail may be fully set and trimmed before the replaced sail is lowered. However, only one mainsail and, except when changing, only one spinnaker shall be carried set at a time.

RULE 50.2 — SPINNAKER POLES; WHISKER POLES

Only one spinnaker pole or whisker pole shall be used at a time except when gybing. When in use, it shall be attached to the foremost mast.

RULE 50.3 — USE OF OUTRIGGERS

(a) No sail shall be sheeted over or through an outrigger, except as permitted in rule 50.3(b) or 50.3(c). An outrigger is any fitting or other device so placed that it could exert outward pressure on a sheet or sail at a point from which, with the boat upright, a vertical line would fall outside the hull or deck. For the purpose of this rule, bulwarks, rails and rubbing strakes are not part of the hull or deck and the following are not outriggers: a bowsprit used to secure the tack of a sail, a bumkin used to sheet the boom of a sail, or a boom of a boomed headsail that requires no adjustment when tacking.

(b) Any sail may be sheeted to or led above a boom that is regularly used for a sail and is permanently attached to the mast from which the head of the sail is set.

(c) A headsail may be sheeted or attached at its clew to a spinnaker pole or whisker pole, provided that a spinnaker is not set.

RULE 50.4 — HEADSAILS

For the purposes of rules 50 and 54 and Appendix G, the difference between a headsail and a spinnaker is that the width of a headsail, measured between the midpoints of its luff and leech, is less than 75% of the length of its foot. A sail tacked down behind the foremost mast is not a headsail.

Note that this rule does not require that a spinnaker pole be used at all when flying a spinnaker! The only pole requirements are in rule 50.2. In other words, you can only use one pole at a time; and when it is "in use;" i.e., projecting the spinnaker or headsail outboard, it must be attached to the mast.

With no requirement to use a pole, boats are free to do "gybe-sets" and "floater-drops." In both of these maneuvers, the spinnaker is set and drawing with no pole attached. In other words, a boat can legally gybe around the windward *mark*, set her spinnaker, fill it, and sail on down the leg with no pole. And likewise, when coming into a leeward *mark*, a boat can legally remove her pole and sail for as long as she chooses before lowering her spinnaker. However, when the pole is down, note that rule 49.2 (Crew Position; Lifelines) forbids competitors from leaning their torsos out over the lifelines "except briefly to perform a necessary task."

"So can a crew member lean out over a boat's lifelines to hold the spinnaker guy after the pole has been removed?"

Yes, but only "briefly." US Sailing Appeal 72 reads, "Without a spinnaker pole, a spinnaker is less efficient and more unstable. As a boat prepares to round a leeward mark, removing the pole is one of the first necessary steps. From that time until the spinnaker is lowered, holding the guy by hand is a less effective but nonetheless useful means of controlling the spinnaker, which remains a "necessary task" even without the pole. The interval of time is normally a brief one, since generally there is no advantage in flying a spinnaker without a pole."

Also note that there is no requirement that the tack of the spinnaker be in "close proximity" to the outboard end of the spinnaker pole. The rationale is that it is generally faster to have the tack close to the outboard end, such that there is no reason to penalize a boat if she chooses not to do so.

Note that rule 86.1(c) (Changes to the Racing Rules) permits class rules to change this rule.

"I see a lot of boats flying asymmetrical spinnakers from bowsprits; I assume this is legal?"

Yes. Rule 50.3(a) specifically states, *"For the purpose of this rule… the following are not outriggers: a bowsprit used to secure the tack of a working sail…"* Rule 50.3 is not broken provided that the bowsprit is used to attach the tack (the windward corner) of the spinnaker or as a lead for a line attached to the tack. Rule 50.3 prohibits "sheeting" a spinnaker with an outrigger; e.g., controlling the clew (the leeward corner) with a sheet led through a bowsprit, because the bowsprit would then be considered an "outrigger."

RULE 55 — TRASH DISPOSAL

A competitor shall not intentionally put trash in the water.

BASIC PRINCIPLES — ENVIRONMENTAL RESPONSIBILITY

Participants are encouraged to minimize any adverse environmental impact of the sport of sailing.

Rule 55 supports the new Basic Principle which states the fast growing view that participants in the sport of sailing should take an active role in protecting the environment. There are many actions that all participants can and should take in that direction, including using refillable instead of disposable water bottles. But most are difficult or impossible to enforce or are not practical for all events. A ban on putting trash in the water, however, is enforceable and easily implemented.

Note, the preamble to Part 4 of *The Racing Rules of Sailing* states that rule 55 *"applies at all times when boats are on the water."* And if the rule is broken when not *racing*, rule 64.1 says, *"If a boat has broken a rule when not racing, her penalty shall apply to the race sailed nearest in time to that of the incident."* So you can be disqualified from a race already sailed or not yet sailed for breaking this rule. Also note that the rule requires that the act of putting trash in the water be **intentional**, to prevent a boat from being penalized, for example, for capsizing and not being able to retrieve objects that might be categorized as trash.

There are many excellent programs now that support this concept. One that is commonly used at US Sailing championships and other regattas is "Clean

Regattas" run by Sailors for the Sea. For more information, contact:

Sailors for the Sea Clean Regattas Program
Sailors for the Sea
449 Thames Street, 300D
Newport, RI 02840

phone: 401 846-8900

info@sailorsforthesea.org
www.sailorsforthesea.org

Hey S, you didn't need to change course to avoid me!
S is right...they've changed rule 18.3(a). PW roke new rule 18.3(a) ecause she forced S to hange course to avoid contact with PL
PW
Yup! And PL gets exonerated under rule 64.1(a) because when PW changed course she forced PL to break rule 18.3(a) which means she did not give PL room to keep clear under rule 16.1

13

Part 5
Protests, Redress, Hearings, Misconduct and Appeals

Part 5 contains all the rules governing who can protest, how to protest, how to ask for redress, how and when a protest or redress hearing should be run, what penalties can be applied and how to appeal (rules 60-71). It is divided into four sections: Section A, Protests; Redress; Rule 69 Action; Section B, Hearings and Decisions; Section C, Gross Misconduct; and Section D, Appeals. I will focus on the Section A and B rules governing *protests* and requests for redress.

Remember that a *protest* is defined as "*An allegation made under rule 61.2 by a boat, a race committee or a protest committee that a boat has broken a **rule**"* (see the definition *Protest*). A *protest*, therefore, is merely a means of bringing a *rules* issue to a hearing after the race where the sailors involved and the members of the protest committee can review the incident and decide how the *rules* apply.

Our sport is premised on competitors doing just that when there is an incident in which neither boat acknowledges being in the wrong. In fact, at the very beginning of the rule book the section entitled Basic Principles; Sportsmanship and the Rules says, "*Competitors in the sport of sailing are governed by a body of **rules** that they are expected to follow **and enforce** (emphasis added)." Protests* that are the result of honest differences of opinions on the *rules* or observations of the incident should never have a negative taint to them. Competitor enforcement of the *rules* is the tradition of our sport, and when the *rules* are not followed, or their application is in question, we owe it to our fellow competitors and ourselves, for the quality and fairness of the racing, to protest.

SECTION A — PROTESTS; REDRESS; RULE 69 ACTION

RULE 60 — RIGHT TO PROTEST; REQUEST REDRESS OR RULE 69 ACTION

RULE 60.1

A boat may

(a) protest another boat, but not for an alleged breach of a rule of Part 2 or rule 31 unless she was involved in or saw the incident; or

(b) request redress.

Any boat that thinks another boat may have broken a *rule* can protest. This can occur during a race, or before or after a race; and it can involve a boat in the same race or one in a different race. Note, however, that the use of the word "may" in rule 60.1 clarifies that it is a boat's choice as to whether or not she protests. A boat cannot be penalized for choosing not to protest.

If you want to protest another boat for breaking a rule of Part 2 (When Boats Meet) or rule 31 (Touching a Mark), you must have been directly involved in the incident or have seen it happen yourself. A *protest* involving a Part 2 rule or rule 31 cannot be initiated by you when you learn about the incident from a "report" by a competitor from another boat in the race, or some other person such as a spectator.

 "What is a 'third-party protest,' and are they allowed?"

If you witness an incident in which you are not involved, and in which you think that at least one of the boats has broken a rule of Part 2 or rule 31, you can protest. It doesn't matter if they have contact or not. In this case you are the "third party." The protest committee will simply call a hearing based on your *protest*, find the facts about what happened in the incident, and penalize any boat that broke a *rule*.

RULE 60.2

A race committee may

(a) protest a boat, but not as a result of information arising from a request for redress or an invalid *protest*, or from a report from an *interested party* other than the representative of the boat herself;

(b) request redress for a boat; or

(c) report to the protest committee requesting action under rule 69.2(a).

However, when the race committee receives a report required by rule 43.1(c) or 78.3, it shall protest the boat.

If the race committee thinks a boat may have broken a *rule*, it may also protest (again, the word "may" is permissive meaning the race committee is under no obligation to protest). Note that it can't protest if it learned of the possible breach from someone who has a close personal interest in the outcome of the protest or who stands to benefit from the protest committee's decision (see the definition *Interested Party*). And it can't protest based on information it learned either in a *protest* that is found to be invalid or in any request for redress.

If the race committee feels a boat may be entitled to redress, it can request redress on behalf of that boat. And if it feels the actions of a boat or competitor should be reviewed under rule 69 (Allegations of Gross Misconduct), it can report that to the protest committee. Finally, the race committee is required to protest if they receive a report from an official inspector or measurer under rule 43.1(c) that a competitor may have broken rule 43 (Competitor Clothing and Equipment) or under rule 78.3 that a boat or its equipment does not comply with the class rules (rule 78, Compliance with Class Rules; Certificates).

"Can the race committee score me DSQ if it thinks it saw me cut or hit
a mark?"

No. A boat cannot be penalized without a protest hearing, with a couple of limited exceptions (rule 63.1, Requirement for a Hearing). If the race committee thinks a boat has broken a *rule*, including for instance not sailing the course correctly or touching a mark, etc., and it thinks the boat should have a hearing to consider being penalized, all it can do is **protest** the boat. The protest committee will then call a hearing, find the facts, decide if the boat broke a *rule*, and penalize her if she did.

If a boat fails to *start* or *finish* (i.e., cross the finishing line) correctly, the race committee can score her DNS or OCS or DNF without a hearing (rule A5, Scores Determined by the Race Committee). Similarly, the race committee can also score a boat worse than her actual finish position when the Z Flag Rule (rule 30.2) or Black Flag Rule (rule 30.3) apply, or when the boat takes a Scoring Penalty (rule 44.3). If a boat feels the race committee has scored her incorrectly, the boat can speak directly with the race committee and/or request redress under rule 62.1(a) (Redress). Rule 90.3(c) says, "*When the race committee determines from its own records or observations that it has scored a boat incorrectly, it shall correct the error and make the corrected scores available to competitors.*"

RULE 60.3

A protest committee may

(a) protest a boat, but not as a result of information arising from a request for redress or an invalid *protest*, or from a report from an *interested party* other than the representative of the boat herself. However, it may protest a boat

    (1) if it learns of an incident involving her that may have resulted in injury or serious damage, or

    (2) If during the hearing of a valid *protest* it learns that the boat, although not a *party* to the hearing, was involved in the incident and may have broken a *rule*;

(b) call a hearing to consider redress; or

(c) act under rule 69.2(a).

Similar to the race committee, the protest committee may also protest a boat that may have broken a *rule*. Again, it can't protest if it learned of the possible breach from an *interested party* (see the definition *Interested Party*), nor based on information it learned either in a *protest* that is found to be invalid, or in any request for redress. If the protest committee feels a boat may be entitled to redress, it can call a hearing to consider redress; and if it believes the actions of a boat or competitor should be reviewed under rule 69 (Allegations of Gross Misconduct), it can call a hearing under rule 69.2(a).

The protest committee can also protest a boat in two other situations. One is when it learns of an incident that may have resulted in injury to a person or serious damage to a boat from **any** source, including from an invalid protest or overhearing competitors discussing an incident in the parking lot. See the discussion of rule 44.1 for a discussion of the terms "injury" and "serious damage."

The other situation is when the protest committee is hearing a valid *protest* and in the course of the hearing it learns that another boat involved in the incident, but not currently a *party* to that hearing, may have broken a *rule* in that incident. If the protest committee wishes to protest that boat, rule 61.1(c) says, *"If the protest committee decides to protest a boat under rule 60.3(a)(2), it shall inform her as soon as reasonably possible, close the current hearing, proceed as required by rules 61.2 and 63, and hear the original and the new protests together."* In other words, the protest committee must stop the current hearing, inform the boat it is being protested **in writing** clearly identifying the reason for the *protest* (rule 61.2, Protest Contents), inform all the boats involved of the time and place of the new hearing, and give the boat time to prepare for the hearing (rule 63.2, Time and Place of the Hearing; Time for Parties to Prepare).

RULE 61 — PROTEST REQUIREMENTS

RULE 61.1 — INFORMING THE PROTESTEE

(a) A boat intending to protest shall inform the other boat at the first reasonable opportunity. When her *protest* will concern an incident in the racing area that she was involved in or saw, she shall hail 'Protest' and conspicuously display a red flag at the first reasonable opportunity for each. She shall display the flag until she is no longer *racing*. However,

   (1) if the other boat is beyond hailing distance, the protesting boat need not hail but she shall inform the other boat at the first reasonable opportunity;

   (2) if the hull length of the protesting boat is less than 6 metres, she need not display a red flag;

   (3) if the incident was an error by the other boat in sailing the course, she need not hail or display a red flag but she shall inform the other

boat before that boat *finishes* or at the first reasonable opportunity after she *finishes*;

(4) if the incident results in damage or injury that is obvious to the boats involved and one of them intends to protest, the requirements of this rule do not apply to her, but she shall attempt to inform the other boat within the time limit of rule 61.3.

(b) If the race committee or protest committee intends to protest a boat concerning an incident the committee observed in the racing area, it shall inform her after the race within the time limit of rule 61.3. In other cases the committee shall inform the boat of its intention to protest as soon as reasonably possible.

When you are involved in or see an incident in the racing area and you want to protest, you have to:

• hail the word "Protest" at the first reasonable opportunity (unless the other boat wouldn't be able to hear your hail in which case you have to tell the other boat at the first reasonable chance you have that you intend to protest them); and

• if you are sailing a boat whose hull is six meters (19.68 feet) or longer, conspicuously display a red flag at the first reasonable opportunity.

Notice that rule 61.1(a) says you "shall" do these things. "Shall" means it is mandatory. If you do not correctly do these two things, your *protest* will not be valid and no hearing on the incident should occur. Rule 63.5 (Validity of the Protest or Request for Redress) states clearly, "*At the beginning of the hearing the protest committee shall take any evidence it considers necessary to decide whether all requirements for the **protest** or request for redress have been met. If they have been met, the **protest** or request is valid and the hearing shall be continued. If not, the committee shall declare the **protest** or request invalid and close the hearing.*"

There are two exception to the hail and flag requirements. If it is "obvious" to the boats involved that the incident results in any damage to a boat or injury to a person, then if one of the boats involved chooses to protest, she does not need to hail "Protest" or fly a flag (rule 61.1(a)(4)). However, she must still try to inform the boat(s) being protested within the time limit for lodging protests that a *protest* will be lodged. The idea is that when there is an incident that clearly results in damage or injury, the boats are clearly aware of it, and should be aware that one or more boats involved broke a *rule*. Often the focus of the situation is on separating the boats, checking the extent of the damage or injury, and getting on with the race if possible, etc. To require competitors to also make mandatory hails and fly flags in order to have the incident go to a protest hearing seemed unnecessary and undesirable. However, to be on the safe side, I would recommend that all boats considering protesting make the required hail and fly the flag if required to ensure that their *protest* will be heard.

The other exception is when you see a boat skip a *mark* or go around a *mark* the wrong way. Rule 61.1(a)(3) says, "*if the incident was an error by the other boat in sailing the course, [a boat intending to protest] need not hail or display a red flag but she shall inform the other boat before that boat finishes or at the first reasonable opportunity after she finishes.*"

THE HAIL

Note that you must use the actual word "Protest." Telling another boat to "do your penalty turns!" does not satisfy this rule. The purpose of the requirement is to be sure that the other boat clearly knows you intend to protest her. As with other mandatory hails in the *rules*, the hail should be loud and clear, and it should be unambiguous as to which boat is being protested. When there could be confusion, I strongly suggest including in the hail the boat's number or name, or the person's name if you know it. Note that if the protest committee decides that you did not hail as required by rule 61.1(a), it is required to declare the protest invalid and close the hearing (rule 63.5, Validity of the Protest or Request for Redress).

The hail must be made at "the first reasonable opportunity" after you become aware of the incident. Though some may exist, it is very difficult to imagine a situation in which the first reasonable opportunity to say the word "Protest" isn't **immediately** after the incident. Remember that you can always decide not to go through with a *protest*, including for the reason that you just aren't sure who it was that fouled you. But if you don't say the word "Protest" at the time of the incident, you lose the opportunity to protest that incident. Therefore, it is always prudent to simply say "Protest" immediately. (See US Sailing Appeal 61.)

Note that the rule anticipates that there may be an instance where the boat you intend to protest is so far away at the time of the incident that there is no way the sailor(s) on that boat could possibly hear a hail. This would depend of course on factors such as the distance between the boats, the amount of wind, and the relationship of the boats to the wind (sound travels farther downwind than upwind). In this case, the rule simply requires you to tell the other boat at the first reasonable chance you have that you intend to protest them. I expect that this exception will typically apply to "third-party" *protests*; i.e., situations where the protestor is not directly involved in the incident but, for instance, sees a boat hit another boat or cut a *mark*.

If you intend to protest based on an incident that either occurred in the racing area without you being aware of it, or did not occur in the racing area, you do not need to say the word "Protest," but you do need to inform the other boat of your intent to protest as soon as is reasonably possible after becoming aware of the incident. The purpose of this rule is to be sure that boats intending to protest make every prompt and reasonable effort to go tell the other boat that a *protest* will be lodged, so that all the boats involved can be prepared and present for the hearing.

 "So is it correct that if I am racing a dinghy I don't need to fly a protest flag to protest; and if that's correct, won't sailors try to get out of protests by saying that they didn't know they were being protested?"

It is correct that if you are racing on a boat less than 20 feet long (6 meters or 19.68 feet to be exact), you do not have to fly a protest flag to protest (unless of course the sailing instructions change rule 61.1(a)). The length refers to the hull length; i.e., from the bow to the stern, and does not include protrusions such as bowsprits, rudders, etc. This will encompass most dinghies, sailboards, catamarans and even some small keel boats.

My opinion is that with no flag requirement, more *protests* will be heard than fewer. Many *protests* get bogged down, and many get disallowed, on the issue of whether the flag was flown quickly enough, leaving the actual *rules* issue unresolved. Not having to endure this frustrating situation should be a welcome relief to competitors and protest committees. Furthermore, often a dinghy was forced to sail a little more slowly or with a little less control while one of its sailors put up the flag, which was both unfair and a reason that often dinghy sailors chose not to protest.

In an incident, the boats are typically near each other such that a quick and audible hail of the word "Protest" should clearly inform the other boat that it is being protested. In college racing, where thousands of races a year have been run successfully for over fifty years with no protest flag requirement, when protestors say they hailed "Protest," the protest committees take them at their word unless the protestee can satisfy the protest committees otherwise. This puts an end to the nefarious claims that the "protestor did not hail." But sailors who say they hailed "Protest" when they know full well that they did not, do themselves and the sport a great disservice, and typically that lack of integrity catches up with them.

THE FLAG

Now, in the event you are required to fly a flag to protest, let's look at the flag requirements (rule 61.1(a), Informing the Protestee). When you are aware of an incident as it occurs in the racing area and want to protest because of it, you must conspicuously display a red flag at the first reasonable opportunity. Again, the purpose of the requirement is to provide a visual signal to the other boat that you intend to protest her. The Appeals are loud and clear throughout that if you are required to fly a flag and do not, then the protest committee cannot hear your *protest*. Notice that even if the incident involves a breach of a class rule or sailing instructions, etc., you must display your flag. (See rule 63.5, Validity of the Protest or Request for Redress, ISAF Case 39 and US Sailing Appeal 67.)

On the other hand, if you intend to protest because of an incident that either occurred in the racing area without you being aware of it, or did not occur in the racing area, you do not need to display a flag. Remember that you do need to inform the competitor that you intend to protest at the first reasonable opportunity after becoming aware of the incident.

"Just how quickly do I need to get my flag up?"

Rule 61.1(a) requires that it be displayed "at the first reasonable opportunity." My best advice is that the "first reasonable opportunity" is normally **immediately** after the incident. Remember that the purpose of the rule is to provide a visual signal to the other boat, and to any other boats in the incident or vicinity, that you intend to protest because of **that** incident. Any delay at all only raises the likelihood that the boat being protested won't be aware of that fact, or that it won't be clear for which incident your flag is being displayed.

The timeliness of the flag issue is the cause of some acrimony in our sport, generally arising when a boat's protest is refused because the protest committee decides that her flag was not displayed soon enough after the incident. Often it is suggested that the flag requirement is less important when the other boat is fully aware of the protesting boat's intent to protest; e.g., after a collision and an immediate hail of "Protest." I agree that it is frustrating when a *protest* is refused on a technicality rather than resolving the rules issue contained in the *protest*. But the *rules* are carefully worded to provide safe and fair racing, and that would be undermined if protest and appeals committees were permitted to overlook the requirements in *rules* when they decide that the "intent" of the *rule* was satisfied.

With a little attention and preparation, each boat can prepare a flag that can be easily displayed (Velcro is wonderful), and find a reasonable and convenient place to store their flag during a race so that members of the crew know where it is and so it can be displayed very quickly after an incident with a minimum of hassle (when all else fails put it in your windsuit pocket or rolled up around your backstay). You may never use it, but if you do and you put it up immediately after an incident, you will not have your *protest* refused for that reason.

As for examples of when it might be reasonable to delay the display of the flag for a brief time, in my opinion it would be reasonable to delay the display of the flag after a big collision until just after you and your crew finish checking to be sure things were okay; or could stop hiking without risk of capsizing, or when setting the spinnaker, when all hands were no longer involved putting it up. However, if after the collision or during the spinnaker set, at least one crew member is not doing anything, it is reasonable to expect that he or she can display the flag. Delaying because the flag is in the ditty bag, which is up in the bow under the anchor, is not reasonable to me. (See US Sailing Appeal 67 and 82).

 "Can I just fly anything red and call it a protest flag?"

Absolutely not. ISAF Case 72 reads, "QUESTION: What is the test of whether an object is a flag within the meaning of rule 61.1(a)? ANSWER: In the context of rule 61.1(a), a flag is used as a signal to communicate the message 'I intend to protest.' Only if the object used as a flag communicates that message, with little or no possibility of causing confusion on the part of those on competing boats, will the object qualify as a flag. A flag must be seen primarily to be a flag." The bottom line is that whatever you display must be RED, and it must be obvious that it's a flag, and not a telltale, baseball-type cap or piece of clothing.

"Does the flag have to be flown on the starboard shroud or anywhere
else in particular?"

No. The flag must simply be "conspicuously displayed." There is no requirement in the rule that the flag need be put anywhere in particular. The test of "conspicuous" is whether the flag is initially highly visible to the protested boat. In many cases the starboard side of the boat may be the worst (least conspicuous) place to display it. Notice also, that the flag can be displayed simply by holding it up and waving it at the other boat, which you can do as you head for the location where you will attach it.

Note that "conspicuous" applies not only to the location of the display but to the actual size of the flag. In US Sailing Appeal 66, the Appeals Committee decided that a two-inch by eight-inch flag on a 40-foot boat was not of sufficient size or of suitable proportions to be "conspicuously displayed."

Also notice that you must keep your flag displayed until you are no longer *racing*; i.e., until you have *finished* and cleared the finishing line and *marks* or retired. If your flag blows off your shroud while you are still *racing*, **you can't protest**. My advice is to devise a good system and carry a spare. If your incident occurs so close to the finishing line that the first reasonable opportunity to display the flag doesn't occur until after you are no longer *racing*, I'd say you still need to display your flag because the incident occurred "in the racing area;" and that it would be prudent, though not required, to ensure that the race committee sees that you have displayed your flag.

"If the race or protest committee is going to protest me, do they have
to hail 'Protest' at the time of the incident as well?"

No. If the incident they observe occurs in the racing area, they need to inform you of their intention to protest you after the race and within the time limit for lodging protests, and they need to deliver their written *protest* to the race office within that time limit as well. If the incident does not occur in the racing area, then they need to inform you as soon as reasonably possible, and deliver their *protest* within two hours of learning of the possible *rules* breach (see rules 61.1(b) and 61.3, Protest Time Limit).

RULE 61.2 – PROTEST CONTENTS

A *protest* shall be in writing and identify

(a) the protestor and protestee;

(b) the incident, including where and when it occurred;

(c) any *rule* the protestor believes was broken; and

(d) the name of the protestor's representative.

However, if requirement (b) is met, requirement (a) may be met at any time before the hearing, and requirements (c) and (d) may be met before or during the hearing.

Rule 61.2 clearly lists the details about the *protest*. Notice that the *protest* must be **in writing**. Also notice that the only detail that cannot be corrected once the time limit for lodging *protests* is past is an omission of a description of the incident itself. Therefore, be sure you clearly identify the incident, including where and when it occurred (ISAF Case 80).

RULE 61.3 – PROTEST TIME LIMIT

A *protest* by a boat, or by the race committee or protest committee about an incident the committee observes in the racing area, shall be delivered to the race office within the time limit stated in the sailing instructions. If none is stated, the time limit is two hours after the last boat in the race *finishes*. Other race committee or protest committee *protests* shall be delivered to the race office no later than two hours after the committee receives the relevant information. The protest committee shall extend the time if there is good reason to do so.

Notice that the first place to look for the time limit for lodging a *protest* is the sailing instructions. If the sailing instructions are silent, then the default time limit in rule 61.3 is "two hours after the last boat in the race *finishes.*"

Also notice that the protest committee **must** extend the time limit is there is a good reason to do so. This may be useful to you if you have made every reasonable effort to deliver your *protest* in time but were unable to do so for good reason.

RULE 62 — REDRESS

RULE 62.1 — A request for redress or a protest committee's decision to consider redress shall be based on a claim or possibility that a boat's score in a race or series has been or may be, through no fault of her own, made significantly worse by

(a) an improper action or omission of the race committee, protest committee, organizing authority, equipment inspection committee or measurement committee for the event, but not by a protest committee decision when the boat was a *party* to the hearing;

(b) injury or physical damage because of the action of a boat that was breaking a rule of Part 2 or of a vessel not *racing* that was required to keep clear;

(c) giving help (except to herself or her crew) in compliance with rule 1.1; or

(d) an action of a boat, or a member of her crew, that resulted in a penalty under rule 2 or a penalty or warning under rule 69.2(c).

"Redress" is a form of compensation the protest committee can give boats when they have lost finishing places or time as a result of certain circumstances that were out of their control. Rule 62.1 lists the four specific circumstances under which a boat can request redress. If something else makes a boat's finishing score worse, it is tough luck. Two examples are (1) when a boat fouls you and the boats get locked together for a time but there is no physical damage or injury; and (2) when a boat fails to give you *mark-room* and you are forced to the wrong side of the *mark* in order not to hit them. These unfortunate situations always remind me of the old saying, "he was in the right as he sped along; but he's just as dead as though he were wrong."

Note that in order to be entitled to redress, your score in the race or series has to have been, or will be, made significantly worse. In other words, if the sailing instructions specify that marks will be yellow and the race committee uses orange marks instead, this is an "improper action;" but if you sailed the course with no confusion, your finishing score wasn't made worse by the "improper action" of the race committee; therefore, you are not entitled to redress.

Finally note that your finishing score has to be worsened by one of the four circumstances in rule 62.1 **and** "through no fault of your own." For instance, if you know you are over the starting line early (OCS) but the race committee fails to signal your OCS properly, and you don't come back and *start*, the race committee made an "improper action," but you also contributed to your OCS score because you knew you had not *started* the race and chose to break rule 28.1 (Sailing the Course) (see ISAF Cases 31 and 71). Another example is when the leeward *mark* is drifting downwind, but instead of rounding it and *finishing*, you drop out of the race and request redress. You caused your finishing score to be DNF, so you cannot get redress for the *mark* being out of position. See US Sailing Appeal 68.

 "OK, so what do I have to do to request redress?"

RULE 62.2 – A request shall be in writing and identify the reason for making it. If the request is based on an incident in the racing area, it shall be delivered to the race office within the protest time limit or two hours after the incident, whichever is later. Other requests shall be delivered as soon as reasonably possible after learning of the reasons for making the request. The protest committee shall extend the time if there is good reason to do so. No red flag is required.

Rule 62.2 says that you have to make a **written** request for redress which clearly identifies the incident you think justifies you receiving redress. You can use the standard protest form available at most regattas, which has a box to check indicating you are requesting redress. Keep in mind, if your request is based on a claim that the race committee did something wrong, you are not "protesting" the race committee; you are simply requesting redress based on their action (see ISAF Case 44). You do not need to fly a red flag or do anything special on the water to request redress. If the incident happened in the racing area, you need to file your request within the protest time limit or two hours after the incident, whichever is later. For other requests, file them as soon as reasonably possible after learning of the reasons for making the request. See ISAF Case 102 and US Sailing Appeal 90.

 "Can you walk me through the four circumstances that might entitle me to redress?"

Sure.

RULE 62.1(a) – These are circumstances where a committee does something it is not supposed to do, or fails to do something it is supposed to do. Note that if the sailing instructions say the race committee "will" do something and it fails to, or does something else instead, that is an "improper action or omission" of the race committee. If the protest committee fails to follow the procedures for a hearing in Part 5, Section B of *The Racing Rules of Sailing*, that too is an "improper action." And if the organizing authority for an event for instance supplies the boats, and one of them is defective, that is an "improper action" of the organizing authority.

Note that if you are a *party* in a hearing and you do not agree with the protest committee decision (as opposed to its procedures), you cannot request redress. Your only two options are to request that the hearing be reopened (see rule 66, Reopening a Hearing), or appeal (see rule 70.1, Appeals and Requests to a National Authority, and Appendix R, Procedures for Appeals and Requests). See also US Sailing Appeal 68 and ISAF Cases 31 and 71.

RULE 62.1(b) – This is the circumstance where your boat has been physically damaged or someone on your boat has been injured by a boat that was required to *keep clear* of you under Part 2 of the racing rules (When Boats Meet) or a non-racing boat required to keep clear under the government right-of-way rules for the area in which you are sailing. Note that this does not apply in the circumstance where a keep-clear boat has made you lose time or positions by forcing you off course or forcing you on the wrong side of a *mark* or even capsizing you. This applies only when something on the boat was physically broken ("damaged") as a direct result of the keep-clear boat, and that damage directly caused the boat to finish worse than she would have had there been no damage (see ISAF Case 110).

RULE 62.1(c) – This is the circumstance where you give assistance to someone in trouble.

Remember, Rule 1.1 (Helping Those in Danger) says, "*A boat or competitor shall give all possible help to any person or vessel in danger.*" When you lose finishing places or time as a result of giving help, you are entitled to compensation ("redress") for that. See the discussion of rule 1.1 and ISAF Case 20.

RULE 62.1(d) – This is the circumstance where someone has done something bad enough to break rule 2 (Fair Sailing) or receive a warning or penalty under rule 69.2(c) (Allegations of Gross Misconduct; Action by a Protest Committee) and their action adversely affected you. An example is a boat cuts a *mark* and sits on your wind causing you to lose ten places. You would need to protest them for breaking rule 28.1 (Sailing the Course) and rule 2, claiming it was an intentional infringement. You could suggest that it also warranted a hearing under rule 69, but that would ultimately be up to the protest committee to decide. Assuming the boat was found to have broken rule 2, and/or received a warning or penalty under rule 69.2(c), and assuming the protest committee decided that the boat's action directly caused your score to be significantly worse through no fault of your own, you are entitled to redress. See ISAF Case 34.

"Thanks. So when the protest committee decides I am entitled to redress, what do they do?"

Once the protest committee decides that a boat is entitled to redress, they turn to rule 64.2 (Decisions on Redress).

RULE 64.2 – When the protest committee decides that a boat is entitled to redress under rule 62, it shall make as fair an arrangement as possible for all boats affected, whether or not they asked for redress. This may be to adjust the scoring (see rule A10 for some examples) or finishing times of boats, to *abandon* the race, to let the results stand or to make some other arrangement. When in doubt about the facts or probable results of any arrangement for the race or series, especially before *abandoning* the race, the protest committee shall take evidence from appropriate sources.

US Sailing Appeal 68 says, "…rule 64.2 requires the protest committee to 'make as fair an arrangement as possible for all boats affected.' This might be to adjust the finishing time, to add some number of places to her actual or average finishing place, to reinstate her in her finishing place, or to make some other adjustment that conforms to rule 64.2." Clearly, rule 64.2 gives a protest committee tremendous discretion to do whatever it thinks is fairest for all the boats that will be affected by the arrangement the protest committee decides to make, whether or not they asked for redress. The last sentence of rule 64.2 reminds protest committees to take appropriate evidence before making its decision when it has some questions as to the facts or probable results of any arrangement for the race or series. See ISAF Cases 31 and 71.

Rule A10 (Guidance on Redress) gives protest committees some suggestions.

A10 — GUIDANCE ON REDRESS

If the protest committee decides to give redress by adjusting a boat's score for a race, it is advised to consider scoring her

(a) **points equal to the average, to the nearest tenth of a point (0.05 to be rounded upward), of her points in all the races in the series except the race in question;**

(b) **points equal to the average, to the nearest tenth of a point (0.05 to be rounded upward), of her points in all the races before the race in question; or**

(c) **points based on the position of the boat in the race at the time of the incident that justified redress.**

"If a boat is requesting redress, am I entitled to be in that hearing and give evidence?"

If the US Sailing prescriptions to rules 60 (Right to Protest; Right to Request Redress or Rule 69 Action) and rule 63.2 (Time and Place of the Hearing; Time for Parties to Prepare) are in effect (and they are in effect in the U.S. unless the sailing instructions specifically say they are not; see rule 88.2, National Prescriptions), then you are allowed to request to be a *party* in that redress hearing.

The prescription to rule 60 says, "*US Sailing prescribes that when redress has been requested or is to be considered, any boat may participate in the hearing provided she makes a written request before the hearing begins. When she does so, the protest committee shall act under rule 60.3(b) to consider redress for her at that hearing.*"

And the prescription to rule 63.2 says, "*US Sailing prescribes that when redress has been requested or is to be considered, the protest committee shall make a reasonable attempt to notify all boats of the time and place of the hearing and the nature of the request or the grounds for considering redress.*

Before holding the hearing, the committee shall allow reasonable time for boats to make written requests to participate."

So when the prescriptions are in effect and the protest committee receives a request for redress, the norm is for it to post a copy of the request on the official notice board with the time and place of the hearing, leaving a reasonable amount of time for sailors to make a written request to participate. All sailors who have made the written request must be made *parties* to the hearing by the protest committee, with the full right to give evidence, ask questions, call witnesses and appeal.

THE RACING RULES OF SAILING

for 2013–2016

Including US Sailing Prescriptions

www.ussailing.org

As the leading authority for the sport, the International Sailing Federation promotes and supports the protection of the environment in all sailing competitions and related activities throughout the world.

CONTACT DETAILS:

US Sailing
Post Office Box 1260
15 Maritime Drive
Portsmouth, RI 02871

Tel	+1 401 683 0800
Fax	+1 401 683 0840
Email	**rules@ussailing.org**
Website	**ussailing.org**

International Sailing Federation
Ariadne House
Town Quay, Southampton
Hampshire SO14 2AQ, United Kingdom

Tel	+44 (0) 2380 635111
Fax	+44 (0) 2380 635789
Email	**secretariat@isaf.co.uk**
Website	**sailing.org**

The Racing Rules of Sailing for 2013–2016
Including US Sailing Prescriptions

ISBN: 978-0-201-10179-9

Issue Date: November 2012
Frequency: Quadrennially
Authorizing Organization: US Sailing
Post Office Box 1260, 15 Maritime Drive
Portsmouth, RI 02871
Issue Number: Issue No. 1

A Message from US Sailing's President

The basic purpose of *The Racing Rules of Sailing* is to keep boats safe and provide fair competition. Many dedicated volunteers have worked hard to update the newest edition of *The Racing Rules of Sailing for 2013–2016*. Please take some time to read through the rules. These rules are updated every four years by the International Sailing Federation (ISAF) and US Sailing. There are changes in each edition, so I encourage all sailors to take some time to refresh your memory, and learn what is new. Many sailors find participating in a rules seminar to be a big help. I like to use small model boats on the dining room table to understand different rules.

Sailing is a complex sport with many different types of boats competing on a variety of levels. Some races are short around the course contests and other races are long ocean passages. Boats themselves are different in nature ranging from small dinghies to large maxi yachts, and windsurfers, kiteboards and multihulls are popular sailing craft as well. Adding to the mix are different disciplines including fleet racing, team racing and match racing. Variations of the rules for different types of racing are included in this rulebook. The index at the end of this volume is a helpful guide when searching for specific definitions or rules.

Participating in a protest hearing is never fun for any of the parties involved. Thankfully, we have written rules to help judges and sailors understand what boat is correct in specific situations. Many of the rules I know best are ones that I have been disqualified for in some race early in my career. Protest hearings are learning experiences. If there is a question about the application of the rules by a protest committee, we have an appeals process, and reading the appeals is a great way to learn the rules. This rulebook is also available as an app from US Sailing. This is an efficient way to find and read the rules.

I have long said that the most important thing in sailing is to simply have fun on the water. *The Racing Rules of Sailing* helps define our routine when competing, and keeps the racing fun. On behalf of US Sailing, I would like to thank the companies advertising in this rulebook for sponsoring *The Racing Rules of Sailing for 2013–2016*.

Sincerely,

Thomas Hubbell, President of US Sailing

Foreword

This 2013–2016 edition of *The Racing Rules of Sailing* was produced by US Sailing under license from the International Sailing Federation (ISAF) and is the result of four years of careful review of the 2009–2012 rules. There are significant changes for 2013–2016, especially in Section C of Part 2 (the rules that apply at Marks and Obstructions) and in the definition *Mark-Room*.

In addition to the ISAF rules, this rulebook contains 'prescriptions', which are rules adopted by US Sailing for events held in the United States. These prescriptions appear throughout this book in *bold italics*. They do not apply when racing at a regatta in another country; in that case, refer to the prescriptions in that country's rulebook.

One new prescription is *Appendix T, Alternative Procedures for Dispute Resolution*. This appendix was written in response to a widespread concern that the rules are not being followed and enforced adequately by competitors, partly because of the daunting structure of protests and penalties. Appendix T provides for voluntary scoring penalties to be taken after finishing, a streamlined procedure for quick protest hearings, and arbitration. These provisions can each be invoked by simple one-line sailing instructions, and we are hoping that organizing authorities will try these new ideas and report back to us with evaluations and comments. If Appendix T is successful, the US Sailing Racing Rules Committee anticipates proposing its provisions to ISAF as international rules for the 2017–2020 *Racing Rules of Sailing*.

Note also that the prescription detailing the US Appeals process has been moved to Appendix R. Appendix F now contains the rules for kiteboard racing.

Many of the rule changes in this book are the result of suggestions from competitors and race officials. The US Sailing Racing Rules Committee welcomes your ideas on how to improve the racing rules for the next rulebook. Please e-mail comments and proposals to rules@ussailing.org, or mail them to the US Sailing Racing Rules Committee, P. O. Box 1260, Portsmouth, RI 02871-0907.

Rob Overton, Chairman, US Sailing Racing Rules Committee
Ben Altman, Jim Capron, David Dellenbaugh, Arthur Engel, Scott Ikle, Matt Knowles, Dick Rose, Mary Savage

Contents

Online Rules Documents

ISAF has established a single internet address at which readers will find links to all the online rules documents mentioned in this book. Those documents are listed below.

The address is: **sailing.org/racingrules/documents**.

Links to documents referred to in US Sailing prescriptions and notes can be found at: **ussailing.org/racingrules/documents**.

Links to other rules documents will also be provided at each of these addresses.

Introduction

The Racing Rules of Sailing includes two main sections. The first, Parts 1–7, contains rules that affect all competitors. The second, the appendices, provides details of rules, rules that apply to particular kinds of racing, and rules that affect only a small number of competitors or officials.

Revision The racing rules are revised and published every four years by the International Sailing Federation (ISAF), the international authority for the sport. This edition becomes effective on 1 January 2013 except that for an event beginning in 2012 the date may be postponed by the notice of race and sailing instructions. Marginal markings indicate important changes to Parts 1–7 and the Definitions of the 2009–2012 edition. No changes are contemplated before 2017, but any changes determined to be urgent before then will be announced through national authorities and posted on the ISAF website.

ISAF Codes The ISAF Eligibility, Advertising, Anti-Doping and Sailor Classification Codes (Regulations 19, 20, 21 and 22) are referred to in the definition *Rule* but are not included in this book because they can be changed at any time. The most recent versions of the codes are available on the ISAF website; new versions will be announced through national authorities.

Cases and Calls The ISAF publishes interpretations of the racing rules in *The Case Book for 2013–2016* and recognizes them as authoritative interpretations and explanations of the rules. It also publishes *The Call Book for Match Racing for 2013–2016* and *The Call Book for Team Racing for 2013–2016*, and it recognizes them as authoritative only for umpired match or team racing. These publications are available on the ISAF website.

Terminology A term used in the sense stated in the Definitions is printed in italics or, in preambles, in bold italics (for example, *racing* and **racing**). 'Racing rule' means a rule in *The Racing Rules of Sailing*. 'Boat' means a sailboat and the crew on board; 'vessel' means any boat or ship. 'Race committee' includes any person or committee performing a race committee function. A 'change' to a *rule* includes an addition to it or deletion of all or part of it. 'National authority' means an ISAF member national authority. Other words and terms are used in the sense ordinarily understood in nautical or general use.

Appendices When the rules of an appendix apply, they take precedence over any conflicting rules in Parts 1–7 and the Definitions. Each appendix is identified by a letter. A reference to a rule in an appendix will contain the letter and the rule number (for example, 'rule A1'). The letters I, O and Q are not used to designate appendices in this book.

Changes to the Rules The prescriptions of a national authority, class rules or the sailing instructions may change a racing rule only as permitted in rule 86.

Changes to National Authority Prescriptions A national authority may restrict changes to its prescriptions as provided in rule 88.2.

***Prescriptions** US Sailing prescriptions are printed in bold italics, except Appendices R, S and T. Those three appendices are US Sailing prescriptions.*

Equal Opportunity

As the national authority for the sport of sailing, US Sailing is committed to providing an equal opportunity to all sailors to participate in the sport of sailing.

Definitions

*A term used as stated below is shown in italic type or, in preambles, in **bold italic** type.*

Abandon A race that a race committee or protest committee *abandons* is void but may be resailed.

Clear Astern and **Clear Ahead; Overlap** One boat is *clear astern* of another when her hull and equipment in normal position are behind a line abeam from the aftermost point of the other boat's hull and equipment in normal position. The other boat is *clear ahead*. They *overlap* when neither is *clear astern*. However, they also *overlap* when a boat between them *overlaps* both. These terms always apply to boats on the same *tack*. They do not apply to boats on opposite *tacks* unless rule 18 applies or both boats are sailing more than ninety degrees from the true wind.

Fetching A boat is *fetching* a *mark* when she is in a position to pass to windward of it and leave it on the required side without changing *tack*.

Finish A boat *finishes* when any part of her hull, or crew or equipment in normal position, crosses the finishing line from the course side. However, she has not *finished* if after crossing the finishing line she

    (a)   takes a penalty under rule 44.2,

    (b)   corrects an error under rule 28.2 made at the line, or

    (c)   continues to sail the course.

Interested Party A person who may gain or lose as a result of a protest committee's decision, or who has a close personal interest in the decision.

Keep Clear A boat *keeps clear* of a right-of-way boat

    (a)   if the right-of-way boat can sail her course with no need to take avoiding action and,

    (b)   when the boats are *overlapped*, if the right-of-way boat can also change course in both directions without immediately making contact.

Leeward and **Windward** A boat's *leeward* side is the side that is or, when she is head to wind, was away from the wind. However, when sailing by the lee or directly downwind, her *leeward* side is the side on which her mainsail lies. The other side is her *windward* side. When two boats on the same *tack overlap*, the one on the *leeward* side of the other is the *leeward* boat. The other is the *windward* boat.

Mark An object the sailing instructions require a boat to leave on a specified side, and a race committee boat surrounded by navigable water from which the starting or finishing line extends. An anchor line or an object attached accidentally to a *mark* is not part of it.

Mark-Room *Room* for a boat to leave a *mark* on the required side. Also,

    (a)   *room* to sail to the *mark* when her *proper course* is to sail close to it, and

    (b)   *room* to round the *mark* as necessary to sail the course.

However, *mark-room* for a boat does not include *room* to tack unless she is *overlapped* inside and to *windward* of the boat required to give *mark-room* and she would be *fetching* the *mark* after her tack.

Obstruction An object that a boat could not pass without changing course substantially, if she were sailing directly towards it and one of her hull lengths from it. An object that can be safely passed on only one side and an area so designated by the sailing instructions are also *obstructions*. However, a boat *racing* is not an *obstruction* to other boats unless they are required to *keep clear* of her or, if rule 23 applies, avoid her. A vessel under way, including a boat *racing*, is never a continuing *obstruction*.

Overlap See **Clear Astern** and **Clear Ahead; Overlap**.

Party A *party* to a hearing is

    (a) for a protest hearing: a protestor, a protestee;

    (b) for a request for redress: a boat requesting redress or for which redress is requested, a race committee acting under rule 60.2(b);

    (c) for a request for redress under rule 62.1(a): the body alleged to have made an improper action or omission;

    (d) a boat or a competitor that may be penalized under rule 69.2.

However, the protest committee is never a *party*.

Postpone A *postponed* race is delayed before its scheduled start but may be started or *abandoned* later.

Proper Course A course a boat would sail to *finish* as soon as possible in the absence of the other boats referred to in the rule using the term. A boat has no *proper course* before her starting signal.

Protest An allegation made under rule 61.2 by a boat, a race committee or a protest committee that a boat has broken a *rule*.

Racing A boat is *racing* from her preparatory signal until she *finishes* and clears the finishing line and *marks* or retires, or until the race committee signals a general recall, *postponement* or *abandonment*.

Room The space a boat needs in the existing conditions, including space to comply with her obligations under the rules of Part 2 and rule 31, while manoeuvring promptly in a seamanlike way.

Rule (a) The rules in this book, including the Definitions, Race Signals, Introduction, preambles and the rules of relevant appendices, but not titles;

    (b) ISAF Regulation 19, Eligibility Code; Regulation 20, Advertising Code; Regulation 21, Anti-Doping Code; and Regulation 22, Sailor Classification Code;

    (c) the prescriptions of the national authority, unless they are changed by the sailing instructions in compliance with the national authority's prescription, if any, to rule 88.2;

    (d) the class rules (for a boat racing under a handicap or rating system, the rules of that system are 'class rules');

    (e) the notice of race;

    (f) the sailing instructions; and

    (g) any other documents that govern the event.

Start A boat *starts* when, having been entirely on the pre-start side of the starting line at or after her starting signal, and having complied with rule 30.1 if it applies, any part of her hull, crew or equipment crosses the starting line in the direction of the first *mark*.

Tack, Starboard or Port A boat is on the *tack, starboard* or *port*, corresponding to her *windward* side.

Windward See **Leeward** and **Windward**.

Zone The area around a *mark* within a distance of three hull lengths of the boat nearer to it. A boat is in the *zone* when any part of her hull is in the *zone*.

Basic Principles

SPORTSMANSHIP AND THE RULES

Competitors in the sport of sailing are governed by a body of *rules* that they are expected to follow and enforce. A fundamental principle of sportsmanship is that when competitors break a *rule* they will promptly take a penalty, which may be to retire.

ENVIRONMENTAL RESPONSIBILITY

Participants are encouraged to minimize any adverse environmental impact of the sport of sailing.

Part 1 — Fundamental Rules

1 SAFETY

1.1 Helping Those in Danger

A boat or competitor shall give all possible help to any person or vessel in danger.

1.2 Life-Saving Equipment and Personal Flotation Devices

A boat shall carry adequate life-saving equipment for all persons on board, including one item ready for immediate use, unless her class rules make some other provision. Each competitor is individually responsible for wearing a personal flotation device adequate for the conditions.

2 FAIR SAILING

A boat and her owner shall compete in compliance with recognized principles of sportsmanship and fair play. A boat may be penalized under this rule only if it is clearly established that these principles have been violated. A disqualification under this rule shall not be excluded from the boat's series score.

3 ACCEPTANCE OF THE RULES

By participating in a race conducted under these racing rules, each competitor and boat owner agrees

(a) to be governed by the *rules*;

(b) to accept the penalties imposed and other action taken under the *rules*, subject to the appeal and review procedures provided in them, as the final determination of any matter arising under the *rules*; and

(c) with respect to any such determination, not to resort to any court of law or tribunal.

4 DECISION TO RACE

The responsibility for a boat's decision to participate in a race or to continue *racing* is hers alone.

5 ANTI-DOPING

A competitor shall comply with the World Anti-Doping Code, the rules of the World Anti-Doping Agency, and ISAF Regulation 21, Anti-Doping Code. An alleged or actual breach of this rule shall be dealt with under Regulation 21. It shall not be grounds for a *protest* and rule 63.1 does not apply.

Part 2 — When Boats Meet

The rules of Part 2 apply between boats that are sailing in or near the racing area and intend to **race**, *are* **racing**, *or have been* **racing**. *However, a boat not* **racing** *shall not be penalized for breaking one of these rules, except rule 24.1.*

When a boat sailing under these rules meets a vessel that is not, she shall comply with the International Regulations for Preventing Collisions at Sea (IRPCAS) *or government right-of-way rules. If the sailing instructions so state, the rules of Part 2 are replaced by the right-of-way rules of the* IRPCAS *or by government right-of-way rules.*

Section A — Right of Way

A boat has right of way over another boat when the other boat is required to **keep clear** *of her. However, some rules in Sections B, C and D limit the actions of a right-of-way boat.*

10   ON OPPOSITE TACKS

When boats are on opposite *tacks*, a *port-tack* boat shall *keep clear* of a *starboard-tack* boat.

11   ON THE SAME TACK, OVERLAPPED

When boats are on the same *tack* and *overlapped*, a *windward* boat shall *keep clear* of a *leeward* boat.

12   ON THE SAME TACK, NOT OVERLAPPED

When boats are on the same *tack* and not *overlapped*, a boat *clear astern* shall *keep clear* of a boat *clear ahead*.

13   WHILE TACKING

After a boat passes head to wind, she shall *keep clear* of other boats until she is on a close-hauled course. During that time rules 10, 11 and 12 do not apply. If two boats are subject to this rule at the same time, the one on the other's port side or the one astern shall *keep clear*.

Section B — General Limitations

14   AVOIDING CONTACT

A boat shall avoid contact with another boat if reasonably possible. However, a right-of-way boat or one entitled to *room* or *mark-room*

(a)   need not act to avoid contact until it is clear that the other boat is not *keeping clear* or giving *room* or *mark-room*, and

(b)   shall be exonerated if she breaks this rule and the contact does not cause damage or injury.

15   ACQUIRING RIGHT OF WAY

When a boat acquires right of way, she shall initially give the other boat *room* to *keep clear*, unless she acquires right of way because of the other boat's actions.

16   CHANGING COURSE

16.1   When a right-of-way boat changes course, she shall give the other boat *room* to *keep clear*.

16.2   In addition, when after the starting signal a *port-tack* boat is *keeping clear* by sailing to pass astern of a *starboard-tack* boat, the *star-board-tack* boat shall not change course if as a result the *port-tack* boat would immediately need to change course to continue *keeping clear*.

17 ON THE SAME TACK; PROPER COURSE

If a boat *clear astern* becomes *overlapped* within two of her hull lengths to *leeward* of a boat on the same *tack*, she shall not sail above her *proper course* while they remain on the same *tack* and *overlapped* within that distance, unless in doing so she promptly sails astern of the other boat. This rule does not apply if the *overlap* begins while the *windward* boat is required by rule 13 to *keep clear*.

Section C — At Marks and Obstructions

Section C rules do not apply at a starting **mark** *surrounded by navigable water or at its anchor line from the time boats are approaching them to* **start** *until they have passed them.*

18 MARK-ROOM

18.1 When Rule 18 Applies

Rule 18 applies between boats when they are required to leave a *mark* on the same side and at least one of them is in the *zone*. However, it does not apply

(a) between boats on opposite *tacks* on a beat to windward,

(b) between boats on opposite *tacks* when the *proper course* at the *mark* for one but not both of them is to tack,

(c) between a boat approaching a *mark* and one leaving it, or

(d) if the *mark* is a continuing *obstruction*, in which case rule 19 applies.

18.2 Giving Mark-Room

(a) When boats are *overlapped* the outside boat shall give the inside boat *mark-room*, unless rule 18.2(b) applies.

(b) If boats are *overlapped* when the first of them reaches the *zone*, the outside boat at that moment shall thereafter give the inside boat *mark-room*. If a boat is *clear ahead* when she reaches the *zone*, the boat *clear astern* at that moment shall thereafter give her *mark-room*.

(c) When a boat is required to give *mark-room* by rule 18.2(b),

  (1) she shall continue to do so even if later an *overlap* is broken or a new *overlap* begins;

  (2) if she becomes *overlapped* inside the boat entitled to *mark-room*, she shall also give that boat *room* to sail her *proper course* while they remain *overlapped*.

However, if the boat entitled to *mark-room* passes head to wind or leaves the *zone*, rule 18.2(b) ceases to apply.

(d) If there is reasonable doubt that a boat obtained or broke an *overlap* in time, it shall be presumed that she did not.

(e) If a boat obtained an inside *overlap* from *clear astern* or by tacking to *windward* of the other boat and, from the time the *overlap* began, the outside boat has been unable to give *mark-room*, she is not required to give it.

18.3 Tacking in the Zone

If a boat in the *zone* passes head to wind and is then on the same *tack* as a boat that is *fetching* the *mark*, rule 18.2 does not thereafter apply between them. The boat that changed *tack*

(a) shall not cause the other boat to sail above close-hauled to avoid contact or prevent the other boat from passing the *mark* on the required side, and

(b) shall give *mark-room* if the other boat becomes *overlapped* inside her.

18.4 Gybing

When an inside *overlapped* right-of-way boat must gybe at a *mark* to sail her *proper course*, until she gybes she shall sail no farther from the *mark* than needed to sail that course. Rule 18.4 does not apply at a gate *mark*.

19 ROOM TO PASS AN OBSTRUCTION

19.1 When Rule 19 Applies

Rule 19 applies between boats at an *obstruction* except when it is also a *mark* the boats are required to leave on the same side. However, at a continuing *obstruction*, rule 19 always applies and rule 18 does not.

19.2 Giving Room at an Obstruction

(a) A right-of-way boat may choose to pass an *obstruction* on either side.

(b) When boats are *overlapped*, the outside boat shall give the inside boat *room* between her and the *obstruction*, unless she has been unable to do so from the time the *overlap* began.

(c) While boats are passing a continuing *obstruction*, if a boat that was *clear astern* and required to *keep clear* becomes *overlapped* between the other boat and the *obstruction* and, at the moment the *overlap* begins, there is not *room* for her to pass between them, she is not entitled to *room* under rule 19.2(b). While the boats remain *overlapped*, she shall *keep clear* and rules 10 and 11 do not apply.

20 ROOM TO TACK AT AN OBSTRUCTION

20.1 Hailing

When approaching an *obstruction*, a boat may hail for *room* to tack and avoid a boat on the same *tack*. However, she shall not hail if

(a) she can avoid the *obstruction* safely without making a substantial course change,

(b) she is sailing below close-hauled, or

(c) the *obstruction* is a *mark* and a boat that is *fetching* it would be required to respond and change course.

20.2 Responding

(a) After a boat hails, she shall give the hailed boat time to respond.

(b) The hailed boat shall respond even if the hail breaks rule 20.1.

(c) The hailed boat shall respond either by tacking as soon as possible, or by immediately replying 'You tack' and then giving the hailing boat *room* to tack and avoid her.

(d) When the hailed boat responds, the hailing boat shall tack as soon as possible.

(e) From the time a boat hails until she has tacked and avoided the hailed boat, rule 18.2 does not apply between them.

20.3 Passing On a Hail to an Additional Boat

When a boat has been hailed for *room* to tack and she intends to respond by tacking, she may hail another boat on the same *tack* for *room* to tack and avoid her. She may hail even if her hail does not meet the conditions of rule 20.1. Rule 20.2 applies between her and the boat she hails.

21 EXONERATION

When a boat is sailing within the *room* or *mark-room* to which she is entitled under a rule of Section C, she shall be exonerated if, in an incident with a boat required to give her that *room* or *mark-room*,

(a)   she breaks a rule of Section A, rule 15 or rule 16, or

(b)   she is compelled to break rule 31.

Section D — Other Rules

When rule 22 or 23 applies between two boats, Section A rules do not.

22   STARTING ERRORS; TAKING PENALTIES; MOVING ASTERN

22.1   A boat sailing towards the pre-start side of the starting line or one of its extensions after her starting signal to *start* or to comply with rule 30.1 shall *keep clear* of a boat not doing so until she is completely on the pre-start side.

22.2   A boat taking a penalty shall *keep clear* of one that is not.

22.3   A boat moving astern through the water by backing a sail shall *keep clear* of one that is not.

23   CAPSIZED, ANCHORED OR AGROUND; RESCUING

If possible, a boat shall avoid a boat that is capsized or has not regained control after capsizing, is anchored or aground, or is trying to help a person or vessel in danger. A boat is capsized when her masthead is in the water.

24   INTERFERING WITH ANOTHER BOAT

24.1   If reasonably possible, a boat not *racing* shall not interfere with a boat that is *racing*.

24.2   Except when sailing her *proper course*, a boat shall not interfere with a boat taking a penalty or sailing on another leg.

Part 3 — Conduct of a Race

25   NOTICE OF RACE, SAILING INSTRUCTIONS AND SIGNALS

25.1   The notice of race and sailing instructions shall be made available to each boat before a race begins.

25.2   The meanings of the visual and sound signals stated in Race Signals shall not be changed except under rule 86.1(b). The meanings of any other signals that may be used shall be stated in the sailing instructions.

25.3   A race committee may display a visual signal by using either a flag or other object of a similar appearance.

26   STARTING RACES

Races shall be started by using the following signals. Times shall be taken from the visual signals; the absence of a sound signal shall be disregarded.

Minutes before starting signal	Visual signal	Sound signal	Means
5*	Class flag	One	Warning*
4	P, I, Z, Z with I, or black flag	One	Preparatory
1	Preparatory flag removed	One long	One minute
0	Class flag removed	One	Starting signal

*or as stated in the sailing instructions

The warning signal for each succeeding class shall be made with or after the starting signal of the preceding class.

27 OTHER RACE COMMITTEE ACTIONS BEFORE THE STARTING SIGNAL

27.1 No later than the warning signal, the race committee shall signal or otherwise designate the course to be sailed if the sailing instructions have not stated the course, and it may replace one course signal with another and signal that wearing personal flotation devices is required (display flag Y with one sound).

27.2 No later than the preparatory signal, the race committee may move a starting *mark*.

27.3 Before the starting signal, the race committee may for any reason *postpone* (display flag AP, AP over H, or AP over A, with two sounds) or *abandon* the race (display flag N over H, or N over A, with three sounds).

28 SAILING THE COURSE

28.1 A boat shall *start*, sail the course described in the sailing instructions and *finish*. While doing so, she may leave on either side a *mark* that does not begin, bound or end the leg she is sailing. After *finishing* she need not cross the finishing line completely.

28.2 A string representing a boat's track from the time she begins to approach the starting line from its pre-start side to *start* until she *finishes* shall, when drawn taut,

(a) pass each *mark* on the required side and in the correct order,

(b) touch each rounding *mark*, and

(c) pass between the *marks* of a gate from the direction of the previous *mark*.

She may correct any errors to comply with this rule, provided she has not *finished*.

29 RECALLS

29.1 Individual Recall

When at a boat's starting signal any part of her hull, crew or equipment is on the course side of the starting line or she must comply with rule 30.1, the race committee shall promptly display flag X with one sound. The flag shall be displayed until all such boats have sailed completely to the pre-start side of the starting line or one of its extensions and have complied with rule 30.1 if it applies, but no later than four minutes after the starting signal or one minute before any later starting signal, whichever is earlier. If rule 30.3 applies this rule does not.

29.2 General Recall

When at the starting signal the race committee is unable to identify boats that are on the course side of the starting line or to which rule 30 applies, or there has been an error in the starting procedure, the race committee may signal a general recall (display the First Substitute with two sounds). The warning signal for a new start for the recalled class shall be made one minute after the First Substitute is removed (one sound), and the starts for any succeeding classes shall follow the new start.

30 STARTING PENALTIES

30.1 I Flag Rule

If flag I has been displayed, and any part of a boat's hull, crew or equipment is on the course side of the starting line or one of its extensions during the last minute before her starting signal, she shall thereafter sail from the course side across an extension to the pre-start side before *starting*.

30.2 Z Flag Rule

If flag Z has been displayed, no part of a boat's hull, crew or equipment shall be in the triangle formed by the ends of the starting line and the first *mark* during the last minute before her starting signal. If a boat breaks this rule and is identified, she shall receive, without a hearing, a 20% Scoring Penalty calculated as stated in rule 44.3(c). She shall be penalized even if the race is restarted or resailed, but not if it is *postponed* or *abandoned* before the starting signal. If she is similarly identified during a subsequent attempt to start the same race, she shall receive an additional 20% Scoring Penalty.

30.3 Black Flag Rule

If a black flag has been displayed, no part of a boat's hull, crew or equipment shall be in the triangle formed by the ends of the starting line and the first *mark* during the last minute before her starting signal. If a boat breaks this rule and is identified, she shall be disqualified without a hearing, even if the race is restarted or resailed, but not if it is *postponed* or *abandoned* before the starting signal. If a general recall is signalled or the race is *abandoned* after the starting signal, the race committee shall display her sail number before the next warning signal for that race, and if the race is restarted or resailed she shall not sail in it. If she does so, her disqualification shall not be excluded in calculating her series score.

31 TOUCHING A MARK

While *racing*, a boat shall not touch a starting *mark* before *starting*, a *mark* that begins, bounds or ends the leg of the course on which she is sailing, or a finishing *mark* after *finishing*.

32 SHORTENING OR ABANDONING AFTER THE START

32.1 After the starting signal, the race committee may shorten the course (display flag S with two sounds) or *abandon* the race (display flag N, N over H, or N over A, with three sounds), as appropriate,

(a) because of an error in the starting procedure,

(b) because of foul weather,

(c) because of insufficient wind making it unlikely that any boat will *finish* within the time limit,

(d) because a *mark* is missing or out of position, or

(e) for any other reason directly affecting the safety or fairness of the competition,

or may shorten the course so that other scheduled races can be sailed. However, after one boat has sailed the course and *finished* within the time limit, if any, the race committee shall not *abandon* the race without considering the consequences for all boats in the race or series.

32.2 If the race committee signals a shortened course (displays flag S with two sounds), the finishing line shall be,

(a) at a rounding *mark*, between the *mark* and a staff displaying flag S;

(b) at a line boats are required to cross at the end of each lap, that line;

(c) at a gate, between the gate *marks*.

The shortened course shall be signalled before the first boat crosses the finishing line.

33 CHANGING THE NEXT LEG OF THE COURSE

The race committee may change a leg of the course that begins at a rounding *mark* or at a gate by changing the position of the next *mark* (or the finishing line) and signalling all boats before they begin the leg. The next *mark* need not be in position at that time.

(a) If the direction of the leg will be changed, the signal shall be the display of flag C with repetitive sounds and either

    (1)   the new compass bearing or

    (2)   a green triangle for a change to starboard or a red rectangle for a change to port.

(b) If the length of the leg will be changed, the signal shall be the display of flag C with repetitive sounds and a '–' if the length will be decreased or a '+' if it will be increased.

(c) Subsequent legs may be changed without further signalling to maintain the course shape.

34 MARK MISSING; *RACE COMMITTEE ABSENT*

If a *mark* is missing or out of position, the race committee shall, if possible,

(a) replace it in its correct position or substitute a new one of similar appearance, or

(b) substitute an object displaying flag M and make repetitive sound signals.

US Sailing prescribes that, if a finishing mark *is missing but another one remains in place, the finishing line is a line through the remaining* mark *at a 90° angle to the last leg and of the shortest practicable length. If the race committee is absent when a boat* finishes, *she should report to the race committee her finishing time and her position in relation to nearby boats at the first reasonable opportunity.*

35 TIME LIMIT AND SCORES

If one boat sails the course as required by rule 28 and *finishes* within the time limit, if any, all boats that *finish* shall be scored according to their finishing places unless the race is *abandoned*. If no boat *finishes* within the time limit, the race committee shall *abandon* the race.

36 RACES RESTARTED OR RESAILED

If a race is restarted or resailed, a breach of a *rule*, other than rule 30.3, in the original race shall not prohibit a boat from competing or, except under rule 30.2, 30.3 or 69, cause her to be penalized.

Part 4 — Other Requirements When Racing

Part 4 rules apply only to boats **racing**. *However, rule 55 applies at all times when boats are on the water.*

40 PERSONAL FLOTATION DEVICES; *LIFE-SAVING EQUIPMENT*

When flag Y is displayed with one sound before or with the warning signal, competitors shall wear personal flotation devices, except briefly while changing or adjusting clothing or personal equipment. Wet suits and dry suits are not personal flotation devices.

US Sailing prescribes that every boat shall carry life-saving equipment conforming to government regulations that apply in the racing area. Go to ussailing.org/racingrules/documents *and click the 'PFD' link for more information.*

41   OUTSIDE HELP

A boat shall not receive help from any outside source, except

(a) help for a crew member who is ill, injured or in danger;

(b) after a collision, help from the crew of the other vessel to get clear;

(c) help in the form of information freely available to all boats;

(d) unsolicited information from a disinterested source, which may be another boat in the same race.

However, a boat that gains a significant advantage in the race from help received under rule 41(a) may be protested and penalized; any penalty may be less than disqualification.

42   PROPULSION

42.1   Basic Rule

Except when permitted in rule 42.3 or 45, a boat shall compete by using only the wind and water to increase, maintain or decrease her speed. Her crew may adjust the trim of sails and hull, and perform other acts of seamanship, but shall not otherwise move their bodies to propel the boat.

42.2   Prohibited Actions

Without limiting the application of rule 42.1, these actions are prohibited:

(a) pumping: repeated fanning of any sail either by pulling in and releasing the sail or by vertical or athwartship body movement;

(b) rocking: repeated rolling of the boat, induced by

(1) body movement,

(2) repeated adjustment of the sails or centreboard, or

(3) steering;

(c) ooching: sudden forward body movement, stopped abruptly;

(d) sculling: repeated movement of the helm that is either forceful or that propels the boat forward or prevents her from moving astern;

(e) repeated tacks or gybes unrelated to changes in the wind or to tactical considerations.

42.3   Exceptions

(a) A boat may be rolled to facilitate steering.

(b) A boat's crew may move their bodies to exaggerate the rolling that facilitates steering the boat through a tack or a gybe, provided that, just after the tack or gybe is completed, the boat's speed is not greater than it would have been in the absence of the tack or gybe.

(c) Except on a beat to windward, when surfing (rapidly accelerating down the front of a wave) or planing is possible, the boat's crew may pull in any sail in order to initiate surfing or planing, but each sail may be pulled in only once for each wave or gust of wind.

(d) When a boat is above a close-hauled course and either stationary or moving slowly, she may scull to turn to a close-hauled course.

(e) If a batten is inverted, the boat's crew may pump the sail until the batten is no longer inverted. This action is not permitted if it clearly propels the boat.

(f) A boat may reduce speed by repeatedly moving her helm.

(g) Any means of propulsion may be used to help a person or another vessel in danger.

(h) To get clear after grounding or colliding with a vessel or object, a boat may use force applied by her crew or the crew of the other vessel and any equipment other than a propulsion engine. However, the use of an engine may be permitted by rule 42.3(i).

(i) Sailing instructions may, in stated circumstances, permit propulsion using an engine or any other method, provided the boat does not gain a significant advantage in the race.

Note: Interpretations of rule 42 are available at the ISAF website or by mail upon request.

43   COMPETITOR CLOTHING AND EQUIPMENT

43.1 (a) Competitors shall not wear or carry clothing or equipment for the purpose of increasing their weight.

(b) Furthermore, a competitor's clothing and equipment shall not weigh more than 8 kilograms, excluding a hiking or trapeze harness and clothing (including footwear) worn only below the knee. Class rules or sailing instructions may specify a lower weight or a higher weight up to 10 kilograms. Class rules may include footwear and other clothing worn below the knee within that weight. A hiking or trapeze harness shall have positive buoyancy and shall not weigh more than 2 kilograms, except that class rules may specify a higher weight up to 4 kilograms. Weights shall be determined as required by Appendix H.

(c) When an equipment inspector or a measurer in charge of weighing clothing and equipment believes a competitor may have broken rule 43.1(a) or 43.1(b) he shall report the matter in writing to the race committee.

43.2 Rule 43.1(b) does not apply to boats required to be equipped with lifelines.

44   PENALTIES AT THE TIME OF AN INCIDENT

44.1 **Taking a Penalty**

A boat may take a Two-Turns Penalty when she may have broken one or more rules of Part 2 in an incident while *racing*. She may take a One-Turn Penalty when she may have broken rule 31. Alternatively, sailing instructions may specify the use of the Scoring Penalty or some other penalty, in which case the specified penalty shall replace the One-Turn and the Two-Turns Penalty. However,

(a) when a boat may have broken a rule of Part 2 and rule 31 in the same incident she need not take the penalty for breaking rule 31;

(b) if the boat caused injury or serious damage or, despite taking a penalty, gained a significant advantage in the race or series by her breach her penalty shall be to retire.

44.2 **One-Turn and Two-Turns Penalties**

After getting well clear of other boats as soon after the incident as possible, a boat takes a One-Turn or Two-Turns Penalty by promptly making the required number of turns in the same direction, each turn including one tack and one gybe. When a boat takes the penalty at or near the finishing line, she shall sail completely to the course side of the line before *finishing*.

44.3 **Scoring Penalty**

(a) A boat takes a Scoring Penalty by displaying a yellow flag at the first reasonable opportunity after the incident.

(b)   When a boat has taken a Scoring Penalty, she shall keep the yellow flag displayed until *finishing* and call the race committee's attention to it at the finishing line. At that time she shall also inform the race committee of the identity of the other boat involved in the incident. If this is impracticable, she shall do so at the first reasonable opportunity and within the time limit for *protests*.

(c)   The race score for a boat that takes a Scoring Penalty shall be the score she would have received without that penalty, made worse by the number of places stated in the sailing instructions. However, she shall not be scored worse than Did Not Finish. When the sailing instructions do not state the number of places, the number shall be the whole number (rounding 0.5 upward) nearest to 20% of the number of boats entered. The scores of other boats shall not be changed; therefore, two boats may receive the same score.

45   HAULING OUT; MAKING FAST; ANCHORING

A boat shall be afloat and off moorings at her preparatory signal. Thereafter, she shall not be hauled out or made fast except to bail out, reef sails or make repairs. She may anchor or the crew may stand on the bottom. She shall recover the anchor before continuing in the race unless she is unable to do so.

46   PERSON IN CHARGE

A boat shall have on board a person in charge designated by the member or organization that entered the boat. See rule 75.

47   LIMITATIONS ON EQUIPMENT AND CREW

47.1   A boat shall use only the equipment on board at her preparatory signal.

47.2   No person on board shall intentionally leave, except when ill or injured, or to help a person or vessel in danger, or to swim. A person leaving the boat by accident or to swim shall be back on board before the boat continues in the race.

48   FOG SIGNALS AND LIGHTS; TRAFFIC SEPARATION SCHEMES

48.1   When safety requires, a boat shall sound fog signals and show lights as required by the *International Regulations for Preventing Collisions at Sea (IRPCAS)* or applicable government rules.

US Sailing prescribes that the use of additional special-purpose lights such as spreader, sail-trim and masthead wind-indicator lights shall not constitute a breach of this rule.

48.2   A boat shall comply with rule 10, Traffic Separation Schemes, of the *IRPCAS*.

49   CREW POSITION; LIFELINES

49.1   Competitors shall use no device designed to position their bodies outboard, other than hiking straps and stiffeners worn under the thighs.

49.2   When lifelines are required by the class rules or the sailing instructions they shall be taut, and competitors shall not position any part of their torsos outside them, except briefly to perform a necessary task. On boats equipped with upper and lower lifelines, a competitor sitting on the deck facing outboard with his waist inside the lower lifeline may have the upper part of his body outside the upper lifeline. If the class rules do not specify the material or minimum diameter of lifelines, they shall comply with the corresponding specifications in the *ISAF Offshore Special Regulations*.

Note: The ISAF Offshore Special Regulations *are available at the ISAF website.*

50   SETTING AND SHEETING SAILS

50.1 Changing Sails

When headsails or spinnakers are being changed, a replacing sail may be fully set and trimmed before the replaced sail is lowered. However, only one mainsail and, except when changing, only one spinnaker shall be carried set at a time.

50.2 Spinnaker Poles; Whisker Poles

Only one spinnaker pole or whisker pole shall be used at a time except when gybing. When in use, it shall be attached to the foremost mast.

50.3 Use of Outriggers

(a) No sail shall be sheeted over or through an outrigger, except as permitted in rule 50.3(b) or 50.3(c). An outrigger is any fitting or other device so placed that it could exert outward pressure on a sheet or sail at a point from which, with the boat upright, a vertical line would fall outside the hull or deck. For the purpose of this rule, bulwarks, rails and rubbing strakes are not part of the hull or deck and the following are not outriggers: a bowsprit used to secure the tack of a sail, a bumkin used to sheet the boom of a sail, or a boom of a boomed headsail that requires no adjustment when tacking.

(b) Any sail may be sheeted to or led above a boom that is regularly used for a sail and is permanently attached to the mast from which the head of the sail is set.

(c) A headsail may be sheeted or attached at its clew to a spinnaker pole or whisker pole, provided that a spinnaker is not set.

50.4 Headsails

For the purposes of rules 50 and 54 and Appendix G, the difference between a headsail and a spinnaker is that the width of a headsail, measured between the midpoints of its luff and leech, is less than 75% of the length of its foot. A sail tacked down behind the foremost mast is not a headsail.

51   MOVABLE BALLAST

All movable ballast, including sails that are not set, shall be properly stowed. Water, dead weight or ballast shall not be moved for the purpose of changing trim or stability. Floorboards, bulkheads, doors, stairs and water tanks shall be left in place and all cabin fixtures kept on board. However, bilge water may be bailed out.

52   MANUAL POWER

A boat's standing rigging, running rigging, spars and movable hull appendages shall be adjusted and operated only by the power provided by the crew.

53   SKIN FRICTION

A boat shall not eject or release a substance, such as a polymer, or have specially textured surfaces that could improve the character of the flow of water inside the boundary layer.

54   FORESTAYS AND HEADSAIL TACKS

Forestays and headsail tacks, except those of spinnaker staysails when the boat is not close-hauled, shall be attached approximately on a boat's centreline.

55   TRASH DISPOSAL

A competitor shall not intentionally put trash in the water.

25, 26, 27

56   FLAGS

US Sailing prescribes that a boat shall not display flags except for signaling. A boat shall not be penalized for breaking this rule without prior warning and opportunity to make correction.

Part 5 — Protest, Redress, Hearings, Misconduct and Appeals

Section A — Protests; Redress: Right to Request Redress or Rule 69 Action

60   RIGHT TO PROTEST; RIGHT TO REQUEST REDRESS OR RULE 69 ACTION

60.1 A boat may

(a)   protest another boat, but not for an alleged breach of a rule of Part 2 or rule 31 unless she was involved in or saw the incident; or

(b)   request redress.

60.2 A race committee may

(a)   protest a boat, but not as a result of information arising from a request for redress or an invalid *protest*, or from a report from an *interested party* other than the representative of the boat herself;

(b)   request redress for a boat; or

(c)   report to the protest committee requesting action under rule 69.2(a).

However, when the race committee receives a report required by rule 43.1(c) or 78.3, it shall protest the boat.

60.3 A protest committee may

(a)   protest a boat, but not as a result of information arising from a request for redress or an invalid *protest*, or from a report from an *interested party* other than the representative of the boat herself. However, it may protest a boat

(1)   if it learns of an incident involving her that may have resulted in injury or serious damage, or

(2)   if during the hearing of a valid *protest* it learns that the boat, although not a *party* to the hearing, was involved in the incident and may have broken a *rule*;

(b)   call a hearing to consider redress; or

(c)   act under rule 69.2(a).

US Sailing prescribes that when redress has been requested or is to be considered, any boat may participate in the hearing provided she makes a written request before the hearing begins. When she does so, the protest committee shall act under rule 60.3(b) to consider redress for her at that hearing.

61   PROTEST REQUIREMENTS

61.1 Informing the Protestee

(a)   A boat intending to protest shall inform the other boat at the first reasonable opportunity. When her *protest* will concern an incident in the racing area that she was involved in or saw, she shall hail 'Protest' and conspicuously display a red flag at the first reasonable opportunity for each. She shall display the flag until she is no longer *racing*. However,

(1) if the other boat is beyond hailing distance, the protesting boat need not hail but she shall inform the other boat at the first reasonable opportunity;

(2) if the hull length of the protesting boat is less than 6 metres, she need not display a red flag;

(3) if the incident was an error by the other boat in sailing the course, she need not hail or display a red flag but she shall inform the other boat before that boat *finishes* or at the first reasonable opportunity after she *finishes*;

(4) if the incident results in damage or injury that is obvious to the boats involved and one of them intends to protest, the requirements of this rule do not apply to her, but she shall attempt to inform the other boat within the time limit of rule 61.3.

(b) If the race committee or protest committee intends to protest a boat concerning an incident the committee observed in the racing area, it shall inform her after the race within the time limit of rule 61.3. In other cases the committee shall inform the boat of its intention to protest as soon as reasonably possible.

(c) If the protest committee decides to protest a boat under rule 60.3(a)(2), it shall inform her as soon as reasonably possible, close the current hearing, proceed as required by rules 61.2 and 63, and hear the original and the new *protests* together.

61.2 Protest Contents

A *protest* shall be in writing and identify

(a) the protestor and protestee;

(b) the incident, including where and when it occurred;

(c) any *rule* the protestor believes was broken; and

(d) the name of the protestor's representative.

However, if requirement (b) is met, requirement (a) may be met at any time before the hearing, and requirements (c) and (d) may be met before or during the hearing.

61.3 Protest Time Limit

A *protest* by a boat, or by the race committee or protest committee about an incident the committee observed in the racing area, shall be delivered to the race office within the time limit stated in the sailing instructions. If none is stated, the time limit is two hours after the last boat in the race *finishes*. Other race committee or protest committee *protests* shall be delivered to the race office no later than two hours after the committee receives the relevant information. The protest committee shall extend the time if there is good reason to do so.

61.4 *Fees for Protests and Requests for Redress*

US Sailing prescribes that no fees shall be charged for protests or requests for redress.

62 REDRESS

62.1 A request for redress or a protest committee's decision to consider redress shall be based on a claim or possibility that a boat's score in a race or series has been or may be, through no fault of her own, made significantly worse by

(a) an improper action or omission of the race committee, protest committee, organizing authority, equipment inspection committee or measurement committee for the event, but not by a protest committee decision when the boat was a *party* to the hearing;

(b) injury or physical damage because of the action of a boat that was breaking a rule of Part 2 or of a vessel not *racing* that was required to keep clear;

(c) giving help (except to herself or her crew) in compliance with rule 1.1; or

(d) an action of a boat, or a member of her crew, that resulted in a penalty under rule 2 or a penalty or warning under rule 69.2(c).

62.2 A request shall be in writing and identify the reason for making it. If the request is based on an incident in the racing area, it shall be delivered to the race office within the protest time limit or two hours after the incident, whichever is later. Other requests shall be delivered as soon as reasonably possible after learning of the reasons for making the request. The protest committee shall extend the time if there is good reason to do so. No red flag is required.

Section B — Hearings and Decisions

63   Hearings

63.1   Requirement for a Hearing

A boat or competitor shall not be penalized without a protest hearing, except as provided in rules 30.2, 30.3, 69, A5 and P2. A decision on redress shall not be made without a hearing. The protest committee shall hear all *protests* and requests for redress that have been delivered to the race office unless it allows a *protest* or request to be withdrawn.

63.2   Time and Place of the Hearing; Time for Parties to Prepare

All *parties* to the hearing shall be notified of the time and place of the hearing, the *protest* or redress information shall be made available to them, and they shall be allowed reasonable time to prepare for the hearing.

US Sailing prescribes that when redress has been requested or is to be considered, the protest committee shall make a reasonable attempt to notify all boats of the time and place of the hearing and the nature of the request or the grounds for considering redress. Before holding the hearing, the committee shall allow reasonable time for boats to make written requests to participate.

63.3   Right to Be Present

(a) The *parties* to the hearing, or a representative of each, have the right to be present throughout the hearing of all the evidence. When a *protest* claims a breach of a rule of Part 2, 3 or 4, the representatives of boats shall have been on board at the time of the incident, unless there is good reason for the protest committee to rule otherwise. Any witness, other than a member of the protest committee, shall be excluded except when giving evidence.

(b) If a *party* to the hearing of a *protest* or request for redress does not come to the hearing, the protest committee may nevertheless decide the *protest* or request. If the *party* was unavoidably absent, the committee may reopen the hearing.

63.4   Interested Party

A member of a protest committee who is an *interested party* shall not take any further part in the hearing but may appear as a witness. Protest committee members must declare any possible self-interest as soon as they are aware of it. A *party* to the hearing who believes a member of the protest committee is an *interested party* shall object as soon as possible.

US Sailing prescribes that when practicable:

(a) no person who brings an incident to the attention of the protest committee or who will give evidence regarding an incident shall be a member of the protest committee for a hearing involving that incident; and

(b) a request for redress based on a protest committee decision shall be heard by a committee that contains no members of the committee that made the original decision.

63.5 Validity of the Protest or Request for Redress

At the beginning of the hearing the protest committee shall take any evidence it considers necessary to decide whether all requirements for the *protest* or request for redress have been met. If they have been met, the *protest* or request is valid and the hearing shall be continued. If not, the committee shall declare the *protest* or request invalid and close the hearing. If the *protest* has been made under rule 60.3(a)(1), the committee shall also determine whether or not injury or serious damage resulted from the incident in question. If not, the hearing shall be closed.

63.6 Taking Evidence and Finding Facts

The protest committee shall take the evidence of the *parties* present at the hearing and of their witnesses and other evidence it considers necessary. A member of the protest committee who saw the incident shall, while the *parties* are present, state that fact and may give evidence. A *party* present at the hearing may question any person who gives evidence. The committee shall then find the facts and base its decision on them.

63.7 Conflict Between the Notice of Race and the Sailing Instructions

If there is a conflict between a rule in the notice of race and one in the sailing instructions that must be resolved before the protest committee can decide a *protest* or request for redress, the committee shall apply the rule that it believes will provide the fairest result for all boats affected.

63.8 Protests Between Boats in Different Races

A *protest* between boats sailing in different races conducted by different organizing authorities shall be heard by a protest committee acceptable to those authorities.

64 DECISIONS

64.1 Penalties and Exoneration

When the protest committee decides that a boat that is a *party* to a protest hearing has broken a *rule* and is not exonerated, it shall disqualify her unless some other penalty applies. A penalty shall be imposed whether or not the applicable *rule* was mentioned in the *protest*. If a boat has broken a *rule* when not *racing*, her penalty shall apply to the race sailed nearest in time to that of the incident. However,

(a) when as a consequence of breaking a *rule* a boat has compelled another boat to break a *rule*, the other boat shall be exonerated.

(b) if a boat has taken an applicable penalty, she shall not be further penalized under this rule unless the penalty for a *rule* she broke is a disqualification that is not excludable from her series score.

(c) if the race is restarted or resailed, rule 36 applies.

64.2 Decisions on Redress

When the protest committee decides that a boat is entitled to redress under rule 62, it shall make as fair an arrangement as possible for all boats affected, whether or not they asked for redress. This may be to adjust the scoring (see rule A10 for some examples) or finishing times of boats, to *abandon* the race, to let the results stand or to make some other arrangement. When in doubt about the facts or probable results of any arrangement for the race or series, especially before *abandoning* the race, the protest committee shall take evidence from appropriate sources.

64.3 Decisions on Protests Concerning Class Rules

(a) When the protest committee finds that deviations in excess of tolerances specified in the class rules were caused by damage or normal wear and do not improve the performance of the boat, it shall not penalize her. However, the boat shall not *race* again until the deviations have been corrected, except when the protest committee decides there is or has been no reasonable opportunity to do so.

(b) When the protest committee is in doubt about the meaning of a class rule, it shall refer its questions, together with the relevant facts, to an authority responsible for interpreting the rule. In making its decision, the committee shall be bound by the reply of the authority.

US Sailing prescribes that the authority responsible for interpreting the rules of a handicap or rating system is the organization that issued the handicap or the rating certificate involved.

(c) When a boat disqualified under a class rule states in writing that she intends to appeal, she may compete in subsequent races without changes to the boat, but shall be disqualified if she fails to appeal or the appeal is decided against her.

(d) Measurement costs arising from a *protest* involving a class rule shall be paid by the unsuccessful *party* unless the protest committee decides otherwise.

65 INFORMING THE PARTIES AND OTHERS

65.1 After making its decision, the protest committee shall promptly inform the *parties* to the hearing of the facts found, the applicable *rules*, the decision, the reasons for it, and any penalties imposed or redress given.

65.2 A *party* to the hearing is entitled to receive the above information in writing, provided she asks for it in writing from the protest committee no later than seven days after being informed of the decision. The committee shall then promptly provide the information, including, when relevant, a diagram of the incident prepared or endorsed by the committee.

65.3 When the protest committee penalizes a boat under a measurement rule, it shall send the above information to the relevant measurement authorities.

66 REOPENING A HEARING

The protest committee may reopen a hearing when it decides that it may have made a significant error, or when significant new evidence becomes available within a reasonable time. It shall reopen a hearing when required by the national authority under rule 71.2 or R5. A *party* to the hearing may ask for a reopening no later than 24 hours after being informed of the decision. When a hearing is reopened, a majority of the members of the protest committee shall, if possible, be members of the original protest committee.

67   DAMAGES

The question of damages arising from a breach of any *rule* shall be governed by the prescriptions, if any, of the national authority.

US Sailing prescribes that:

(a)   A boat that retires from a race or accepts a penalty does not, by that action alone, admit liability for damages.

(b)   A protest committee shall find facts and make decisions only in compliance with the rules. *No protest committee or US Sailing appeal authority shall adjudicate any claim for damages. Such a claim is subject to the jurisdiction of the courts.*

(c)   A basic purpose of the rules *is to prevent contact between boats. By participating in an event governed by the* rules, *a boat agrees that responsibility for damages arising from any breach of the* rules *shall be based on fault as determined by application of the* rules, *and that she shall not be governed by the legal doctrine of 'assumption of risk' for monetary damages resulting from contact with other boats.*

Note: There is no rule 68.

Section C — Gross Misconduct

69   ALLEGATIONS OF GROSS MISCONDUCT

69.1   Obligation not to Commit Gross Misconduct

(a)   A competitor shall not commit gross misconduct, including a gross breach of a *rule*, good manners or sportsmanship, or conduct bringing the sport into disrepute. Throughout rule 69, 'competitor' means a member of the crew, or the owner, of a boat.

(b)   An allegation of a breach of rule 69.1(a) shall be resolved in accordance with the provisions of rule 69.

69.2   Action by a Protest Committee

(a)   When a protest committee, from its own observation or a report received from any source, believes that a competitor may have broken rule 69.1(a), it may call a hearing. If the protest committee decides to call a hearing, it shall promptly inform the competitor in writing of the alleged breach and of the time and place of the hearing. If the competitor provides good reason for being unable to attend the hearing, the protest committee shall reschedule it.

(b)   A protest committee of at least three members shall conduct the hearing, following the procedures in rules 63.2, 63.3(a), 63.4 and 63.6.

(c)   If it is established to the comfortable satisfaction of the protest committee, bearing in mind the seriousness of the alleged misconduct, that the competitor has broken rule 69.1(a), it shall either

(1)   warn the competitor or

(2)   impose a penalty by excluding the competitor and, when appropriate, disqualifying a boat, from a race or the remaining races or all races of the series, or by taking other action within its jurisdiction. A disqualification under this rule shall not be excluded from the boat's series score.

If the standard of proof in this rule conflicts with the laws of a country, the national authority may, with the approval of the ISAF, change it with a prescription to this rule.

35, 36, 37

(d) The protest committee shall promptly report a penalty, but not a warning, to the national authorities of the venue, of the competitor and of the boat owner. If the protest committee is an international jury appointed by the ISAF under rule 89.2(b), it shall send a copy of the report to the ISAF.

(e) If the competitor does not provide good reason for being unable to attend the hearing and does not come to it, the protest committee may conduct it without the competitor present. If the committee does so and penalizes the competitor, it shall include in the report it makes under rule 69.2(d) the facts found, the decision and the reasons for it.

(f) If the protest committee chooses not to conduct the hearing without the competitor present or if the hearing cannot be scheduled for a time and place when it would be reasonable for the competitor to attend, the protest committee shall collect all available information and, if the allegation seems justified, make a report to the relevant national authorities. If the protest committee is an international jury appointed by the ISAF under rule 89.2(b), it shall send a copy of the report to the ISAF.

(g) When the protest committee has left the event and a report alleging a breach of rule 69.1(a) is received, the race committee or organizing authority may appoint a new protest committee to proceed under this rule.

69.3 Action by a National Authority or Initial Action by the ISAF

(a) When a national authority or the ISAF receives a report alleging a breach of rule 69.1(a) or a report required by rule 69.2(d) or 69.2(f), it shall conduct an investigation, in accordance with its established procedures, and, when appropriate, conduct a hearing. It may then take any disciplinary action within its jurisdiction it considers appropriate against the competitor or boat, or other person involved, including suspending eligibility, permanently or for a specified period of time, to compete in any event held within its jurisdiction, and suspending ISAF eligibility under ISAF Regulation 19. The national authority shall promptly inform the other national authorities involved and the ISAF of its decision and reasons, even if its decision is to take no further action.

(b) The national authority of a competitor shall also suspend the ISAF eligibility of the competitor as required in ISAF Regulation 19.

(c) The national authority shall promptly report a suspension of eligibility under rule 69.3(a) to the ISAF, and to the national authorities of the person or the owner of the boat suspended if they are not members of the suspending national authority.

69.4 Subsequent Action by the ISAF

Upon receipt of a report required by rule 69.3(c) or ISAF Regulation 19, or following its own action under rule 69.3(a), the ISAF shall inform all national authorities, which may also suspend eligibility for events held within their jurisdiction. The ISAF Executive Committee shall suspend the competitor's ISAF eligibility as required in ISAF Regulation 19 if the competitor's national authority does not do so.

Section D — Appeals

70 APPEALS AND REQUESTS TO A NATIONAL AUTHORITY

70.1 (a) Provided that the right of appeal has not been denied under rule 70.5, a *party* to a hearing may appeal a protest committee's decision or its procedures, but not the facts found.

(b) A boat may appeal when she is denied a hearing required by rule 63.1.

70.2 A protest committee may request confirmation or correction of its decision.

70.3 An appeal under rule 70.1 or a request by a protest committee under rule 70.2 shall be sent to the national authority with which the organizing authority is associated under rule 89.1. However, if boats will pass through the waters of more than one national authority while *racing*, the sailing instructions shall identify the national authority to which appeals or requests are required to be sent.

70.4 A club or other organization affiliated to a national authority may request an interpretation of the *rules*, provided that no *protest* or request for redress that may be appealed is involved. The interpretation shall not be used for changing a previous protest committee decision.

70.5 There shall be no appeal from the decisions of an international jury constituted in compliance with Appendix N. Furthermore, if the notice of race and the sailing instructions so state, the right of appeal may be denied provided that

(a) it is essential to determine promptly the result of a race that will qualify a boat to compete in a later stage of an event or a subsequent event (a national authority may prescribe that its approval is required for such a procedure);

US Sailing prescribes that its approval is required. Go to ussailing.org/racing-rules/documents *and click the 'No Appeal' link for more information or to obtain approval.*

(b) a national authority so approves for a particular event open only to entrants under its own jurisdiction; or

(c) a national authority after consultation with the ISAF so approves for a particular event, provided the protest committee is constituted as required by Appendix N, except that only two members of the protest committee need be International Judges.

70.6 Appeals and requests shall conform to Appendix R

71   NATIONAL AUTHORITY DECISIONS

71.1 No *interested party* or member of the protest committee shall take any part in the discussion or decision on an appeal or a request for confirmation or correction.

71.2 The national authority may uphold, change or reverse the protest committee's decision; declare the *protest* or request for redress invalid; or return the protest or request for the hearing to be reopened, or for a new hearing and decision by the same or a different protest committee. When the national authority decides that there shall be a new hearing, it may appoint the protest committee.

71.3 When from the facts found by the protest committee the national authority decides that a boat that was a *party* to a protest hearing broke a *rule*, it shall penalize her, whether or not that boat or that *rule* was mentioned in the protest committee's decision.

71.4 The decision of the national authority shall be final. The national authority shall send its decision in writing to all *parties* to the hearing and the protest committee, who shall be bound by the decision.

38, 39, 40

Part 6 — Entry and Qualification

75 ENTERING A RACE

75.1 To enter a race, a boat shall comply with the requirements of the organizing authority of the race. She shall be entered by

(a) a member of a club or other organization affiliated to an ISAF member national authority,

(b) such a club or organization, or

(c) a member of an ISAF member national authority.

75.2 Competitors shall comply with ISAF Regulation 19, Eligibility Code.

76 EXCLUSION OF BOATS OR COMPETITORS

76.1 The organizing authority or the race committee may reject or cancel the entry of a boat or exclude a competitor, subject to rule 76.3, provided it does so before the start of the first race and states the reason for doing so. On request the boat shall promptly be given the reason in writing. The boat may request redress if she considers that the rejection or exclusion is improper.

US Sailing prescribes that an organizing authority or race committee shall not reject or cancel the entry of a boat or exclude a competitor eligible under the notice of race and sailing instructions for an arbitrary or capricious reason or for reason of race, color, religion, national origin, gender, sexual orientation, or age.

76.2 The organizing authority or the race committee shall not reject or cancel the entry of a boat or exclude a competitor because of advertising, provided the boat or competitor complies with ISAF Regulation 20, Advertising Code.

76.3 At world and continental championships no entry within stated quotas shall be rejected or cancelled without first obtaining the approval of the relevant ISAF Class Association (or the Offshore Racing Council) or the ISAF.

77 IDENTIFICATION ON SAILS

A boat shall comply with the requirements of Appendix G governing class insignia, national letters and numbers on sails.

78 COMPLIANCE WITH CLASS RULES; CERTIFICATES

78.1 A boat's owner and any other person in charge shall ensure that the boat is maintained to comply with her class rules and that her measurement or rating certificate, if any, remains valid.

78.2 When a *rule* requires a valid certificate to be produced or its existence verified before a boat *races*, and this cannot be done, the boat may *race* provided that the race committee receives a statement signed by the person in charge that the boat has a valid certificate. If the certificate is not produced or verified before the end of the event, the boat shall be disqualified from all races of the event.

78.3 When an equipment inspector or a measurer for an event decides that a boat or personal equipment does not comply with the class rules, he shall report the matter in writing to the race committee.

79 CLASSIFICATION

If the notice of race or class rules state that some or all competitors must satisfy classification requirements, the classification shall be carried out as described in ISAF Regulation 22, Sailor Classification Code.

80   ADVERTISING

A boat and her crew shall comply with ISAF Regulation 20, Advertising Code.

81   RESCHEDULED EVENT

When an event is rescheduled to dates different from the dates stated in the notice of race, all boats entered shall be notified. The race committee may accept new entries that meet all the entry requirements except the original deadline for entries.

82   *INDEMNIFICATION OR HOLD HARMLESS AGREEMENTS*

US Sailing prescribes that the organizing authority shall not require a competitor to assume any liabilities of the organizing authority, race committee, protest committee, host club, sponsors, or any other organization or official involved with the event. (This is commonly referred to as an 'indemnification' or 'hold harmless' agreement.) Go to ussailing.org/ racing rules/documents *and click the 'Indemnification' link for more information.*

Part 7 — Race Organization

85   GOVERNING RULES

The organizing authority, race committee and protest committee shall be governed by the *rules* in the conduct and judging of races.

86   CHANGES TO THE RACING RULES

86.1   A racing rule shall not be changed unless permitted in the rule itself or as follows:

(a)   Prescriptions of a national authority may change a racing rule, but not the Definitions; a rule in the Introduction; Sportsmanship and the Rules; Part 1, 2 or 7; rule 42, 43, 69, 70, 71, 75, 76.3, 79 or 80; a rule of an appendix that changes one of these rules; Appendix H or N; or ISAF Regulation 19, 20, 21 or 22.

(b)   Sailing instructions may change a racing rule by referring specifically to it and stating the change, but not rules 76.1 or 76.2, Appendix R, or a rule listed in rule 86.1(a).

(c)   Class rules may change only racing rules 42, 49, 50, 51, 52, 53 and 54. Such changes shall refer specifically to the rule and state the change.

86.2   In exception to rule 86.1, the ISAF may in limited circumstances (see ISAF Regulation 28.1.3) authorize changes to the racing rules for a specific international event. The authorization shall be stated in a letter of approval to the event organizing authority and in the notice of race and sailing instructions, and the letter shall be posted on the event's official notice board.

86.3   If a national authority so prescribes, the restrictions in rule 86.1 do not apply if rules are changed to develop or test proposed rules. The national authority may prescribe that its approval is required for such changes.

US Sailing prescribes that proposed rules may be tested, but only in local races. However, proposed rules may also be tested at other events if, for each event, the organizing authority first obtains written permission from US Sailing and the proposed rules are included in the notice of race and sailing instructions. Go to ussailing.org/racingrules/documents *and click the 'Experimental Rules' link for more information.*

42, 43, 44, 45

87   CHANGES TO CLASS RULES

The sailing instructions may change a class rule only when the class rules permit the change, or when written permission of the class association for the change is displayed on the official notice board.

88   NATIONAL PRESCRIPTIONS

88.1   The prescriptions that apply to an event are the prescriptions of the national authority with which the organizing authority is associated under rule 89.1. However, if boats will pass through the waters of more than one national authority while *racing*, the sailing instructions shall identify the prescriptions that will apply and when they will apply.

88.2   The sailing instructions may change a prescription. However, a national authority may restrict changes to its prescriptions with a prescription to this rule, provided the ISAF approves its application to do so. The restricted prescriptions shall not be changed by the sailing instructions.

US Sailing prescribes that sailing instructions shall not change or delete rule 61.4, Appendix R, or its prescriptions to rules 40, 67, 70.5(a) or 76.1. However, for an international event the prescription to rule 40 may be deleted.

89   ORGANIZING AUTHORITY; NOTICE OF RACE; APPOINTMENT OF RACE OFFICIALS

89.1   Organizing Authority

Races shall be organized by an organizing authority, which shall be

(a) the ISAF;

(b) a member national authority of the ISAF;

(c) an affiliated club;

(d) an affiliated organization other than a club and, if so prescribed by the national authority, with the approval of the national authority or in conjunction with an affiliated club;

(e) an unaffiliated class association, either with the approval of the national authority or in conjunction with an affiliated club;

(f) two or more of the above organizations;

(g) an unaffiliated body in conjunction with an affiliated club where the body is owned and controlled by the club. The national authority of the club may prescribe that its approval is required for such an event; or

(h) if approved by the ISAF and the national authority of the club, an unaffiliated body in conjunction with an affiliated club where the body is not owned and controlled by the club.

In rule 89.1, an organization is affiliated if it is affiliated to the national authority of the venue; otherwise the organization is unaffiliated. However, if boats will pass through the waters of more than one national authority while *racing*, an organization is affiliated if it is affiliated to the national authority of one of the ports of call.

89.2   Notice of Race; Appointment of Race Officials

(a) The organizing authority shall publish a notice of race that conforms to rule J1. The notice of race may be changed provided adequate notice is given.

(b) The organizing authority shall appoint a race committee and, when appropriate, appoint a protest committee and umpires. However, the race committee, an international jury and umpires may be appointed by the ISAF as provided in the ISAF regulations.

90   RACE COMMITTEE; SAILING INSTRUCTIONS; SCORING

90.1   Race Committee

The race committee shall conduct races as directed by the organizing authority and as required by the *rules*.

90.2   Sailing Instructions

(a) The race committee shall publish written sailing instructions that conform to rule J2.

(b) When appropriate, for an event where entries from other countries are expected, the sailing instructions shall include, in English, the applicable national prescriptions.

(c) Changes to the sailing instructions shall be in writing and posted on the official notice board before the time stated in the sailing instructions or, on the water, communicated to each boat before her warning signal. Oral changes may be given only on the water, and only if the procedure is stated in the sailing instructions.

90.3   Scoring

(a) The race committee shall score a race or series as provided in Appendix A using the Low Point System, unless the sailing instructions specify some other system. A race shall be scored if it is not *abandoned* and if one boat sails the course in compliance with rule 28 and *finishes* within the time limit, if any, even if she retires after *finishing* or is disqualified.

(b) When a scoring system provides for excluding one or more race scores from a boat's series score, the score for disqualification under rule 2; rule 30.3's last sentence; rule 42 if rule P2.2 or P2.3 applies; or rule 69.2(c)(2) shall not be excluded. The next-worse score shall be excluded instead.

(c) When the race committee determines from its own records or observations that it has scored a boat incorrectly, it shall correct the error and make the corrected scores available to competitors.

91   PROTEST COMMITTEE

A protest committee shall be

(a) a committee appointed by the organizing authority or race committee, or

(b) an international jury appointed by the organizing authority or as prescribed in the ISAF regulations. It shall be composed as required by rule N1 and have the authority and responsibilities stated in rule N2. A national authority may prescribe that its approval is required for the appointment of international juries for races within its jurisdiction, except ISAF events or when inter-national juries are appointed by the ISAF under rule 89.2(b).

Appendix A — Scoring

See rule 90.3.

A1 NUMBER OF RACES

The number of races scheduled and the number required to be completed to constitute a series shall be stated in the sailing instructions.

A2 SERIES SCORES

Each boat's series score shall be the total of her race scores excluding her worst score. (The sailing instructions may make a different arrangement by providing, for example, that no score will be excluded, that two or more scores will be excluded, or that a specified number of scores will be excluded if a specified number of races are completed. A race is completed if scored; see rule 90.3(a).) If a boat has two or more equal worst scores, the score(s) for the race(s) sailed earliest in the series shall be excluded. The boat with the lowest series score wins and others shall be ranked accordingly.

A3 STARTING TIMES AND FINISHING PLACES

The time of a boat's starting signal shall be her starting time, and the order in which boats *finish* a race shall determine their finishing places. However, when a handicap or rating system is used a boat's corrected time shall determine her finishing place.

A4 LOW POINT SYSTEM

The Low Point System will apply unless the sailing instructions specify another system; see rule 90.3(a).

A4.1 Each boat *starting* and *finishing* and not thereafter retiring, being penalized or given redress shall be scored points as follows:

Finishing place	Points
First	1
Second	2
Third	3
Fourth	4
Fifth	5
Sixth	6
Seventh	7
Each place thereafter	Add 1 point

A4.2 A boat that did not *start*, did not *finish*, retired or was disqualified shall be scored points for the finishing place one more than the number of boats entered in the series. A boat that is penalized under rule 30.2 or that takes a penalty under rule 44.3(a) shall be scored points as provided in rule 44.3(c).

A5 SCORES DETERMINED BY THE RACE COMMITTEE

A boat that did not *start*, comply with rule 30.2 or 30.3, or *finish*, or that takes a penalty under rule 44.3(a) or retires, shall be scored accordingly by the race committee without a hearing. Only the protest committee may take other scoring actions that worsen a boat's score.

A6.1 If a boat is disqualified from a race or retires after *finishing*, each boat with a worse finishing place shall be moved up one place.

A6.2 If the protest committee decides to give redress by adjusting a boat's score, the scores of other boats shall not be changed unless the protest committee decides otherwise.

A7 RACE TIES

If boats are tied at the finishing line or if a handicap or rating system is used and boats have equal corrected times, the points for the place for which the boats have tied and for the place(s) immediately below shall be added together and divided equally. Boats tied for a race prize shall share it or be given equal prizes.

A8 SERIES TIES

A8.1 If there is a series-score tie between two or more boats, each boat's race scores shall be listed in order of best to worst, and at the first point(s) where there is a difference the tie shall be broken in favour of the boat(s) with the best score(s). No excluded scores shall be used.

A8.2 If a tie remains between two or more boats, they shall be ranked in order of their scores in the last race. Any remaining ties shall be broken by using the tied boats' scores in the next-to-last race and so on until all ties are broken. These scores shall be used even if some of them are excluded scores.

A9 RACE SCORES IN A SERIES LONGER THAN A REGATTA

For a series that is held over a period of time longer than a regatta, a boat that came to the starting area but did not *start,* did not *finish*, retired or was disqualified shall be scored points for the finishing place one more than the number of boats that came to the starting area. A boat that did not come to the starting area shall be scored points for the finishing place one more than the number of boats entered in the series.

A10 GUIDANCE ON REDRESS

If the protest committee decides to give redress by adjusting a boat's score for a race, it is advised to consider scoring her

(a) points equal to the average, to the nearest tenth of a point (0.05 to be rounded upward), of her points in all the races in the series except the race in question;

(b) points equal to the average, to the nearest tenth of a point (0.05 to be rounded upward), of her points in all the races before the race in question; or

(c) points based on the position of the boat in the race at the time of the incident that justified redress.

A11 SCORING ABBREVIATIONS

These scoring abbreviations shall be used for recording the circumstances described:

DNC Did not *start*; did not come to the starting area

DNS Did not *start* (other than DNC and OCS)

OCS Did not *start*; on the course side of the starting line at her starting signal and failed to *start*, or broke rule 30.1

ZFP 20% penalty under rule 30.2

BFD   Disqualification under rule 30.3

SCP   Took a Scoring Penalty under rule 44.3(a)

DNF   Did not *finish*

RET   Retired

DSQ   Disqualification

DNE   Disqualification (other than DGM) not excludable under rule 90.3(b)

DGM   Disqualification for gross misconduct not excludable under
         rule 90.3(b)

RDG   Redress given

DPI   Discretionary penalty imposed

US Sailing Note on Scoring a Long Series: The scoring systems in Appendix A may be inappropriate for a long series, such as a club's season championship held over several weeks or months, in which some boats do not compete in all of the races and in which more boats compete in some races than in others. Go to **ussailing.org/racingrules/documents** *and click the 'Scoring a Long Series' link for an explanation of the scoring problems that occur in such series, alternative scoring systems, and language for sailing instructions to implement them.*

Appendix B — Windsurfing Competition Rules

Windsurfing races shall be sailed under The Racing Rules of Sailing *as changed by this appendix. The term 'boat' elsewhere in the racing rules means 'board' or 'boat' as appropriate. The term 'heat' means one elimination race, a 'round' consists of several heats, and an 'elimination series' consists of one or more rounds. However, in speed competition, a 'round' consists of one or more speed 'runs'.*

A windsurfing event can include one or more of the following disciplines or their formats:

Discipline	Formats
Racing	*Course racing; Slalom; Marathon*
Expression	*Marathon Wave performance; Freestyle*
Speed	*Offshore Speed Course; Speed Crossings; Alpha Speed Course*

In racing or expression competition, boards may compete in elimination series, and only a limited number of them may advance from round to round. A marathon race is a race scheduled to last more than one hour.

In expression competition a board's performance is judged on skill and variety rather than speed and is organized using elimination series. Either wave performance or freestyle competition is organized, depending on the wave conditions at the venue.

In speed competition a board's performance is based on her speed over a measured course. Boards take turns sailing runs over the course.

CHANGES TO THE DEFINITIONS

The definitions *Mark-Room,* and *Tack, Starboard* or *Port* are deleted and replaced by:

Mark-Room *Mark-Room for a board is* room *to sail her* proper course *to* round or pass the *mark*. However, *mark-room* for a board does not include *room* to tack unless she is *overlapped* inside and to *windward* of the board required to give *mark-room* and she would be *fetching* the *mark* after her tack.

Tack, Starboard or Port A board is on the *tack, starboard* or *port*, corresponding to the competitor's hand that would be nearer the mast if the competitor were in normal sailing position with both hands on the wishbone and arms not crossed. A board is on *starboard tack* when the competitor's right hand would be nearer the mast and is on *port tack* when the competitor's left hand would be nearer the mast.

The definition *Zone* is deleted. Add the following definitions:

About to Round or Pass A board is *about to round or pass* a *mark* when her *proper course* is to begin to manoeuvre to round or pass it.

Capsized A board is *capsized* when her sail or the competitor is in the water.

B1   CHANGES TO THE RULES OF PART 1

[No changes.]

B2   CHANGES TO THE RULES OF PART 2

13   WHILE TACKING

Rule 13 is changed to:

After a board passes head to wind, she shall *keep clear* of other boards until her sail has filled. During that time rules 10, 11 and 12 do not apply. If two boards are subject to this rule at the same time, the one on the other's port side or the one astern shall *keep clear*.

16   CHANGING COURSE

Add new rule 16.3:

16.3 When, at the warning signal, the course to the first *mark* is ninety degrees or more from the true wind, a right-of-way board shall not change course during the last minute before her starting signal if as a result the other board would need to take immediate action to avoid contact.

17   ON THE SAME TACK; PROPER COURSE

Rule 17 is deleted.

18   MARK-ROOM

Rule 18 is changed as follows:

The first sentence of rule 18.1 is changed to:

Rule 18 begins to apply between boards when they are required to leave a *mark* on the same side and at least one of them is *about to round or pass* it. The rule no longer applies after the board entitled to *mark-room* has passed the *mark*.

Rule 18.2(b) is changed to:

(b) If boards are *overlapped* when the first of them is *about to round or pass* the *mark*, the outside board at that moment shall thereafter give the inside board *mark-room*. If a board is *clear ahead* when she is *about to round or pass* the *mark*, the board *clear astern* at that moment shall thereafter give her *mark-room*.

Rule 18.2(c) is changed to:

(c) When a board is required to give *mark-room* by rule 18.2(b), she shall continue to do so even if later an *overlap* is broken or a new *overlap* begins. However, if the board entitled to *mark-room* passes head to wind, rule 18.2(b) ceases to apply.

18.3 Tacking in the Zone
Rule 18.3 is deleted.

18.4 Gybing or Bearing Away
Rule 18.4 is changed to:

When an inside *overlapped* right-of-way board must gybe or bear away at a *mark* to sail her *proper course*, until she gybes or bears away she shall sail no farther from the *mark* than needed to sail that course. Rule 18.4 does not apply at a gate *mark*.

23 CAPSIZED; AGROUND; RESCUING
Rule 23 is changed to:

23.1 If possible, a board shall avoid a board that is *capsized* or has not regained control after *capsizing*, is aground, or is trying to help a person or vessel in danger.

23.2 If possible, a board that is *capsized* or aground shall not interfere with another board.

24 INTERFERING WITH ANOTHER BOARD; SAIL OUT OF WATER
Add new rule 24.3:

24.3 In the last minute before her starting signal, a board shall have her sail out of the water and in a normal position, except when accidentally *capsized*.

B3 CHANGES TO THE RULES OF PART 3

31 TOUCHING A MARK
Rule 31 is deleted.

B4 CHANGES TO THE RULES OF PART 4

42 PROPULSION
Rule 42 is changed to:

A board shall be propelled only by the action of the wind on the sail, by the action of the water on the hull and by the unassisted actions of the competitor. However, significant progress shall not be made by paddling, swimming or walking.

43 COMPETITOR CLOTHING AND EQUIPMENT
Rule 43.1(a) is changed to:

(a) Competitors shall not wear or carry clothing or equipment for the purpose of increasing their weight. However, a competitor may wear a drinking container that shall have a capacity of at least one litre and weigh no more than 1.5 kilograms when full.

44 PENALTIES AT THE TIME OF AN INCIDENT
Rule 44 is changed to:

44.1 Taking a Penalty
A board may take a 360°-Turn Penalty when she may have broken one of more rules of Part 2 in an incident while *racing*. Sailing instructions may specify the use of some other penalty. However, if the board caused injury or serious damage or, despite taking a penalty, gained a significant advantage in the race or series by her breach her penalty shall be to retire.

54, 55, 56

44.2 360°-Turn Penalty

After getting well clear of other boards as soon after the incident as possible, a board takes a 360°-Turn Penalty by promptly making a 360° turn with no requirement for a tack or a gybe. When a board takes the penalty at or near the finishing line, she shall sail completely to the course side of the line before *finishing*.

PART 4 RULES DELETED

Rules 43.2, 44.3, 45, 47.2, 48.1, 49, 50, 51, 52 and 54 are deleted.

B5 CHANGES TO THE RULES OF PART 5

60 RIGHT TO PROTEST; RIGHT TO REQUEST REDRESS OR RULE 69 ACTION

Rule 60.1(a) is changed by deleting 'or saw'.

61 PROTEST REQUIREMENTS

The first three sentences of rule 61.1(a) are changed to:

A board intending to protest shall inform the other board at the first reasonable opportunity. When her *protest* will concern an incident in the racing area that she was involved in or saw, she shall hail 'Protest'. She shall also inform the race committee of her intention to protest as soon as practicable after she *finishes* or retires.

62 REDRESS

Add new rule 62.1(e):

(e) *capsizing* because of the action of a board that was breaking a rule of Part 2.

64 DECISIONS

Rule 64.3(b) is changed to:

(b) When the protest committee is in doubt about a matter concerning the measurement of a board, the meaning of a class rule, or damage to a board, it shall refer its questions, together with the relevant facts, to an authority responsible for interpreting the rule. In making its decision, the committee shall be bound by the reply of the authority.

B6 CHANGES TO THE RULES OF PART 6

78 COMPLIANCE WITH CLASS RULES; CERTIFICATES

Add to rule 78.1: 'When so prescribed by the ISAF, a numbered and dated device on a board and her centreboard, fin and rig shall serve as her measurement certificate.'

B7 CHANGES TO THE RULES OF PART 7

90 RACE COMMITTEE; SAILING INSTRUCTIONS; SCORING

The last sentence of rule 90.2(c) is changed to: 'Oral instructions may be given only if the procedure is stated in the sailing instructions.'

B8 CHANGES TO APPENDIX A

A1 NUMBER OF RACES; OVERALL SCORES

Rule A1 is changed to:

The number of races scheduled and the number required to be completed to constitute a series shall be stated in the sailing instructions. If an event includes more than one discipline or format, the sailing instructions shall state how the overall scores are to be calculated.

A2   SERIES SCORES

Rule A2 is changed to:

Each board's series score shall be the total of her race scores excluding her

(a)   worst score when from 5 to 11 races have been completed, or

(b)   two worst scores when 12 or more races have been completed.

(The sailing instructions may make a different arrangement. A race is completed if scored; see rule 90.3(a).) If a board has two or more equal worst scores, the score(s) for the race(s) sailed earliest in the series shall be excluded. The board with the lowest series score wins and others shall be ranked accordingly.

A8   SERIES TIES

Rule A8 is changed to:

A8.1   If there is a series-score tie between two or more boards, they shall be ranked in order of their best excluded race score.

A8.2   If a tie remains between two or more boards, each board's race scores, including excluded scores, shall be listed in order of best to worst, and at the first point(s) where there is a difference the tie shall be broken in favour of the board(s) with the best score(s). These scores shall be used even if some of them are excluded scores.

A8.3   If a tie still remains between two or more boards, they shall be ranked in order of their scores in the last race. Any remaining ties shall be broken by using the tied boards' scores in the next-to-last race and so on until all ties are broken. These scores shall be used even if some of them are excluded scores.

B9   CHANGES TO APPENDIX G

G1   ISAF CLASS BOARDS

Rule G1.1(a) is changed to:

(a)   the insignia denoting her class. The insignia shall not refer to anything other than the manufacturer or class and, if it is not an abstract design, it shall not consist of more than two letters and three digits.

Rule G1.3(a) is changed to:

(a)   The class insignia shall be displayed once on each side of the sail in the area above a line projected at right angles from a point on the luff of the sail one-third of the distance from the head to the wishbone. The national letters and sail numbers shall be in the central third of that part of the sail above the wishbone, clearly separated from any advertising. They shall be black and applied back to back on an opaque white back-ground. The background shall extend a minimum of 30 mm beyond the characters. There shall be a '–' between the national letters and the sail number, and the spacing between characters shall be adequate for legibility.

The first sentence of rule G1.3(b) is deleted. Rules G1.3(c), G1.3(d) and G1.3(e) are deleted.

B10   CHANGES TO RULES FOR EVENTS THAT INCLUDE ELIMINATION SERIES

29   RECALLS

For a race of an elimination series that will qualify a board to compete in a later stage of an event, rule 29 is changed to:

(a) When at a board's starting signal any part of her hull, crew or equipment is on the course side of the starting line, the race committee shall signal a general recall.

(b) If the race committee acts under rule 29.1(a) and the board is identified, she shall be disqualified without a hearing, even if the race is *abandoned*. The race committee shall hail or display her sail number, and she shall leave the course area immediately. If the race is restarted or resailed, she shall not sail in it.

(c) If the race was completed but was later *abandoned* by the protest committee, and if the race is resailed, a board disqualified under rule 29.1(b) may sail in it.

37   ELIMINATION SERIES INCLUDING HEATS

Add new rule 37:

Rule 37 applies in elimination series in which boards compete in heats.

37.1   Elimination Series Procedure

(a) Competition shall take the form of one or more elimination series. Each of them shall consist of either rounds in a single elimination series where only a number of the best scorers advance, or rounds in a double elimination series where boards have more than one opportunity to advance.

(b) Boards shall sail one against another in pairs, or in groups determined by the elimination ladder. The selected form of competition shall not be changed while a round remains uncompleted.

37.2   Seeding and Ranking Lists

(a) When a seeding or ranking list is used to establish the heats of the first round, places 1–8 (four heats) or 1–16 (eight heats) shall be distributed evenly among the heats.

(b) For a subsequent elimination series, if any, boards shall be reassigned to new heats according to the ranking in the previous elimination series.

(c) The organizing authority's seeding decisions are final and are not grounds for a request for redress.

37.3   Heat Schedule

The schedule of heats shall be posted on the official notice board no later than 30 minutes before the starting signal for the first heat.

37.4   Advancement and Byes

(a) In racing and expression competition, the boards in each heat to advance to the next round shall be announced by the race committee no later than 10 minutes before the starting signal for the first heat. The number advancing may be changed by the protest committee as a result of a redress decision.

(b) In expression competition, any first-round byes shall be assigned to the highest-seeded boards.

(c) In wave performance competition, only the winner of each heat shall advance to the next round.

(d) In freestyle competition, boards shall advance to the next round as follows: from an eight-board heat, the best four advance, and the winner will sail against the fourth and the second against the third; from a four-board heat, the best two advance and will sail against each other.

37.5   Finals

(a) The final shall consist of a maximum of three races. The race committee shall announce the number of races to be sailed in the final no later than 5 minutes before the warning signal for the first final race.

(b) A runners-up final may be sailed after the final. All boards in the semi-final heats that failed to qualify for the final may compete in it.

63 HEARINGS

For a race of an elimination series that will qualify a board to compete in a later stage of an event, rules 61.2 and 65.2 are deleted and rule 63.6 is changed to:

63.6 *Protests* and requests for redress need not be in writing; they shall be made orally to a member of the protest committee as soon as reasonably possible following the race. The protest committee may take evidence in any way it considers appropriate and may communicate its decision orally.

70 APPEALS AND REQUESTS TO A NATIONAL AUTHORITY

Rule 70.5(a) is changed to:

(a) it is essential to determine promptly the result of a race of an elimination series that will qualify a board to compete in a later stage of an event;

A2 SERIES SCORES

Rule A2 is changed to:

Each board's elimination series score shall be the total of her race scores excluding her

(a) worst score when 3 or 4 races are completed,

(b) two worst scores when from 5 to 7 races are completed,

(c) three worst scores when 8 or more races are completed.

Each board's final series score shall be the total of her race scores excluding her worst score when 3 races are completed. (The sailing instructions may make a different arrangement. A race is completed if scored; see rule 90.3(a).) If a board has two or more equal worst scores, the score(s) for the race(s) sailed earliest in the series shall be excluded. The board with the lowest series score wins and others shall be ranked accordingly.

A4 LOW POINT SYSTEM

Add at the end of the first sentence of rule A4.2: 'or, in a race of an elimination series, the number of boards in that heat'.

Add new rule A4.3:

A4.3 When a heat cannot be completed, the points for the unscored places shall be added together and divided by the number of places in that heat. The resulting number of points, to the nearest tenth of a point (0.05 to be rounded upward), shall be given to each board entered in the heat.

B11 CHANGES TO RULES FOR EXPRESSION COMPETITION

Add the following definitions:

Coming In and *Going Out* A board sailing in the same direction as the incoming surf is *coming in*. A board sailing in the direction opposite to the incoming surf is *going out*.

Jumping A board is *jumping* when she takes off at the top of a wave while *going out*.

Overtaking A board is *overtaking* from the moment she gains an *overlap* from *clear astern* until the moment she is *clear ahead* of the *overtaken* board.

Possession The first board sailing shoreward immediately in front of a wave has *possession* of that wave. However, when it is impossible to determine which board is first the *windward* board has *possession*.

61, 62, 63

Recovering   A board is *recovering* from the time her sail or, when water-starting, the competitor is out of the water until she has steerage way.

Surfing   A board is *surfing* when she is on or immediately in front of a wave while *coming in*.

Transition   A board changing *tacks*, or taking off while *coming in*, or one that is not *surfing*, *jumping*, *capsized* or *recovering* is in *transition*.

PART 2 – WHEN BOARDS MEET

The rules of Part 2 are deleted and replaced by:

(a) COMING IN AND GOING OUT

A board *coming in* shall *keep clear* of a board *going out*. When two boards are *going out* or *coming in* while on the same wave, or when neither is *going out* or *coming in*, a board on *port tack* shall *keep clear* of the one on *starboard tack*.

(b) BOARDS ON THE SAME WAVE, COMING IN

When two or more boards are on a wave *coming in*, a board that does not have *possession* shall *keep clear*.

(c) CLEAR ASTERN, CLEAR AHEAD AND OVERTAKING

A board *clear astern* and not on a wave shall *keep clear* of a board *clear ahead*. An *overtaking* board that is not on a wave shall *keep clear*.

(d) TRANSITION

A board in *transition* shall *keep clear* of one that is not. When two boards are in *transition* at the same time, the one on the other's port side or the one astern shall *keep clear*.

(e) JUMPING

A board that is *jumping* shall *keep clear* of one that is not.

26   STARTING AND ENDING HEATS

Rule 26 is changed to:

Heats shall be started and ended by using the following signals:

(a) STARTING A HEAT

Each flag shall be removed when the next flag is displayed.

Minutes before starting signal	Visual signal	Sound signal	Means
Beginning of transition period	Heat number with red flag	One	Warning
1	Yellow flag	One	Preparatory
0	Green flag	One	Starting signal

(b) ENDING A HEAT

Minutes before ending signal	Visual signal	Sound signal	Means
1	Green flag removed	One	End warning
0	Red flag	One	Ending signal

38   REGISTRATION; COURSE AREA; HEAT DURATION; ADVANCEMENT AND BYES

Add new rule 38:

(a) Boards shall register with the race committee the colours and other particulars of their sails, or their identification according to another method stated in the sailing instructions, no later than the starting signal for the heat two heats before their own.

(b) The course area shall be defined in the sailing instructions and posted on the official notice board no later than 10 minutes before the starting signal for the first heat. A board shall be scored only while sailing in the course area.

(c) Any change in heat duration shall be announced by the race committee no later than 15 minutes before the starting signal for the first heat in the next round.

(d) Rule 37.4 in rule B10 applies.

41   OUTSIDE HELP

Change the number of rule 41 to 41.1 and add new rule 41.2:

41.2 An assistant may provide replacement equipment to a board. The assistant shall not interfere with other competing boards. A board whose assistant interferes with another board may be penalized at the discretion of the protest committee.

APPENDIX A – SCORING

The rules of Appendix A are deleted and replaced by:

A1   EXPRESSION COMPETITION SCORING

(a) Expression competition shall be scored by a panel of three judges. However, the panel may have a greater odd number of members, and there may be two such panels. Each judge shall give points for each manoeuvre based on the scale stated in the sailing instructions.

(b) The criteria of scoring shall be decided by the race committee and announced on the official notice board no later than 30 minutes before the starting signal for the first heat.

(c) A board's heat standing shall be determined by adding together the points given by each judge. The board with the highest score wins and others shall be ranked accordingly.

(d) Both semi-final heats shall have been sailed for an elimination series to be valid.

(e) Except for members of the race committee responsible for scoring the event, only competitors in the heat shall be allowed to see judges' score sheets for the heat. Each score sheet shall bear the full name of the judge.

(f) Scoring decisions of the judges shall not be grounds for a request for redress by a board.

A2   SERIES TIES

(a) In a heat, if there is a tie in the total points given by one or more judges, it shall be broken in favour of the board with the higher single score in the priority category. If the categories are weighted equally, in wave performance competition the tie shall be broken in favour of the board with the higher single score in wave riding, and in freestyle competition in favour of the board with the higher score for overall impression. If a tie remains, in wave performance competition it shall be broken in favour of the board with the higher single score in the category without priority, and in freestyle competition it shall stand as the final result.

(b) If there is a tie in the series score, it shall be broken in favour of the board that scored better more times than the other board. All scores shall be used even if some of them are excluded scores.

(c) If a tie still remains, the heat shall be resailed. If this is not possible, the tie shall stand as the final result.

B12 CHANGES TO RULES FOR SPEED COMPETITION
PART 2 – WHEN BOARDS MEET

The rules of Part 2 are deleted and replaced by:

PART 2 – GENERAL RULES

(a) WATER STARTING

A board shall not water start on the course or in the starting area, except to sail off the course to avoid boards that are making, or about to make, a run.

(b) LEAVING THE COURSE AREA

A board leaving the course area shall *keep clear* of boards making a run.

(c) COURSE CONTROL

When the race committee points an orange flag at a board, she is penalized and the run shall not be counted.

(d) RETURNING TO THE STARTING AREA

A board returning to the starting area shall keep clear of the course.

(e) MAXIMUM NUMBER OF RUNS FOR EACH BOARD

The maximum number of runs that may be made by each board in a round shall be announced by the race committee no later than 15 minutes before the starting signal for the first round.

(f) DURATION OF A ROUND

The duration of a round shall be announced by the race committee no later than 15 minutes before the starting signal for the next round.

(g) CONDITIONS FOR ESTABLISHING A RECORD

The minimum distance for a world record is 500 metres. Other records may be established over shorter distances. The course shall be defined by posts and transits ashore or by buoys afloat. Transits shall not converge.

(h) VERIFICATION RULES

(1) An observer appointed by the World Sailing Speed Record Council shall be present and verify run times and speeds at world record attempts. The race committee shall verify run times and speeds at other record attempts.

(2) A competitor shall not enter the timing control area or discuss any timing matter directly with the timing organization. Any timing question shall be directed to the race committee.

26 STARTING AND ENDING A ROUND

Rule 26 is changed to:

Rounds shall be started and ended by using the following signals. Each flag shall be removed when the next flag is displayed.

(a) STARTING A ROUND

Signal	Flag	Means
Stand-by	AP flag	Course closed. Races are *postponed*
Course closed	Red flag	Course closed; will open shortly
Preparatory	Red and yellow flag	Course will open in 5 minutes
Starting	Green flag	Course is open

(b) ENDING A ROUND

Signal	Flags	Means
End warning	Green and yellow flag	Course will be closed in 5 minutes
Extension	Yellow flag	Current round extended by 15 minutes
Round ended	Red flag	A new round will be started shortly

64 DECISIONS

Rule 64.1 is deleted and replaced by.

64.1 Penalties

(a) If a board fails to comply with a rule, she may be warned. If a board is warned a second time during the same round, she shall be excluded by the race committee from the remainder of the round A list of the sail numbers of boards that have received warnings or have been excluded shall be posted on a notice board near the finishing line.

(b) A board observed in the course area after having been excluded from a round shall be excluded from the competition without a hearing, and none of her previous times or results shall be valid.

(c) Any breach of the verification rules may result in exclusion from one or more rounds or from the competition.

APPENDIX A — SCORING

The rules of Appendix A are deleted and replaced by:

A1 SPEED COMPETITION SCORING

(a) On Standard Offshore Speed Courses, the speeds of a board's fastest two runs in a round shall be averaged to determine her standing in that round. The board with the highest average wins and others shall be ranked accordingly. If boards are tied, the tie shall be broken in favour of the board with the fastest run in the round.

(b) On Speed Crossings and Alpha Speed Courses, boards shall be ranked based on their fastest run in the round.

(c) If there is a series-score tie between two or more boards, it shall be broken in favour of the board(s) with the fastest run during the competition. If a tie remains, it shall be broken by applying rules A8.2(b) and (c) in rule B8.

Appendix C — Match Racing Rules

Match races shall be sailed under The Racing Rules of Sailing *as changed by this appendix. Matches shall be umpired unless the notice of race and sailing instructions state otherwise.*

Note: A Standard Notice of Race, Standard Sailing Instructions, and Match Racing Rules for Blind Competitors are available at the ISAF website.

C1 TERMINOLOGY

'Competitor' means the skipper, team or boat as appropriate for the event. 'Flight' means two or more matches started in the same starting sequence.

C2 CHANGES TO THE DEFINITIONS AND THE RULES OF PARTS 2 AND 4

C2.1 The definition *Finish* is changed to:

A boat *finishes* when any part of her hull crosses the finishing line in the direction of the course from the last *mark* after completing any penalties. However, when penalties are cancelled under rule C7.2(d) after one or both boats have *finished* each shall be recorded as *finished* when she crossed the line.

C2.2 Add to the definition *Proper Course*: 'A boat taking a penalty or manoeuvring to take a penalty is not sailing a *proper course.*'

C2.3 In the definition *Zone* the distance is changed to two hull lengths.

C2.4 Rule 13 is changed to:

13   WHILE TACKING OR GYRING

13.1 After a boat passes head to wind, she shall *keep clear* of other boats until she is on a close-hauled course.

13.2 After the foot of the mainsail of a boat sailing downwind crosses the centreline she shall *keep clear* of other boats until her mainsail has filled or she is no longer sailing downwind.

13.3 While rule 13.1 or 13.2 applies, rules 10, 11 and 12 do not. However, if two boats are subject to rule 13.1 or 13.2 at the same time, the one on the other's port side or the one astern shall *keep clear*.

C2.5 Rule 16.2 is deleted.

C2.6 Rule 18.2(e) is changed to: 'If a boat obtained an inside *overlap* and, from the time the *overlap* began, the outside boat has been unable to give *mark-room*, she is not required to give it.'

C2.7 Rule 18.3 is changed to:

If a boat in the *zone* passes head to wind and is then on the same *tack* as a boat that is *fetching* the *mark*, rule 18.2 does not thereafter apply between them. If, once the boat that changed *tack* has completed her tack,

(a) the other boat cannot by luffing avoid becoming *overlapped* inside her, she is entitled to *mark-room*;

(b) the other boat can by luffing avoid becoming *overlapped* inside her, the boat that changed *tack* is entitled to *mark- room.*

C2.8 When rule 20 applies, the following arm signals by the helmsman are required in addition to the hails:

(a) for 'Room to tack', repeatedly and clearly pointing to windward; and

(b) for 'You tack', repeatedly and clearly pointing at the other boat and waving the arm to windward.

C2.9 Rule 22.3 is changed to: 'A boat moving astern through the water shall *keep clear* of one that is not.'

C2.10 Rule 24.1 is changed to: 'If reasonably possible, a boat not *racing* shall not interfere with a boat that is *racing* or an umpire boat.'

C2.11 Add new rule 24.3: 'When boats in different matches meet, any change of course by either boat shall be consistent with complying with a *rule* or trying to win her own match.'

C2.12 Add to the preamble of Part 4: 'Rule 42 shall also apply between the warning and preparatory signals.'

C2.13 Rule 42.2(d) is changed to: 'sculling: repeated movement of the helm to propel the boat forward;'.

C3   RACE SIGNALS AND CHANGES TO RELATED RULES

C3.1   Starting Signals

The signals for starting a match shall be as follows. Times shall be taken from the visual signals; the failure of a sound signal shall be disregarded. If more than one match will be sailed, the starting signal for one match shall be the warning signal for the next match.

Time in minutes	Visual signal	Sound signal	Means
10	Flag F displayed	One	Attention signal
6	Flag F removed	None	
5	Numeral pennant displayed*	One	Warning signal
4	Flag P displayed	One	Preparatory signal
2	Blue or yellow flag or both displayed**	One**	End of pre-start entry time
1	Flag P removed	One long	
0	Warning signal removed	One	Starting signal

* Within a flight, numeral pennant 1 means Match 1, pennant 2 means Match 2, etc., unless the sailing instructions state otherwise.

** These signals shall be made only if one or both boats fail to comply with rule C4.2. The flag(s) shall be displayed until the umpires have signalled a penalty or for one minute, whichever is earlier.

C3.2   Changes to Related Rules

(a) Rule 29.1 is changed to:

    (1) When at a boat's starting signal any part of her hull, crew or equipment is on the course side of the starting line or one of its extensions, the race committee shall promptly display a blue or yellow flag identifying the boat with one sound. The flag shall be displayed until the boat is completely on the pre-start side of the starting line or one of its extensions or until two minutes after her starting signal, whichever is earlier.

    (2) When after her starting signal a boat sails from the pre-start side to the course side of the starting line across an extension without having *started* correctly, the race committee shall promptly display a blue or yellow flag identifying the boat. The flag shall be displayed until the boat is completely on the pre-start side of the starting line or one of its extensions or until two minutes after her starting signal, whichever is earlier.

(b) In the race signal AP the last sentence is changed to: 'The attention signal will be made 1 minute after removal unless at that time the race is *postponed* again or *abandoned*.'

(c) In the race signal N the last sentence is changed to: 'The attention signal will be made 1 minute after removal unless at that time the race is *abandoned* again or *postponed*.'

C3.3   Finishing Line Signals

The race signal Blue flag or shape shall not be used.

C4   REQUIREMENTS BEFORE THE START

C4.1   At her preparatory signal, each boat shall be outside the line that is at a 90° angle to the starting line through the starting *mark* at her assigned end. In the pairing list, the boat listed on the left-hand side is assigned the port end and shall display a blue flag at her stern while *racing*. The other boat is assigned the starboard end and shall display a yellow flag at her stern while *racing*.

C4.2   Within the two-minute period following her preparatory signal, a boat shall cross and clear the starting line, the first time from the course side to the pre-start side.

C5 SIGNALS BY UMPIRES

C5.1 A green and white flag with one long sound means 'No penalty.'

C5.2 A blue or yellow flag identifying a boat with one long sound means 'The identified boat shall take a penalty by complying with rule C7.'

C5.3 A red flag with or soon after a blue or yellow flag with one long sound means 'The identified boat shall take a penalty by complying with rule C7.3(d).'

C5.4 A black flag with a blue or yellow flag and one long sound means 'The identified boat is disqualified, and the match is terminated and awarded to the other boat.'

C5.5 One short sound means 'A penalty is now completed.'

C5.6 Repetitive short sounds mean 'A boat is no longer taking a penalty and the penalty remains.'

C5.7 A blue or yellow flag or shape displayed from an umpire boat means 'The identified boat has an outstanding penalty.'

C6 PROTESTS AND REQUESTS FOR REDRESS BY BOATS

C6.1 A boat may protest another boat

   (a) under a rule of Part 2, except rule 14, by clearly displaying flag Y immediately after an incident in which she was involved;

   (b) under any rule not listed in rule C6.1(a) or C6.2 by clearly displaying a red flag as soon as possible after the incident.

C6.2 A boat may not protest another boat under

   (a) rule 14, unless damage or injury results;

   (b) a rule of Part 2, unless she was involved in the incident;

   (c) rule 31 or 42; or

   (d) rule C4 or C7.

C6.3 A boat intending to request redress because of circumstances that arise before she *finishes* or retires shall clearly display a red flag as soon as possible after she becomes aware of those circumstances, but no later than two minutes after *finishing* or retiring.

C6.4 (a) A boat protesting under rule C6.1(a) shall remove flag Y before or as soon as possible after the umpires' signal.

   (b) A boat protesting under rule C6.1(b) or requesting redress under rule C6.3 shall, for her *protest* or request to be valid, keep her red flag displayed until she has so informed the umpires after *finishing* or retiring. No written *protest* or request for redress is required.

C6.5 **Umpire Decisions**

   (a) After flag Y is displayed, the umpires shall decide whether to penalize any boat. They shall signal their decision in compliance with rule C5.1, C5.2 or C5.3. However, when the umpires penalize a boat under rule C8.2 and in the same incident there is a flag Y from a boat, the umpires may disregard the flag Y.

   (b) The red-flag penalty in rule C5.3 shall be used when a boat has gained a controlling position as a result of breaking a *rule*, but the umpires are not certain that the conditions for an additional umpire-initiated penalty have been fulfilled.

C6.6 **Protest Committee Decisions**

   (a) The protest committee may take evidence in any way it considers appropriate and may communicate its decision orally.

(b) If the protest committee decides that a breach of a *rule* has had no significant effect on the outcome of the match, it may

(1) impose a penalty of one point or part of one point;

(2) order a resail; or

(3) make another arrangement it decides is equitable, which may be to impose no penalty.

(c) The penalty for breaking rule 14 when damage or injury results will be at the discretion of the protest committee, and may include exclusion from further races in the event.

C7 PENALTY SYSTEM

C7.1 Deleted Rule

Rule 44 is deleted.

C7.2 All Penalties

(a) A penalized boat may delay taking a penalty within the limitations of rule C7.3 and shall take it as follows:

(1) When on a leg of the course to a windward *mark*, she shall gybe and, as soon as reasonably possible, luff to a close-hauled course.

(2) When on a leg of the course to a leeward *mark* or the finishing line, she shall tack and, as soon as reasonably possible, bear away to a course that is more than ninety degrees from the true wind.

(b) Add to rule 2: 'When *racing*, a boat need not take a penalty unless signalled to do so by an umpire.'

(c) A boat completes a leg of the course when her bow crosses the extension of the line from the previous *mark* through the *mark* she is rounding, or on the last leg when she *finishes*.

(d) A penalized boat shall not be recorded as having *finished* until she takes her penalty and sails completely to the course side of the line and then *finishes*, unless the penalty is cancelled before or after she crosses the finishing line.

(e) If a boat has one or two outstanding penalties and the other boat in her match is penalized, one penalty for each boat shall be cancelled except that a red-flag penalty shall not cancel or be cancelled by another penalty.

(f) If a boat has more than two outstanding penalties, the umpires shall signal her disqualification under rule C5.4.

C7.3 Penalty Limitations

(a) A boat taking a penalty that includes a tack shall have the spinnaker head below the main-boom gooseneck from the time she passes head to wind until she is on a close-hauled course.

(b) No part of a penalty may be taken inside the *zone* of a rounding *mark* that begins, bounds or ends the leg the boat is on.

(c) If a boat has one outstanding penalty, she may take the penalty any time after *starting* and before *finishing*. If a boat has two outstanding penalties, she shall take one of them as soon as reasonably possible, but not before *starting*.

(d) When the umpires display a red flag with or soon after a penalty flag, the penalized boat shall take a penalty as soon as reasonably possible, but not before *starting*.

C7.4 Taking and Completing Penalties

(a) When a boat with an outstanding penalty is on a leg to a windward *mark* and gybes, or is on a leg to a leeward *mark* or the finishing line and passes head to wind, she is taking a penalty.

(b)   When a boat taking a penalty either does not take the penalty correctly or does not complete the penalty as soon as reasonably possible, she is no longer taking a penalty. The umpires shall signal this as required by rule C5.6.

(c)   The umpire boat for each match shall display blue or yellow flags or shapes, each flag or shape indicating one outstanding penalty. When a boat has taken a penalty, or a penalty has been cancelled, one flag or shape shall be removed, with the appropriate sound signal. Failure of the umpires to signal correctly shall not change the number of penalties outstanding.

C8   PENALTIES INITIATED BY UMPIRES

C8.1   Rule Changes

(a)   Rules 60.2(a) and 60.3(a) do not apply to *rules* for which penalties may be imposed by umpires.

(b)   Rule 64.1(a) is changed so that the provision for exonerating a boat may be applied by the umpires without a hearing, and it takes precedence over any conflicting rule of this appendix.

C8.2   When the umpires decide that a boat has broken rule 31, 42, C4, C7.3(c) or C7.3(d) she shall be penalized by signalling her under rule C5.2 or C5.3. However, if a boat is penalized for breaking a rule of Part 2 and if she in the same incident breaks rule 31, she shall not be penalized for breaking rule 31. Furthermore, a boat that displays an incorrect flag or does not display the correct flag shall be warned orally and given an opportunity to correct the error before being penalized.

C8.3   When the umpires decide that a boat has

(a)   gained an advantage by breaking a *rule* after allowing for a penalty,

(b)   deliberately broken a *rule*, or

(c)   committed a breach of sportsmanship,

she shall be penalized under rule C5.2, C5.3 or C5.4.

C8.4   If the umpires or protest committee members decide that a boat may have broken a *rule* other than those listed in rules C6.1(a) and C6.2, they shall so inform the protest committee for its action under rule 60.3 and rule C6.6 when appropriate.

C8.5   When, after one boat has *started*, the umpires are satisfied that the other boat will not *start*, they may signal under rule C5.4 that the boat that did not *start* is disqualified and the match is terminated.

C8.6   When the match umpires, together with at least one other umpire, decide that a boat has broken rule 14 and damage resulted, they may impose a points-penalty without a hearing. The competitor shall be informed of the penalty as soon as practicable and, at the time of being so informed, may request a hearing. The protest committee shall then proceed under rule C6.6. Any penalty decided by the protest committee may be more than the penalty imposed by the umpires. When the umpires decide that a penalty greater than one point is appropriate, they shall act under rule C8.4.

C9   REQUESTS FOR REDRESS OR REOPENING; APPEALS; OTHER PROCEEDINGS

C9.1   There shall be no request for redress or an appeal from a decision made under rule C5, C6, C7 or C8. In rule 66 the third sentence is changed to: 'A *party* to the hearing may not ask for a reopening.'

C9.2   A competitor may not base a request for redress on a claim that an action by an official boat was improper. The protest committee may decide to consider giving redress in such circumstances but only if it believes that an official boat, including

an umpire boat, may have seriously interfered with a competing boat.

C9.3   No proceedings of any kind may be taken in relation to any action or non-action by the umpires, except as permitted in rule C9.2.

C10   SCORING

C10.1   The winning competitor of each match scores one point (half a point each for a dead heat); the loser scores no points.

C10.2   When a competitor withdraws from part of an event the scores of all completed races shall stand.

C10.3   When a single round robin is terminated before completion, or a multiple round robin is terminated during the first round robin, a competitor's score shall be the average points scored per match sailed by the competitor. However, if any of the competitors have completed less than one third of the scheduled matches, the entire round robin shall be disregarded and, if necessary, the event declared void. For the purposes of tie-breaking in rule C11.1(a), a competitor's score shall be the average points scored per match between the tied competitors.

C10.4   When a multiple round robin is terminated with an incomplete round robin, only one point shall be available for all the matches sailed between any two competitors, as follows:

Number of matches completed between any two competitors	Points for each win
1	One point
2	Half a point
3	A third of a point
(etc.)	

C10.5   In a round-robin series,
   (a)   competitors shall be placed in order of their total scores, highest score first;
   (b)   a competitor who has won a match but is disqualified for breaking a *rule* against a competitor in another match shall lose the point for that match (but the losing competitor shall not be awarded the point); and
   (c)   the overall position between competitors who have sailed in different groups shall be decided by the highest score.

C10.6   In a knockout series the sailing instructions shall state the minimum number of points required to win a series between two competitors. When a knockout series is terminated it shall be decided in favour of the competitor with the higher score.

C11   TIES

C11.1   Round-Robin Series

In a round-robin series competitors are assigned to one or more groups and scheduled to sail against all other competitors in their group one or more times. Each separate stage identified in the event format shall be a separate round-robin series irrespective of the number of times each competitor sails against each other competitor in that stage.

Ties between two or more competitors in a round-robin series shall be broken by the following methods, in order, until all ties are broken. When one or more ties are only partially broken, rules C11.1(a) to C11.1(e) shall be reapplied to them.

Ties shall be decided in favour of the competitor(s) who

(a)   placed in order, has the highest score in the matches between the tied competitors;

(b)   when the tie is between two competitors in a multiple round robin, has won the last match between the two competitors;

(c)   has the most points against the competitor placed highest in the round-robin series or, if necessary, second highest, and so on until the tie is broken. When two separate ties have to be resolved but the resolution of each depends upon resolving the other, the following principles shall be used in the rule C11.1(c) procedure:

  (1)   the higher-place tie shall be resolved before the lower- place tie, and

  (2)   all the competitors in the lower-place tie shall be treated as a single competitor for the purposes of rule C11.1(c);

(d)   applying rule C10.5(c), has the highest place in the after different groups, irrespective of the number of competitors in each group;

(e)   has the highest place in the most recent stage of the event (fleet race, round robin, etc.).

C11.2   Knockout Series

Ties (including 0–0) between competitors in a knockout series shall be broken by the following methods, in order, until the tie is broken. The tie shall be decided in favour of the competitor who

(a)   has the highest place in the most recent round-robin series, applying rule C11.1 if necessary;

(b)   has won the most recent match in the event between the tied competitors.

C11.3   Remaining Ties

When rule C11.1 or C11.2 does not resolve a tie,

(a)   if the tie needs to be resolved for a later stage of the event (or another event for which the event is a direct qualifier), the tie shall be broken by a sail-off when practicable. When the race committee decides that a sail-off is not practicable, the tie shall be decided in favour of the competitor who has the highest score in the round-robin series after eliminating the score for the first race for each tied competitor or, should this fail to break the tie, the second race for each tied competitor and so on until the tie is broken. When a tie is partially resolved, the remaining tie shall be broken by reapplying rule C11.1 or C11.2.

(b)   to decide the winner of an event that is not a direct qualifier for another event, or the overall position between competitors eliminated in one round of a knockout series, a sail-off may be used (but not a draw).

(c)   when a tie is not broken any monetary prizes or ranking points for tied places shall be added together and divided equally among the tied competitors.

Appendix D — Team Racing Rules

Team races shall be sailed under The Racing Rules of Sailing *as changed by this appendix.*

D1   CHANGES TO THE RACING RULES

D1.1   Definitions and the Rules of Parts 2 and 4

(a)   In the definition *Zone* the distance is changed to two hull lengths.

(b)   Rule 18.2(b) is changed to:

If boats are *overlapped* when the first of them reaches the *zone*, the out-side boat at that moment shall thereafter give the inside boat *mark-room*. If a boat is *clear ahead* when she reaches the *zone*, or she later becomes *clear ahead* when another boat passes head to wind, the boat *clear astern* at that moment shall thereafter give her *mark-room*.

(c)   Rule 18.4 is deleted.

(d)   When rule 20 applies the following arm signals by the helmsman are required in addition to the hails:

(1)   for 'Room to tack', repeatedly and clearly pointing to windward; and

(2)   for 'You tack', repeatedly and clearly pointing at the other boat and waving the arm to windward.

Sailing instructions may delete this requirement.

(e)   Add new rule 24.3: 'A boat that has *finished* shall not act to interfere with a boat that has not *finished*.'

(f)   Add new rule 24.4: 'When boats in different races meet, any change of course by either boat shall be consistent with complying with a *rule* or trying to win her own race.'

(g)   Add to rule 41:

(e)   help from another boat on her team provided electronic communication is not used.

(h)   Rule 45 is deleted.

D1.2   Protests and Requests for Redress

(a)   Rule 60.1 is changed to:

A boat may

(a)   protest another boat, but not for an alleged breach of a rule of Part 2 unless she was involved in the incident or the incident involved contact between members of the other team; or

(b)   request redress.

(b)   Rule 61.1(a) is changed so that a boat may remove her red flag after it has been conspicuously displayed.

(c)   A boat intending to request redress for an incident in the racing area shall display a red flag at the first reasonable opportunity after the incident. She shall display the red flag until it is acknowledged by the race committee or by an umpire.

(d)   The race committee or protest committee shall not protest a boat for breaking a rule of Part 2 or rule 31 or 42 except

(1)   based on evidence in a report from an umpire after a black and white flag has been displayed; or

(2)   under rule 14 upon receipt of a report from any source alleging damage or injury.

(e)   *Protests* and requests for redress need not be in writing. The protest com-mittee may take evidence in any way it considers appropriate and may communicate its decision orally.

(f)   A boat is not entitled to redress based on damage or injury caused by another boat on her team.

(g)   When a supplied boat suffers a breakdown, rule D5 applies.

D1.3   Penalties

(a)   Rule 44.1 is changed to:

A boat may take a One-Turn Penalty when she may have broken one or more rules of Part 2, or rule 31 or 42, in an incident while *racing*. However, when she may have broken a rule of Part 2 and rule 31 in the same incident she need not take the penalty for breaking rule 31.

(b)   A boat may take a penalty by retiring, in which case she shall notify the race committee as soon as possible and 6 points shall be added to her score.

(c)   There shall be no penalty for breaking a rule of Part 2 when the incident is between boats on the same team and there is no contact.

D2   UMPIRED RACES

D2.1   When Rule D2 Applies

Rule D2 applies to umpired races. Races to be umpired shall be identified either in the sailing instructions or by the display of flag U no later than the warning signal.

D2.2   Protests by Boats

When a boat protests under a rule of Part 2 or under rule 31 or 42 for an incident in the racing area, she is not entitled to a hearing and the following applies:

(a)   She shall hail 'Protest' and conspicuously display a red flag at the first reasonable opportunity for each.

(b)   The boats shall be given time to respond. A boat involved in the incident may respond by promptly taking an appropriate penalty or clearly indicating that she will do so as soon as possible.

(c)   If no boat takes a penalty, an umpire shall decide whether to penalize any boat.

(d)   If more than one boat broke a rule and was not exonerated, an umpire may penalize any boat that broke a rule and did not take an appropriate penalty.

(e)   An umpire shall signal a decision in compliance with rule D2.4.

(f)   A boat penalized by an umpire shall take a Two-Turns Penalty.

D2.3   Penalties Initiated by an Umpire

An umpire may penalize a boat without a *protest* by another boat, or report the incident to the protest committee, or both, when the boat

(a)   breaks rule 31 or 42 and does not take a penalty;

(b)   breaks a rule of Part 2 and makes contact with another boat on her team or with a boat in another race, and no boat takes a penalty;

(c)   breaks a *rule* and her team gains an advantage despite her, or another boat on her team, taking a penalty;

(d)   breaks rule 14 and there is damage or injury;

(e)   clearly indicates that she will take a One-Turn Penalty, and then fails to do so;

(f)   fails to take a penalty signalled by an umpire; commits a breach of sportsmanship.

The umpire shall signal a decision in compliance with rule D2.4. A boat penalized by an umpire shall take a Two-Turns Penalty except that, when an umpire hails a number of turns, the boat shall take that number of One-Turn Penalties.

D2.4   Signals by an Umpire

An umpire shall signal a decision with one long sound and the display of a flag as follows:

(a)   For no penalty, a green and white flag.

(b)   To penalize one or more boats, a red flag. The umpire shall hail or signal to identify each boat penalized.

(c)   To report the incident to the protest committee, a black and white flag.

D2.5   Two-Flag Protest Procedure

This rule applies only if the sailing instructions so state and it then replaces rule D2.2.

When a boat protests under a rule of Part 2 or under rule 31 or 42 for an incident in the racing area, she is not entitled to a hearing and the following applies:

(a) She shall hail 'Protest' and conspicuously display a red flag at the first reasonable opportunity for each.

(b) The boats shall be given time to respond. A boat involved in the incident may respond by promptly taking an appropriate penalty or clearly indicating that she will do so as soon as possible.

(c) If the protested boat fails to respond, the protesting boat may request a decision by conspicuously displaying a yellow flag and hailing 'Umpire'.

(d) An umpire shall then decide whether to penalize any boat.

(e) An umpire shall signal a decision in compliance with rule D2.4.

(f) If a boat hails for an umpire decision without complying with the protest procedure, an umpire shall signal No Penalty.

(g) A boat penalized by an umpire shall take a Two-Turns Penalty.

D2.6   Limited Umpiring

This rule applies only if the sailing instructions so state and it then changes rules D2.2 and D2.5.

When a boat protests and either there is no decision signalled, or an umpire displays a yellow flag with one long sound signalling he has insufficient facts to make a decision, the protesting boat is entitled to a hearing.

D2.7   Limitations on Other Proceedings

A decision, action or non-action of an umpire shall not be

(a) grounds for redress,

(b) subject to an appeal under rule 70, or

(c) grounds for *abandoning* a race after it has started.

The protest committee may decide to consider giving redress when it believes that an official boat, including an umpire boat, may have seriously interfered with a competing boat.

D3   SCORING A RACE

D3.1   (a) Each boat *finishing* a race shall be scored points equal to her finishing place. All other boats shall be scored points equal to the number of boats entitled to *race*.

(b) When a boat is scored OCS, 10 points shall be added to her score unless she retired as soon as possible after the starting signal.

(c) When a boat fails to take a penalty imposed by an umpire at or near the finishing line, she shall be scored points for last place and other scores shall be adjusted accordingly.

(d) When a protest committee decides that a boat that is a *party* to a protest hearing has broken a *rule* and is not exonerated,

(1) if the boat has not taken a penalty, 6 points shall be added to her score;

(2) if the boat's team has gained an advantage despite any penalty taken or imposed, the boat's score may be increased;

(3) when the boat has broken rule 1 or 2, rule 14 when she has caused damage or injury, or a *rule* when not *racing*, half or more race wins may be deducted from her team, or no penalty may be imposed. Race wins deducted shall not be awarded to any other team.

D3.2 When all boats on one team have *finished*, retired or failed to *start*, the other team's boats *racing* at that time shall be scored the points they would have received had they *finished*.

D3.3 The team with the lower total points wins the race. If the totals are equal, the team that does not have first place wins.

D4 SCORING A SERIES

D4.1 Terminology

In a round-robin series teams are assigned to one or more groups and scheduled to sail against all other teams in their group one or more times. In a knock-out series teams are scheduled to sail in matches; a match is one or more races between two teams.

D4.2 Terminating a Series

(a) The race committee may terminate a series at any reasonable time taking into account the entries, weather, time constraints and other relevant factors.

(b) When a round-robin series is terminated, any round-robin in the series in which 80% or more of the full schedule of races has been completed shall be scored as complete; if fewer races have been completed, the round-robin shall be excluded from the results, but may be used to break ties.

D4.3 Scoring a Round-Robin Series

In a round-robin series the teams shall be ranked in order of number of race wins, highest number first. If the teams in a round-robin group have not completed an equal number of races, they shall be ranked in order of the percentage of races won, highest number first.

D4.4 Ties in a Completed Round-Robin Series

Ties in a completed round-robin series shall be broken using only the results in the series, in order,

(a) the highest number of race wins in all races between the tied teams;
(b) the lowest total points scored in all races between the tied teams;
(c) if two teams remain tied, the winner of the last race between them;
(d) the lowest average points scored in all races against common opponents;
(e) a sail-off if possible, otherwise a game of chance.

If a tie is partially broken by one of these, the remaining tie shall be broken by starting again at rule D4.4(a).

D4.5 Ties in an Incomplete Series

If a round-robin series is not completed, teams shall be ranked according to the results from all completed round-robins in the series. Ties shall be broken whenever possible using the results from races between the tied teams in the incomplete round-robin. Other ties shall be broken in accordance with rule D4.4.

D4.6 Scoring a Knock-Out Series

The winner of a match is the first team to score the number of race wins stated in the sailing instructions.

D4.7 Incomplete Knock-Out Series

If a match in a knock-out series is not completed (including 0-0), the result of the match shall be determined using, in order,

(a) the higher number of race wins in the incomplete match;
(b) the higher number of race wins in all races between the teams in the event;
(c) the higher place in the most recent round-robin series, applying D4.4(a) if necessary;

(d)   the winner of the most recent race between the teams.

If this rule fails to determine a result, the series shall be tied unless the sailing instructions provide for some other result.

D5   BREAKDOWNS WHEN BOATS ARE SUPPLIED BY THE ORGANIZING AUTHORITY

D5.1   Rule D5 applies when boats are supplied by the organizing authority.

D5.2   When a boat suffers a breakdown in the racing area, she may request a score change by displaying a red flag at the first reasonable opportunity after the breakdown until it is acknowledged by the race committee or by an umpire. If possible, she shall continue *racing*.

D5.3   The race committee shall decide requests for a score change in accordance with rules D5.4 and D5.5. It may take evidence in any way it considers appropriate and may communicate its decision orally.

D5.4   When the race committee decides that the team's finishing position was made significantly worse, that the breakdown was through no fault of the crew, and that in the same circumstances a reasonably competent crew would not have been able to avoid the breakdown, it shall make as equitable a decision as possible. This may be to *abandon* and resail the race or, when the boat's finishing position was predictable, award her points for that position. Any doubt about a boat's position when she broke down shall be resolved against her.

D5.5   A breakdown caused by defective supplied equipment or a breach of a *rule* by an opponent shall not normally be determined to be the fault of the crew, but one caused by careless handling, capsizing or a breach by a boat on the same team shall be. If there is doubt, it shall be presumed that the crew are not at fault.

Appendix E — Radio Sailing Racing Rules

Radio sailing races shall be sailed under The Racing Rules of Sailing *as changed by this appendix.*

E1   CHANGES TO THE DEFINITIONS, TERMINOLOGY AND THE RULES OF PARTS 1, 2 AND 7

E1.1   Definitions

Add to the definition *Interested Party*: 'but not a competitor when acting as an observer'.

In the definition *Zone* the distance is changed to four hull lengths.

Add new definition:

Disabled   A boat is *disabled* while she is unable to continue in the heat.

E1.2   Terminology

The Terminology paragraph of the Introduction is changed so that:

(a)   'Boat' means a sailboat controlled by radio signals and having no crew. However, in the rules of Part 1 and Part 5, rule E6 and the definitions *Party* and *Protest*, 'boat' includes the competitor controlling her.

(b)   'Competitor' means the person that controls a boat using radio signals.

(c)   In the racing rules, but not in its appendices, replace the noun 'race' with 'heat'. In Appendix E a race consists of one or more heats and is completed when the last heat in the race is completed.

E1.3   Rules of Parts 1, 2 and 7

(a)   Rule 1.2 is deleted.

(b)   In rule 20, hails and replies shall be made by the competitor controlling the boat.

(c)   Rule 23 is changed to: 'If possible, a boat shall avoid a boat that is *disabled.'*

(d)   Rule 90.2(c) is changed to:

Changes to the sailing instructions may be communicated orally to all affected competitors before the warning signal of the relevant race or heat. When appropriate, changes shall be confirmed in writing.

E2   ADDITIONAL RULES WHEN RACING

*Rule E2 applies only while boats are **racing**.*

E2.1   Hailing Requirements

(a)   A hail shall be made so that the competitors to whom the hail is directed might reasonably be expected to hear it.

(b)   The individual digits of a boat's sail number shall be hailed; for example 'one five', not 'fifteen'.

E2.2   Giving Advice

A competitor shall not give tactical or strategic advice to a competitor controlling a boat that is *racing*.

E2.3   Boat Out of Radio Control

A competitor who loses radio control of his boat shall promptly hail and repeat '(The boat's sail number) out of control' and the boat shall retire.

E2.4   Transmitter Aerials

If a transmitter aerial is longer than 200mm when extended, the extremity shall be adequately protected.

E2.5   Radio Interference

Transmission of radio signals that cause interference with the control of other boats is prohibited. A competitor that has broken this rule shall not *race* again until permitted to do so by the race committee.

E3   CONDUCT OF A RACE

E3.1   Control Area

The sailing instructions may specify a control area; if not specified, it shall be unrestricted. Competitors shall be in this area when controlling boats that are *racing*, except briefly to handle and then release or relaunch the boat.

E3.2   Launching Area

The sailing instructions may specify a launching area and its use; if not specified it shall be unrestricted.

E3.3   Course Board

The sailing instructions may require the course to be displayed on a board and, if so, the board shall be located in or adjacent to the control area.

E3.4   Starting and Finishing

(a)   Rule 26 is changed to:

Heats shall be started using warning, preparatory and starting signals at one-minute intervals. During the minute before the starting signal, additional sound or oral signals shall be made at ten-second intervals, and during the final ten seconds at one-second intervals. Each signal shall be timed from the beginning of its sound.

(b)   The starting and finishing lines shall be between the course sides of the starting and finishing *marks*.

E3.5   **Individual Recall**

Rule 29.1 is changed to:

When at a boat's starting signal any part of the boat is on the course side of the starting line, or when she must comply with rule 30.1, the race committee shall promptly hail 'Recall (sail numbers)' and repeat the hail as appropriate.

E3.6   **General Recall**

Rule 29.2 is changed to:

When at the starting signal the race committee is unable to identify boats that are on the course side of the starting line or to which rule 30 applies, or there has been an error in the starting procedure, the race committee may hail and repeat as appropriate 'General recall' and make two loud sounds. The preparatory signal for a new start will normally be made shortly thereafter.

E3.7   **Black Flag Rule**

When the race committee informs a boat that she has broken rule 30.3, the boat shall immediately leave the course area.

E3.8   **Other Changes to the Rules of Part 3**

(a)   Rules 30.2 and 33 are deleted.

(b)   All race committee signals shall be made orally or by other sounds. No visual signals are required unless specified in the sailing instructions.

(c)   Courses shall not be shortened.

(d)   Rule 32.1(b) is changed to: 'because of foul weather or thunderstorms,'.

E4   **RULES OF PART 4**

E4.1   **Deleted Rules in Part 4**

Rules 40, 43, 44.3, 45, 47, 48, 49, 50, 52 and 54 are deleted.

E4.2   **Outside Help**

Rule 41 is changed to:

A boat or the competitor controlling her shall not receive help from any outside source, except

(a)   when the competitor is ill, injured or in danger;

(b)   when her hull, rig or appendages are entangled with another boat, help from the other competitor;

(c)   help in the form of information freely available to all competitors.

E4.3   **Taking a Penalty**

Rule 44.1 is changed to:

A boat may take a One-Turn Penalty when she may have broken one or more rules of Part 2, or rule 31, in an incident while *racing*. However,

(a)   when she may have broken a rule of Part 2 and rule 31 in the same incident she need not take the penalty for breaking rule 31;

(b)   if the boat gained a significant advantage in the heat or race by her breach despite taking a penalty, her penalty shall be an additional One-Turn Penalty;

(c)   if the boat caused serious damage, or as a result of breaking a rule of Part 2 she caused another boat to become *disabled* and retire, her penalty shall be to retire.

E4.4   Person in Charge

Rule 46 is changed to: 'The member or organization that entered the boat shall designate the competitor. See rule 75.'

E5   RACING WITH OBSERVERS AND UMPIRES

E5.1   Observers

(a) The race committee may appoint observers, who may be competitors.

(b) Observers shall hail the sail numbers of boats that make contact with a *mark* or another boat and shall repeat the hail as appropriate.

(c) At the end of a heat, observers shall report to the race committee all unresolved incidents, and any failure to sail the course as required by rule 28.

E5.2   Umpired Races

The International Radio Sailing Association Addendum Q shall apply to umpired races. Races to be umpired may be identified in the sailing instructions or orally before the warning signal.

Note: The addendum is available at the website: **radiosailing.org.**

E5.3   Rules for Observers and Umpires

Observers and umpires shall be located in the control area. They shall not use any aid or device that gives them a visual advantage over competitors.

E6   PROTESTS AND REQUESTS FOR REDRESS

E6.1   Right to Protest

Rule 60.1 is changed to:

A boat may

(a) protest another boat, but not for an alleged breach of a rule of Part 2, 3 or 4 unless she was scheduled to sail in that heat; or

(b) request redress.

However, a boat or competitor may not protest for an alleged breach of rules E2 or E3.7.

E6.2   Protest for a Rule Broken by a Competitor

When a race committee or protest committee learns that a competitor may have broken a *rule*, it may protest the boat controlled by that competitor.

E6.3   Informing the Protestee

Rule 61.1(a) is changed to:

A boat intending to protest shall inform the other boat at the first reasonable opportunity. When her *protest* concerns an incident in the racing area that she was involved in or saw, she shall hail twice '(Her own sail number) protest (the sail number of the other boat)'.

E6.4   Informing the Race Committee

A boat intending to protest or request redress about an incident in the racing area or control area shall inform the race officer as soon as reasonably possible after *finishing* or retiring.

E6.5   Time Limits

A *protest*, request for redress or request for reopening shall be delivered to the race officer no later than ten minutes after the last boat in the heat *finishes* or after the relevant incident, whichever is later.

E6.6   Redress

Add to rule 62.1:

(e)   external radio interference acknowledged by the race committee, or

(f)   becoming *disabled* and as a result retiring because of the action of a boat that was breaking a rule of Part 2 or of a vessel not *racing* that was required to keep clear.

E6.7   Right to Be Present

In rule 63.3(a) 'the representatives of boats shall have been on board' is changed to 'the representative of each boat shall be the competitor controlling her'.

E6.8   Taking Evidence and Finding Facts

Add to rule 63.6:

When the *protest* concerns an alleged breach of a rule of Part 2, 3 or 4, any witness shall have been in the control area at the time of the incident. If the witness is a competitor who was not acting as an observer, he shall also have been scheduled to race in the relevant heat.

E6.9   Decisions on Redress

Add to rule 64.2:

If a boat is given redress because she was damaged, her redress shall include reasonable time, but not more than 30 minutes, to make repairs before her next heat.

E7   PENALTIES

When a protest committee decides that a boat that is a *party* to a protest hearing has broken a *rule* other than a rule of Part 2, 3 or 4, it shall either

(a)   disqualify her or add any number of points (including zero and fractions of points) to her score. The penalty shall be applied, if possible, to the heat or race in which the *rule* was broken; otherwise it shall be applied to the next heat or race for that boat. When points are added, the scores of other boats shall not be changed; or

(b)   require her to take one or more One-Turn Penalties that shall be taken as soon as possible after the starting signal of her next heat that is started and not subsequently recalled or *abandoned*.

However, if the boat has broken a rule in Appendix G or rule E8, the protest committee shall act in accordance with rule G4.

E8   CHANGES TO APPENDIX G, IDENTIFICATION ON SAILS

(a)   The first paragraph of rule G1.1 is changed to:

Every boat of a class administered or recognised by the International Radio Sailing Association shall display a sail number on both sides of each sail. Class insignia and national letters shall be displayed on mainsails as stated in rules G1.1(a), G1.1(b), E8(d) and E8(e).

(b)   Rule G1.1(c) is changed to:

(1)   A sail number, which shall be the last two digits of the boat registration number or the competitor's or owner's personal number, allotted by the relevant issuing authority.

(2)   When possible, there shall be space in front of a sail number for a numeric prefix.

(3)   When the sail number is in the range '00' to '09', the initial '0' shall be omitted and the remaining digit positioned to allow space for both a prefix and a suffix.

(4)   '0' shall not be used as a prefix.

(5) When there is a conflict between sail numbers or a sail number might be misread, the race committee may require that the sail numbers on one or more boats be changed to a numeric alternative.

(6) Any changed sail number shall become the sail number for the event.

(c) The sentence after rule G1.1(c) is deleted.

(d) Rule G1.2(b) is changed to:

The height of characters and distance between them on the same and opposite sides of the sail shall be as follows:

	Minimum	*Maximum*
Class insignia:		
Except where positioned back to back, shortest distance between insignia on opposite sides of sail	20 mm	
Sail numbers:		
Height of characters	100 mm	110 mm
Shortest distance between adjoining characters on same side of sail	20 mm	30 mm
Shortest distance between sail numbers on opposite sides of sail and between sail numbers and other identification	60 mm	
National letters:		
Height of characters	60 mm	70 mm
Shortest distance between adjoining characters on same side of sail	13 mm	23mm
Shortest distance between national letters on opposite sides of sail	40 mm	

(e) Rule G1.3 is changed to:

(1) Class insignia may be positioned back to back on opposite sides of the sail where the design coincides. Otherwise class insignia, sail numbers and national letters shall be positioned at different heights, with those on the starboard side being uppermost.

(2) On a mainsail, sail numbers shall be positioned above the national letters and below the class insignia.

(3) Sail numbers shall be positioned on a mainsail above the line perpendicular to the luff through the quarter leech point.

(f) Where the size of a sail makes it impossible to comply with rule E8(b), the minimum dimensions in rule E8(d) or the positioning requirements in rule E8(e)(3), exceptions are permitted in the following order of priority:

(1) omission of national letters;

(2) position of the mainsail sail numbers lower than the line perpendicular to the luff through the quarter leech point;

(3) reduction of the shortest distance between sail numbers on opposite sides of the sail provided the shortest distance is not less than 20 mm;

(4) reduction of the height of sail numbers.

Appendix F — Kiteboarding Racing Rules

Kiteboard course races shall be sailed under The Racing Rules of Sailing *as changed by this appendix. The term 'boat' elsewhere in the racing rules means 'kiteboard' or 'boat' as appropriate.*

Note: Rules for other kiteboard racing formats (such as Kitecross, Slalom, Boarder X) or other kiteboard competitions (such as Freestyle, Wave, Speed) are not included in this appendix. Links to current versions of these rules can be found on the ISAF website.

CHANGES TO THE DEFINITIONS

The definitions *Finish, Keep Clear, Leeward* and *Windward, Mark-Room, Obstruction, Start,* and *Tack, Starboard* or *Port* are changed to:

Finish A kiteboard *finishes* when, while the competitor is in contact with the hull, any part of her hull, or the competitor in normal position, crosses the finishing line from the course side. However, she has not *finished* if after crossing the finishing line she

(a) takes a penalty under rule 44.2,

(b) corrects an error under rule 28.2 made at the line, or

(c) continues to sail the course.

Keep Clear A kiteboard *keeps clear* of a right-of-way kiteboard

(a) if the right-of-way kiteboard can sail her course with no need to take avoiding action and,

(b) when the kiteboards are *overlapped*, if the right-of-way kiteboard can also, without immediately making contact, change course in both directions or move her kite in any direction.

Leeward and **Windward** A kiteboard's *leeward* side is the side that is or, when she is head to wind, was away from the wind. However, when sailing by the lee or directly downwind, her *leeward* side is the side on which her kite lies. The other side is her *windward* side. When two kiteboards on the same *tack* overlap, the one whose hull is on the *leeward* side of the other's hull is the *leeward* kiteboard. The other is the *windward* kiteboard.

Mark-Room *Mark-Room* for a kiteboard is *room* to sail her *proper course* to round or pass the *mark*. However, *mark-room* for a kiteboard does not include *room* to tack unless the kiteboard is *overlapped* inside and to *windward* of the kiteboard required to give *mark-room* and she would be *fetching* the *mark* after her tack.

Obstruction An object that a kiteboard could not pass without changing course substantially, if she were sailing directly towards it and 10 metres from it. An object that can be safely passed on only one side and an area so designated by the sailing instructions are also *obstructions*. However, a kiteboard *racing* is not an *obstruction* to other kiteboards unless they are required to *keep clear* of her or, if rule 23 applies, avoid her. A vessel under way, including a kiteboard *racing*, is never a continuing *obstruction*.

Start A kiteboard *starts* when, her hull and the competitor having been entirely on the pre-start side of the starting line at or after her starting signal, and having complied with rule 30.1 if it applies, any part of her hull, or the competitor crosses the starting line in the direction of the first *mark*.

Tack, Starboard or **Port** A kiteboard is on the *tack, starboard* or *port*, corresponding to the competitor's hand that would be forward if the competitor were in normal riding position (riding heel side with both hands on the control bar and arms not crossed). A kiteboard is on *starboard tack* when the competitor's right hand would be forward and is on the *port tack* when the competitor's left hand would be forward.

The definition *Zone* is deleted.

Add the following definitions:

About to Round or Pass A kiteboard is *about to round or pass* a *mark* when her *proper course* is to begin to manoeuvre to round or pass it.

Capsized A kiteboard is *capsized* if
(a) her kite is in the water,
(b) her lines are tangled with another kiteboard's lines, or
(c) the competitor has, clearly by accident and for a significant period of time,
    (1) fallen into the water or
    (2) become disconnected from the hull.

Jumping A kiteboard is *jumping* when her hull, its appendages and the competitor are clear of the water.

Looping A kite is *looping* when it is being flown in a single loop or in a pattern of repeated loops, clockwise, counterclockwise or alternating between the two.

F1 CHANGES TO THE RULES OF PART 1
[No changes.]

F2 CHANGES TO THE RULES OF PART 2

13 EXCEPTIONS TO RULES 10, 11 AND 12
Rule 13 is changed to:

13.1 When a kiteboard changes *tack* on an upwind leg, she shall *keep clear* of other kiteboards until she is moving on a close-hauled course. During that time rules 10, 11 and 12 do not apply. If two kiteboards are subject to this rule at the same time, the one on the other's port side or the one astern shall *keep clear*.

13.2 If two kiteboards converge while sailing downwind and it is not possible under rule 10, 11 or 12 to determine which one has right of way,
    (a) if they are *overlapped*, the one on the other's starboard side shall *keep clear*.
    (b) if they are not *overlapped*, the one *clear astern* shall *keep clear*.

16 CHANGING COURSE OR KITE POSITION
Rule 16 is changed to:

16.1 When a right-of-way kiteboard changes course or the position of her kite, she shall give the other kiteboard *room* to *keep clear*.

16.2 In addition, when after the starting signal a *port-tack* kiteboard is *keeping clear* by sailing to pass astern of a *starboard-tack* kiteboard, the *starboard-tack* kiteboard shall not change course or the position of her kite if as a result the *port-tack* kiteboard would immediately need to change course or the position of her kite to continue *keeping clear*.

17 ON THE SAME TACK; PROPER COURSE
Rule 17 is deleted.

18 MARK-ROOM
Rule 18 is changed as follows:

The first sentence of rule 18.1 is changed to:

Rule 18 begins to apply between kiteboards when they are required to leave a *mark* on the same side and at least one of them is *about to round or pass* it. The rule no longer applies after the kiteboard entitled to *mark-room* has passed the *mark*.

Rule 18.2(b) is changed to:

(b)   If kiteboards are *overlapped* when the first of them is *about to round or pass* the *mark*, the outside kiteboard at that moment shall thereafter give the inside kiteboard *mark-room*. If a kiteboard is *clear ahead* when she is *about to round or pass* the *mark*, the kiteboard *clear astern* at that moment shall thereafter give her *mark-room*.

Rule 18.2(c) is changed to:

(c)   When a kiteboard is required to give *mark-room* by rule 18.2(b), she shall continue to do so even if later an *overlap* is broken or a new *overlap* begins.

18.3   Tacking in the Zone

Rule 18.3 is deleted.

18.4   Gybing or Bearing Away

Rule 18.4 is changed to:

When an inside *overlapped* right-of-way kiteboard must gybe or bear away at a *mark* to sail her *proper course*, until she gybes or bears away she shall sail no farther from the *mark* than needed to sail that course. Rule 18.4 does not apply at a gate *mark*.

22   STARTING ERRORS; TAKING PENALTIES; JUMPING

Rule 22.3 is changed and new rules 22.4 and 22.5 are added:

22.3   During the last minute before her starting signal, a kiteboard that stops, slows down significantly, or one that is not making significant forward progress shall *keep clear* of all others unless she is accidentally *capsized*.

22.4   A kiteboard that is *jumping* shall *keep clear* of one that is not.

22.5   When sailing downwind, if one kiteboard is *looping* her kite and another is not, the kiteboard that is *looping* her kite shall *keep clear* of the one that is not.

23   CAPSIZED OR AGROUND; RESCUING

Rule 23 is changed to:

23.1   If possible, a kiteboard shall avoid a kiteboard that is *capsized* or has not regained control after *capsizing*, is aground, or is trying to help a person or vessel in danger.

23.2   A kiteboard that is *capsized* or aground shall not interfere with another kiteboard.

F3   CHANGES TO THE RULES OF PART 3

30   STARTING PENALTIES

In rule 30.3, 'sail number' is changed to 'competitor number'.

31   TOUCHING A MARK

Rule 31 is deleted.

F4   CHANGES TO THE RULES OF PART 4

41   OUTSIDE HELP

Add new rules 41(e) and 41(f):

(e)   help from another competitor in the same race to assist a relaunch;

(f)   help to change equipment, but only in the launching area.

42   PROPULSION

Rule 42 is changed to:

A kiteboard shall be propelled only by the action of the wind on the kite, by the action of the water on the hull and by the unassisted actions of the competitor. However, the competitor shall not make significant progress by paddling, swimming or walking.

43   COMPETITOR CLOTHING AND EQUIPMENT

Rule 43.1(a) is changed to:

(a)   Competitors shall not wear or carry clothing or equipment for the purpose of increasing their weight. However, a competitor may wear a drinking container that shall have a capacity of at least one litre and weigh no more than 1.5 kilograms when full.

44   PENALTIES AT THE TIME OF AN INCIDENT

Rule 44 is changed to:

44.1   Taking a Penalty

A kiteboard may take a 360°-Turn Penalty when she may have broken one or more rules of Part 2 in an incident while *racing*. Sailing instructions may specify the use of some other penalty. However, if the kiteboard caused injury or serious damage or, despite taking a penalty, gained a significant advantage in the race or series by her breach her penalty shall be to retire.

44.2   360°-Turn Penalty

After getting well clear of other kiteboards as soon after the incident as possible, a kiteboard takes a 360°-Turn Penalty by promptly making a 360° turn with her hull in the water and with no requirement for a tack or a gybe. When a kiteboard takes the penalty at or near the finishing line, she shall sail completely to the course side of the line before *finishing*.

PART 4 RULES DELETED

Rules 43.2, 44.3, 45, 47, 48.1, 49, 50, 51, 52 and 54 are deleted.

F5   CHANGES TO THE RULES OF PART 5

61   PROTEST REQUIREMENTS

Rule 61.1(a) is changed to:

(a)   A kiteboard intending to protest shall inform the other kiteboard at the first reasonable opportunity. When her *protest* will concern an incident in the racing area that she was involved in or saw, she shall hail 'Protest'. She shall also inform the race committee of her intention to protest as soon as practicable after she *finishes* or retires.

62   REDRESS

Add new rule 62.1(e):

(e)   *capsizing* because of the action of a kiteboard that was breaking a rule of Part 2.

63   HEARINGS

For a race of an elimination series that will qualify a kiteboard to compete in a later stage of an event, rules 61.2 and 65.2 are deleted and rule 63.6 is changed to:

63.6   *Protests* and requests for redress need not be in writing; they shall be made orally to a member of the protest committee as soon as reasonably possible following the race. The protest committee may take evidence in any way it considers appropriate and may communicate its decision orally.

70   APPEALS AND REQUESTS TO A NATIONAL AUTHORITY

Rule 70.5(a) is changed to:

(a)   it is essential to determine promptly the result of a race of an elimination series that will qualify a kiteboard to compete in a later stage of
an event;

F6   CHANGES TO THE RULES OF PART 6

[No changes.]

F7   CHANGES TO THE RULES OF PART 7

90   RACE COMMITTEE; SAILING INSTRUCTIONS; SCORING

The last sentence of rule 90.2(c) is changed to: 'Oral instructions may be
given only if the procedure is stated in the sailing instructions.'

F8   CHANGES TO APPENDIX A

A1   NUMBER OF RACES; OVERALL SCORES

Rule A1 is changed to:

The number of races scheduled and the number required to be completed
to constitute a series shall be stated in the sailing instructions. If an event
includes more than one discipline or format, the sailing instructions shall
state how the overall scores are to be calculated.

A8   SERIES TIES

Rule A8 is changed to:

A8.1   If there is a series-score tie between two or more kiteboards, it shall be
broken in favour of the kiteboard(s) with the best single excluded race
score(s).

A8.2   If a tie remains between two or more kiteboards, each kiteboard's race
scores shall be listed in order of best to worst, and at the first point(s)
where there is a difference the tie shall be broken in favour of the kite-
board(s) with the best score(s). These scores shall be used even if
some of them are excluded scores.

A8.3   If a tie still remains between two or more kiteboards, they shall be ranked
in order of their scores in the last race. Any remaining ties shall be broken
by using the tied kiteboards' scores in the next-to-last race and so on until
all ties are broken. These scores shall be used even if some of them are
excluded scores.

F9   CHANGES TO APPENDIX G

Appendix G is changed to:

Appendix G – Identification on Competitors

G1   Every kiteboard shall be identified as follows:

(a)   Each competitor shall be provided with and wear a shirt with a
personal competition number of no more than three digits.

(b)   The numbers shall be displayed on the front and back of the shirts
and be at least 15 cm high.

(c)   The numbers shall be Arabic numerals, all of the same solid colour,
clearly legible and in a commercially available typeface giving the
same or better legibility as Helvetica. The colour of the numbers
shall contrast with the colour of the shirt.

Appendix G — Identification on Sails

See rule 77.

G1 ISAF CLASS BOATS

G1.1 Identification

Every boat of an ISAF Class shall carry on her mainsail and, as provided in rules G1.3(d) and G1.3(e) for letters and numbers only, on her spinnaker and headsail

(a) the insignia denoting her class;

(b) at all international events, except when the boats are provided to all competitors, national letters denoting her national authority from the table below. For the purposes of this rule, international events are ISAF events, world and continental championships, and events described as international events in their notices of race and sailing instructions; and

(c) a sail number of no more than four digits allotted by her national authority or, when so required by the class rules, by the class association. The four-digit limitation does not apply to classes whose ISAF membership or recognition took effect before 1 April 1997. Alternatively, if permitted in the class rules, an owner may be allotted a personal sail number by the relevant issuing authority, which may be used on all his boats in that class.

Sails measured before 31 March 1999 shall comply with rule G1.1 or with the rules applicable at the time of measurement.

Note: An up-to-date version of the table below is available on the ISAF website.

NATIONAL SAIL LETTERS

National authority	Letters	National authority	Letters
Algeria	ALG	Cayman Islands	CAY
American Samoa	ASA	Chile	CHI
Andorra	AND	China, PR	CHN
Angola	ANG	Chinese Taipei	TPE
Antigua	ANT	Colombia	COL
Argentina	ARG	Cook Islands	COK
Armenia	ARM	Croatia	CRO
Aruba	ARU	Cuba	CUB
Australia	AUS	Cyprus	CYP
Austria	AUT	Czech Republic	CZE
Azerbaijan	AZE	Denmark	DEN
Bahamas	BAH	Djibouti	DJI
Bahrain	BRN	Dominican Republic	DOM
Barbados	BAR	Ecuador	ECU
Belarus	BLR	Egypt	EGY
Belgium	BEL	El Salvador	ESA
Belize	BIZ	Estonia	EST
Bermuda	BER	Fiji	FIJ
Brazil	BRA	Finland	FIN
British Virgin Islands	IVB	France	FRA
Bulgaria	BUL	Georgia	GEO
Canada	CAN	Germany	GER

National authority	Letters	National authority	Letters
Great Britain	GBR	Namibia	NAM
Greece	GRE	Netherlands	NED
Grenada	GRN	Netherlands Antilles	AHO
Guam	GUM	New Zealand	NZL
Guatemala	GUA	Norway	NOR
Hong Kong	HKG	Oman	OMA
Hungary	HUN	Pakistan	PAK
Iceland	ISL	Palestine	PLE
India	IND	Papua New Guinea	PNG
Indonesia	INA	Paraguay	PAR
Ireland	IRL	Peru	PER
Israel	ISR	Philippines	PHI
Italy	ITA	Poland	POL
Jamaica	JAM	Portugal	POR
Japan	JPN	Puerto Rico	PUR
Kazakhstan	KAZ	Qatar	QAT
Kenya	KEN	Romania	ROU
Korea, DPR	PRK	Russia	RUS
Korea, Republic of	KOR	Samoa	SAM
Kosovo	KOS	San Marino	SMR
Kuwait	KUW	Senegal	SEN
Kyrgyzstan	KGZ	Serbia	SRB
Latvia	LAT	Seychelles	SEY
Lebanon	LIB	Singapore	SIN
Libya	LBA	Slovak Republic	SVK
Liechtenstein	LIE	Slovenia	SLO
Lithuania	LTU	Solomon Islands	SOL
Luxembourg	LUX	South Africa	RSA
Macedonia (FYRO)	MKD	Spain	ESP
Madagascar	MAD	Sri Lanka	SRI
Malaysia	MAS	St Lucia	LCA
Malta	MLT	Sudan	SUD
Mauritius	MRI	Sweden	SWE
Mexico	MEX	Switzerland	SUI
Micronesia (FSo)	FSM	Tahiti	TAH
Moldova	MDA	Tanzania	TAN
Monaco	MON	Thailand	THA
Montenegro	MNE	Trinidad & Tobago	TRI
Morocco	MAR	Tunisia	TUN
Mozambique	MOZ	Turkey	TUR
Myanmar	MYA	Uganda	UGA

National authority	Letters	National authority	Letters
Ukraine	UKR	Vanuatu	VAN
United Arab Emirates	UAE	Venezuela	VEN
United States of America	USA	Vietnam	VIE
Uruguay	URU	Zimbabwe	ZIM
US Virgin Islands	ISV		

G1.2 Specifications

(a) National letters and sail numbers shall be in capital letters and Arabic numerals, clearly legible and of the same colour. Commercially available typefaces giving the same or better legibility than Helvetica are acceptable.

(b) The height of characters and space between adjoining characters on the same and opposite sides of the sail shall be related to the boat's overall length as follows:

Overall length	Minimum height	Minimum space between characters and from edge of sail
under 3.5 m	230 mm	45 mm
3.5 m – 8.5 m	300 mm	60 mm
8.5 m – 11 m	375 mm	75 mm
over 11 m	450 mm	90 mm

G1.3 Positioning

Class insignia, national letters and sail numbers shall be positioned as follows:

(a) Except as provided in rules G1.3(d) and G1.3(e), class insignia, national letters and sail numbers shall, if possible, be wholly above an arc whose centre is the head point and whose radius is 60% of the leech length. They shall be placed at different heights on the two sides of the sail, those on the starboard side being uppermost.

(b) The class insignia shall be placed above the national letters. If the class insignia is of such a design that two of them coincide when placed back to back on both sides of the sail, they may be so placed.

(c) National letters shall be placed above the sail number.

(d) The national letters and sail number shall be displayed on the front side of a spinnaker but may be placed on both sides. They shall be displayed wholly below an arc whose centre is the head point and whose radius is 40% of the foot median and, if possible, wholly above an arc whose radius is 60% of the foot median.

(e) The national letters and sail number shall be displayed on both sides of a headsail whose clew can extend behind the mast 30% or more of the main-sail foot length. They shall be displayed wholly below an arc whose centre is the head point and whose radius is half the luff length and, if possible, wholly above an arc whose radius is 75% of the luff length.

G2 OTHER BOATS

Other boats shall comply with the rules of their national authority or class association in regard to the allotment, carrying and size of insignia, letters and numbers. Such rules shall, when practicable, conform to the above requirements.

US Sailing prescribes that unless otherwise stated in her class rules, the sails of a boat that is not in an ISAF International Class or Recognized Class shall comply with rule G1. However, offshore racing boats not in a class that is subject to rule G1 shall carry numbers allotted by US Sailing on mainsails, spinnakers and each overlapping headsail having a luff-perpendicular measurement exceeding 130% of the base of the foretriangle. This rule applies only to a boat whose owner's national authority is US Sailing. Go to ussailing.org/racingrules/documents *and click the 'Sail Numbers' link for the full text of the Sail Numbering System for offshore racing boats in the United States or for an application for a sail number.*

G3   CHARTERED OR LOANED BOATS

When so stated in the notice of race or sailing instructions, a boat chartered or loaned for an event may carry national letters or a sail number in contravention of her class rules.

G4   WARNINGS AND PENALTIES

When a protest committee finds that a boat has broken a rule of this appendix, it shall either warn her and give her time to comply or penalize her.

G5   CHANGES BY CLASS RULES

ISAF Classes may change the rules of this appendix provided the changes have first been approved by the ISAF.

Appendix H — Weighing Clothing and Equipment

See rule 43. This appendix shall not be changed by sailing instructions or prescriptions of national authorities.

H1   Items of clothing and equipment to be weighed shall be arranged on a rack. After being saturated in water the items shall be allowed to drain freely for one minute before being weighed. The rack must allow the items to hang as they would hang from clothes hangers, so as to allow the water to drain freely. Pockets that have drain-holes that cannot be closed shall be empty, but pockets or items that can hold water shall be full.

H2   When the weight recorded exceeds the amount permitted, the competitor may rearrange the items on the rack and the equipment inspector or measurer shall again soak and weigh them. This procedure may be repeated a second time if the weight still exceeds the amount permitted.

H3   A competitor wearing a dry suit may choose an alternative means of weighing the items.

    (a)   The dry suit and items of clothing and equipment that are worn outside the dry suit shall be weighed as described above.

    (b)   Clothing worn underneath the dry suit shall be weighed as worn while *racing*, without draining.

    (c)   The two weights shall be added together.

Appendix J — Notice of Race and Sailing Instructions

See rules 89.2(a) and 90.2. The term 'race' includes a regatta or other series of races.

J1 **NOTICE OF RACE CONTENTS**

J1.1 The notice of race shall include the following information:

(1) the title, place and dates of the race and name of the organizing authority;

(2) that the race will be governed by the *rules* as defined in *The Racing Rules of Sailing*;

(3) a list of any other documents that will govern the event (for example, *The Equipment Rules of Sailing*, to the extent that they apply), stating where or how each document or a copy of it may be seen;

(4) the classes to race, any handicap or rating system that will be used and the classes to which it will apply, conditions of entry and any restrictions on entries;

(5) the times of registration and warning signals for the practice race, if one is scheduled, and the first race, and succeeding races if known.

J1.2 The notice of race shall include any of the following that will apply and that would help competitors decide whether to attend the event or that conveys other information they will need before the sailing instructions become available:

(1) identification of any racing rules that will be changed (see rule 86), a summary of the changes, and a statement that the changes will appear in full in the sailing instructions (also, if rule 86.2 applies, include the statement from ISAF authorizing the change);

(2) that boats will be required to display advertising chosen and supplied by the organizing authority (see rule 80 and ISAF Regulation 20, Advertising Code) and other information related to Regulation 20;

(3) any classification requirements that some or all competitors must satisfy (see rule 79 and ISAF Regulation 22, Sailor Classification Code);

(4) for an event where entries from other countries are expected, any national prescriptions that may require advance preparation (see rule 88);

(5) the procedures for registration or entry, including fees and any closing dates;

(6) an entry form, to be signed by the boat's owner or owner's representative, containing words such as 'I agree to be bound by *The Racing Rules of Sailing* and by all other *rules* that govern this event.';

(7) equipment inspection, measurement procedures or requirements for measurement certificates or for handicap or rating certificates;

(8) the time and place at which the sailing instructions will be available;

(9) changes to class rules, as permitted under rule 87, referring specifically to each rule and stating the change;

(10) the courses to be sailed;

(11) the penalty for breaking a rule of Part 2, other than the Two-Turns Penalty;

(12) denial of the right of appeal, subject to rule 70.5;

(13) the scoring system, if different from the Low Point System in Appendix A, the number of races scheduled and the minimum number that must be completed to constitute a series;

(14) for chartered or loaned boats, whether rule G3 applies;

(15) prizes.

J2   SAILING INSTRUCTION CONTENTS

J2.1   The sailing instructions shall include the following information:

(1) that the race will be governed by the *rules* as defined in *The Racing Rules of Sailing*;

(2) a list of any other documents that will govern the event (for example, *The Equipment Rules of Sailing*, to the extent that they apply);

(3) the schedule of races, the classes to race and times of warning signals for each class;

(4) the course(s) to be sailed, or a list of *marks* from which the course will be selected and, if relevant, how courses will be signalled;

(5) descriptions of *marks*, including starting and finishing *marks*, stating the order in which *marks* are to be passed and the side on which each is to be left and identifying all rounding *marks* (see rule 28.2);

(6) descriptions of the starting and finishing lines, class flags and any special signals to be used;

(7) the time limit, if any, for *finishing*;

(8) the handicap or rating system to be used, if any, and the classes to which it will apply;

(9) the scoring system, if different from the Low Point System in Appendix A, included by reference to class rules or other *rules* governing the event, or stated in full. State the number of races scheduled and the minimum number that must be completed to constitute a series.

J2.2   The sailing instructions shall include those of the following that will apply:

(1) that boats will be required to display advertising chosen and supplied by the organizing authority (see rule 80 and ISAF Regulation 20, Advertising Code) and other information related to Regulation 20;

(2) replacement of the rules of Part 2 with the right-of-way rules of the *International Regulations for Preventing Collisions at Sea* or other government right-of-way rules, the time(s) or place(s) they will apply, and any night signals to be used by the race committee;

(3) changes to the racing rules permitted by rule 86, referring specifically to each rule and stating the change (also, if rule 86.2 applies, include the statement from ISAF authorizing the change);

(4) changes to the national prescriptions (see rule 88.2);

(5) prescriptions that will apply if boats will pass through the waters of more than one national authority while *racing*, and when they will apply (see rule 88.1);

(6) when appropriate, at an event where entries from other countries are expected, a copy in English of the national prescriptions that will apply;

(7) changes to class rules, as permitted under rule 87, referring specifically to each rule and stating the change;

(8) restrictions controlling changes to boats when supplied by the organizing authority;

(9) procedures for equipment inspection or measurement;

(10) location(s) of official notice board(s);

(11) procedure for changing the sailing instructions;

(12) procedure for giving oral changes to the sailing instructions on the water (see rule 90.2(c));

(13) safety requirements, such as requirements and signals for personal flotation devices, check-in at the starting area, and check-out and check-in ashore;

(14)   declaration requirements;

(15)   signals to be made ashore and location of signal station(s);

(16)   the racing area (a chart is recommended);

(17)   approximate course length and approximate length of windward legs;

(18)   description of any area designated by the race committee to be an
        obstruction (see the definition *Obstruction*);

(19)   the time limit, if any, for the first boat to *finish* and the time limit, if any,
        for boats other than the first boat to *finish*;

(20)   time allowances;

(21)   the location of the starting area and any restrictions on entering it;

(22)   any special procedures or signals for individual or general recall;

(23)   boats identifying *mark* locations;

(24)   any special procedures or signals for changing a leg of the course
        (see rule 33);

(25)   any special procedures for shortening the course or for *finishing* a short-
        ened course;

(26)   restrictions on use of support boats, plastic pools, radios, etc.; on trash
        disposal; on hauling out; and on outside assistance provided to a boat
        that is not *racing*;

(27)   the penalty for breaking a rule of Part 2, other than the Two-Turns Penalty;

(28)   whether Appendix P will apply;

(29)   when and under what circumstances propulsion is permitted under
        rule 42.3(i);

(30)   time limits, place of hearings, and special procedures for *protests*, requests
        for redress or requests for reopening;

(31)   if rule N1.4(b) will apply, the time limit for requesting a hearing under that
        rule;

(32)   denial of the right of appeal, subject to rule 70.5;

(33)   when required by rule 70.3, the national authority to which appeals and
        requests may be sent;

(34)   the national authority's approval of the appointment of an international jury,
        when required under rule 91(b);

(35)   substitution of competitors;

(36)   the minimum number of boats appearing in the starting area required for
        a race to be started;

(37)   when and where races *postponed* or *abandoned* for the day will be sailed;

(38)   tides and currents;

(39)   prizes;

(40)   other commitments of the race committee and obligations of boats.

Appendix K — Notice of Race Guide

*This guide provides a notice of race designed primarily for major championship
regattas for one or more classes. It therefore will be particularly useful for world,
continental and national championships and other events of similar importance.
It can be downloaded from the ISAF website as a basic text for producing a
notice of race for any particular event.*

*The guide can also be useful for other events. However, for such events some
of the paragraphs will be unnecessary or undesirable. Organizing authorities
should therefore be careful in making their choices.*

This guide relates closely to Appendix L, Sailing Instructions Guide, and its expanded version Appendix LE on the ISAF website, the introduction to which contains principles that also apply to a notice of race.

*To use this guide, first review rule J1 and decide which paragraphs will be needed. Paragraphs that are required by rule J1.1 are marked with an asterisk (*). Delete all inapplicable or unnecessary paragraphs. Select the version preferred where there is a choice. Follow the directions in the left margin to fill in the spaces where a solid line (___) appears and select the preferred wording if a choice or option is shown in brackets ([...]).*

After deleting unused paragraphs, renumber all paragraphs in sequential order. Be sure that paragraph numbers are correct where one paragraph refers to another.

The items listed below, when applicable, should be distributed with the notice of race, but should not be included as numbered paragraphs in the notice.

1   *An entry form, to be signed by the boat's owner or owner's representative, containing words such as 'I agree to be bound by* The Racing Rules of Sailing *and by all other rules that govern this event.'*

2   *For an event where entries from other countries are expected, the applicable national prescriptions in English.*

3   *List of sponsors, if appropriate.*

4   *Lodging and camping information.*

5   *Description of meal facilities.*

6   *Race committee and protest committee members.*

7   *Special mooring or storage requirements.*

8   *Sail and boat repair facilities and ship's chandlers.*

9   *Availability of chartered or loaned boats and whether rule G3 will apply.*

On separate lines, insert the full name of the regatta, the inclusive dates from measurement or the practice race until the final race or closing ceremony, the name of the organizing authority, and the city and country.	_____ _____ _____ _____

NOTICE OF RACE

1   RULES

1.1* The regatta will be governed by the rules as defined in *The Racing Rules of Sailing*.

Use the first sentence if appropriate. Insert the name. List by number and title the prescriptions that will not apply (see rule 88). Use the second sentence if it applies and if entries from other countries are expected, and state the relevant prescriptions in full.

1.2 [The following prescriptions of the _____ national authority will not apply: _____.] [The prescriptions that may require advance preparation are stated in full below.]

(OR)

Use if appropriate, but only if the national authority for the venue of the event has not adopted a prescription to rule 88.

1.2 No national prescriptions will apply.

List by name any other documents that govern the event; for example, The Equipment Rules of Sailing, to the extent that they apply.

1.3* _____ will apply.

See rule 86. Insert the rule number(s) and summarize the changes.

1.4 Racing rule(s) _____ will be changed as follows: _____. The changes will appear in full in the sailing instructions. The sailing instructions may also change other racing rules.

Insert the rule number(s) and class name. Make a separate statement for the rules of each class.

1.5 Under rule 87, rule(s) _____ of the _____ class rules [will not apply] [is (are) changed as follows: ___].

1.6 If there is a conflict between languages the English text will take precedence.

2 **ADVERTISING**

See ISAF Regulation 20, Advertising Code. Include other applicable information related to Regulation 20.

2.1 Competitor advertising will be restricted as follows: _____.

See ISAF Regulation 20.

2.2 Boats [shall] [may] be required to display advertising chosen and supplied by the organizing authority.

3* **ELIGIBILITY AND ENTRY**

Insert the class(es).

3.1 The regatta is open to all boats of the _____ class(es).

(OR)

Insert the class(es) and eligibility requirements.

3.1 The regatta is open to boats of the _____ class(es) that _____.

Insert the postal, fax and e-mail addresses and entry closing date.

3.2 Eligible boats may enter by completing the attached form and sending it, together with the required fee, to _____ by _____.

Insert any conditions.

3.3 Late entries will be accepted under the following conditions: _____.

Insert any restrictions.

3.4 The following restrictions on the number of boats apply: _____.

4 **CLASSIFICATION**

Insert any requirements.

The following classification requirements will apply (see rule 79): _____.

5   FEES

Insert all required fees for racing.

5.1 Required fees are as follows:

Class	Fee

*Insert optional fees
(for example, for
social events).*

5.2 Other fees:

**6   QUALIFYING SERIES AND
      FINAL SERIES**

*Use only when a class is divided
into fleets racing a qualifying series
and a final series.*

The regatta will consist of a qualifying
series and a final series.

7   SCHEDULE

Insert the day, date and times.

7.1* Registration:

Day and date _____

From _____ To _____

Insert the day, date and times.

7.2 Measurement and inspection:

Day and date _____

From _____ To _____

*Revise as desired and insert the
dates and classes. Include a practice
race if any. When the series consists
of qualifying races and final races,
specify them. The schedule can
also be given in an attachment.*

7.3* Dates of racing:

Date	Class _____	Class _____
_____	racing	racing
_____	racing	reserve day
_____	reserve day	racing
_____	racing	racing
_____	racing	racing

Insert the classes and numbers.

7.4 Number of races:

Class	Number	Races per day

Insert the time.

7.5* The scheduled time of the warning signal
for the [practice race] [first race] [each
day] is _____.

8   MEASUREMENTS

Each boat shall produce a valid
[measurement] [rating] certificate.

(OR)

*List the measurements with
appropriate references to the
class rules.*

Each boat shall produce a valid [measure-
ment] [rating] certificate. In addition the
following measurements [may] [will]
be taken: _____.

9   SAILING INSTRUCTIONS

Insert the time, date and location.

The sailing instructions will be available after _____ on _____ at _____.

10   VENUE

Insert a number or letter. Provide a marked map with driving instructions.

10.1 Attachment _____ shows the location of the regatta harbour.

Insert a number or letter. Provide a marked map or chart.

10.2 Attachment _____ shows the location of the racing areas.

11   THE COURSES

Include the description.

The courses to be sailed will be as follows: _____.

(OR)

Insert a number or letter. A method of illustrating various courses is shown in Addendum A of Appendix L or LE. Insert the course length if applicable.

The diagrams in Attachment _____ show the courses, including the approximate angles between legs, the order in which marks are to be passed, and the side on which each mark is to be left. [The approximate course length will be _____.]

12   PENALTY SYSTEM

Include paragraph 12.1 only when the Two-Turns Penalty will not be used. Insert the number of places or describe the penalties.

12.1 The Scoring Penalty, rule 44.3, will apply. The penalty will be _____ places.

(OR)

12.1 The penalties are as follows: _____.

Insert the class(es).

12.2 For the _____ class(es) rule 44.1 is changed so that the Two-Turns Penalty is replaced by the One-Turn Penalty.

Include only if the protest committee is an international jury or another provision of rule 70.5 applies.

12.3 Decisions of the [protest committee] [international jury] will be final as provided in rule 70.5.

13   SCORING

Include only if the Low Point System of Appendix A will not be used. Describe the system.

13.1 The scoring system is as follows: _____.

Insert the number.

13.2 _____ races are required to be completed to constitute a series.

Insert the numbers throughout.

13.3 (a) When fewer than _____ races have been completed, a boat's series score will be the total of her race scores.

(b) When from _____ to _____ races have been completed, a boat's series score will be the total of her race scores excluding her worst score.

(c) When _____ or more races have been completed, a boat's series score will be the total of her race scores excluding her two worst scores.

Insert the identification markings. National letters are suggested for international events.

14 SUPPORT BOATS

Support boats shall be marked with _____.

15 BERTHING

Boats shall be kept in their assigned places while they are in the [boat park] [harbour].

16 HAUL-OUT RESTRICTIONS

Keelboats shall not be hauled out during the regatta except with and according to the terms of prior written permission of the race committee.

17 DIVING EQUIPMENT AND PLASTIC POOLS

Underwater breathing apparatus and plastic pools or their equivalent shall not be used around keelboats between the preparatory signal of the first race and the end of the regatta.

Insert any alternative text that applies. Describe the radio communication bands or frequencies that will be used or allowed.

18 RADIO COMMUNICATION

Except in an emergency, a boat shall neither make radio transmissions while racing nor receive radio communications not available to all boats. This restriction also applies to mobile telephones.

If perpetual trophies will be awarded state their complete names.

19 PRIZES

Prizes will be given as follows: _____.

The laws applicable to the venue in which the event is held may limit disclaimers. Any disclaimer should be drafted to comply with those laws.

20 DISCLAIMER OF LIABILITY

Competitors participate in the regatta entirely at their own risk. See rule 4, Decision to Race. The organizing authority will not accept any liability for material damage or personal injury or death sustained in conjunction with or prior to, during, or after the regatta.

Insert the currency and amount.

21 INSURANCE

Each participating boat shall be insured with valid third-party liability insurance with a minimum cover of _____ per incident or the equivalent.

Insert necessary contact information.

22 FURTHER INFORMATION

For further information please contact _____.

Appendix L — Sailing Instructions Guide

This guide provides a set of tested sailing instructions designed primarily for major championship regattas for one or more classes. It therefore will be particularly useful for world, continental and national championships and other events of similar importance. The guide can also be useful for other events; however, for such events some of these instructions will be unnecessary or undesirable. Race officers should therefore be careful in making their choices.

An expanded version of the guide, Appendix LE, is available on the ISAF website. It contains provisions applicable to the largest and most complicated multi-class events, as well as variations on several of the sailing instructions recommended in this appendix. It will be revised from time to time, to reflect advances in race management techniques as they develop, and can be downloaded as a basic text for producing the sailing instructions for any particular event. Appendix L can also be downloaded from the ISAF website.

The principles on which all sailing instructions should be based are as follows:

1   They should include only two types of statement: the intentions of the race committee and protest committee and the obligations of competitors.

2   They should be concerned only with racing. Information about social events, assignment of moorings, etc., should be provided separately.

3   They should not change the racing rules except when clearly desirable. (When they do so, they must follow rule 86 by referring specifically to the rule being changed and stating the change.)

4   They should not repeat or restate any of the racing rules.

5   They should not repeat themselves.

6   They should be in chronological order; that is, the order in which the competitor will use them.

7   They should, when possible, use words or phrases from the racing rules.

To use this guide, first review rule J2 and decide which instructions will be needed. Instructions that are required by rule J2.1 are marked with an asterisk (*). Delete all inapplicable or unnecessary instructions. Select the version preferred where there is a choice. Follow the directions in the left margin to fill in the spaces where a solid line (___) appears and select the preferred wording if a choice or option is shown in brackets ([. . .]).

After deleting unused instructions, renumber all instructions in sequential order. Be sure that instruction numbers are correct where one instruction refers to another.

***US Sailing Note**: US Sailing has produced a guide to simplified sailing instructions suitable for events such as club or local regattas. Go to **ussailing.org/racingrules/ documents** and click the 'Simple SIs' link to read and download this guide.*

On separate lines, insert the full name of the regatta, the inclusive dates from measurement or the practice race until the final race or closing ceremony, the name of the organizing authority, and the city and country.

_____

_____

_____

_____

SAILING INSTRUCTIONS

1   RULES

1.1*   The regatta will be governed by the rules as defined in *The Racing Rules of Sailing*.

Use the first sentence if appropriate.
Insert the name. List by number
and title the prescriptions that will
not apply (see rule 88.2). Use the
second sentence if it applies and
if entries from other national
authorities are expected, and
state the prescriptions in full.
Include the prescriptions in
English when appropriate
(see rule 90.2(b)).

1.2 [The following prescriptions of the _____ national authority will not apply: _____.]
[The prescriptions that will apply are stated in full below.]

(OR)

Use if appropriate, but only if the
national authority for the venue
of the event has not adopted a
prescription to rule 88.

1.2 No national prescriptions will apply.

List by name any other documents
that govern the event; for example,
The Equipment Rules of Sailing,
to the extent that they apply.

1.3* _____ will apply.

See rule 86. Either insert here
the rule number(s) and state the
changes, or, if not using this
instruction, do the same in each
instruction that changes a rule.

1.4 Racing rule(s) _____ will be changed as follows: _____.

Insert the rule number(s) and class
name. Make a separate statement
for the rules of each class.

1.5 Under rule 87, rule(s) _____ of the _____ class rules [will not apply] [is (are) changed as follows: ___].

1.6 If there is a conflict between languages the English text will take precedence.

2 **NOTICES TO COMPETITORS**

Insert the location(s).

Notices to competitors will be posted on the official notice board(s) located at _____.

3 **CHANGES TO SAILING INSTRUCTIONS**

Change the times if different.

Any change to the sailing instructions will be posted before 0900 on the day it will take effect, except that any change to the schedule of races will be posted by 2000 on the day before it will take effect.

4 **SIGNALS MADE ASHORE**

Insert the location.

4.1 Signals made ashore will be displayed at _____.

Insert the number of minutes.

4.2 When flag AP is displayed ashore, '1 minute' is replaced with 'not less than _____ minutes' in the race signal AP.

(OR)

Insert the number of minutes.

4.2 Flag D with one sound means 'The warning signal will be made not less than _____

minutes after flag D is displayed.'
[Boats are requested not to leave
the harbour until this signal is made.]'

4.3 When flag Y is displayed ashore, rule 40
applies at all times while afloat. This
changes the Part 4 preamble.

5   SCHEDULE OF RACES

Revise as desired and insert
the dates and classes. Include
a practice race if any. When the
series consists of qualifying races
and final races, specify them.
The schedule can also be
given in an attachment.

5.1* Dates of racing:

Date	Class _____	Class _____
_____	racing	racing
_____	racing	reserve day
_____	reserve day	racing
_____	racing	racing
_____	racing	racing

Insert the classes and numbers.

5.2* Number of races:

Class	Number	Races per day
_____	_____	_____
_____	_____	_____

One extra race per day may be sailed,
provided that no class becomes more
than one race ahead of schedule and the
change is made according to instruction 3.

Insert the time.

5.3* The scheduled time of the warning signal
for the first race each day is _____.

5.4 To alert boats that a race or sequence of
races will begin soon, the orange starting
line flag will be displayed with one sound
for at least five minutes before a warning
signal is displayed.

Insert the time.

5.5 On the last day of the regatta no warning
signal will be made after _____.

This is a US Sailing prescription.

5.6 *Flag A displayed, with no sound, while*
boats are finishing means 'No more
racing today.'

6*   **CLASS FLAGS**

Insert the classes and names
or descriptions of the flags.

Class flags will be:

Class	Flag
_____	_____
_____	_____
_____	_____

7   RACING AREAS

Insert a number or letter.

Attachment _____ shows the location
of racing areas.

8   THE COURSES

Insert a number or letter.
A method of illustrating various courses is shown in Addendum A.
Insert the course length if applicable.

8.1* The diagrams in Attachment ____ show the courses, including the approximate angles between legs, the order in which marks are to be passed, and the side on which each mark is to be left. [The approximate course length will be _____.]

8.2 No later than the warning signal, the race committee signal boat will display the approximate compass bearing of the first leg.

8.3 Courses will not be shortened. This changes rule 32.

Include only when changing positions of marks is impracticable.

8.4 Legs of the course will not be changed after the preparatory signal. This changes rule 33.

9   MARKS

Change the mark numbers as needed and insert the descriptions of the marks. Use the second alternative when Marks 4S and 4P form a gate, with Mark 4S to be left to starboard and Mark 4P to port.

9.1* Marks 1, 2, 3 and 4 will be _____.

(OR)

9.1* Marks 1, 2, 3, 4S and 4P will be _____.

(OR)

Insert the number or letter used in instruction 8.1.

9.1* Marks are described in Attachment _____.

Unless it is clear from the course diagrams, list the marks that are rounding marks.

9.2 The following marks are rounding marks: _____.

Insert the descriptions of the marks.

9.3 New marks, as provided in instruction 12.1, will be _____.

Describe the starting and finishing marks: for example, the race committee signal boat at the starboard end and a buoy at the port end. Instruction 11.2 will describe the starting line and instruction 13 the finishing line.

9.4* The starting and finishing marks will be _____.

Include if instruction 12.2 is included.

9.5 A race committee boat signalling a change of a leg of the course is a mark as provided in instruction 12.2.

10   AREAS THAT ARE OBSTRUCTIONS

Describe each area by its location and any easily recognized details of appearance.

The following areas are designated as obstructions: _____.

11   THE START

Include only if the asterisked option in rule 26 will be used. Insert the number of minutes.

11.1 Races will be started by using rule 26 with the warning signal made _____ minutes before the starting signal.

(OR)

Describe any starting system other than that stated in rule 26.

11.1 Races will be started as follows: _____. This changes rule 26.

11.2* The starting line will be between staffs displaying orange flags on the starting marks.

(OR)

11.2* The starting line will be between a staff displaying an orange flag on the starting mark at the starboard end and the course side of the port-end starting mark.

(OR)

Insert the description.

11.2* The starting line will be _____.

11.3 Boats whose warning signal has not been made shall avoid the starting area during the starting sequence for other races.

Insert the number of minutes.

11.4 A boat starting later than _____ minutes after her starting signal will be scored Did Not Start without a hearing. This changes rule A4.

May be used as an alternative to rule 30.3

11.5 If flag U has been displayed as the preparatory signal, no part of a boat's hull, crew or equipment shall be in the triangle formed by the ends of the starting line and the first mark during the last minute before her starting signal. If a boat breaks this rule, and is identified, she shall be disqualified without a hearing but not if the race is restarted or resailed or postponed or abandoned before the starting signal. This changes rule 26.

Insert the channel number .

11.6 If any part of a boat's hull, crew or equipment is on the course side of the starting line during the two minutes before her starting signal and she is identified, the race committee will attempt to broadcast her sail number on VHF channel _____. Failure to make a broadcast or to time it accurately will not be grounds for a request for redress. This changes rule 62.1(a).

12   CHANGE OF THE NEXT LEG OF THE COURSE

12.1 To change the next leg of the course, the race committee will move the original mark (or the finishing line) to a new position.

(OR)

Sailing Instructions Guide

12.1 To change the next leg of the course, the race committee will lay a new mark (or move the finishing line) and remove the original mark as soon as practicable. When in a subsequent change a new mark is replaced, it will be replaced by an original mark.

When instruction 12.2 is included, instruction 9.5 must also be included. Reverse 'port' and 'starboard' when the mark is to be left to starboard.

12.2 Except at a gate, boats shall pass between the race committee boat signalling the change of the next leg and the nearby mark, leaving the mark to port and the race committee boat to starboard. This changes rule 28.

13* THE FINISH

The finishing line will be between staffs displaying orange flags on the finishing marks.

(OR)

The finishing line will be between a staff displaying an orange flag on the finishing mark at the starboard end and the course side of the port-end finishing mark.

(OR)

Insert the description.

The finishing line will be _____.

14   PENALTY SYSTEM

14.1 The Scoring Penalty, rule 44.3, will apply. The penalty will be _____ places.

(OR)

Include instruction 14.1 only when the Two-Turns Penalty will not be used. Insert the number of places or describe the penalties.

14.1 The penalties are as follows: _____.

Insert the class(es).

14.2 For the _____ class(es) rule 44.1 is changed so that the Two-Turns Penalty is replaced by the One-Turn Penalty.

Unless all of Appendix P applies, state any restrictions.

14.3 Appendix P will apply [as changed by instruction(s) [14.2] [and] [14.4]].

Recommended only for junior events.

14.4 Rule P2.3 will not apply and rule P2.2 is changed so that it will apply to any penalty after the first one.

15   TIME LIMITS AND TARGET TIMES

Insert the classes and times. Omit the Mark 1 time limit and target time if inapplicable.

15.1* Time limits and target times are as follows:

Class	Time limit	Mark 1 time limit	Target time
_____	_____	_____	_____
_____	_____	_____	_____
_____	_____	_____	_____

If no boat has passed Mark 1 within the Mark 1 time limit the race will be abandoned. Failure to meet the target time will not be grounds for redress. This changes rule 62.1(a).

Insert the time (or different times for different classes).

15.2 Boats failing to finish within _____ after the first boat sails the course and finishes will be scored Did Not Finish without a hearing. This changes rules 35, A4 and A5.

16   PROTESTS AND REQUESTS FOR REDRESS

State the location if necessary.

16.1 Protest forms are available at the race office[, located at _____]. Protests and requests for redress or reopening shall be delivered there within the appropriate time limit.

Change the time if different.

16.2 For each class, the protest time limit is 90 minutes after the last boat has finished the last race of the day or the race committee signals no more racing today, whichever is later.

Change the posting time if different. Insert the protest room location and, if applicable, the time for the first hearing.

16.3 Notices will be posted no later than 30 minutes after the protest time limit to inform competitors of hearings in which they are parties or named as witnesses. Hearings will be held in the protest room, located at _____, beginning at [the time posted] [_____].

16.4 Notices of protests by the race committee or protest committee will be posted to inform boats under rule 61.1(b).

16.5 A list of boats that, under instruction 14.3, have been penalized for breaking rule 42 will be posted.

16.6 Breaches of instructions 11.3, 18, 21, 23, 24, 25, 26 and 27 will not be grounds for a protest by a boat. This changes rule 60.1(a). Penalties for these breaches may be less than disqualification if the protest committee so decides.

16.7 On the last scheduled day of racing a request for reopening a hearing shall be delivered

(a) within the protest time limit if the requesting party was informed of the decision on the previous day;

Change the time if different.

(b) no later than 30 minutes after the requesting party was informed of the decision on that day.

This changes rule 66.

16.8 On the last scheduled day of racing a request for redress based on a protest committee decision shall be delivered no later than 30 minutes after the decision was posted. This changes rule 62.2.

Include only if rule 70.5 applies.

16.9 Decisions of the [protest committee] [international jury] will be final as provided in rule 70.5.

This is a US Sailing prescription.

16.10 ***If the race committee posts a list of boats scored OCS, ZFP or BFD on the official notice board before the protest time limit, a request for redress based on such a posted score shall be made no later than one hour after the protest time limit. This changes the first sentence of rule 62.2.***

17   SCORING

Include only if the Low Point System of Appendix A will not be used. Describe the system.

17.1* The scoring system is as follows: _____.

Insert the number.

17.2* _____ races are required to be completed to constitute a series.

Insert the numbers throughout.

17.3 (a) When fewer than _____ races have been completed, a boat's series score will be the total of her race scores.

(b) When from _____ to _____ races have been completed, a boat's series score will be the total of her race scores excluding her worst score.

(c) When _____ or more races have been completed, a boat's series score will be the total of her race scores excluding her two worst scores.

18   SAFETY REGULATIONS

Insert the procedure for check-out and check-in.

18.1 Check-Out and Check-In: _____.

18.2 A boat that retires from a race shall notify the race committee as soon as possible.

19   REPLACEMENT OF CREW OR EQUIPMENT

19.1 Substitution of competitors will not be allowed without prior written approval of the [race committee] [protest committee].

19.2 Substitution of damaged or lost equipment will not be allowed unless authorized by the [race committee] [protest committee]. Requests for substitution shall be made to the committee at the first reasonable opportunity.

20   EQUIPMENT AND MEASUREMENT CHECKS

A boat or equipment may be inspected at any time for compliance with the class rules and sailing instructions. On the water, a boat can be instructed by a race committee equipment inspector or measurer to proceed immediately to a designated area for inspection.

21   EVENT ADVERTISING

See ISAF Regulation 20.4. Insert necessary information on the display of event advertising material.

Boats shall display event advertising supplied by the organizing authority as follows: _____.

22   OFFICIAL BOATS

Insert the descriptions. If appropriate, use different identification markings for boats performing different duties.

Official boats will be marked as follows: _____.

23   SUPPORT BOATS

23.1 Team leaders, coaches and other support personnel shall stay outside areas where boats are racing from the time of the preparatory signal for the first class to start until all boats have finished or retired or the race committee signals a postponement, general recall or abandonment.

Insert the identification markings. National letters are suggested for international events.

23.2 Support boats shall be marked with _____.

24   TRASH DISPOSAL

Trash may be placed aboard support or official boats.

25   HAUL-OUT RESTRICTIONS

Keelboats shall not be hauled out during the regatta except with and according to the terms of prior written permission of the race committee.

26   DIVING EQUIPMENT AND PLASTIC POOLS

Underwater breathing apparatus and plastic pools or their equivalent shall not be used around keelboats between the preparatory signal of the first race and the end of the regatta.

27   RADIO COMMUNICATION

Insert any alternative text that applies. Describe the radio communication bands or frequencies that will be used or allowed.

Except in an emergency, a boat shall neither make radio transmissions while racing nor receive radio communications not available to all boats. This restriction also applies to mobile telephones.

*If perpetual trophies will be awarded
state their complete names.*

*The laws applicable to the venue
in which the event is held may limit
disclaimers. Any disclaimer should
be drafted to comply with those
laws.*

Insert the currency and amount.

28   PRIZES

Prizes will be given as follows: _____.

29   DISCLAIMER OF LIABILITY

Competitors participate in the regatta
entirely at their own risk. See rule 4,
Decision to Race. The organizing authority
will not accept any liability for material
damage or personal injury or death
sustained in conjunction with or prior
to, during, or after the regatta.

30   INSURANCE

Each participating boat shall be insured
with valid third-party liability insurance
with a minimum cover of _____ per
incident or the equivalent.

ADDENDUM A — ILLUSTRATING THE COURSE

Shown here are diagrams of course shapes. The boat's track is represented by a discontinuous line so that each diagram can describe courses with different numbers of laps. If more than one course may be used for a class, state how each particular course will be signalled.

A Windward-Leeward Course
Start – 1 – 2 – 1 – 2 – Finish

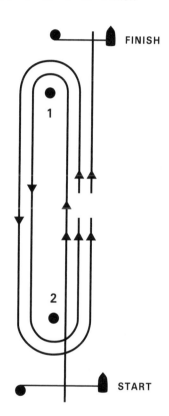

Options for this course include

(1)   increasing or decreasing the number of laps,

(2)   deleting the last windward leg,

(3)   using a gate instead of a leeward mark,

(4)   using an offset mark at the windward mark, and

(5)   using the leeward and windward marks as starting and finishing marks.

A Triangle-Windward-Leeward Course

Start − 1 − 2 − 3 − 1 − 3 − Finish

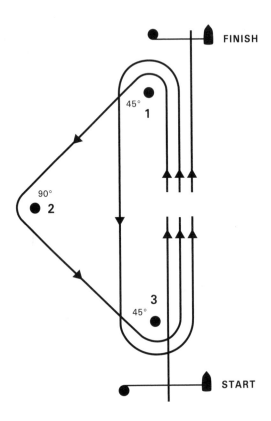

Options for this course include

(1) increasing or decreasing the number of laps,

(2) deleting the last windward leg,

*(3) varying the interior angles of the triangle
(45°− 90°− 45° and 60°− 60°− 60° are common),*

(4) using a gate instead of a leeward mark for downwind legs,

(5) using an offset mark at the beginning of downwind legs, and

*(6) using the leeward and windward marks as starting and
finishing marks.*

Be sure to specify the interior angle at each mark.

Trapezoid Courses

Start − 1 − 2 − 3 − 2 − 3 − Finish   Start − 1 − 4 − 1 − 2 − 3 − Finish

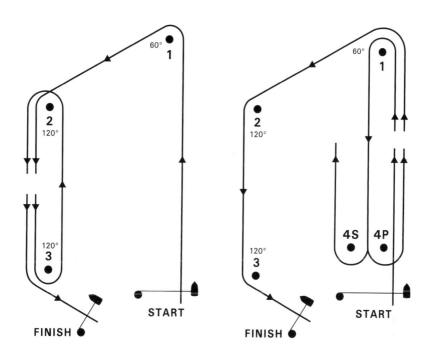

Options for these courses include

(1)   adding additional legs,

(2)   replacing the gate shown by a single mark, or using a gate also in the outer loop,

(3)   varying the interior angles of the reaching legs,

(4)   using an offset mark at the beginning of downwind legs, and

(5)   finishing boats upwind rather than on a reach.

Be sure to specify the interior angle of each reaching leg.

ADDENDUM B — BOATS PROVIDED BY THE ORGANIZING AUTHORITY

The following sailing instruction is recommended when all boats will be provided by the organizing authority. It can be changed to suit the circumstances. When used, it should be inserted after instruction 3.

4   BOATS

4.1   Boats will be provided for all competitors, who shall not modify them or cause them to be modified in any way except that

(a) a compass may be tied or taped to the hull or spars;

(b) wind indicators, including yarn or thread, may be tied or taped anywhere on the boat;

(c) hulls, centreboards and rudders may be cleaned, but only with water;

(d) adhesive tape may be used anywhere above the water line; and

(e) all fittings or equipment designed to be adjusted may be adjusted, provided that the class rules are complied with.

4.2   All the equipment provided with the boat for sailing purposes shall be in boat while afloat.

4.3   The penalty for not complying with one of the above instructions will be disqualification from all races sailed in which the instruction was broken.

4.4   Competitors shall report any damage or loss of equipment, however slight, to the organizing authority's representative immediately after securing the boat ashore. The penalty for breaking this instruction, unless the protest committee is satisfied that the competitor made a determined effort to comply, will be disqualification from the race most recently sailed.

4.5   Class rules requiring competitors to be members of the class association will not apply.

Appendix M — Recommendations for Protest Committees

This appendix is advisory only; in some circumstances changing these procedures may be advisable. It is addressed primarily to protest committee chairmen but may also help judges, protest committee secretaries, race committees and others connected with protest and redress hearings.

In a protest or redress hearing, the protest committee should weigh all testimony with equal care; should recognize that honest testimony can vary, and even be in conflict, as a result of different observations and recollections; should resolve such differences as best it can; should recognize that no boat or competitor is guilty until a breach of a *rule* has been established to the satisfaction of the protest committee; and should keep an open mind until all the evidence has been heard as to whether a boat or competitor has broken a *rule*.

M1   PRELIMINARIES (may be performed by race office staff)

- Receive the *protest* or request for redress.
- Note on the form the time the *protest* or request is delivered and the protest time limit.
- Inform each *party*, and the race committee when necessary, when and where the hearing will be held.

M2   BEFORE THE HEARING

M2.1   Make sure that

- each *party* has a copy of or the opportunity to read the *protest* or request for redress and has had reasonable time to prepare for the hearing.
- no member of the protest committee is an *interested party*. Ask the *parties* whether they object to any member. When redress is requested under rule 62.1(a), a member of the race committee should not be a member of the protest committee.
- only one person from each boat (or *party*) is present unless an interpreter is needed.
- all boats and people involved are represented. If they are not, however, the committee may proceed under rule 63.3(b).
- boats' representatives were on board when required (rule 63.3(a)). When the *parties* were in different races, both organizing authorities must accept the composition of the protest committee (rule 63.8). In a measurement *protest* obtain the current class rules and identify the authority responsible for interpreting them (rule 64.3(b)).

M2.2   Determine if any members of the protest committee saw the incident. If so, require each of them to state that fact in the presence of the *parties* (rule 63.6).

M3   THE HEARING

M3.1   Check the validity of the *protest* or request for redress.

- Are the contents adequate (rule 61.2 or 62)?
- Was it delivered in time? If not, is there good reason to extend the time limit (rule 61.3 or 62.2)?
- When required, was the protestor involved in or a witness to the incident (rule 60.1(a))?
- When necessary, was 'Protest' hailed and, if required, a red flag displayed correctly (rule 61.1(a))?
- When the flag or hail was not necessary, was the protestee informed?
- Decide whether the *protest* or request for redress is valid (rule 63.5).
- Once the validity of the *protest* or request has been determined, do not let the subject be introduced again unless truly new evidence is available.

M3.2   Take the evidence (rule 63.6).

- Ask the protestor and then the protestee to tell their stories. Then allow them to question one another. In a redress matter, ask the *party* to state the request.
- Invite questions from protest committee members.
- Make sure you know what facts each *party* is alleging before calling any witnesses. Their stories may be different.
- Allow anyone, including a boat's crew, to give evidence. It is the *party* who normally decides which witnesses to call, although the protest committee may also call witnesses (rule 63.6). The question asked by a *party* 'Would you like to hear N?' is best answered by 'It is your choice.'
- Call each *party's* witnesses (and the protest committee's if any) one by one. Limit *parties* to questioning the witness(es) (they may wander into general statements).
- Invite the protestee to question the protestor's witness first (and vice versa). This prevents the protestor from leading his witness from the beginning.
- Allow members of the protest committee who saw the incident to give evidence (rule 63.6), but only while the *parties* are present. Members

who give evidence may be questioned, should take care to relate all they
know about the incident that could affect the decision, and may remain
on the protest committee (rule 63.3(a)).

- Try to prevent leading questions or hearsay evidence, but if that is impossible discount the evidence so obtained.
- Accept written evidence from a witness who is not available to be questioned only if all *parties* agree. In doing so they forego their rights to question that witness (rule 63.6).
- Ask one member of the committee to note down evidence, particularly times, distances, speeds, etc.
- Invite first the protestor and then the protestee to make a final statement of her case, particularly on any application or interpretation of the *rules*.

M3.3 Find the facts (rule 63.6).
- Write down the facts; resolve doubts one way or the other.
- Call back *parties* for more questions if necessary.
- When appropriate, draw a diagram of the incident using the facts you have found.

M3.4 Decide the *protest* or request for redress (rule 64).
- Base the decision on the facts found (if you cannot, find some more facts).
- In redress cases, make sure that no further evidence is needed from boats that will be affected by the decision.

M3.5 Inform the *parties* (rule 65).
- Recall the *parties* and read them the facts found, conclusions and *rules* that apply, and the decision. When time presses it is permissible to read the decision and give the details later.
- Give any *party* a copy of the decision on request. File the *protest* or request for redress with the committee records.

M4   **REOPENING A HEARING (rule 66)**

M4.1 When a *party*, within the time limit, has asked for a hearing to be reopened, hear the *party* making the request, look at any video, etc., and decide whether there is any significant new evidence that might lead you to change your decision. Decide whether your interpretation of the *rules* may have been wrong; be open-minded as to whether you have made a mistake. If none of these applies refuse to reopen; otherwise schedule a hearing.

M4.2 Evidence is 'new'
- if it was not reasonably possible for the *party* asking for the reopening to have discovered the evidence before the original hearing,
- if the protest committee is satisfied that before the original hearing the evidence was diligently but unsuccessfully sought by the *party* asking for the reopening, or
- if the protest committee learns from any source that the evidence was not available to the *parties* at the time of the original hearing.

M5   **GROSS MISCONDUCT (rule 69)**

M5.1 An action under this rule is not a *protest,* but the protest committee gives its allegations in writing to the competitor before the hearing. The hearing is conducted under the same rules as other hearings but the protest committee must have at least three members (rule 69.2(b)). Use the greatest care to protect the competitor's rights.

M5.2 A competitor or a boat cannot protest under rule 69, but the protest form of a competitor who tries to do so may be accepted as a report to the protest committee, which can then decide whether or not to call a hearing.

M5.3 When it is desirable to call a hearing under rule 69 as a result of a Part 2 incident, it is important to hear any boat-vs.-boat *protest* in the normal way, deciding which boat, if any, broke which *rule*, before proceeding against the competitor under this rule.

M5.4 Although action under rule 69 is taken against a competitor, not a boat, a boat may also be penalized (rule 69.2(c)).

M5.5 The protest committee may warn the competitor (rule 69.2(c)(1)), in which case no report is to be made (rule 69.2(d)). When a penalty is imposed and a report is made as required by rule 69.2(d) or 69.2(f), it may be helpful to recommend whether or not further action should be taken.

M6 **APPEALS (rule 70 and Appendix R)**

When decisions can be appealed,

- retain the papers relevant to the hearing so that the information can easily be used for an appeal. Is there a diagram endorsed or prepared by the protest committee? Are the facts found sufficient? (Example: W as there an *overlap*? Yes or No. 'Perhaps' is not a fact found.) Are the names of the protest committee members and other important information on the form?
- comments by the protest committee on any appeal should enable the appeals committee to picture the whole incident clearly; the appeals committee knows nothing about the situation.

M7 **PHOTOGRAPHIC EVIDENCE**

Photographs and videos can sometimes provide useful evidence but protest committees should recognize their limitations and note the following points:

- The *party* producing the photographic evidence is responsible for arranging the viewing.
- View the video several times to extract all the information from it.
- The depth perception of any single-lens camera is very poor; with a telephoto lens it is non-existent. When the camera views two *overlapped* boats at right angles to their course, it is impossible to assess the distance between them. When the camera views them head on, it is impossible to see whether an *overlap* exists unless it is substantial.
- Ask the following questions:
  - Where was the camera in relation to the boats?
  - Was the camera's platform moving? If so in what direction and how fast?
  - Is the angle changing as the boats approach the critical point? Fast panning causes radical change.
  - Did the camera have an unrestricted view throughout?

Appendix N — International Juries

See rules 70.5 and 91(b). This appendix shall not be changed by sailing instructions or national prescriptions.

N1 **COMPOSITION, APPOINTMENT AND ORGANIZATION**

N1.1 An international jury shall be composed of experienced sailors with excellent knowledge of the racing rules and extensive protest committee experience. It shall be independent of and have no members from the race committee, and be appointed by the organizing authority, subject to approval by the national authority if required (see rule 91(b)), or by the ISAF under rule 89.2(b).

N1.2 The jury shall consist of a chairman, a vice chairman if desired, and other members for a total of at least five. A majority shall be International Judges.

The jury may appoint a secretary, who shall not be a member of the jury.

N1.3   No more than two members (three, in Groups M, N and Q) shall be from the same national authority.

N1.4   (a)   The chairman of a jury may appoint one or more panels composed in compliance with rules N1.1, N1.2 and N1.3. This can be done even if the full jury is not composed in compliance with these rules.

   (b)   The chairman of a jury of fewer than ten members may appoint two or three panels of at least three members each, of which the majority shall be Inter-national Judges. Members of each panel shall be from at least three different national authorities except in Groups M, N and Q, where they shall be from at least two different national authorities. If dissatisfied with a panel's decision, a *party* is entitled to a hearing by a panel composed in compliance with rules N1.1, N1.2 and N1.3, except concerning the facts found, if requested within the time limit specified in the sailing instructions.

N1.5   When a full jury, or a panel, has fewer than five members, because of illness or emergency, and no qualified replacements are available, it remains properly constituted if it consists of at least three members and if at least two of them are International Judges. When there are three or four members they shall be from at least three different national authorities except in Groups M, N and Q, where they shall be from at least two different national authorities.

N1.6   When the national authority's approval is required for the appointment of an international jury (see rule 91(b)), notice of its approval shall be included in the sailing instructions or be posted on the official notice board.

N1.7   If the jury or a panel acts while not properly constituted, its decisions may be appealed.

N2   RESPONSIBILITIES

N2.1   An international jury is responsible for hearing and deciding all *protests*, requests for redress and other matters arising under the rules of Part 5. When asked by the organizing authority or the race committee, it shall advise and assist them on any matter directly affecting the fairness of the competition.

N2.2   Unless the organizing authority directs otherwise, the jury shall decide

   (a)   questions of eligibility, measurement or boat certificates; and

   (b)   whether to authorize the substitution of competitors, boats or equipment when a *rule* requires such a decision.

N2.3   The jury shall also decide matters referred to it by the organizing authority or the race committee.

N3   PROCEDURES

N3.1   Decisions of the jury, or of a panel, shall be made by a simple majority vote of all members. When there is an equal division of votes cast, the chairman of the meeting may cast an additional vote.

N3.2   When it is considered desirable that some members not participate in discussing and deciding a *protest* or request for redress, and no qualified replacements are available, the jury or panel remains properly constituted if at least three members remain and at least two of them are International Judges.

N3.3   Members shall not be regarded as *interested parties* (see rule 63.4) by reason of their nationality.

N3.4   If a panel fails to agree on a decision it may adjourn, in which case the chairman shall refer the matter to a properly constituted panel with as many members as possible, which may be the full jury.

Appendix P — Special Procedures for Rule 42

All or part of this appendix applies only if the sailing instructions so state.

P1   SIGNALLING A PENALTY

A member of the protest committee or its designated observer who sees a boat breaking rule 42 may penalize her by, as soon as reasonably possible, making a sound signal, pointing a yellow flag at her and hailing her sail number, even if she is no longer *racing*. A boat so penalized shall not be penalized a second time under rule 42 for the same incident.

P2   PENALTIES

P2.1   First Penalty

When a boat is first penalized under rule P1 her penalty shall be a Two-Turns Penalty under rule 44.2. If she fails to take it she shall be disqualified without a hearing.

P2.2   Second Penalty

When a boat is penalized a second time during the regatta, her penalty shall be to promptly retire from the race. If she fails to take it she shall be disqualified without a hearing and her score shall not be excluded.

P2.3   Third and Subsequent Penalties

When a boat is penalized a third or subsequent time during the regatta, she shall promptly retire from the race. If she does so her penalty shall be disqualification without a hearing and her score shall not be excluded. If she fails to do so her penalty shall be disqualification without a hearing from all races in the regatta, with no score excluded, and the protest committee shall consider calling a hearing under rule 69.2(a).

P3   POSTPONEMENT, GENERAL RECALL OR ABANDONMENT

If a boat has been penalized under rule P1 and the race committee signals a *postponement*, general recall or *abandonment*, the penalty is cancelled, but it is still counted to determine the number of times she has been penalized during the regatta.

P4   REDRESS LIMITATION

A boat shall not be given redress for an action by a member of the protest committee or its designated observer under rule P1 unless the action was improper due to a failure to take into account a race committee signal or a class rule.

P5   FLAGS O AND R

(a) If the class rules permit pumping, rocking and ooching when the wind speed exceeds a specified limit, the race committee may signal that those actions are permitted, as specified in the class rules, by displaying flag O no later than the warning signal.

(b) If the wind speed exceeds the specified limit after the starting signal, the race committee may display flag O with repetitive sounds at a *mark* to signal to a boat that the actions are permitted, as specified in the class rules, after she has passed the *mark*.

(c) If the wind speed becomes less than the specified limit after flag O was displayed, the race committee may display flag R with repetitive sounds at a *mark* to signal to a boat that rule 42, as changed by the class rules, applies after she has passed the *mark*.

Appendix R — Procedures for Appeals and Requests

This appendix is a US Sailing prescription.

See rules 70 and 71. This appendix replaces Appendix R as adopted by the International Sailing Federation for the purpose of creating a two-level appeals system. The US Sailing Appeals Committee acts as the national authority under rule 71. An association appeals committee may act as permitted by rule 71.2 and shall act as required by rule 71.3, subject to further appeal as provided in rule R7.1(a).

Frequently Asked Questions (FAQ) on the appeals system and their answers, including advice on how to prepare an appeal, can be found on the US Sailing website. Go to **ussailing.org/racingrules/documents** *and click the 'Appeals FAQ' link.*

R1 WHERE TO SEND AN APPEAL OR REQUEST

R1.1 All appeals and requests shall be sent to the Race Administration Director at US Sailing, at either P.O. Box 1260 or 15 Maritime Drive, Portsmouth, RI 02871, or by e-mail to RaceAdmin@ussailing.org.

R1.2 Except as provided in rule R1.4, the director will forward an appeal of a decision of a protest committee or a request by a protest committee for confirmation or correction of its decision to the association appeals committee for the place in which the event was held. However, such an appeal or request arising from an event conducted under the procedural rules of the Intercollegiate Sailing Association or the Interscholastic Sailing Association will be forwarded to the association appeals committee for the ICSA and ISSA.

R1.3 The director will forward an appeal of a decision of an association appeals committee, a request by an association appeals committee for confirmation or correction of its decision, and a request for an interpretation of *rules* to the US Sailing Appeals Committee.

R1.4 The director will forward an appeal of a decision of a protest committee acting under rule 69.1, an appeal of a decision of a protest committee of a US Sailing national championship, and a request by such a committee for confirmation or correction of its decision to the US Sailing Appeals Committee.

R2 TO APPEAL OR MAKE A REQUEST

R2.1 To appeal,
(a) no later than 15 days after receiving the written decision being appealed or a protest committee's decision not to reopen a hearing, the appellant shall send an appeal and a copy of the decision to US Sailing. The appeal shall state why the appellant believes the committee's decision or its procedures were incorrect;
(b) when the hearing required by rule 63.1 has not been held within 30 days after a *protest* or request for redress was delivered, the appellant shall, within a further 15 days, send an appeal with a copy of the *protest* or request and any relevant correspondence. The appeals committee to which the appeal is forwarded shall extend the time if there is good reason to do so; or
(c) when the protest committee fails to comply with rule 65, the appellant shall, within a reasonable time after the hearing, send an appeal with a copy of the *protest* or request and any relevant correspondence.

If a copy of the *protest* or request is not available, the appellant shall instead send a statement of its substance.

R2.2   The appellant shall also send, with the appeal or as soon as possible thereafter, all of the following documents and information available:

    (a)   the written *protest*(s) or request(s) for redress;

    (b)   if the appeal is from a decision of an association appeals committee, the written decision of the protest committee and the appeal to the association appeals committee;

    (c)   a diagram, prepared or endorsed by the protest committee, that shows

        (1)   the positions of all boats involved at relevant times, and their tracks;

        (2)   the course to the next *mark* and its required side;

        (3)   the speed and direction of the wind;

        (4)   any relevant *mark, obstruction* or *zone*; and

        (5)   if relevant, the depth of the water and the speed and direction of any current;

    (d)   the notice of race, sailing instructions, any other documents governing the event, and any changes to them;

    (e)   the names, mailing addresses and e-mail addresses of the *parties* to the hearing, the chairman of the protest committee and, if relevant, the chairman of the association appeals committee; and

    (f)   any other relevant documents.

R2.3   To request confirmation or correction of its decision, a protest committee or association appeals committee shall send to US Sailing a copy of its decision and all relevant documents and comments (see rule R2.2).

R2.4   To request an interpretation of the *rules*, a club or other organization affiliated to US Sailing shall send its request to US Sailing. The request shall include assumed facts and be endorsed by an officer of the club or organization. A US Sailing committee is considered to be an organization affiliated to US Sailing.

R3   **FEES**

R3.1   If the appeal or request is being made to an association appeals committee (see rule R1.2), US Sailing charges no fee for forwarding that appeal or request. However, an association appeals committee may charge a fee, in which case the association appeals committee will send a notice to the appellant (or, for a request, to the protest committee) stating the fee, to whom the fee is payable, and the address to which the fee must be sent.

R3.2   If the appeal is being made to the US Sailing Appeals Committee (see rules R1.3 and R1.4) by a member of US Sailing or another national authority, US Sailing charges a fee of $25. The fee is $75 for all others.

R3.3   A fee of $25 is charged for a request for an interpretation of the rules, but there is no fee for such a request from a US Sailing committee. There is no fee for a request from an association appeals committee for confirmation or correction of its decision.

R3.4   If a fee is required for an appeal or request, it must be received before the appeal or request will be considered. For appeals and requests made to the US Sailing Appeals Committee, the fee can be paid by check to 'US Sailing' or electronically as described in the Appeals FAQ.

R4   **NOTIFICATION OF THE COMMITTEE WHOSE DECISION IS BEING APPEALED**

     Upon receipt of an appeal, the appeals committee shall send a copy of the appeal to the committee whose decision is being appealed, asking it for any documents required by rule R2.2 not supplied by the appellant.

R5 COMMITTEE RESPONSIBILITIES

R5.1 Protest Committee

A protest committee whose decision is being appealed shall supply the documents requested under rule R4 and any facts or other information requested under rule R5.4. If directed to do so by the appeals committee, it shall conduct a hearing, or reopen the hearing, of the protest or request for redress, or conduct a hearing to consider redress.

R5.2 Association Appeals Committee

(a) The association appeals committee shall send to all *parties* to the hearing, and to the committee whose decision is being appealed or reviewed, copies of all relevant documents, comments and clarifications it has received, except those supplied by that *party* or committee.

(b) The association appeals committee shall send its decision in writing to all *parties* to the hearing and the protest committee.

(c) An association appeals committee shall consider an appeal it has refused to decide if directed to do so by the US Sailing Appeals Committee.

R5.3 US Sailing Appeals Committee

The US Sailing Appeals Committee shall send to all *parties* to the hearing, to the protest committee and to the association appeals committee whose decision is being appealed or reviewed, copies of all relevant documents, comments and clarifications it has received, except those supplied by that party or committee.

R5.4 Inadequate Facts; Reopening

An appeals committee shall accept the protest committee's finding of facts except when it decides they are inadequate. In that case it shall require the protest committee to provide additional facts or other information, or to reopen the hearing and report any new finding of facts, and the protest committee shall promptly do so.

R6 COMMENTS

The *parties* to the hearing, the protest committee and, if relevant, the association appeals committee may make comments on the appeal or request, on any of the documents listed in rule R2.2, and on any clarifications received under rule R7.2(d). Comments shall be sent in writing to the appeals committee no later than 15 days after the *party* or committee receives the document. The appeals committee need not consider comments sent after that time or comments on comments.

R7 PROVISIONS IN ADDITION TO THOSE OF RULES 70 AND 71

R7.1 Right to Appeal or Request Confirmation or Correction

(a) A *party* to a hearing may appeal an association appeals committee's decision.

(b) An association appeals committee may request confirmation or correction of its decision (see rule R2.3).

R7.2 Other Provisions

(a) No member of the association appeals committee shall take part in the discussion or decision on an appeal or a request for confirmation or correction to the US Sailing Appeals Committee.

(b) An appeals committee may direct a protest committee to conduct a hearing to consider redress for an appellant or other boats.

(c) The US Sailing Appeals Committee may direct an association appeals committee to consider an appeal it has refused to decide.

(d) An appeals committee may seek clarifications of *rules* governing the event from organizations that are not *parties* to the hearing.

R8 EXPEDITED APPEALS

An expedited appeals system, which can only be used at US Sailing Protected Competitions (see US Sailing Regulation 12.03), can be found on the US Sailing website. Go to **ussailing.org/racingrules/documents** and click the 'Expedited Appeals' link.

Appendix S — Sound-Signal Starting System

This appendix is a US Sailing prescription.

US Sailing prescribes that, when the sailing instructions so indicate, the Sound-Signal Starting System described below shall be used. This system is recommended primarily for small-boat racing and makes it unnecessary for competitors to use stopwatches. Supplemental visual course and recall signals are also recommended when practicable.

S1 Course and postponement signals may be made orally.

S2 Audible signals shall govern, even when supplemental visual signals are also used.

S3 The starting sequence shall consist of the following sound signals made at the indicated times:

Signal	Sound	Time before start
Warning	3 long	3 minutes
Preparatory	2 long	2 minutes
	1 long, 3 short	1 minute, 30 seconds
	1 long	1 minute
	3 short	30 seconds
	2 short	20 seconds
	1 short	10 seconds
	1 short	5 seconds
	1 short	4 seconds
	1 short	3 seconds
	1 short	2 seconds
	1 short	1 second
Starting	1 long	0

S4 Signals shall be timed from their commencement.

S5 A series of short signals may be made before the sequence begins in order to attract attention.

S6 Individual recalls shall be signalled by the hail of the sail number (or some other clearly distinguishing feature) of each recalled boat. Flag X need not be displayed.

S7 Failure of a competitor to hear an adequate course, postponement, starting sequence or recall signal shall not be grounds for redress.

Appendix T – Alternative Procedures for Dispute Resolution

This appendix is a US Sailing prescription.

One or more sections of this appendix apply only if the sailing instructions so state.

The rules in this appendix are intended to improve compliance with the Basic Principle, Sportsmanship and the Rules, and may be used for fleets of boats in major or minor events.

Sections A and B provide alternative penalties that encourage competitors to take a penalty when they may have broken a rule of Part 2 or rule 31. They can be used together or individually.

Sections C and D each provide a modified hearing procedure that is less formal and less time-consuming than the usual hearing procedure. They are designed to encourage boats to enforce the rules by protesting. Sections C and D are not designed to be used at the same event, but either Section C or Section D may be used with Section A or B, or with both. Note however that, if Section D is used, Section B automatically applies.

Please report your experiences with and evaluations of these rules to US Sailing by sending an e-mail to rules@ussailing.org.

Section A — Penalties While Racing

If Section A applies, rule T1 shall be included in the sailing instructions.

T1 PENALTIES AT THE TIME OF THE INCIDENT

The first two sentences of rule 44.1 are changed to: 'A boat may take a One-Turn Penalty when she may have broken a rule of Part 2 or rule 31 while *racing*. However, when she may have broken a rule of Part 2 while in the *zone* around a *mark* other than a starting *mark*, her penalty shall be a Two-Turns Penalty.'

Section B — Post-Race Penalties

T2 PENALTIES TAKEN AFTER A RACE

After a race, a boat that may have broken a rule of Part 2 or rule 31 while *racing* may take a Post-Race Penalty for that incident. The penalty shall be a Scoring Penalty, calculated as stated in rule 44.3(c). However, rules 44.1(a) and (b) apply. A boat takes a Post-Race Penalty by informing the race committee in writing and identifying the race number and when and where the incident occurred.

T2.1 The Post-Race Penalty shall be

(a) 20%, if taken before the protest time limit, or

(b) 30%, if taken after the protest time limit but before the beginning of a hearing involving the incident.

Section C — Expedited Hearings

T3 INFORMING THE RACE COMMITTEE

A boat intending to protest or request redress based on an incident in the racing area that she is involved in or sees shall, at the first reasonable opportunity after she *finishes*, inform the race committee at the finishing line of her intent to protest or request redress and, when applicable, the identity of the protestee.

T4   CHANGES IN HEARING PROCEDURES

This rule applies to all hearings except hearings under rule 69.

T4.1   If the protest committee is able to assemble the *parties* to a hearing before the *protest* or redress time limit, it may begin the hearing and may waive the requirements of rule 61.2 or 62.2.

T4.2   The US Sailing prescriptions to rules 60, 63.2 and 63.4 are deleted.

T4.3   Rule 63.5 is changed to: 'At the beginning of the hearing, if there is no objection, the *protest* or request is valid and the hearing shall be continued. If an objection is made, the protest committee shall take any evidence . . . [*no further change*].'

T4.4   Insert a new sentence after the third sentence of rule 63.6: 'However, the committee may limit the number of witnesses and the time during which *parties* may present evidence and ask questions.'

T4.5   The first sentence of rule 65.2 is changed to: 'A *party* to the hearing is entitled to receive the above information in writing, provided she asks the protest committee for it no later than thirty minutes after being informed of the decision or coming ashore following the last race of the day, whichever is later.'

T4.6   The third sentence of rule 66 is changed to: 'A *party* to the hearing may not ask for a reopening.'

Section D — Arbitration

When Section D applies, a boat may take the applicable Post-Race Penalty in Section B without participating in an arbitration meeting.

T5   PROTEST ARBITRATION

T5.1   An arbitration meeting will be held prior to a protest hearing for each incident resulting in a *protest* by a boat involving a rule of Part 2 or rule 31, but only if each *party* is represented by a person who was on board at the time of the incident. No witnesses will be permitted. However, if the arbitrator decides that rule 44.1(b) may apply or that arbitration is not appropriate, the meeting will not be held, and if a meeting is in progress, it will be closed.

T5.2   Based on the evidence given by the representatives, the arbitrator will offer an opinion as to what the protest committee is likely to decide:

(a)   the *protest* is invalid,

(b)   no boat will be penalized for breaking a rule, or

(c)   one or more boats will be penalized for breaking a rule, identifying the boats and the penalties.

T5.3   A boat that may have broken a rule may take a Post-Race Penalty as provided in Section B. However, the penalty in rule T2.2(a) is available only until the protest time limit or until the beginning of the arbitration meeting, whichever is earlier. During a meeting, a boat may take a penalty by acknowledging her acceptance of the penalty in writing.

T5.4   If a boat asks to withdraw her *protest*, the arbitrator may act on behalf of the protest committee in accordance with rule 63.1 to accept the withdrawal.

Protest Form

US SAILING   also for requests for redress and reopening
www.ussailing.org

Fill in and check as appropriate

Date and time received _____

Received by _____ Filing no. _____

Protest time limit _____

---

1. EVENT _____ Organizing authority _____ Date _____ Race no. _____

2. TYPE OF HEARING

☐ Protest by boat against boat

☐ Protest by race committee against boat

☐ Protest by protest committee
   against boat

☐ Request for redress by boat or race committee

☐ Consideration of redress by protest committee

☐ Request by boat or race committee to reopen hearing

☐ Consideration of reopening by protest committee

3. BOAT PROTESTING, OR REQUESTING REDRESS OR REOPENING

Class _____ Sail no. _____ Boat's name _____

Represented by _____ Tel. _____ E-mail _____

4. BOAT(S) PROTESTED OR BEING CONSIDERED FOR REDRESS

Class _____ Sail no. _____ Boat's name _____

5. INCIDENT

Time and place of incident _____

Rule(s) alleged to have been broken _____ Witness(es) _____

6. INFORMING PROTESTEE   How did you inform the protestee of your intention to protest?

☐ By hailing When? _____ Word(s) used _____

☐ By displaying a red flag When? _____

☐ By informing him/her in some other way Give details _____

---

7. DESCRIPTION OF INCIDENT (use another sheet if necessary)	Diagram: one square = one hull length Show position of boats, wind and current direction, marks.

❏ Withdrawal requested; signature _____ ❏ Withdrawal permitted

❏ Protest, or request for redress or reopening, received within time limit ❏ Time limit extended

Protestor, or party requesting redress or reopening, represented by _____

Other party, or boat being considered for redress, represented by _____

Names of witnesses _____

Interpreters _____ **Remarks**

No objection about interested party . . . . _____

Written protest or request identifies incident . . . . _____

'Protest' hailed at first reasonable opportunity . . . . _____

No hail needed; protestee informed at first . . . . _____
reasonable opportunity

Red flag conspicuously displayed at first . . . . _____
reasonable opportunity

❏ **Protest or request valid; hearing will continue**   ❏ **Protest or request invalid; hearing is closed**

FACTS FOUND

❏ Diagram of boat _____ is endorsed by committee   ❏ Committee's diagram is attached

CONCLUSIONS AND RULES THAT APPLY

DECISION

Protest: ❏ dismissed   Boat(s) _____ is (are)   ❏ disqualified from race(s) _____
                                                          ❏ penalized as follows _____

Redress: ❏ not given   ❏ given as follows _____

Request to reopen a hearing: ❏ denied ❏ granted	**Written decision requested**
PROTEST COMMITTEE	When _____
Members _____	By whom _____
Chairman's signature _____ Date & time _____	Date provided _____

Index

References are to rule numbers (for example, 27.3), appendices and their rule numbers (for example, C or E3.5), and sections of the book (for example, Introduction, Race Signals). Defined terms appear in *italics*. Appendices K, L and M are not indexed except for their titles. *US Sailing prescriptions are not indexed.*

About the Author

DAVE PERRY grew up sailing on Long Island Sound. Learning to sail in Sunfish, Blue Jays and Lightnings from his parents and in the junior program at the Pequot Yacht Club in Southport, Connecticut, he won the Clinton M. Bell Trophy for the best junior record on L.I.S. in 1971. While at Yale (1973-1977) he was captain of the National Championship Team in 1975, and was voted All-American in 1975 and 1977.

Other racing accomplishments include: 1st, 1978 Tasar North Americans; 5th, 1979 Laser Worlds; 1st, 1979 Soling Olympic Pre-Trials (crew); 10th overall, 1981 SORC (crew); 3rd, 1982 Soling Worlds; 1st, 1982, 2006, 2008 and 2011 U.S. Match Racing Championship (POW); 1st, 1983 Star South American Championship (crew); 1st, 1983 and 1984 Congressional Cup; 2nd, 1984 Soling Olympic Trials; 6th, 1985 Transpac Race (crew); 1st, 1988 and 1992 Knicker-bocker Match Race Cup; 1st, 1994, 1999 and 2003 Ideal 18 North American Champion-ship; 1st, 2007 South American Match Racing Championship and 1st, 2010 Detroit Cup (Match Racing).

Dave has been actively working for the sport since 1977. He has led hundreds of US Sailing instructional seminars in over 50 one-design classes; directed U.S. Olympic Yacht-ing Committee Talent Development Clinics; coached the 1981 World Champion U.S. Youth Team; and given seminars in Japan, Australia, Sweden, Argentina, Brazil and Canada. He has been the Youth Representative on the US Sailing Board of Directors and the Chair-man of the U.S. Youth Championship Committee, and has served on the following other US Sailing committees: Match Racing, Olympic, Training, Class Racing and O'Day Cham-pionship. He is currently a member of the US Sailing Appeals Committee and a US Sailing Senior Certified Judge.

In 1992 he was voted into the *Sailing World* Hall of Fame; in 1994 he received an honorary Doctorate of Education from Piedmont College; in 1995 he became the first recipient of US Sailing's Captain Joe Prosser Award for exceptional contribution to sailing education; and in March 2001 Dave received the W. Van Alan Clarke, Jr. Trophy, US Sail-ing's national award for sportsmanship. He was the Director of Athletics at Greens Farms Academy, a K-12 coed independent day school in Westport, Connecticut from 1986-2006; and has served as the Rules Advisor to *Victory Challenge* (the Swedish 2007 America's Cup challenger) and *Artemis Racing* (the Swedish 2013 America's Cup challenger), Coach for women's match racing for the 2009-2012 U.S. Sailing Team, and Rules Advisor for the U.S. Olympic Sailing Team in 2008 and 2012.

About the Illustrator

BRAD DELLENBAUGH grew up in Fairfield, Connecticut where he learned to sail at the Pequot Yacht Club. He has been coaching and teaching sailing for over 35 years. Presently the Sailing Director at the New York Yacht Club based in Newport, Rhode Island, Brad has coached the offshore sailing team at the U.S. Naval Academy in Annapolis from 1992-2005, the intercollegiate team at Brown University from 1980-1990, as well as the U.S. Women's team from 1984-1987. From 1977-1980 he coached the sailing team at the Hotchkiss School in addition to teaching in the art department, and taught junior sailing from 1973 through 1982 on Long Island Sound. He continues to lecture frequently on racing tactics and the rules.

An avid racer, Brad has been involved in three Olympic campaigns in the Soling class (including one with Dave in 1981-1984), as well as serving as tactician or helmsman in numerous national, continental and world championships in a wide variety of one-designs and offshore boats. He has won the 1987 and 1988 US Sailing Team Racing Championship, the 1989 J/24 World Championship, the 1990 and 1991 J/22 World Championships and the 1997 US Sailing Prince of Wales Match Racing Championship. He is an International Judge and Umpire and has served as the rules advisor to *Young America* and the U.S. Olympic Sailing Team in 2000, as an umpire for the Louis Vuitton and America's Cup in 2002-2003, as the chief umpire for the America's Cup in 2006-2007 and as an umpire in the 2011-2012 America's Cup World Series.

Brad graduated from Brown University with a major in fine arts and has pursued this interest as a freelance artist, illustrating for a number of sailing magazines and books.

Protest Form

SAILING also for requests for redress and reopening
www.ussailing.org

Fill in and check as appropriate

Date and time received _____

Received by _____ Filing no. _____

Protest time limit _____

---

1. EVENT _____ Organizing authority _____ Date _____ Race no. _____

2. TYPE OF HEARING

☐ Protest by boat against boat

☐ Protest by race committee against boat

☐ Protest by protest committee against boat

☐ Request for redress by boat or race committee

☐ Consideration of redress by protest committee

☐ Request by boat or race committee to reopen hearing

☐ Consideration of reopening by protest committee

3. BOAT PROTESTING, OR REQUESTING REDRESS OR REOPENING

Class _____ Sail no. _____ Boat's name _____

Represented by _____ Tel. _____ E-mail _____

4. BOAT(S) PROTESTED OR BEING CONSIDERED FOR REDRESS

Class _____ Sail no. _____ Boat's name _____

5. INCIDENT

Time and place of incident _____

Rule(s) alleged to have been broken _____ Witness(es) _____

6. INFORMING PROTESTEE   How did you inform the protestee of your intention to protest?

☐ By hailing When?_____ Word(s) used _____

☐ By displaying a red flag When?_____

☐ By informing him/her in some other way Give details _____

---

7. DESCRIPTION OF INCIDENT
(use another sheet if necessary)

Diagram: one square = one hull length
Show position of boats, wind and
current direction, marks.

T4   CHANGES IN HEARING PROCEDURES

This rule applies to all hearings except hearings under rule 69.

T4.1   If the protest committee is able to assemble the *parties* to a hearing before the *protest* or redress time limit, it may begin the hearing and may waive the requirements of rule 61.2 or 62.2.

T4.2   The US Sailing prescriptions to rules 60, 63.2 and 63.4 are deleted.

T4.3   Rule 63.5 is changed to: 'At the beginning of the hearing, if there is no objection, the *protest* or request is valid and the hearing shall be continued. If an objection is made, the protest committee shall take any evidence . . . [*no further change*].'

T4.4   Insert a new sentence after the third sentence of rule 63.6: 'However, the committee may limit the number of witnesses and the time during which *parties* may present evidence and ask questions.'

T4.5   The first sentence of rule 65.2 is changed to: 'A *party* to the hearing is entitled to receive the above information in writing, provided she asks the protest committee for it no later than thirty minutes after being informed of the decision or coming ashore following the last race of the day, whichever is later.'

T4.6   The third sentence of rule 66 is changed to: 'A *party* to the hearing may not ask for a reopening.'

Section D — Arbitration

When Section D applies, a boat may take the applicable Post-Race Penalty in Section B without participating in an arbitration meeting.

T5   PROTEST ARBITRATION

T5.1   An arbitration meeting will be held prior to a protest hearing for each incident resulting in a *protest* by a boat involving a rule of Part 2 or rule 31, but only if each *party* is represented by a person who was on board at the time of the incident. No witnesses will be permitted. However, if the arbitrator decides that rule 44.1(b) may apply or that arbitration is not appropriate, the meeting will not be held, and if a meeting is in progress, it will be closed.

T5.2   Based on the evidence given by the representatives, the arbitrator will offer an opinion as to what the protest committee is likely to decide:

(a)   the *protest* is invalid,

(b)   no boat will be penalized for breaking a rule, or

(c)   one or more boats will be penalized for breaking a rule, identifying the boats and the penalties.

T5.3   A boat that may have broken a rule may take a Post-Race Penalty as provided in Section B. However, the penalty in rule T2.2(a) is available only until the protest time limit or until the beginning of the arbitration meeting, whichever is earlier. During a meeting, a boat may take a penalty by acknowledging her acceptance of the penalty in writing.

T5.4   If a boat asks to withdraw her *protest*, the arbitrator may act on behalf of the protest committee in accordance with rule 63.1 to accept the withdrawal.